ALSO BY JUSTIN WOLFF

Richard Caton Woodville:
American Painter, Artful Dodger

THOMAS HART BENTON

THOMAS HART BENTON

A LIFE

JUSTIN WOLFF

FARRAR, STRAUS AND GIROUX   NEW YORK

Farrar, Straus and Giroux
18 West 18th Street, New York 10011

Grateful acknowledgment is made for permission to reprint excerpts from the following previously published material:

"Stieglitz" by Gertrude Stein. Reprinted by permission of the Estate of Gertrude Stein, through its Literary Executor, Mr. Stanford Gann, Jr., of Levin & Gann, P.A.

"Visiting Thomas Hart Benton and His Wife in Kansas City" by Robert Bly. Copyright © 1975 by Robert Bly. Reprinted by permission of Georges Borchardt, Inc., for Robert Bly.

All art by Thomas Hart Benton copyright © T. H. Benton and R. P. Benton Testamentary Trusts / UMB Bank Trustee / Licensed by VAGA, New York, N.Y.

Library of Congress Cataloging-in-Publication Data
Wolff, Justin P.
    Thomas Hart Benton : a life / Justin Wolff. — 1st ed.
      p.   cm.
    Includes bibliographical references and index.
    ISBN 978-0-374-19987-6 (alk. paper)
    1. Benton, Thomas Hart, 1889–1975.   2. Painters—United States—Biography.   I. Benton, Thomas Hart, 1889–1975.   II. Title.
ND237.B47W65 2012
759.13—dc23
[B]
2011034925

Designed by Jonathan D. Lippincott

www.fsgbooks.com

1   2   3   4   5   6   7   8   9   10

FOR MY MOTHER AND FATHER

The stuff of this America which I know directly and immediately is to me more important . . . than all the art of the past.

—Thomas Hart Benton

CONTENTS

ACKNOWLEDGMENTS

I am immensely grateful to those generous institutions and organizations that awarded me funding while I was working on this book. I am especially thankful for a yearlong research fellowship from the National Endowment for the Humanities. I am grateful as well for funding from the Society for the Preservation of American Modernists and, at the University of Maine, Orono, the Faculty Research Funds Program, the College of Liberal Arts and Sciences, and the Department of Art.

I owe my biggest debt to the community of scholars whose analyses of Thomas Hart Benton preceded mine. For sharing research discoveries, offering criticisms, and responding to my phone calls and e-mails, I am particularly beholden to Henry Adams, Margi Conrads, Erika Doss, Randall Griffey, and Leo Mazow—all of whose insights are reflected throughout my book. In addition, I am grateful for the wisdom of Matthew Baigell, Austen Barron Bailly, Marianne Berardi, Emily Braun, Elizabeth Broun, Ken Burns, Polly Burroughs, Creekmore Fath, Vivien Fryd, Karal Ann Marling, Bob Priddy, and Michael Szalay. For their participation on a Benton panel I chaired at the College Art Association's annual conference in 2006, I thank John X. Christ, Roberta Smith Favis, Randall C. Griffin, Leo Mazow, and Kristina Wilson. I am also grateful for the helpful conversations I had with Debra Bricker Balkan, Betsy Kennedy, Lauren Lessing, and Jake Wien. I want to express my appreciation as well to Jessie Benton, who kindly and patiently answered my queries about her father.

As any scholar will tell you, research libraries and archive collections perform an enormous service in making their holdings available to researchers. For their research assistance, I am grateful to the staff of the Department of American Art at the Nelson-Atkins Museum of Art in Kansas City; the staff of the Spencer Art Reference Library at the Nelson-Atkins, especially Jeffrey Weidman and Holly Wright; the offices of the Archives of American Art in Washington, D.C., and New York City; and Jan Leonard of the Thomas Hart and Rita Piacenza Benton Testamentary Trusts at UMB Bank, Kansas City.

My editors at Farrar, Straus and Giroux, Courtney Hodell and Mark Krotov, have worked tirelessly on behalf of this book, and I am enormously appreciative of their diligence and patience. I am also thankful for the careful work of my copy editor, Ingrid Sterner, and my production editor, Susan Goldfarb. I would like to acknowledge as well Josh Kendall, who got this project started. In addition, I am grateful to my agent, Sarah Chalfant, and her assistants at the Wylie Agency.

Finally, I want to thank my supportive colleagues in the Department of Art at the University of Maine. Their good cheer and encouragement have been remarkable. And to my family, Megan, Ruby, and Oscar—wow . . . thank you.

THOMAS HART BENTON

PROLOGUE: SKETCHES FROM LIFE

In the summer of 1920, when he was thirty-one, Thomas Hart Benton and his future wife, Rita Piacenza, visited Martha's Vineyard for the first time. They both lived in Manhattan, where Benton had been painting since 1912 and twenty-year-old Rita was taking art classes and designing sewing patterns. Looking to escape the heat of the city, they rented a farmhouse and a barn with some friends in the town of Chilmark. Tom and Rita loved the area so much that six years later, they bought land near Menemsha Pond, where they spent almost every summer until their deaths in 1975. *Menemsha* means "still water" in the language of the Wampanoag Indians, and on calm days the pond is the picture of serenity: cranes feed on sand eels in its ring of marsh grass, and ospreys swoop in and out of high-perched nests. Benton often swam in the Atlantic while Rita gathered cranberries, beach plums, and wild grapes. The couple's two children—Thomas, known as T.P., and Jessie— ran wild across Chilmark's hills and beaches. The island, Benton avowed, "occasioned one of the greatest changes in my life": it cleared his view of the world and inspired him. It was, he added, "the only place I ever found peace."

Benton also claimed that his painting matured once he discovered the Vineyard's windblown landscape and Yankee villagers. During their third summer on the island, in 1922, Benton painted *Self-Portrait with Rita*, which shows the couple on a beach near the Gay Head cliffs, on the southwestern tip of the Vineyard. At the time, he was abandoning abstract painting for a realist style influenced by Renaissance, mannerist, and baroque artists. In fact, *Self-Portrait with Rita* was a debut of sorts, a calculated presentation of his newfound aesthetic, which he fashioned from the influence of the muscular figures of Michelangelo and Peter Paul Rubens and the attenuated forms of Jacopo Pontormo and Parmigianino. Benton continued working in this style, with a few modifications, for the rest of his long career; his easel paintings and murals depict similarly robust figures situated in stylized landscapes, cityscapes, or interiors.

The painting introduces what would become Benton's trademark dynamism; it is distinguished by undulating forms, as in the globular clouds and complementary convexities and concavities—what Benton called "bumps and hollows"—evident in the deep contours of his chiseled chest. The push and pull of the forms continues across the entire composition, which is animated by contrasts between light and dark, between recessive and dominant space. There's a stirring organic quality to their figures as well, as if Tom and Rita have absorbed into their bodies the vitality of nature itself. Benton represents himself as a modern Poseidon, modeled by and just risen from the ocean glimpsed to his right. Rita, who sits in front of him, recalls the Madonnas in mannerist paintings; her strong, elongated figure appears to have been cut by the same ocean forces that pound at the Gay Head cliffs seen behind them. Benton was sure he'd found his style, and the painting was his proclamation to the art world that it had better pay attention.

But the painting introduced more than just a style. It also revealed a philosophy of art that Benton would work his whole life to promote. This had to do with notions about the experience of place that were emerging at the time in the pragmatist philosophy of John Dewey (who would become enormously influential to Benton), the writings of the historian Lewis Mumford, and art and literary criticism more generally. Benton was attracted to pragmatism—a distinctly American philosophy that shows how knowledge relates to practical purposes and maintains that intellectual ideas are only valid if they have human utility. Pragmatist thinkers reject abstraction and absolutism in favor of concreteness and action; they are interested in how knowledge is an instrument for adapting to environments rather than for elaborating theories. Benton fashioned from these principles an idiosyncratic worldview that had a lot in common with phenomenology, another modern philosophy. Phenomenology elevates immediate experiences over reflective analysis of those experiences. It's a doctrine that is more interested in how we process what Martin Heidegger calls "being-in-the-world" at the moment that we're actually in it rather than after the fact. The concept of "experience" was crucial to Benton's attitudes about art, and he used the term often to explain his belief that art ought to represent life as it is actually lived in a particular environment. Art, according to Benton, should be instrumental (a favorite term of Dewey's) and work to clarify ordinary experiences rather than interrogate the mysteries of the world. Based on such philosophies, Benton concluded that art should be realistic, not abstract, and that it should serve practical rather than intellectual ends.

These attitudes are represented in *Self-Portrait with Rita*. The painting is less an emotional expression about a day spent at a Vineyard beach than it is a testament to how the island shore has acted on him and Rita. They are at home in the world, in close contact with their milieu, and they have achieved this in the same way that anybody might— simply by being there and remaining open to what the environment offers them. The painting appears to promise a similar reconciliation with nature to anyone who cares to look for it. It's for these reasons that during the late 1920s and the 1930s Benton became such a popular painter, for it seemed that he was more interested in common American experiences than in what many deemed the elitist aesthetic theories of avant-garde artists who sought to justify experimentation and abstraction with a specialized professional language. For many, then, Benton was one of them: he spoke their language, painted their lives, and believed wholeheartedly in the significance of their experiences.

Being-in-the-world, though, was rarely so easy for Benton. He was embroiled in controversy almost constantly, and the confidence that he wears so comfortably in the painting proved hard to come by and even harder to maintain. Of the many antagonisms Benton experienced during his life, none exasperated him more than the harsh criticism he received from the radical Left during the 1930s. Occasionally, his skirmishes with leftist artists stemmed from personal differences, but the principal grievance of his critics was that his hale and hearty realism was clichéd. The Marxist art historian Meyer Schapiro, for instance, excoriated Benton's apparent nationalism and "strong and masculine" figures, which he felt were dangerously similar to the xenophobia and idealizing style of fascist art. That Benton believed such arguments were idiotic, and said so again and again, didn't help matters. Like anyone, Benton wanted to live in harmony with his time and place; that he often failed, or was misunderstood, is what makes his such a human story.

•

My first brush with Benton came in the late 1990s, when I was researching a project at the Archives of American Art. The New York offices are just across the street from the AXA Equitable Tower, where Benton's famous mural *America Today* (1930), originally made for the New School for Social Research in New York, has been on view since 1985. Even a casual acquaintance with him elicits strong responses, and so it was with me. I knew that he was from Missouri, had painted several murals, was Jackson Pollock's teacher, and, like Grant Wood and John Steuart Curry, was a popular painter of the American scene during the Depression years. I also knew that he was infamously pugnacious; had a reputation for making outlandish comments about modern art, museums, and homosexuals; and had said nasty things about two artists—Alfred Stieglitz and Stuart Davis—whom I knew more about and happened to admire. So I'd dismissed him as a conservative crank.

Nevertheless, I liked what I'd seen of his paintings. They certainly didn't strike me as beautiful (in the way that a painting by, say, John Singer Sargent is beautiful) or as awesomely intricate (like a Cézanne painting), but I did find them entertaining. At any rate, Benton was not on my mind the rainy day when, taking a break from research, I wandered into the AXA lobby to stretch my legs. The panels of the *America Today* mural, which had been restored in the mid-1980s, floored me. I was caught up in their bold color and dynamic, swirling energy and engrossed by their vignettes of muscular figures dancing, singing, drinking, and conversing. What impressed me most, however, was the degree to which the mural surpassed merely entertaining narrative. It possesses a palpable urgency; more than just a reflection of the progressive social and industrial life of its moment, the vital mural manages to take on a life of its own and stand out as living history.

Benton is often seen as a populist, but that term is notoriously slippery. For one, it works equally well for fascism, communism, and democracy. Benton's brand of populism was especially fickle: he changed his politics, could sound liberal or conservative, was decidedly intellectual (despite his claims to the contrary), and received as much criticism as praise from reviewers. So where is the ideological homogeneity, conformity, and uniform appeal that supposedly make up the popular?

Well, first of all, it's worth reminding oneself that an artist and his art are distinct entities. Truth be told, Benton's art, as rich and dynamic as it may be, is not as paradoxical as the man was. Though art critics and art historians find much to analyze in his paintings, one doesn't require their arbitrations to appreciate a Benton painting. Furthermore, the term "populism" has had various connotations at different times and in different places. In the United States during the Depression, politicians, philosophers, writers, and artists conceived of populism as any agenda that expressed sympathy for human suffering, outrage over economic greed, and a desire for pragmatic rather than radical reform. And in this particular place, at this particular time, most groups agreed—hence the election of Franklin Delano Roosevelt in 1932. Admittedly, this is only a schematic definition of Depression-era populism, but it's a fair one, I think, and one that Benton conformed to. He and his art were sympathetic to the plight of the common man, disparaging of special interests, and reformist but not extreme. In her landmark study of Benton's work, the art historian Erika Doss uses the term "producerism" to characterize his populist reformism. Rather than emphasize the plight of Americans during the Depression—as his social realist peers did—he attempted to illustrate pragmatic responses to it and in so doing resuscitated Jeffersonian agrarianism and Yankee ingenuity for the twentieth century. Because these were familiar historical concepts, they were, for a period anyway, when the times called for them, popular. Benton was also popular because he appeared common; that is, he denigrated anything that struck him as alienating—cities, intellectualism, museums, critics, and the soul-destroying consequences of endless economic expansion and mindless labor. He was devoted to American democracy, and his art drew on both low culture's profanity and middlebrow culture's wholesomeness. Genteel culture, however, because elite, was off-limits.

"I believe I have wanted, more than anything else," Benton writes, "to make pictures, the imagery of which would carry unmistakably American meanings for Americans and for as many of them as possible." His desire to be the most American artist may seem brazen and imperious, and at times it most definitely was, but it was also consistent with the quixotic ambitions of many modern American artists and writers to represent the essences of their subjects, be they flowers, skyscrapers, or farmers. Georgia O'Keeffe famously described many of her peers as being motivated to uncover "the Great American Thing." "They talked so often," she recalled in her autobiography, "of writing the Great American Novel—the Great American Play—the Great American Poetry."

In late May 1940, Jackson Pollock, seven years away from becoming the most famous painter in America, was dismissed from the Federal Art Project, a division of the New Deal's Works Progress Administration. Though the setback was temporary (he had worked on the project for his allotted eighteen months and would reapply successfully), Pollock was upset to find himself without a paycheck. Then, a week later, in early June, he learned that his friend Helen Marot had died. Marot, who was introduced to Pollock by Benton, Pollock's teacher at the Art Students League in New York during the 1930s, was an advocate of Jungian theory and had guided Pollock into psychotherapy for treatment of alcoholism and depression. These misfortunes devastated Pollock, and his biographers speculate that the day Marot died was the same day he descended into a drunken fury and "destroyed dozens of his own paintings, slashing them repeatedly with a kitchen knife and throwing the shreds out the window, where they floated to the street like multicolored streamers." According to Reuben Kadish, a sculptor friend of Pollock's, he reserved a special hostility for his Bentonesque paintings—canvases from the 1930s that were influenced by Benton's trademark style, a dynamic and mannered realism. "He didn't want the world to see that he had any contact with Benton," Kadish explained.

Pollock's young therapist, Joseph Henderson, though concerned about the incident, concluded that it was little more than "a truly glorious wake [for] a special friend." This infamous episode, however, was about more than mourning the death of Marot: Pollock, who had been growing increasingly resentful of Benton's influence on him, mutilated his paintings to express the dissatisfaction he felt with his mentor and the realistic representations of the American scene that Benton worked so hard to promote. The incident can be interpreted, then, as a moment of Oedipal rage, another gesture by an abstract expressionist painter to dismiss popular pictorial modes in favor of experimental and confessional styles. Either way, Pollock was rejecting Benton, the famous regionalist painter who just six years earlier was featured on the cover of

Time magazine and was among the most renowned artists in the world. Despite these successes, Benton had become the favorite target of leftist critics and proponents of abstract art, one more manifestation of the stunning turnaround his reputation would undergo in the 1940s. However, Benton's reputation had been the subject of much debate for a long time, and his reversal of fortune had more to do with his ornery personality and shifts in American political and social theory around World War II than it did with Pollock's often sensational stunts. Nevertheless, and though he was thick-skinned and resilient, Benton was certainly hurt by Pollock's theatrical denunciation of his influence and worried that he might lose another good friend, which happened to be a sad but persistent theme of his life.

Benton had dramatic relationships with other students as well. He often treated his pupils like family—as siblings and sometimes as children—and for him a family wasn't something to surrender to but something to wrestle with. But Benton taught during the 1930s and 1940s, just when teaching in the arts was going through a massive change. The logic of apprenticeship and patrimony in the arts disintegrated right before his eyes. Figuratively speaking, Pollock and other abstract expressionists were the last sons in American art; literally, they were the last apprentices. In the 1960s, Andy Warhol's Factory—with its capricious posturing and ironic attitudes regarding celebrity—became the new paradigm for art training in America. Seen in this light, Benton's pugnaciousness was a symptom not so much of his personal weaknesses as of a dying era. Camaraderie, mentorship, and Oedipal furor have largely vanished as generative forces in American art.

But throughout his life Benton probably spent more time on the offensive than he did defending himself. His poor judgment, profanity, and belligerent baiting of any artist walking a different stylistic or ideological path scandalized New Yorkers, New Englanders, and Missourians equally. Over the years he opposed abstract art, curators, homosexuals, intellectuals, Harvard, New York City, Kansas City, women, and old friends like Stieglitz and Mumford, to name a few. An atavistic drive compelled him to measure each person he met, each painting or idea he made or encountered, against a dogged ethos distilled from egomania, pragmatism, and populism. Despite his modest midwestern fashion—his denim, gingham, and flannel—and his "realism," Benton was not simple.

At the same time, his purposeful figures and his own industriousness—he worked fast, drove all over the country to observe American folk, built his own houses, taught himself to play the harmonica, raised kids, fished, and rafted white water—assuaged a generalized anxiety among average folk and critics alike. The Depression, based as it was in a speculative economy, demonstrated to many Americans that their nation had grown too conceptual; Benton, a populist artisan, reminded Americans of their original, if also mythical, sense of themselves as robust and self-reliant people. He also read ravenously, devouring books by Thoreau, Whitman, and Twain (he illustrated an edition of *Adventures of Huckleberry Finn*), and pictured himself as another great narrator of American stories.

Benton was, above all, a paradox: Born into modernity, he happened to inherit from his political family a philosophy of Jeffersonian populism. He was also a communist turned patriot, treacherous but loyal, humorous but melancholy, and a skeptic with a strain of progressivism. These paradoxes, however, didn't reveal themselves neatly; they unfolded as capriciously as his century did. Benton lived his moment; he tried everything the century offered—sometimes all at once. He was among the most prolific American artists of the twentieth century and painted or sketched daily from 1907 until his death in 1975. He painted massive murals in New York City, for the New School for Social Research and the Whitney Museum of American Art; in Chicago, for the Indiana pavilion at the 1933 World's Fair; in Missouri, for the state capitol, the Truman Library, and the centennial of the city of Joplin; and in Nashville, for the Country Music Hall of Fame. He produced hundreds of canvases, including abstract color experiments, heroic and pseudo-socialist figure compositions, western landscapes, and sentimental scenes of everyday life in the Midwest. He made thousands of drawings and nearly one hundred lithographs of the citizens he met on numerous trips to the Deep South, to the Ozarks, and down Missouri rivers. In New York and Kansas City, he taught such famous artists as Pollock and Fairfield Porter. Finally, he wrote almost as much as he painted—essays on the practice of art and the political ideologies of the modern era; reviews of the work of his peers; memoirs (two autobiographies and numerous essays on his life in Paris, New York, and Missouri); and dozens of articles.

He also played a central role in virtually every cultural and political drama of his day: he returned from Paris a bohemian—"*le petit Balzac*," they called him; then, in New York, he rode the wave of radical Marxism; later, he allied with kinds of New Deal liberalism, pragmatism, and social conservatism. In the end, however, one tenet endured through it all. Benton always distrusted—*detested*—power and privilege and superiority. He was a Democrat. In this, he believed he was safe; it was, he thought, enough to live democratically rather than radically. But it wasn't enough. And because he was self-confident, and because he knew politics (it was in his blood, as his father was a U.S. congressman and his great-uncle had been a famed U.S. senator), when Benton was called up short, when he was blindsided by politics, he got hurt. Then he'd dig in, lash out, and say awful, foolish things. He'd drift in the dangerous waters of ideology.

But to view Benton clearly, in all of his contrasting guises, one must resist the urge to type him and instead simply set him loose on the stage of his times and try to keep up, to trace him as he injures, insults, and delights us.

The critic Jed Perl says that two other critics, Edmund Wilson and Lionel Trilling, "make a fascinating pair." Wilson, Perl writes, explained his interest in his subjects, whereas Trilling explained his subjects' interests. Benton was like Wilson in that he claimed to represent his subjects' wishes and anxieties but really represented his own. On occasion this aspect of Benton's work got him in trouble, especially when he insisted that his paintings were authentic expressions of his subjects' inner lives rather than of his own attitudes. Benton reminds one of another writer of his era, John Dos Passos, who also experimented with a variety of political positions and constructed his *U.S.A.* trilogy from bits of popular culture—newsreels and photographs, for example. Benton similarly patched together his paintings from little bits—the drawings and sketches he made while traveling throughout the United States, the characters from folk songs and literature, and the stuff of history, myth, and Hollywood. Just as Dos Passos's works have amplitude about them, Benton's have breadth and expansiveness. Despite his crotchety ways, Benton possessed an enormous curiosity, mining fiction, the news, and films for subjects. Wilson, however, was critical of Dos Passos for the same reasons many critics panned Benton. After reading the trilogy, Wilson sent the author a letter. "You yourself seem to enjoy life more than most people," he wrote, "and are by way of being a brilliant talker; but you tend to make your characters talk clichés, and they always get a bad egg for breakfast." One frequent knock on Benton has been that despite his apparent inquisitiveness about people and their customs, he tended to stereotype his figures and limit them to certain behaviors and attitudes. Of course, he didn't see it this way.

In the early 1920s, after experimenting for fifteen years with various abstract styles (cubism, pointillism, synchromism), Benton started making realist pictures. By 1924 he was painting colorful canvases that teem with muscular figures who, in the tradition of American heroes from history and literature (Natty Bumppo, Daniel Boone, Thoreau, Ishmael, Tom Sawyer, cowboys, Indians), snub society and subsist on nature. Armed with a brazen outward confidence—a notorious family attribute—Benton believed that he belonged to this line of courageous men. Critics called his style "regionalism," an awkward, confining term, because Benton's intentions weren't parochial at all, but broad and national. "The name Regionalism suggested too narrow a range of inspiration to be quite applicable," he wrote in 1951. "I was after a picture of America in its entirety . . . I ranged from north and south and from New York to Hollywood and back and forth in legend and history."

So another paradox of his career is that he was a "regional" painter but a nomadic person. With romantic images of Pappy Wise, his maternal grandfather and a frontiersman, and the recent death of his father on his mind, Benton started "going places," as he liked to call it, in 1924. He went anywhere he believed he might find the roots of his people, whom he imagined to be tenant farmers, trappers, miners, tobacco growers, banjo players, and barge captains. From way upstate New York to the Deep South and the Rockies, Benton walked or hitched in search of Americans. In order to distinguish himself from artists and writers who surveyed the same outposts, such as Walker Evans and James Agee, with strictly reformist agendas—what Benton called "uplift psychologies"—he claimed not "to give a damn what people thought, how they ate their eggs or approached their females, how they voted, or what devious business they were involved in. I took them as they came and got along with them as best I could."

•

Thomas Hart Benton Day—May 12, 1962—was a wholesome mash of idolatry and civic pride. Benton hadn't visited his boyhood home of Neosho, Missouri, for fifty years, and he was greeted by more people, eight thousand, than lived in the town. "This was very much of an affair," Benton remembered, "the kind that, with bands and parading beauties, is often enough given for politicians and soldiers, but never, at least before this one, for a picture painter." The homecoming, according to *The New York Times*, rivaled that of Dwight Eisenhower, who a week earlier had lamented the state of modern art at the opening of his presidential library in Abilene, Kansas. Accompanied by his wife, Rita, daughter, Jessie, and friends Bess and Harry Truman, Benton pulled into town on a four-car Kansas City Southern Lines train; when a whistle signaled their arrival, a National Guard unit and the Neosho High School band snapped to attention. Benton, carrying a gold-headed cane, alighted from the train into the hot mid-morning sun, the band jumped into "Let a Smile Be Your Umbrella," and two local belles in throwback dresses grabbed his arms and escorted him through the throngs to a convoy led by two convertibles, a 1929 Peerless and a 1923 Franklin.

The Bentons' open car, stopping occasionally for autograph seekers, nudged through the crowd and crawled around the town square, followed at a respectable distance by the Trumans' automobile. The procession eventually made its way to the high school gym, where the honoree attended a roast-beef lunch with childhood friends, and then to Flower Box Square at the courthouse, where he was feted by local fiddlers, pickers, folk dancers, and a troupe of Pawnee dancers. Benton and his entourage then arrived at the Neosho Municipal Auditorium, where "near bedlam broke out" among the "noisy and unruly crowd" before Truman unveiled a portrait of Benton and proclaimed him "the greatest artist of this century." Benton, who a year earlier had completed a mural for the Truman Library in Independence, Missouri, demurred, calling the proposition "debatable." As the party wrapped up, Benton retreated to a clover patch behind the city hall where he chatted with an old friend, Brummett Echohawk, the Pawnee Indian who had helped him find Native American models for some of his murals.

An hour later, a tired and cranky Benton sat at a press conference. Did he remember the Neosho of his youth?

"I've written it all down in a book," he snapped, "and I hope you buy it."

Which of your paintings do you like best?

"I haven't done it yet."

Why didn't you come back to Neosho earlier?

"I was never invited."

So it was that Tom Benton turned his magnificent homecoming into a forum for airing grievances. Though he once said that art "would appear to almost guarantee a life of peace and quiet," he also confessed, "[I]t never did for me."

PART ONE

BEFORE NEW YORK

1

NEOSHO

In a 1972 interview, Thomas Hart Benton was asked if being named after his great-uncle, the boisterous nineteenth-century senator, had built into him "a kind of compulsion for greatness." "No, I would not believe that at all," he responded. And though Benton continually rebuffed the pleas of his father, a U.S. congressman, that he practice either law or politics, the truth is that he never lacked self-confidence or a sense of purpose. At the age of seventeen, he boasted to his mother, "I am bound to be successful. I have the fullest confidence in myself." That his renown would be marked by controversy was virtually preordained. In an unpublished memoir written late in life, Benton explained that his was a "family fated, it would seem, for turmoil. I was raised in a family environment which conditioned me very early in my life to accept strife and argument as basic factors of existence."

Senator Thomas Hart Benton is an American icon, the sort of man who typifies the tales of audacity often told in high school history books. In his biography of the senator, Theodore Roosevelt described him as "a man of high principle and determined courage." "Old Bullion"—a nickname the senator earned for his devotion to hard-money currency—"was deeply imbued with the masterful, overbearing spirit of the West,—a spirit whose manifestations are not always agreeable, but the possession of which is certainly a most healthy sign of the virile strength of a young community." As much as any figure of the day, Senator Benton has come to stand for the vigorous republicanism of early America; though aristocratic by nature, he rallied his considerable might behind small farmers, tradespeople, landowner rights, and a just economic system. Though "not necessarily one of 'the people,'" one historian explains, he was their "defender."

The senator was born in Orange County, North Carolina, on March 14, 1782. His mother, a forceful, educated Virginian and a widow, moved her family to a plot bequeathed by her husband on the western slope of the Appalachian Mountains in southeastern Tennessee. On this frontier land, in the midst of Cherokee settlements, the family built roads, mills, and a plantation, which eventually became part of the small town of Benton. The nearest city, Nashville, 180 miles to the northwest, was, according to Roosevelt, a savage place where horse racing, cockfighting, gambling, whiskey, and "the various coarse vices which masquerade as pleasures in frontier towns, all throve in rank luxuriance." The young would-be senator took to these vices with gusto and witnessed many street fights, stabbings, and murders.

These skills served him well during two infamous duels. The second took place in September 1817, after he'd moved to St. Louis to practice law and founded a newspaper, the *Missouri Inquirer*, which advocated statehood for the Missouri Territory. Benton challenged Charles Lucas, a St. Louis lawyer, to a fight to the death in 1816, after Lucas insulted him during a case before the circuit court. Lucas refused the challenge but further antagonized Benton during the August election of 1817, when he accused him of not paying his taxes. Old Bullion countered that he would not answer charges made by "any puppy who may happen to run across my path." The duel occurred on a small patch of land in the Mississippi River, soon to be dubbed Bloody Island. At a distance of thirty feet, Benton wounded Lucas in the throat and was himself grazed by a bullet. Lucas claimed satisfaction, but Benton was bloodthirsty. On September 26, 1817, after Lucas had recovered enough to return to work, he received a note from the senator demanding another duel. The next day the two met again, at a distance of ten feet. Lucas missed and Benton killed him with a bullet to the chest.

But even before the Lucas incident, Benton was notorious for his combativeness. Before he moved to Missouri, at the outset of the War of 1812, General Andrew Jackson appointed him his aide-de-camp, with the rank of lieutenant colonel, and dispatched him to languish in the safety of Washington—his orders were to assuage anxieties about the firebrand general. Already frustrated by his posting far from the field of battle, Benton was sensitive to any perceived slight, so when he learned about an insult to his brother Jesse, perpetrated by William Carroll, a soldier under Jackson's command, he flew into a rage. Jackson—himself no stranger to physical violence (he had already killed a man in a duel and was inclined to cane his foes)—publicly threatened to horsewhip his impudent colonel and scolded him in a letter: "It is the character of a man of honor . . . not to quarrel and brawl like fish women." Justice-minded, Benton and Jesse arrived at the Nashville Inn on September 4, 1813, to settle the score. Jackson was skinny and Benton thick and broad, but "in capacity for blind fury, utter recklessness and iron-willed determination, neither man had a superior."

Brandishing a whip, Jackson charged Benton, yelling, "Now defend yourself, you damned rascal!" According to Roosevelt, "The details were so intricate that probably not even the participants themselves knew exactly what had taken place . . . At any rate, Jackson was shot and Benton was pitched headlong downstairs, and all the other combatants were more or less damaged; but it ended in Jackson being carried off by his friends" and Benton ceremoniously breaking his commanding officer's sword over his knee, "leaving the Bentons masters of the field, where they strutted up and down and indulged in a good deal of loud bravado." Content with their victory, the Benton brothers retreated to Missouri.

After killing Lucas, Benton cooled down and committed himself to the political battleground. Missouri's second Democratic senator, Benton served six consecutive terms, from 1821 to 1851, winning support by bringing a mixture of grandiosity and pragmatism to bear on an era of expansion; in his long, passionate stump speeches, delivered in a "jabbing, repetitive" style and "roaring voice," Benton linked frontier life to Union principles. Like his grandnephew later, the senator was wary of centralized power and devoted to America's democratic experiment, which he saw as nothing less than a revolution in the service of humanity.

What Roosevelt admired most about Senator Benton was that he refused to endorse the spread of slavery, even when his constituents wanted him to, and so "bravely [accepted] defeat as the alternative . . . going down without flinching a hair's breadth from the ground on which he always stood." Roosevelt probably gives him too much credit, for the senator never anticipated that slavery would tear his party apart. But as James Polk came to power, "Union Democracy" receded into the realm of impractical idealism, and party members split into factions— separatists on one side and Free-Soilers on the other. Senator Benton, in Roosevelt's words, had now entered "the heroic part of his career." The senator, though, was guided not by a philosophy of racial harmony but by a love for the Union—"the world's last hope for free government on the earth"—and pragmatism. He reasoned that economic concerns would settle the matter: one day, he hoped, it would be cheaper to hire a man than to own him. But when it became clear that the debate about whether to annex Texas was in fact a debate about whether to grant the South's agenda federal license, and thus permit the spread of slavery to new territories, Old Bullion dug in. "I shall not fall upon my sword," he threatened, "but I shall save it, and save myself for another day, and for another use—for the day when the battle of the disunion of these States is to be fought—not with words, but with iron."

Though Senator Benton served as the chief military adviser to President Polk during the Mexican War, by backing Oregon's wish to bar slavery from its territory, he prompted an all-out effort within the Democratic Party to scuttle his bid for reelection in 1850. The senator stumped across Missouri, addressing crowds with high rhetoric and claiming that he "would sooner sit in council with the six thousand dead who had died of cholera in St. Louis [in 1849], than go into convention with such a gang of scamps [the Democrats] . . . Even the election of Whigs will be a triumph over them—a victory in behalf of the Union—and that is the over-ruling consideration." His constituents, however, saw such bombastic oratory as a graver threat to the Union than the spread of slavery, and he was defeated.

The senator's actions during the slavery debate illustrate a paradox of character that manifested itself in the careers of his descendants, most notably Maecenas Benton, a U.S. representative from Missouri during the late nineteenth century, and Maecenas's son Thomas Hart Benton. Though generally understood as men motivated first by regional concerns—as advocates for farmers, small-business owners, and settlers—all three Bentons desired national attention. A common misconception about regionalism is that it was an isolationist doctrine, but as practiced by these three men, it was rarely escapist; each of them viewed the local as a reflection of a broader republican state. The purpose of any given region, like Missouri, was to exemplify how a nation guided by democratic principles might function. The senator, according to his grandnephew, "helped, with pompous phrase but determined will, to lay the hand of the West on eastern political policy." All Bentons, he added, relied on "power" rather than "God" to enact and justify their superiority. The Benton men craved national authority and, contrary to popular opinion, often belittled and condescended to small-town attitudes. Benton, the painter, believed, for instance, that his father alienated his constituents in rural Missouri, thus costing himself reelection, by donning the fashions and habits of a "tidewater aristocrat," his term for privileged and socially poised Chesapeake easterners. The same was true, and more so, of our Benton: he was torn apart by the competing allures of rural Missouri and cosmopolitan New York.

Maecenas Eason Benton, "the Colonel," left southwest Missouri for Tennessee after the Civil War, "knocking the snakes . . . out of his horse's path with a long stick." Though M.E., as he was also called, served with the Confederate army and fought at Shiloh under General Nathan Bedford Forrest, he was not in fact a colonel; the title was simply a common sobriquet for southern gentlemen. The Tennessee Bentons were "an individualistic and cocksure people" who "nursed their idiosyncrasies and took no advice"; M.E., "a slice of the block," was born in northwestern Tennessee in 1848 and attended school in Missouri. Even as a boy he exhibited a "splendid American fighting spirit." After the war, the Colonel earned a law degree at Cumberland University, in Lebanon, Tennessee; moved to Neosho in 1869; and established a fashionable law practice, enticing clients with rollicking stories and a "full measure of political ability." Possessed of a wonderful memory, and an expert eater, drinker, and stump speaker, the Colonel prospered in both the Missouri bar and the state Democratic Party. He made his debut in politics when he was elected prosecuting attorney of Newton County, and his party loyalty earned him an appointment as a U.S. district attorney during Grover Cleveland's first term, from 1885 to 1889. The Colonel further distinguished himself in 1887, when he took on a murderous gang of vigilantes, known as the Bald Knobbers, who, under the leadership of the ruthless Nat Kinney, terrorized the outsiders who settled in Missouri after the war. Benton recalled that for many years after prosecuting the gang, the Colonel would close all the cedar shutters in their glamorous house each evening, paranoid that vengeful gang members intended to kill his family.

In general, though, Neosho was a gentle place—a town, Benton explains, "addicted" to celebrations. Today it calls itself the Flower Box City. The seat of Newton County in the Hickory Creek valley, Neosho had been a fertile habitat for Native tribes on account of its abundant springs and during Benton's childhood was rich with Indian lore. It was just miles from the Nations, since the early nineteenth century the prescribed homeland of displaced tribes, including Cherokees, Choctaws, Chickasaws, Creeks, and Seminoles. (The land, as these stories go, was later seized upon the formation of the state of Oklahoma, in 1907.) Before the Civil War, pioneers from Kentucky and Tennessee settled among the oaks, walnuts, and hickories that grew along the region's creeks; during the war, Neosho saw its share of skirmishes and was situated close enough to the Battle of Pea Ridge (1862)—in which over five thousand soldiers died and Missouri was secured for the Union—that it switched hands between the Confederate army and "the federals" several times.

Neosho reconstructed well, however, and by the time the Colonel hung his shingle outside a downtown office, the town was almost two thousand strong, and commerce was slowly displacing the horrific war as the business of the day. In typically terse but imagistic prose, Benton recollects the Neosho of his childhood:

> In the middle eighteen-nineties, when I first began to take notice of things, it was far off from the lines of continental travel and had an old-fashioned flavor. Its people took their time. Old soldiers of the Civil War sat around in the shade of store awnings or lounged about the livery stables, which were, in the horse-and-buggy civilization of the time, important centers of reminiscence and debate . . . Confederate and Union gatherings occurred every year and the square would be full of veterans, with imprecise triangles of old men's tobacco spit staining their white or grizzled beards. They lived over again their bloody youth. They used to congregate in the law office of my father . . . These old war birds of the Great Struggle were a constant part of my early environment and when, years later, I painted a picture depicting the departure of the doughboys of the sixties for the front, I painted them as grizzled and toothless old men. I knew . . . them as such.

But Neosho was a modern town as well: it was home to a bountiful strawberry industry and the country's first federal fish hatchery, established in 1888. These two institutions represented more than a growing economy in Neosho; they were manifestations of a profound change in small midwestern towns during the Gilded Age—a shift from agrarianism to "civic scientific management" and "corporate capitalism." Both Benton and his father bemoaned these changes.

Though the Colonel drank and smoked with "clients" in his downtown office, he wasn't content to live among the people. When he was thirty-nine and still a bachelor, he built a massive house atop a hill outside of town. Oak Hill, as the house was called, was situated amid a grove of majestic oaks and had all the amenities: a coal furnace in the basement for central heat, a cistern with a charcoal and gypsum filtration system for drinking water, a large kitchen with a bread oven, a parlor, a library, and a tin-lined bathtub. Each side of the house had a porch, the one in front affording a view down a long valley to town, the one in back leading out to a stretch of land with a glass conservatory for exotic plants, flower and vegetable gardens, a smokehouse, a chicken coop, a half-acre pig lot, and a barn with a hayloft, where young Tom and friends staged circuses and theatrical productions. In 1887 a proud Colonel moved into Oak Hill with his brother Sam and sisters Fanny and Dolly, both spinsters.

Soon after, a twenty-two-year-old Texan named Elizabeth "Lizzie" Wise—a "tall willowy black-haired . . . and brown-eyed beauty"—arrived in Neosho to visit a sister, Emma, who had married a local horse trader named Jim McElhany. Uncle Jim, "the top town sport," donned a brown derby hat, rather than a more fashionable broad-brimmed felt hat, and played poker and shot dice. The Colonel had little use for Uncle Jim, a Republican, but he admired Lizzie, who sang and tinkled at the piano, and put politics aside long enough to court her. They were married in Waxahachie, Texas, on June 24, 1888. Back at Oak Hill, there was an enormous soiree—"an epoch in Neosho receptions." Based on Benton's paintings, one might imagine a pig roast or hoedown, but a gleeful account of the party in *The Newton County Saga* paints a picture of an aristocratic celebration that evening. "The night was dark, the clouds and fog thick," the reporter begins, a bit ominously, but "the turrets, corridors, and halls of Oak Hill were ablaze with light and generous welcome":

> Col. Benton like one of the old barons, was blithe and gay, keeping the festal holiday. Carriage after carriage rolled up, and for

two hours emptied precious freight of admiring friends, and friendly guests, enfolded and wrapped; they were bundled into the reception room, where the light, warmth and gentle hands unfolded their wings, as delicate butterflies of fashion . . . So much was to be said and done, that it is a late hour, too, before the guests had arisen from the banquet, spread profusely and richly with the most tempting viands and luxuries.

Attendees included Missouri's Democratic senator George Vest; Congressman James Burnes; the U.S. marshal Elijah Gates and his seventeen deputies; and "the Fifteen Bachelors of Neosho." Lizzie Benton wore an elegant reception dress "of pale blue ottoman silk, with [a] train of pale and . . . blue striped moiré."

The Colonel naively imagined that his new bride would share Oak Hill with his sisters, but as Benton explained, once his mother "got her papers, she spit the bit of the marriage vow out of her mouth and asserted herself." Though both families were of hardy frontier stock, the Wises and the Bentons were philosophically and spiritually incompatible: the Wises labored outdoors, "were able to choose their lives and maintain them, keep them going as they wanted," and, unlike the Bentons, refused to appeal to any force other than God. Pappy Wise, Lizzie's father, was an odd man who "made his own deals with the masters of the Universe," dressed in black from head to toe, and wore a long white beard. Born in Kentucky, Pappy Wise had been an itinerant laborer; he'd rafted lumber in New Orleans and farmed hogs in Missouri. After the Civil War, during which he'd been a saddlemaker for the Confederate army, Pappy Wise constructed and sold wagons, plows, and other farm equipment in Waxahachie. Later he moved outside town to a cotton farm where he made violins; in the evenings he and his daughters picked up their instruments and played hymns, jigs, and reels. Young Tom occasionally visited the Wise farm with his mother, and his impressions of the property's teetering structures fed his artistic imagination, serving as models for the buildings in so many of his paintings and lithographs. "The farm house was painted white," he once recollected, "but all the other structures . . . were of raw wood greyed and warped by the Texas sun. Most of them had cracks and fissures through which the eternal Texas wind moaned and whistled and cried."

By all accounts Lizzie was spoiled and stubborn. Benton always described his mother as demanding: she was, he explained, "proud, intensely self-concerned, given to religious imaginings, high strung, with an innate sense of personal superiority." Mildred Benton Small, Tom's youngest sister, claimed that her mother once said to her, "I've never met anyone I thought was superior to me." Much to the Colonel's chagrin, his wife began feuding with his sisters the moment she moved into Oak Hill. Long after her husband's death, Lizzie continued to speak spitefully about those first days in the house. "Oh, they hated me," she told her son. "But I taught them a lesson. I got the horrid things before your father and I told him, it's them or it's me, mister. Throw them out of the house or I'll go back to Texas." So not long after moving into Oak Hill, she watched as Fanny, Dolly, and Uncle Sam hauled their bags down the valley into town, where they occupied an apartment next door to the Colonel's office. Uncle Sam, who kept his hunting dogs in a wood-lot adjacent to Oak Hill, returned occasionally to take young Tom on tours of the town in a small wagon, but the sisters stayed away for good, and the house was officially turned over to the Wise women. When Uncle Jim was off on horse business, Aunt Em visited the Bentons and helped with sewing and other chores around the house, though her implicit ambition was to school the family in the Bible. Taking their cue from Pappy Wise, Lizzie and Aunt Em practiced an improvised kind of Baptist faith; as Benton remembered it, "The women . . . found themselves appointed brides of Christ . . . and saved from the hell fires to which most other human beings, especially women not of the Wise family, were destined." After supper each evening the sisters gathered the family in the parlor and passed the Bible in a circle, sharing reading duties until bedtime; the women enjoyed such spirituality, but the Colonel and his children didn't pay it much mind. Years later Mildred speculated that her mother knew this and only made them read in order to teach them proper English. Maybe so, but religion was a topic on which Lizzie and her children never reached an agreement.

Lizzie and M.E. had a miserable marriage: they fought about money and were sexually incompatible. She could charm his clients and constituents at parties and political meetings, but her haughtiness eventually turned them off, contributing to the Colonel's political defeat. Though the Colonel also had a touch of superiority, he could play the part of a commoner, whereas Lizzie dreamed of a life in the city. The Colonel was also ugly—portly, sometimes sloppy, and always smelling of booze and tobacco—and apparently repulsed his wife. "My father," Benton explained, "was not, in any sense, a romantic figure, short, thick necked, with a reddish skin, a red beard and a protruding belly. A heavy eater, he was . . . an equally heavy drinker . . . It is hard to imagine him paying any kind of delicate courtship." Mildred put it more harshly, confessing, "I never had any feeling for my father except being scared to death of that raging voice . . . [He] was the original chauvinist pig." Lizzie, meanwhile, didn't abide "physical intimacies" of any kind. "As a little toddler," Benton recalled, "I was more than once frightened by my mother's protesting screams when my father entered her room at night." None of their children remembers a tender moment between them, and Benton, in fact, undertook his final memoir in part to explain his parents' unhappiness. In the prologue to "The Intimate Story," his unpublished autobiography, he explained that his parents often "annoyed" and "embarrassed" him, but "in spite of that I have a profound sympathy for them and for the unhappy ways in which they ended their lives, one choking to death with throat cancer, deserted by the female members of his family, the other dying in an insane asylum, also deserted. I think I have more sympathy for my father who knew he was deserted than for my mother who did not."

Tom, the sad couple's first child, was born at Oak Hill on April 15, 1889. "The boy," the Colonel boasted to Dr. Wills, "is worth his weight in gold." Though they had three more children—Mary Elizabeth, or "Mamie," Nathaniel, and Mildred—the proud parents had the highest hopes for Tom; he would embody, they believed, the best of the superior qualities circulating in the Benton and Wise blood. But Tom, though whip smart, inherited some less desirable traits as well: like his great-uncle and his mother, he possessed an occasionally absurd stubbornness and an almost deranged sense of destiny. The great emotional crisis of Benton's youth was his relationship with his father, the problem being that they never agreed on where this destiny led. In his memoirs, Benton builds the struggle between himself and his father into an epic Oedipal drama. "From the moment of my birth," he writes, "my future was laid out in my father's mind. A Benton male could be nothing but a lawyer—first because the law was the only field worthy of the attention of responsible and intelligent men, and second because it led naturally to political power." But the Colonel began to have doubts about his son early—Tom was argumentative, skeptical, and wary of his father's cronies—and made his suspicions known.

Aunt Mariah Watkins, a popular black midwife in Neosho, cared for the boy. Born into slavery in St. Louis in 1824, Aunt Mariah had her two children taken from her when she was a young woman. After escaping from her master, she settled in Neosho and made a living delivering and mothering babies of the town's well-to-do citizens. Her most famous charge was the frail George Washington Carver, who traced his moral and spiritual character back to her matronly guardianship of him. Dubbed the "midwife to greatness," her trademark was an "immaculate white apron, bordered with crocheted lace, which billowed out from her ample waist." When Aunt Mariah walked down the street in Neosho with her black medicine kit, all the kids in town formed a line behind her, believing "she had a baby in the bag and was going . . . to find a home for it."

Aunt Mariah bathed, clothed, and "whacked" Tom until he was five. As he remembered it, she was big, "up and down, forwards and backwards," and strong—she "could run down a chicken before it knew it was being chased." The only woman, according to Benton, who showed the Colonel any respect, Aunt Mariah also ran errands for the family. She drove into town from Oak Hill in a buggy, "the seat barely holding her," pulled by a yellow pony.

Home for the summers from Washington, D.C., where his father served as a U.S. representative from 1897 to 1905, Tom swam with his pals—as Tom Sawyer and Huck Finn did—at Ten Foot and Round Bend, perfect holes in Neosho's Hickory Creek. One boyhood friend, Walter Stroop, recalled that they also swam in Shoal Creek and would ride logs downstream. "We had no business doing that," Stroop explains. "Shoal Creek was bank-full and swift. But there wasn't anything we wouldn't try." Often the boys simply idled on the grassy riverbanks, where, mimicking the grown men they observed loafing on the town square, they shot the breeze and jawed plugs of tobacco. In the afternoons they explored caves, hunted cottonmouths and copperheads, and sprinted alongside trains making their way into town. According to Stroop, the boys always remained a step ahead of B. J. Pearlman, the town's frustrated marshal.

Benton's memoirs tell all the typical stories: he steps on a black snake in the backyard, gets his foot stomped by a horse, observes his father shouting commands at some "negroes" who were slicing a hog suspended from a tree, rides around town with his mother in a buggy pulled by a big white horse named Rex, and is wrapped in icy sheets after catching scarlet fever. In the autumn, Benton reminisces, there were hunts "where you ran in the dark of night with kerosene lanterns," guided by the barks and howls of Uncle Sam's dogs, in search of treed possum. The Colonel, however, who gave Tom a .22 rifle when Tom was six, was said to be embarrassed that his boy was "game-shy," the consequence, apparently, of a sad episode with a blue jay that had been pecking at Oak Hill's eaves. By most accounts, though, Tom was a tough boy: the Neosho papers documented his resilience and quick recovery from numerous injuries, like when he cracked his head open on a rock in Hickory Creek or scraped his knees dodging a speeding train.

Another favorite pastime was staging plays and circuses in Oak Hill's barn. Curious about life on the Nations, the boys had a passion for Indian themes. Though the tribes came into Neosho on the Fourth of July and entertained the young ones with elaborate powwows, these rituals weren't fierce enough for the boys, who had something more primal in mind. And so with their parents in attendance, Tom and his friends put on wild performances. They'd strip to their underwear, adorn their bodies with burned cork and pokeberry tattoos, and "jump and howl" around the barn.

Unlike Twain's restless boys, Tom didn't mind work. Neosho was located in the heart of the Ozark berry belt, and beginning in late May, Tom, Johnny Robison, and Bill Duff joined other children picking strawberries. Tom prided himself on being the swiftest "strawberry gaumer" in the field, a skill for which he was rewarded with six cents and a sticky glaze of berry juice on his limbs and clothes. In addition, his mother and father devised numerous chores to instill in him some "Missouri values." In the summer, for instance, he cleaned the stables at Oak Hill and tended to the Colonel's horses and cows.

Though Benton would emerge as a diligent and inspirational teacher, he always hated school. His philosophy of art was based on an abiding faith in practical instruction, yet from early childhood he distrusted doctrines. His memoirs, which describe the influence of Aunt Mariah and the books his father gave him to read, imply that he was home-schooled, when in fact he attended an intermediate school affiliated with Neosho's Scarritt Collegiate Institute, a training ground for young preachers run by the Methodist Episcopal Church. Tom was dissatisfied with his instructors and classmates, whom he felt were beneath him, and one day he came home bearing the news that he'd been promoted to a higher grade. His proud parents bought him the necessary books only to learn a few days later that they'd been duped. Tom saw the world—what he knew of it, anyway—as his classroom. He learned about politics and the social relations of men at Neosho's town square and on the campaign trail with the Colonel. Between the ages of seven and fifteen, Tom traveled with his father all over Missouri by horse and buggy, lodging in backwoods hotels and farms and hobnobbing, as Benton's friend and principal defender, Thomas Craven, put it, with "men in wide black hats, blue-eyed women in sunbonnets, hillbillies, babies, and seedy pettifoggers."

The Colonel was elected president of the Democratic State Convention in 1890 and first campaigned for U.S. Congress in 1896. He was an important figure in state politics, and though he remained a loyal Democrat throughout his career and was a protégé of George Vest's—an anti-imperialist and the author of a famous speech in favor of a fifty-dollar damage award for the owner of Old Drum (an opportunistic dog that was murdered for eating too many of a neighbor's sheep)—he also endorsed populist causes, most notably monetary reform. As a supporter of William Jennings Bryan, the Populist *and* Democratic candidate for president in 1896, the Colonel primarily targeted eastern plutocrats, bankers, and railroad magnates. Champ Clark, a Democratic lawyer and newspaper editor who served in Congress alongside the Colonel and was speaker from 1911 to 1919, was another close friend. These men shared a talent for speechifying and often congregated to brainstorm the urgent questions of the day. "Our dinner table," Benton remembers, "was always surrounded with arguing, expository men who drank heavily, ate heartily, and talked long over fat cigars."

Surely playing fast and loose with the true complexity of the Colonel's attitudes, Benton consistently claimed that his father's political philosophy began and ended with Thomas Jefferson. He began describing his father this way in the 1930s, at a moment in his career when it seemed advantageous to portray himself as the heir to an agrarian ideology. Mildred, however, described the Colonel's politics a bit more precisely. "My father was a Populist in a true sense," she said. "He was trying to fight off modernization and keep the agricultural focus in the center of this nation." According to the literary historian Russel B. Nye, "The problem, as the Midwest conceived it, was to reaffirm eighteenth-century democratic faith and to preserve it against the rising tide of skepticism, cynicism, and, as they called it, 'plutocracy.' But how could an agrarian democracy exist in an industrialized America? How could the political philosophy of Jefferson and Jackson be grafted onto the system of Spencer, Darwin, and Rockefeller?"

Bryan, the Boy Orator of the Platte, was an avid free-silver reformer and advocate for farmers and industrial workers who often quoted one of Andrew Jackson's more famous mottoes: "Equal rights to all and special privileges to none." Bryan also cited Senator Benton's praise of Jackson in his famous "Cross of Gold" speech, delivered at the Democratic National Convention in Chicago in 1896. With Tom at his side, the Colonel took Bryan's message via bumpy dirt roads to his constituents at camp meetings, noisy, boisterous affairs staged on grounds decorated with flags, posters, and red, white, and blue bunting. The meetings were early incarnations of the Chautauqua conventions (fervent summer lyceums for adult education first conducted at Lake Chautauqua in New York) that had become a staple of midwestern life by 1900. The traveling "tent-show" Chautauquas of the Midwest were less high-minded—according to Nye, they "could be incredibly cheap and tedious, with Kaffir choirs, Swiss bell-ringers, chalk-talk artists, and performing dogs . . . in the dripping Midwest heat"—but equally didactic. Both Bryan and Champ Clark became frequent speakers at Chautauqua events, and it was from these men that "millions of Americans got their first ideas of tariffs and tax policy . . . of Wall Street and the trusts."

The Colonel was also a gifted speaker and stood out as one of a few men able to awaken Missouri crowds during the 1890s, which was apparently an "uphill struggle" for most politicians of the time, who had to resort to "scramble[d] allusions" and "flight[s] of metaphor" to rouse their constituents. As one historian explains, while populist candidates failed to effectively communicate a radical message of class struggle to Missouri farmers, they did succeed in compelling Democratic candidates, like the Colonel, to develop a more radical rhetoric. In the 1890s and early years of the twentieth century, Democrats developed a pragmatic solution—called the Missouri Idea—that urged farmers and small-business owners to "make law into the major weapon for popular restraint of wealthy and powerful commercial and political leaders." As a lawyer, the Colonel was a logical choice for a leadership role on this progressive Democratic platform. Arriving at the rallies, he would disembark from his buggy and, with "blaring horns and smashing drums . . . [and] a great public 'hurrah'" chasing him, "shake everybody's hand and get slobbered over by . . . sticky babies." Time and again, Benton recalled, his father mounted improvised stages to campaign at the top of his voice. Meanwhile, with a few coins in his pocket, Tom roamed among barbecue pits, lemonade stands, fortune-tellers, shooting stands, and medicine shows. He was particularly fond of "spinnin' jennies," mule-powered merry-go-rounds, and on one occasion he accosted his father onstage just as he was preparing to deliver one of his rousing speeches.

"Hold on Dad. Hold on," Tom pleaded. "Gimme a quarter to ride the Spinnin' Jenny!"

The Colonel's face flushed, and he let out a belly laugh. "I guess you all know that's my boy Tom," he told the crowd, which erupted in applause.

It's not hard to imagine how stimulated a boy might feel standing next to his father, together working an ardent crowd. Not all fathers are publicly adored—or if they are, not all sons are there to witness it. Benton recalled that he saw his father's companionship during these days as a "promise of adventure and excitement in unfamiliar places." Years later, in *A Social History of the State of Missouri* (1936), his controversial mural for the Missouri State Capitol in Jefferson City, Benton represented what he remembered from those exhilarating childhood experiences. One panel, *Politics, Farming, and Law in Missouri*, illustrates, among other things, a political rally like the ones he attended in his youth. A speaker stands at a rostrum in front of a poster of Champ Clark and, one arm raised for dramatic effect, addresses the crowd. Tellingly, the audience is not yet moved by the speech, and Benton offers a few clues to explain the crowd's reticence. All around, dutiful Missourians engage in the labor and chores of daily life—sawing logs, hunting, dishing out food, even changing diapers. But their elders, sitting on benches and focusing on the speech, appear skeptical, unable to reconcile the politician's words with the work being performed by the responsible, productive citizens behind them. The speaker's challenge is to persuade the audience that his allegiance is not just to Clark and his cronies, who sit on the stage behind him, but also to the working class. Since the speaker is in fact the Colonel, it would have been easy for Benton to depict a more receptive crowd, one at the very least moving in rhythm with the oratory. But they sit perfectly still. What makes the scene poignant is that Benton is more interested in the hard sell of politics—and surely his father lost a crowd now and again—than in quaint family legends. One doubts that young Tom comprehended such nuances, but as a mature artist at the height of his career he managed to describe the push and shove of campaigning. The laboring figures may be muscular and heroic, but the solemn audience is the detail that best commemorates the Colonel's kind of work.

The Colonel craved campaigning and political ballyhoo. "The activity," Benton recalls, "was the breath of his life. It was not the holding of office but the getting of office that brought out from within him the grand drive, the expansiveness, the *go* that electrifies existence." Young Tom also enjoyed the spectacle but still could not shake the feeling that he was a disappointment to his father. "There was much about my unfolding character that did not fit in with [my father's] conception of a budding lawyer," he explains. "I was argumentative enough but I could not be induced to study and I had a low taste for creek-bank company. I preferred the town bums and the colored boys to the governors, senators, and judges who used to sit at our table."

The Colonel was a positivist who believed wholeheartedly that politics was the finest instrument for advancing social improvement. But his son wasn't so sure. This attitude was a natural consequence of Benton's instinctive skepticism, which was abetted later by witnessing his father's political defeat in the 1904 elections and his firsthand experience of the ruthless economic and class divisions in America's big cities. By many standards the Colonel was an admirable figure, at least in terms of his professional accomplishments: he had friends and influence. But Tom wasn't seduced, in part because of a distaste for politics. Such an explanation might surprise observers of Benton's life and art, both of which were deeply attuned to party politics. Indeed, during the 1920s and 1930s, Benton was more than a casual participant in political debates; he was an engaged artist who wrote articulately and passionately about Marxism and American liberalism and was a key player in the ideological skirmishes in New York over the practicality of radicalism. But Benton had learned to be political only after moving to New York in 1912, and in two thoughtful essays written later in life, he explains his reasons for turning away from active political debate. As Benton saw it, he was betrayed by the radicals and politicians he had once supported, and so he came to distrust politics, which he saw as corrupt. "Looking back," he writes, "it is amazing to think how much violence and hate . . . [was] generated by mere political attitudes."

Tom was a lonely boy, and pop psychologists might be tempted to ascribe his youthful contrarianism to his awkward appearance and being, as he puts it, "a variant of our stock." He was short, about five and a half feet, and much was made of his not resembling a Benton. One Neosho native recalls that he hated being called "Tommy" and got in fistfights over it; another explains that he always came home from Washington looking "different" from the other boys. The Colonel, meanwhile, did little to allay his son's insecurities. Tom was walking downtown one day, wearing a kilt and tam-o'-shanter, likely owing to his mother's Scottish heritage, when the Colonel, strolling with a friend, saw him strutting down the street and exclaimed, "Look what I've produced!" Another time, when a lady cousin visited Oak Hill, the Colonel lined up his children for inspection. Nathaniel, Mamie, and Mildred were strawberry blonds, but Tom, who had dark eyes and olive skin, resembled his mother. "Well, Cousin Maecenas," the cousin said, singling out the stout Tom, "they're all Bentons but that one. He seems to be a stray."

Mildred, however, was impressed by Tom's appearance and once claimed that he was "a very beautiful young child" with a powerful torso and arms—not "a little man at all." She agreed, however, that he was "very pugnacious, yes, very pugnacious, even as a young person," and concluded, coldly, "I didn't like him or dislike him." In truth, Tom didn't feel liked. In a devastating recollection he describes growing painfully self-conscious of his perceived idiosyncrasies and developing a "defensive defiance, especially in the presence of my elders":

> My father said that I rarely looked a man in the eye on being presented to him, and that if I did, it seemed as if I were getting ready to hit him with a rock. Actually, violence was frequently on my mind because I didn't like the way so many of Dad's

friends looked me over. Smart, shrewd men could tell at a glance that I would never make a lawyer. Dad's cronies loved him, and I always felt that they were sorry he had such a queer duck for a son.

In Washington, the Colonel tried in vain to mold his son in his own image by assigning him a variety of books to read. He had a substantial library of biographies and historical texts, some of which, according to Benton, contained "over-romantic reports of our history . . . that the young could get hold of." But Benton claims to have labored through several of the books—including *Pilgrim's Progress, Plutarch's Lives,* a life of Jefferson, and Senator Benton's *Thirty Years' View* and *Abridgment of the Debates of Congress*—and preferred "the dime novels hid out in the barn." The Colonel believed his plan to edify Tom was working when the boy started to browse the library on his own and would retreat to his hideouts with a few books under his arm. He was furious to learn later that Tom used the books for another purpose—to find inspiration for his real passion: drawing.

Polly Burroughs, one of Benton's biographers, recounts that he once told her that he had a "psychological failing" as a boy; he suffered, she explains, "dream-like spells where he sat, entranced, staring at the design, color, and texture of things for hours on end." Lizzie was convinced that her son was a genius and, against the Colonel's wishes, encouraged his talent for art. She told Gilberta Goodwin, a New York artist and Martha's Vineyard neighbor of Benton's, that when Tom was just eighteen months old, she held him up to a window to look at the rising moon. Lizzie explained that upon viewing the glowing orb in the dark sky, Tom uttered his first sentence: "What is it?" This curiosity about the "what" of things manifested itself from a young age in sketches and drawings. Tom drew the typical subjects—Indians, trains, and legendary feats, such as Custer's Last Stand, a favorite topic. What the Colonel didn't know at first was that his son found these subjects in his library; Tom copied many of his pictures from illustrations in books like John Clark Ridpath's *History of the World*.

Tom's very first drawings were of the locomotives he observed entering the Neosho depot. "Engines," he recalls, "were the most impressive things that came into my childhood . . . [T]o . . . see them come in, belching black smoke, with their big headlights shining and their bells ringing and their pistons clanking, gave me a feeling of stupendous drama . . . I scrawled crude representations of them over everything." Even as a boy Benton thought big: he composed his first mural when he was just six or seven. Oak Hill had a large stairway that led from the lower hall to the second floor, and soon after the wall of the stairway had been dressed in a cream-colored wallpaper, he defaced it with a long freight train drawn in charcoal. The mural began at the foot of the stairs with a caboose and ended at the top with an engine "puffing long strings of black smoke." The reception of this drawing, Benton explains, "was the first intimation I received of the divergency of view on the subject of mural decoration." Lizzie and the Colonel weren't impressed, and Tom was obliged to erase the mural with bread crumbs.

At first the Colonel saw no harm in Tom's scribblings, but when the boy's drawings began attracting the attention of Lizzie and family friends, he was outraged and started to lecture his son about the "futile ends of lazy habits." Benton outlines his father's objections in *An Artist in America*:

> Dad was profoundly prejudiced against artists, and with some reason. The only ones he had ever come across were the mincing, bootlicking portrait painters of Washington who hung around the skirts of women at receptions and lisped a silly jargon about grace and beauty. Dad was utterly contemptuous of them and labeled them promptly as pimps. He couldn't think of a son of his having anything to do with their profession. But I had drawn pictures all my life. It was a habit and Dad's disapproval didn't affect me in the least. I didn't think of being an artist. I just drew because I liked to do so.

As was his habit in his memoirs, Benton misrepresents the matter here. Not only did he work tirelessly in his letters home to convince his parents that being a painter was a noble and relevant vocation, but his later attitudes about artists, especially effeminate modern ones, were similar to the Colonel's. One ugly habit of Benton's was to occasionally mimic the rhetoric and arguments of the very men—including his father—he claimed were devoid of reason. During the 1930s, the mature Benton sounded a lot like the Colonel, and a lot like a hypocrite, especially when he repeatedly baited art critics and museum "pretty boy[s]" with "delicate wrists." But when Benton was young, art was just another subject that he and the Colonel disagreed about, and their disputes only grew in frequency and fervor once the family moved to Washington.

2

WASHINGTON, D.C.

In late 1897 the Bentons moved into a house on A Street, just behind the brand-new Library of Congress building and a short walk from the Capitol. Tom badly missed Neosho, particularly his friends and Indian pony, and in a letter to his friend John Robison, written soon after he arrived in Washington, he begged for news from home. But he also bragged about seeing a twenty-five-foot cannon at the "Navy Yart [sic]" and a performance of *Jack and the Beanstalk* at "the grand Opera house." Benton later described the Washington of that time more soberly, as a "leisurely place" and a quaint "brick-and-stone, horse-and-buggy town."

The Colonel's office, situated in the back of the house on A Street, was full of noise and smoke, a circumstance that Lizzie briefly tolerated. Though she desired a more glamorous life in the capital, she subdued her instinctive superiority—at first, anyway—and played the role of plain old Lizzie in order to support her husband's reputation as a man of the people. But she especially liked it when congressmen reminded her that the "ugliest man in Congress had the most beautiful wife." The Colonel, according to one observer, could "outtalk, outlaugh, and outdrink any of his colleagues"; Lizzie and M.E. were "the beauty and the beast."

Though the Colonel never distinguished himself as a major force in Congress (his service was limited to sitting on the House committees on Appropriations and Indian Affairs), because he was a gifted spokesman, his Democratic colleagues called on him to promote the party position on the major issues of the day—farm debt, tariffs, free silver, and U.S. imperialism in Cuba and the Philippines. Regarding the latter issue, which Democrats believed funneled capital away from their constituents, the Colonel argued that "the money power" coerced "this republican Government . . . to go into world politics, spit on our great past, and deny liberty to a struggling people." During his second term, Congressman Benton spoke on the floor on behalf of his beleaguered constituents—those planters saddled by the high-rate loans disbursed by eastern banks—when he attacked the gold standard as "un-American, un-businesslike, unconstitutional, and hurtful to the wealth producers of our country"; he argued that free silver—essentially the ability for, say, a farmer to deposit silver bullion and receive in return a like weight in silver coins, as was the case with gold—would prevent the "enslavement of the farmer, miner, country merchant, small banker, mechanic, and day laborer to the money power." A dozen years earlier, President Cleveland nearly fired the Colonel from his post as U.S. attorney for the Western District of Missouri after he made impolitic remarks regarding the president's coziness with the "gold bugs of Wall Street": he told a crowd of Democrats that free silver would eradicate these "leeches that suck the blood of the honest yeomanry of the west." Such speeches demonstrated the Colonel's allegiance to William Jennings Bryan's brand of idealistic populism, which was based, despite the evolution of the American economy, on an appealing republicanism that imagined the yeoman as the most virtuous of all citizens. Even after Bryan's defeat in the 1896 presidential election, the Colonel remained loyal to him, going so far as to predict that he'd win the next election.

In his unpublished memoir, Benton astutely summarized his father's political ideology: "The public image he presented was that of a man of the people, a plain, straight forward small town lawyer, and therefore the best fitted to represent the people's interest. In accordance with the populist line he was against big bankers, big railroad magnates, big corporations (TRUSTS) and above all against the corruptions and the nefarious influence of the rich Eastern society."

Regardless of what he said, the Colonel was no farmer, and neither was his son. Glancing at his paintings and murals, many have been tempted to mythologize Benton as the heir to a cropper ideology and a "chronicler of America's folk heritage." But such portrayals ignore two essential facts: first, the Colonel's populist rhetoric masked his sense of himself as an aristocrat especially suited to representing producers and farmers from a position of privilege, and, second, his son's presentation of himself as an outsider artist was a ploy to distinguish himself from the artists he associated with in New York. In fact, Benton was one of them: his concerns were largely aesthetic, and he wanted to be a "modern" artist (though one who, like his father, spoke for the disempowered). The challenge for father and son was representing this constituency without sacrificing what they believed was their superiority. Both wanted to be popular, not backward; both struggled mightily to seem so, albeit for different reasons; and both resented the struggle. Populist dogmas have always been hard to perfect, especially for those who deem themselves better than the average man.

Lizzie, meanwhile, grew restless. She was a social woman, not a political one, and quickly wearied of performing the ceremonies of a country wife. Just months after moving to A Street, she realized their address wasn't as chic as it might be, which upset her because she had a sense of entitlement, owing to Senator Benton's legacy in Washington, and plans to host many parties. The Colonel had no desire to move and initially was amused by his wife's aspirations, but the issue festered, and Lizzie grew more desperate to exploit the family name. Soon the A Street parlor was a combat zone: Lizzie demanded more elegant furniture, more fashionable dresses (from Paris!), new table settings, and finely engraved stationery ("Mrs. Elizabeth W. Benton"). The Colonel protested, citing, in vain, the impressions of his Missouri friends. His fears turned to panic when Lizzie introduced her pretentious habits to Neosho, where they returned each summer. Benton recalls, for instance, that he and the Colonel were humiliated when, back in Missouri, Lizzie would "dress herself, and her two daughters, in their most expensive and fashionable Washington clothes and walk around the square like a queen with her little princesses, bowing to the men and haughtily waving a gloved hand to the women." Also, while it had been customary at Oak Hill to serve supper all at once, filling the table with bounty from the backyard farm, after the first winter in Washington Lizzie hung new wallpaper in the Oak Hill dining room and instructed Berry, their black servant, to serve their meals in courses when guests were over. Beginning in the summer of 1899, Neosho townsfolk began referring to the Bentons as "mighty uppity," and the Colonel appealed to his wife, "It's these folks who send us [to Washington], Mizzuz. Don't shame them."

The Benton biographer Henry Adams recounts a dramatic story that Benton told, very matter-of-factly, in "The Intimate Story." Some time before their second year in Washington, Adams says, Tom walked into the parlor and discovered his mother "prostrate on the floor, with only the whites of her eyes showing." Apparently, Lizzie had passed out from rage after M.E. once again refused to move to a new address. The Colonel, "red and grim-faced, hurriedly explained that she had fainted and pushed the boy out of the room." The theatrics weakened the Colonel's resolve, however, and the family moved into a new house, at 1723 Q Street, when they returned to Washington for their second winter.

A few years before this incident, a peevish Henry Adams (the great nineteenth-century historian and, coincidentally, an ancestor and namesake of Benton's biographer) had returned to Washington from abroad and was taken aback by the merry mood in the city. "In Washington," Adams wrote after his visit, referring to himself in the third person, "he saw plenty of reasons for staying dead . . . Slowly, a certain society had built itself up about the Government; houses had been opened and there was much dining; much calling; much leaving of cards." When Lizzie got back to Washington, she hired a butler, purchased a carriage that remained on call to taxi her to teas and parties, and started traveling to Baltimore once a week to study piano with Ernest Hutcheson at the distinguished Peabody Conservatory of Music. (The stubbornly commonsensical Colonel begrudged Lizzie even this pleasure. "Play a tune once in a while," he barked from his study when she rehearsed her scales.) But her persistence eventually earned the family a few social triumphs: for one, her charms apparently beguiled the Roosevelts, who moved into the White House after President McKinley's assassination in September 1901. Theodore Roosevelt had written a biography of Senator Thomas Hart Benton in 1886 and was naturally curious about his descendants (and it didn't hurt that Roosevelt was softer on Democrats than his predecessor had been). Best of all for the Bentons, Mrs. Roosevelt loved to throw lavish parties—fetes, it so happened, that coincided with the emergence in Washington society of Jessie and Juliet Frémont, the beautiful granddaughters of John Charles Frémont, the awesome explorer and surveyor, and his wife, Jessie Ann Benton Frémont, a daughter of Senator Benton's and a cultural and social force in her own right. The Frémont name was still prominent in Washington at the turn of the century, and while the Bentons were there, one could read about Jessie and Juliet almost weekly. The local papers reported on what they wore (one evening "Miss Juliet" dressed in "a directoire gown of white chiffon, embroidered in roman floss in rich heavy lines, which formed a plastron about the low bodice and extended in deep point down the front of the skirt") and where they wore it (at Miss Ethel Roosevelt's White House debutante ball, for instance). To keep apace, Lizzie ordered new clothes for Mamie and Mildred, who had vivid memories of her mother in Washington:

> I like best to think of her coming down the stone steps of our house in Washington. She is wearing the hat with the bird of paradise on it; one white-gloved hand is holding up her trailing skirt, the other is in her ermine muff. Mrs. Rixey's carriage, with its pair of fine bays, is waiting at the curb. The footman holds open the carriage door and touches Mother's elbow as she steps in. I am five years old and I see this from the parlor window. Mother and Mrs. Rixey are going calling.

In the spring of 1902, the Bentons enjoyed their proudest moment in Washington. Lizzie's father, the grizzled Pappy Wise, visited from Texas, and the Colonel arranged for him to be honored in the House of Representatives. Pappy—with his long white beard and in his customary black outfit—cut a figure on the House floor, and the Colonel, Benton tells us, extolled the old man's rugged life in a moving speech:

> The old man . . . unwound his tall, spare body . . . and stood up looking straight ahead of him. The entire house rose and bowed and then broke into a thunderous clapping. My mother wept with pride. She did not realize that what these men were acclaiming was a world that she, and many of them too, were doing their best to destroy, the world of the plain straightforward old frontiersman who, axe and adze in hand, had laid the foundations of America. Running into machine like controls of their political behaviors . . . these men of the 1902 Congress rose to pay their respects to a better time and maybe to a fuller man than they could ever hope to be.

The move to Washington did little to placate the antagonism between Tom and the Colonel. Father and son enjoyed their last intimate contact during the summer of 1900, an election year, when they traveled together through the upper Ozarks and made a memorable rafting trip down the Gasconade River, a gentle, northerly flowing river lined with caves, bluffs, hardwood forests, and small villages. Benton reflected on this journey in his memoirs and viewed it as a turning point in his relationship with his father. In *An Artist in America,* he explains, "I had come to see myself as somehow or other involved in his activities, tied to his life. As I grew up and he began to be dissatisfied with my ways and lectured me, I learned to let his admonitions go in one ear and out the other."

Though the Colonel was hard on his son and cruel about his interest in art, Tom's petulance and arrogance annoyed everyone in the family except for Lizzie. Mildred recalled that he was "very tender with our mother. He never misbehaved in any way at all in our mother's presence . . . [She] was the only person he really loved, I guess. And he was the only person she really loved." Benton admitted there was some truth to Mildred's impression; he recalled how his mother was especially cruel to his brother, Nat, for no reason other than that his reddish hair and bug eyes reminded her of her husband. She would shove Nat away and then torment him when he ran to his father for consolation. This spiteful bickering and playing of favorites occasionally degenerated into spectacular showdowns. By the time Tom was thirteen, he'd gotten in the habit of interrupting his father at the dinner table. As the Colonel addressed the family, Tom would interject, "Well, I don't believe that's the way it was," or, "I don't read it that way." Congressman Benton would lose his temper and shout across the table, "Git out you two bit pipsqueak." Mildred corroborated these stories, describing how her father would order Tom away from the dinner table to take a walk around the block and cool off. Tom "was very sure that he was always right, and he was very talkative," she said. "He insisted on 'What I think,' and 'What I do,' and 'What I will do,' and it was always, as my father said, 'I,' 'I,' 'I.' My father called him 'Big I.'"

Tom felt the Colonel was unfair and perplexing. Simply put, he couldn't figure out his father, whom many have described as maddeningly erratic. On the one hand, the Colonel was genial with company; on the other hand, he was irritable and withdrawn when alone with his family. "At Oak Hill, his father was a nitpicker and faultfinder who criticized nearly everything Tom did," Adams explains. In public, though, the Colonel "encouraged the boy's argumentative traits." According to Benton, this hypocrisy was indicative of a more fundamental split in his father's character; the Colonel, he believed, struggled to reconcile his roles as a gentleman and an everyman:

> Now, my Dad was a Democrat, but like his idol, Thomas Jefferson, he had certain reservations about gentility and honorable company. These reservations were, however, purely conceptual, abstract, ideal, for he himself made no actual reservations in the selection of his own associates . . . Dad belonged to a race of men who, with Andrew Jackson, could brawl all over the race tracks and barrooms of Tennessee, shooting, stabbing, and cussing each other, and yet who were capable of maintaining to the death their good breeding and their assumptions of aristocracy . . . [I]t was mainly to attitude that Dad referred when he began looking skeptically at me. I didn't perform according to the standards which his attitude set up as proper. He never thought of his own unconventional ways of being and doing.

Tom regretted his poor relationship with his father. He knew he was lucky to travel with his dad among the river valleys and hills of southwestern Missouri, but in 1928, when he attempted to contextualize his turn away from abstract painting toward "historical conceptions," he wrote, "I was raised in an atmosphere of violent political opinions . . . This was always going on at the dinner table . . . and though it didn't have meaning for me in a political sense, it did have significance of an emotional sort."

As Tom entered adolescence, he and his father had an awkward relationship based on mutual distrust. They'd pass each other in the halls of Oak Hill or 1723 Q Street with barely a word. They only spoke to squabble: Tom was smug; the Colonel was unforgiving. What the Colonel anticipated would be a bond based on filial devotion, fatherly advice, and ancestral customs became a sad drama of recalcitrance. Though Benton's memoirs demonstrate that he preserved a begrudging respect for his father, they also contradict the popular notion that he revered his family's political legacy.

•

Even as his relationship with his father descended into juvenile bickering, Tom matured into a smart and gifted young man. He was educated at home by a female tutor during the family's first year in Washington; later, he enrolled in the Force School, where the Roosevelts' son Quentin, who was several years younger than Tom, was also a student. During his free time, Tom accompanied Lizzie to the Library of Congress, where he wandered the stacks in search of books more interesting than the political texts the Colonel assigned him to read. "I ran into the *Arabian Nights* in an awful hurry," Benton told an interviewer. "We had a big fracas about that when my father found it." After M.E. confiscated the book and replaced it with Senator Benton's *Debates of Congress*, Tom and John Rixey arranged a complicated system whereby they passed another copy of the illicit book—as well as cigarettes and editions of the *Police Gazette*, a tabloid with lurid reports on murders, prostitution, and boxing matches—to each other between their neighboring bedroom windows. Back in Neosho, the Colonel, nervous about the malignant influence of Washington on his son's character, arranged various menial jobs for him. When he was fifteen, for instance, Tom drove a delivery wagon for the local hardware store. As he waited at the train station for the arrival of his freight, boxes of nails and tools, he killed the time by smoking a pipe, a new habit that drew stares from the locals but that neither of his parents objected to, which Tom saw as a small victory.

Lizzie and the Colonel did squabble over Tom's growing passion for art, however. After moving to Washington, he continued to draw obsessively, and as earlier his favorite subjects were Indians and trains. Every spring Tom and Lizzie traveled by train to Waxahachie to visit Pappy Wise, and Tom was mesmerized by the awesome steam engines. From Neosho they would take the Frisco to Oklahoma, where they'd transfer to the Katy Flyer. In one remarkable drawing, made when he was nine, Tom depicts the Katy Flyer from three vantage points. The drawing illustrates his fascination with the mechanics of trains, with the pumping of their pistons and turning of their wheels. "I liked steam engines," Benton said, "because their movements were presented to the eye very clearly . . . But after we got into the highly industrial world we live in now the mechanical power is disguised so there's no more interest in it." He also had a "spell of mythology" and drew sketches of subjects from *Beowulf* and Greek and Rhine legends. Thomas Craven came across a trove of these pen-and-ink drawings and remarked that they "show an almost incredible proficiency for a boy of fourteen . . . Benton has always maintained that his facility is the reward of hard labor. He is not altogether right—he was a born draftsman."

John Franklin Rixey, a Democratic congressman from Virginia, and his wife, Ellen Barbour Rixey, were the Bentons' neighbors and closest friends in Washington, and Mrs. Rixey frequently accompanied Lizzie on her sojourns around the city. The Rixeys noticed Tom's talent and arranged for him to take art lessons from a Washington lady who designed place cards for society parties. He quickly tired of her prim sensibility and signed up for art classes at the Corcoran School of Art, which offered instruction to children on Saturday mornings. The school, which opened in 1890, was affiliated with the Corcoran Gallery of Art, an impressive museum showcasing the private collection of William Wilson Corcoran. The instructors obliged the young students to sketch geometric figures and wood cubes, "the very appearance of which," he remembers, "was forbidding." Tom preferred copying images from books and popular prints to the drudgery of academic training, and he attended classes sporadically. He was an assiduous student of these prints—*Custer's Last Fight*, for instance, a chromolithograph published in 1896 by Anheuser-Busch, which grossly romanticized the appearance of both Custer and his enemies, and various representations of the blowing up of the USS *Maine* in Havana Harbor in 1898. Benton always admitted that his drawings of these historical subjects were embellished. "What I didn't know about ships," he recalls, "I concealed with violent explosions full of spread-eagle men, fragments of smokestack and rigging." He continues:

> I had seen plenty of Indians in my time but they were of the sort that hung around the railroad stations of Indian Territory watching the trains. They were slouchy fellows in checked or red shirts who wore tall-crowned black hats . . . Except for . . . the color of their skin, and a certain solemnity, they were in no way different from the loafers around Neosho. They didn't wear feathers nor did they ever let out any war whoops that weren't generated in libations of corn whisky. They did no scalping and stole no

babies to bring up as members of their tribe. They were too tame for me, so I closed my eyes to what I knew and retreated into the ideal.

Benton adds a sad story about a visit to the 1904 St. Louis World's Fair, where he saw, for "two bits," Geronimo—"stories of whose ferocity had so often stimulated my imagination." But the Apache warrior was ferocious no more, of course—"there was only apathy." He was brought to the fair from prison in Oklahoma to sign autographs for a dime and was "a tired old man who gave bored answers to questions" and who wore, humiliatingly, "a long blue Army coat with brass buttons."

As Craven notes, Benton's early drawings, viewed in retrospect, aren't just juvenile, penny-a-picture doodles. One can infer from Benton's drawings two types of training—the lessons in geometry at the Corcoran and the idealized sketches of popular subjects—and find in them the foundations of his artistic principles. First, geometry was a key component of his aesthetic principle of "bumps and hollows," a technique whereby exaggerated convexities and concavities render volume as if it were pulsing dynamically. In his first official artist's statement, written in 1916 for the exhibition catalog for the Forum Exhibition of Modern American Painters in New York, Benton explains this theory: "I may speak generally of my aim as being toward the achievement of a compact, massive, and rhythmical composition of forms in which tactile sensations of alternate bulgings and recessions shall be exactly related to the force of the line limiting the space in which these activities take place." These "bulgings and recessions" were decidedly sculptural forms inspired by Renaissance statuary and Michelangelo's muscular figures. Benton's primary goal as a painter, he said again and again, was to enliven fundamental forms, to give the shapes we experience every day an aesthetic dynamism so we might encounter them anew.

Benton's style was also affected by his encounter with the tremendous paintings decorating the walls of the Thomas Jefferson Building, the Library of Congress structure completed just as he arrived in Washington. Tom was astonished by the building's architectural details—its lunettes, mosaics, marble, and, of course, murals. The golden dome of the library was visible from the Bentons' front steps, and he wrote to his friends in Neosho extolling its beauty. Commissioned in 1895 and finished in early 1897, these murals astounded the first visitors to the library. Its planners and architects were lucky because the completion of the building coincided with the grand style of the so-called American Renaissance. During the late nineteenth century, painters such as Kenyon Cox and Elihu Vedder were producing large-scale allegorical murals and paintings for public and private buildings and were a natural choice to decorate the Library of Congress.

Cox's murals *The Arts* and *The Sciences* were installed in the Southwest Gallery on the Jefferson Building's second floor; the pairing of "art" and "science" was a logical one that emphasized the nation's foundation in positivism and reason. Vedder's mural series *Government*, which graced the entrance to the Main Reading Room, was more impressively executed and thought out. The series treats, in a traditional way, what was deemed a timely topic: the effects of good and bad government on society. The central lunette, *Government*, is flanked on the left by paintings depicting *Corrupt Legislation* and its consequence *Anarchy*; on the right, by *Good Administration* and its corollary *Peace and Prosperity*.

Benton told an interviewer, "The first paintings that I ever noticed in my life were the murals in the Library of Congress, as a seven- or eight-year-old boy. I would say . . . that they must have had an effect on me." Vedder's murals seem quaint and escapist today—an allusion to distant and ideal republics—but to Tom they were utterly new and contemporary: not only did they correspond to the concerns of Congress during an era when big money was seen as a threat to the country's republican heritage, they reverberated with what he heard at the dinner table, the Colonel's lectures on the dangers of corruption and the justice of Jeffersonian ideas about agrarian prosperity. One incident demonstrates the extent of Tom's familiarity with the murals. He and the Colonel were leading a delegation of Missourians on a tour of the Jefferson Building when one asked about the murals. The Colonel was stumped, but Tom cut in and gave a small speech explaining in detail the entire narrative program of Vedder's series. The delegate was impressed by the boy's knowledge and asked how he'd obtained it.

"Well," Tom responded, "I read books once in a while."

"That boy don't waste his time, does he M.E.?" the man asked a red-faced Colonel.

It's fair to say, however, that Tom was less impressed by the content of Vedder's simple allegory than by other aspects of the murals, especially their scale, placement, and production. Unlike previous mural projects, the Jefferson Building murals weren't merely decoration for the architectural surface but as dynamic and functional a part of the structure as its columns, staircases, and stacks; the very purpose of such a massive library—to bolster responsible, informed governance and citizenship—was embodied in these public murals as well as in its books. One of Benton's favorite targets in later years was the increasing privatization of the art world; he frequently accused museums and curators of holding art hostage and keeping it, in fact and in spirit, hidden from citizens. These murals, however, were there to remind both politicians and the public of the purpose of republican governments—to serve the people. This democratic principle was also evident in the manner in which the murals were made. Though the Bentons arrived in Washington just after their completion, it was common knowledge that the murals had been produced by cooperative, bustling teams of artists, artisans, and laborers. One visitor who witnessed the construction of the murals in the summer of 1896 reported:

> Here was an immense scaffolding rising a hundred feet or more to the base of the dome, and high above that, as I looked up, I saw the iron elliptical truss-work that swung from the platform of the scaffolding to the top of the dome, carrying ladders and landing places to the crown of the lantern, 160 feet from the floor. Scores of skilled workmen were carving, fitting, and polishing. Some were perched high in the drum of the dome; others were setting mosaics and laying marble floors . . . The artists, like the workmen, were in overalls, and the atmosphere of the place seemed impregnated with the spirit of art and labor. It was something as it must have been in Florence or Venice in the Renaissance.

Though his boisterous scenes were a far cry from Vedder's classicized fables, Benton honored them years later when, as a teacher and a muralist, he alluded to the artisanal methods and apprenticeship system of the Renaissance to glorify the cooperative aspects of the production and reception of art.

As inspired as Benton may have been by the Jefferson Building murals, he claims not to have thought about being a painter until years later, when he was a student at the Art Institute of Chicago, in 1907. His passion remained drawing, especially pen-and-ink sketches. Benton cites as his main influence Clifford Berryman, the popular political caricaturist for *The Washington Post* when the Bentons were in town. A Democrat, Berryman made a living satirizing politicians from both the Democratic Party and the GOP. On the occasion of his eightieth birthday, in 1949, Berryman received a congratulatory letter from Harry Truman, one of his favorite subjects, stating, "Presidents, Senators, and even Supreme Court Justices come and go but the [Washington] Monument and Berryman stand." Berryman's drawings were almost always humorous. He drew irreverent scenes depicting Teddy Roosevelt and others with gigantic heads, tousled, windswept hair, and buffoonish costumes. Tom copied these subjects and imitated Berryman's crosshatching style; soon he was making his own original drawings on Capitol Hill. "When my father would take me up to the House," Benton recalled, "I'd sit there for hours sketching the congressmen, especially Uncle Joe Cannon, the famous speaker. I'll bet I drew him a hundred times."

Here, too, one is tempted to perceive an antecedent to Benton's mature manner, as he did, once declaring, "It is plain to me that the whole range of my aesthetic experience was foreshadowed by . . . the first seventeen years of my life." Along with his volumetric "bumps and hollows" and his public-mindedness, an essential element of his subject matter was a folksy, ground-level humor. From the moment he first encountered these cartoons, Benton sketched caricatures of family and friends, even of himself. His taste for stereotype, which Stuart Davis so loathed, can be traced back to his ardor for Berryman's caricatures. And even more fundamental is the devotion Tom showed to his craft during these early years. He didn't draw because he was bored; neither did he get bored of drawing. From the beginning he was obsessed, and it's this desire we ought to imagine; it's what distinguished him from his family when he was a boy and from his peers when he was a man. "As far back as I remember I drew pictures," Benton explained to the art historian Matthew Baigell. "But all children draw pictures. So I was not too unusual. What is unusual is that I kept it up. And this is what makes an artist. A permanent interest in visible things, a strong desire or will to create them and (in my case) to represent them." Describing Benton's sketching trips to the Ozarks and the Deep South during the

1920s, the art historian Karal Ann Marling explains that for Benton "sketches preserved that sense of the real, but drawing itself—the chatting, and the looking, and the pull of the pencil on the page—had a special kind of authenticity."

No matter which way the winds of criticism blew, whether in his favor or smack into his face, Benton sketched or painted every day. But regardless of how enthusiastic Tom was about art, high or low, the Colonel remained unmoved. Though the Wises liked art and Lizzie saw herself as a woman of "taste" who cultivated an "aesthetic responsiveness," Benton claimed that his father sustained "a Puritan aversion to images." Sadly, things would get worse. Whatever token of sympathy M.E. had for his boy and his interests was overwhelmed by the depression he tumbled into after losing his seat in Congress—to a Republican.

The humiliating defeat came in 1904. Labor radicals in the Midwest— energized by Eugene Debs, the Socialist candidate for president, and the triumphant strikes he organized—demanded more than Democrats could offer. Republicans, meanwhile, were successfully luring wary farmers away from the Democratic Party, which was unable to articulate a philosophy on labor that was sufficiently distinct from yet on par with radicalism; in addition, it was split on the party candidate for governor of Missouri and was being served with bribery and fraud indictments. In short, the political climate in Missouri had become a mess, and this demanded from the Colonel nimbler campaigning than he was capable of. The extent of the Colonel's position regarding unions and strikes was "You do not bite the hand that feeds you." Another matter on the table during the election was the railroad industry, especially its voracious corporate executives, who lobbied for local tax relief and development easements and then stuck it to farmers and passengers with inflated rates for shipping and travel. Benton recalls one stop in particular on this difficult campaign. The Colonel had just finished a rally speech on Jefferson's farmer when a young man asked, "Why do you, a farmer's Congressman, ride the trains on passes, when the railroads oppress us with their rates?" M.E. flushed and bumbled before scolding the concerned man, telling him he was a "trouble making Socialist trying to undermine his betters."

The Colonel may have lost his pragmatic touch during this reelection bid, but in fairness to him he'd seen it coming; the year before, he'd announced that he didn't want to run again, but upon hearing this confession, Lizzie went into "hysterics and faints," called him a coward, and accused him of bankrupting their children's future. So the Colonel soldiered on, going so far as permitting Lizzie, who anticipated another victory, to return to Washington with the kids in the fall of 1904. As a result, M.E. suffered the humiliating defeat alone.

3

JOPLIN

On Christmas Day of 1904, just after the Colonel's election defeat, Ellen Maury Slayden, the wife of a Texas congressman, attended an eggnog party in Georgetown and ran into Lizzie Benton. Slayden remarked in her journal that Lizzie "leaned against the wall dead white, as if she would faint, her pallor not relieved by the glow of the deep red velvet hat and dress in which, like Mary Queen of Scots, she had arrayed herself for her execution." Lizzie couldn't bear the shame of the Colonel's loss and refused to acknowledge that she'd have to abandon her teas and carriages and music lessons. At first she lobbied the Colonel to stay in Washington and establish a law practice; when this didn't work, she spoiled her children with gifts and demanded that they persuade their father to see things her way. But M.E. had some fight left and resolved to return to Oak Hill: the people whose opinions he cared most about were in Neosho, and even though he could have established a viable practice in Washington, he felt obliged to return home and regain their respect.

Initially, Tom was unmoved by the loss; he was more interested in wrestling than in his father's political career or his mother's social angst. It wasn't until his sixteenth birthday party, in the spring of 1905, that the meaning of the Colonel's defeat became clear to him. Lizzie walked into the party with a cake and announced grimly, "This is your last Washington birthday, Tom," before running from the room, sobbing in her hands. By early summer the Bentons were back at Oak Hill unpacking their belongings. Lizzie continued to despair and eventually took to bed; the diagnosis was a nervous breakdown. Her sisters were summoned and spent days kneeling at her bedside appealing to God for her recovery.

The Colonel finally cracked as well. Scared about his future and wounded by Lizzie's collapse, he withdrew from his family and developed what now seem obsessive-compulsive rituals. Benton recalls being puzzled by his behavior: my father, he writes, "was at times a secretive man, inwardly turned, and, although he had a great belly laugh, was not always quite happy. He was addicted to odd and inexplicable ways of self-communion." Once back in Neosho, the Colonel stopped using the indoor toilet and developed the peculiar habit of retreating to Oak Hill's outhouse, situated in a wooded lot, where he sat adding and subtracting enormous numbers: "The walls of our privy, the backs of our books, and the edges of newspapers were covered with them—column after column." No amount of cajoling budged him. Even as clients waited for him and servants called his name, the Colonel hid in the outhouse, scribbling and erasing. "No one ever found out what it was all about," Benton concludes, and during the year following his defeat, he adds, "[we] drifted apart . . . so I scarcely knew him."

As his parents regressed into their eccentricities, Benton struck out on his own. He was a young man now—no longer a "two bit pipsqueak"—who had, as he puts it, "all the cockiness of my fifteen years sitting on my shoulders." Though he attended high school for a year in Neosho, most of his education was extracurricular; the only work he remembers doing that year was writing a long biography of Napoleon, a project he undertook on his own initiative. He spent his afternoons bumming around the town square, scowling at anyone who caught his eye. By his own admission he was pugnacious and tense; the Neosho boys viewed him skeptically, and he desired to reestablish himself. He didn't help himself much when one Sunday evening in June 1905 he walked downtown wearing an outfit his mother had bought him in Washington. The very weird sight of this short, surly boy with clenched fists strutting by the Bank of Neosho in a shimmering silk shirt, blue blazer with mother-of-pearl buttons, and white slacks caught the eye of one Harry Hargrove, who was obliged by his gang to smear his boot on Benton's pants. Benton went berserk and bloodied Hargrove's nose before pinning him in the dirt with a wrestling move he had learned at the Force School. A zealous marshal rounded up the boys and dragged them into court, where a judge fined Benton eight dollars and let Hargrove walk. "The damned scoundrels," a paranoid Colonel responded, "trying to get at me through my boy."

Benton worked on his wrestling and boxing techniques at the gymnasium on the square and then challenged the boys to meet him at Big

Spring Park, where he defended himself with "slashing attack[s] to the stomach." On those occasions when he was injured, he'd respond, "I don't pay that no mind." But Benton eventually earned the grudging respect of the local boys. They came to tolerate his odd habits and fashions, and even peered over his shoulder as he sketched the swimming hole at Hickory Creek. Soon he was up to more customary kinds of adolescent high jinks: loafing around the square, ogling girls, sharing lewd jokes. He also learned to drink: "I found my way through the back doors of the saloons and learned . . . to stand up to the bar and wash down a jigger of whisky with salted beer." In the fall of 1905, Benton and his friend Sterling Price made fools of themselves at the annual Seneca-Neosho high school football game. They raided Price's father's store and got away with a jug of rock-candy whiskey, which they killed as they drove a horse-drawn buggy the sixteen miles to Seneca; on arrival they lost control of the buggy, which the horse steered into the middle of the football field. They fell off the wagon and rolled around the fifty-yard line in drunken hysterics. As punishment the boys were obliged to attend temperance sermons by Neosho preachers.

The next summer Benton had another adventure. Eager to bust out of provincial Neosho, he and another friend, Johnny Smith, "hooked a southbound freight . . . and experimented with bumming." They rode an open boxcar through the night, watching the moon rise in Missouri and the sun come up in Arkansas. A brakeman found the two young men and booted them off the train in the middle of the woods. They followed the tracks to the nearest town and spent the day in a creek bed waiting around for a return train. Because Benton became an avid chronicler and player of American folk music, it's hard to resist thinking here of Woody Guthrie—who, in turn, illustrated his books with Bentonesque sketches. The two men had a lot in common politically and stylistically, and both used trains to symbolize what one historian has called a "faux-naive" rhetoric meant to substantiate their identification with "dispossessed Okies and the working classes." Guthrie, too, rode trains wherever they were going: "I'm gonna hug her breast till I find out where she's bound." Benton put it this way: "The itch to be on the go was strong with me, and I grew more restless every month."

His naughty ways likely owed something to his encounter with Missouri's greatest fictional heroes, Tom Sawyer and Huck Finn. Upon his return to Neosho, Benton renewed his friendship with Wellesby Benton. Wellesby's father, a Neosho doctor, had an impressive library where the boys lost themselves in fantastic tales by Alexandre Dumas and Edgar Allan Poe. It was also in Dr. Benton's library that the boys first read Mark Twain's *Adventures of Huckleberry Finn*, and, not surprisingly, Benton frequently identified Huck as a kind of doppelgänger. "I was raised among people who talked the language of Huck Finn's people, who thought like them, and acted like them," Benton explains. "I am in that book just as the book, after all these years of reading it, is in me."

Between 1939 and 1944, just a few years after executing *A Social History of the State of Missouri*, Benton illustrated editions of *The Adventures of Tom Sawyer, Adventures of Huckleberry Finn*, and *Life on the Mississippi*. It has become something of a cliché to describe Benton's youth as a reification of the fictional lives of Twain's boys. Compared with Tom Sawyer's and Huck Finn's boyhoods, Benton's was certainly a privileged one, but there was more to the comparison than the boys' mischievous ways. "For Huck," Robert Penn Warren observed, "the discovery of reality, as opposed to illusion, will mean freedom." The same was true of young Tom Benton: he saw through the chimera of politics, much to his father's dismay, and recoiled from bluster; he sensed that something was amiss with the world, especially with its hierarchies and with the conventional wisdom of its elders.

Benton grew up between the Missouri and the Mississippi Rivers, as did Twain, and as a boy (and later as a grown man), he let his imagination loose on their great expanses. "Down the river is freedom from consequence," Benton writes in *An Artist in America*:

> All one has to do is jump in a skiff at night, and by the morrow be beyond reach of trouble. In the past . . . fellows who had been too handy with a knife or gun . . . could float off into a new world and begin again . . . [T]he river waters are suggestive of release . . . The thought of floating effortlessly away on running water has an irresistible charm. In *Huckleberry Finn*, Mark Twain has caught the spirit of this, and back of the adventures of Huck and Jim . . . there is always the moving river and the promises and hopes that lie around its unfolding bends.

Though he hadn't been able to fully unfasten himself from his family and the expectations they had of him, Benton made sure that his illustrations of Tom and Huck depicted boys who were unfettered and, in the frontier tradition, sui generis. In his illustration of the white-washing scene from *Tom Sawyer*, for example, he shows Ben Rogers—the boy who demands the brush from Sawyer—hard at work on the fence. Sawyer, meanwhile, enjoys his break: he sits on the barrel in the shade, dangles his legs, and munches on an apple. Benton teases from the scene a nice bit of symbolism. Twain describes the fence as an "un-whitewashed" and "far-reaching continent," and as Benton imagines it, Ben has splashed a representation of the eastern half of the United States on the fence, an image that the relaxed Sawyer luxuriates in, daydream-ing of walking its roads and crossing its rivers. Benton turns the day's labor into an invocation to voyage beyond the bonds of boyhood. Such illustrations capture well the spirit of Twain's own description of Huck Finn in *Tom Sawyer*:

> Huckleberry came and went, at his own free will. He slept on doorsteps in fine weather and in empty hogsheads in wet; he did not have to go to school or to church, or call any being mas-ter or obey anybody; he could go fishing or swimming when and where he chose, and stay as long as it suited him; nobody for-bade him to fight; he could sit up as late as he pleased; he was always the first boy that went barefoot in the spring and the last to resume leather in the fall; he never had to wash, nor put on clean clothes; he could swear wonderfully. In a word, every-thing that goes to make life precious that boy had.

Benton started reading serious literature during the summer of 1905, when he had idle time before starting work as the errand boy on a Neo-sho surveying crew. He met a local law student who was four years older and the owner of an alluring library. This anonymous young man, who impressed Benton with his analytical mind and irreverent attitudes about religion, invited him to spend evenings discussing the books of Emerson, Twain, Darwin, Robert Green Ingersoll, and Elbert Hubbard. Ingersoll, known as "the great agnostic," was an eloquent and iconoclas-tic orator who attacked orthodoxy: in lectures such as "The Gods," "Some Mistakes of Moses," and "Suicide and Sanity," he enunciated the bases for his skepticism and humanism. "The foundation of supersti-tion is ignorance, the superstructure is faith and the dome is a vain hope," Ingersoll professed to audiences in 1898. "Superstition is the child of ignorance and the mother of misery." In his last public lecture, delivered in Boston in 1899, Ingersoll posed the question "What is religion?" His answer was no-nonsense: "Religion teaches the slave-virtues—obedience, humility, self-denial, forgiveness, non-resistance . . . Religion does not teach self-reliance, independence, manliness, courage, self-defence."

Hubbard was the successful soap salesman who, in 1895, founded the Roycroft Press and the associated self-sufficient community that preached a rugged individualism and established its own farms, blacksmith shop, and bank. The Roycrofters advocated social reform through an arts and crafts ethos, and if it weren't for the quality of their craftsmanship, the community and its teachings wouldn't have been nearly as popular as they were. Hubbard, who by coincidence was the uncle of one of Benton's mentors in Paris, was a weak writer, and even his best-selling pamphlet A Message to Garcia, published in 1899, makes one squirm. It's a sentimental ode to hard work and to loyalty between employer and employee that butchers Jefferson's notions about the yeoman. "It is not book-learning young men need, nor instruction about this and that," Hubbard admonishes, "but a stiffening of the vertebrae which will cause them to be loyal to a trust, to act promptly, concentrate their energies [and] do the thing." Hubbard's promise that honest, scrupulous men were "wanted in every city, town, and village" likely placated the drifting young artist's anxieties upon his return to Neosho, when he was sixteen and searching for meaningful work. Ingersoll's message, by contrast, galvanized Benton at a time when he was increasingly skeptical of Lizzie's notions about God. Recalling his conversations with this anonymous law student, Benton wrote, "I would never become, as he was, a militant atheist . . . but I would never again have any . . . fears of hell."

Given Benton's love of books, attraction to big ideas, and aptitude as a writer, it's surprising that he wasn't a more engaged student, but he was dreamy and distracted by an intrinsic "uneasiness." After the Bentons returned to Neosho, one man in particular seemed to comprehend Tom's true nature and was the first person to urge him to flee the town and pursue an artist's life in the city. This was Mr. Calhoun, the music tutor Lizzie had hired to teach her piano. Once a week Calhoun came down to Neosho from Carthage—a town about thirty miles to the north that was enlivened by the tinkling of ragtime piano—and he quickly took an interest in Tom, whom he deemed a skilled draftsman. He exhorted Lizzie to let Tom travel to Paris to live "*la vie de bohème*," and though this was impossible at the time, Calhoun's encouragement confirmed what Benton already suspected—that he was wasting his time in Neosho.

In May 1906, seventeen and having barely passed on to the next grade, Benton saw an opportunity when his cousin Willie McElhany visited Oak Hill. The son of Jim McElhany and Emma (Lizzie's sister), Willie lived in Joplin and worked as a surveyor in the mines. Situated in the southwest corner of the state between Neosho and Carthage, Joplin had opened to mining after the Civil War and was flooded by immigrants hoping to cash in on the boom. Though the mining industry within the city limits had gone bust before Benton moved there, lead and zinc saturated the rock around the city, and by the turn of the century ten thousand miners lived in the region. Downtown Joplin was the hub of the tristate district and had numerous newspapers and banks, which capitalized on the financing and administration of mining. It was also a boisterous city that saw its share of labor unrest, socialist agitation, and horrible racial violence. In 1903, for instance, just one year after Langston Hughes was born there, Joplin was plagued by a string of terrible crimes, including the murder of two policemen and the retaliatory lynching of a black man named Thomas Gilyard, who was strung from a downtown telephone pole and shot three times, over the protestations of a local attorney and the mayor-elect. In the ensuing riot, several houses were burned to the ground, and many blacks fled the city. After visiting Oak Hill, Willie promptly wrote to Lizzie and the Colonel to say that he could get Tom work as a surveyor in Joplin. They resisted, citing the city's rough-and-tumble reputation and the rumors about Willie's older brother Roy, who also lived in Joplin and was reputed to be a womanizer and a pimp. But they were eventually swayed by their son's pleas and Mr. Calhoun's pledge to check in on the boy periodically.

Benton was seventeen, though, and quickly surrendered to the tempting vices of city life. His parents, it turns out, had been right to worry. His first task was to find work, and with Willie at his side he toiled at the scorching mines marking property boundaries. It was a nasty, sweaty job that required lots of walking "in the burning sun of the diggings, over shale and crushed rock which shimmered in the heat and burned through the leather of our boots." After three weeks of this work without a day off, Benton quit. Besides labor and racial tensions, the city's founders had to contend with a boom in the number of saloons that served hard-nosed miners and unscrupulous businessmen, saloons that contributed to Joplin's reputation as a hub not just of commerce but of gambling and prostitution. "The saloon doors—and there were plenty of them—swung constantly," Benton remembers. "Money was being made, and all the devices of our rough-and-ready civilization were set up to see that it was spent." Ever vigilant about the whereabouts of family friends, Benton, "in an independent frame of mind," visited the saloons to drink beer and plug his hard-earned nickels into slot machines. It was in one of these saloons that he had his first experience in the "mysteries of sex": after a night drinking with a friend, Benton yielded to a "black-haired young slut" in a "flaming red kimono." The underappreciated lady took the young lad upstairs and coaxed a performance out of him. When it was done, she brought Benton downstairs, pushed him into the center of the room, and announced, with a curtsy, "The kid has been fucked."

Likely dazed, Benton arranged a meeting with Mr. Calhoun, who had promised to check up on him, in a "dim" downtown hotel. Calhoun plied Benton with Benedictine aperitifs and wine. As Benton described it, "Although my head was a little turned with wine, I caught the strange way he was looking at me. His eyes were girls' eyes, when they want to tease you, wide open, clear and looking as if they were going to melt." Benton fled the hotel, "revolted," and never saw Mr. Calhoun again.

The most infamous saloon in Joplin was the elegantly debauched House of Lords, which served big steaks to businessmen negotiating deals above the din of the house orchestra and rented upstairs rooms to miners looking for a place to play cards and rendezvous with the house ladies. It was also the setting of an oft-told story about how Benton earned his first paying job as an artist. One Saturday night, a few weeks after getting to town, he was sitting alone at the bar, nursing a beer and ogling a notorious painting that hung on the saloon wall. As Benton describes it, this was by the standards of the time a risqué picture: it depicted a naked, masked woman reclining on a daybed and bleeding to death from a knife wound. A caption explained that her murderer, who stood behind her poised to turn the weapon on himself, was her brother. Apparently, the siblings had committed incest at a masked ball, and upon discovering their blunder, the brother saw only one way to atone for the unnatural act. "I must have got sufficiently absorbed in this masterpiece to attract attention," Benton wrote later, "for I became aware of some laughing down the bar . . . and turned to meet a line of grinning fellows." As was his custom, Benton wasn't willing to laugh at himself and insisted that he was studying the picture because he was an artist and "wanted to see how it was done."

"So, you're an artist, Shorty?" one of his tormenters asked.

"Yes, by God! I am," Benton replied.

He claims that this impromptu declaration "tied together the loose strings of all the purposeless activities of my adolescence" and "threw me back on the only abilities that distinguished me from the run of boys." The episode, he insists, was a "quirk of fate" that "made a professional artist of me in a short half-hour," for one of the men accepted his challenge and demanded to know where he worked. When Benton answered that he was in town to find employment, the man said that a new newspaper, the *Joplin American*, had its offices just down the street and was looking for an artist. The man was even willing to take Benton there that very minute. "I went, strangely enough, with perfect confidence," Benton recalls.

The two men walked up a steep stairway leading to the paper's second-story offices. The room, which smelled of "printer's ink, hot iron, and oil," was occupied by a single man with a gray beard. Benton announced that if the paper needed an artist, he was the man for the job. The editor chuckled and stared back at him for an awkward minute before saying that he would give him work on the condition that he go across the street and sketch a likeness of the town druggist. "By the grace of God," Benton returned to the office with a reasonable portrait and was offered a wage of fourteen dollars a week.

Benton worked for the *Joplin American* for the remainder of the summer. Each week the editors asked him to draw a caricature of a prominent city member. In the fashion of Clifford Berryman, his sketches placed oversized heads on small bodies—"I would start with the nose and hang the other features on it." He'd hit the streets each week looking for a suitable subject and "under the red-hot corrugated iron roof of the office" would translate his pencil sketch into an ink draw- ing. When his work was done, Benton set out for the House of Lords, where he "clamped [his] foot importantly on the bar rail . . . and drank beer." And he wasn't alone anymore, either. He had befriended the pa- per's cub reporter, Ben H. Reese, and together they rented a room on Joplin's south side and spent their idle hours in the saloons. It was a splendid summer. "Everything was jake," Benton wrote. "I was a man— and free."

In his letters home, Benton made sure to impress on his parents that he had outgrown bumpkinish Neosho and was engaging in manly en- tertainments. In one particularly colorful letter to the Colonel, written on *Joplin American* letterhead, he bragged about the paper's ability to monitor the great boxing matches of the day. The city, Benton ex- plained, had just been captivated by the Labor Day title bout between two legendary boxers, Battling Nelson and Joe Gans. The slight Nelson was renowned for his capacity to absorb poundings; Gans, meanwhile, who was black, had been described by the *St. Louis Post-Dispatch* a day before the fight as "easily the fastest and cleverest man of his weight in the world" who "can hit like a mule kicking with either hand." During the bout, Benton told his father, a man from the paper with a deep bass voice read the returns from each round to a swelling crowd. At sundown, Benton observed over two thousand people in the streets cheering for Nelson to beat the "nigger." After an epic forty-two rounds, Nelson lost the fight on a foul; he'd hit Gans with a low blow. "Everyone was disap- pointed," Benton reported, "except of course the niggers. I was afraid the white people would kill a few of them and I'm pretty sure they would if the niggers had offered to do anything."

That letter, of September 1906, turned out to be Benton's last from Joplin. During a weekend trip home to Oak Hill, the Colonel pointed out that it was school time and that cartooning wasn't the kind of em- ployment he'd envisioned for his son. Moreover, the Colonel fretted, Joplin "offered too many opportunities for a seventeen-year-old boy to go to hell." After several hours of spectacular bickering, Benton and his parents reached an odd compromise: if he agreed to quit the *Joplin American* and enroll in military school for a year, they would consider allowing him to go to Chicago and study at the School of the Art Insti- tute. So, just like that, Benton explains, he found himself "strutting around in a gray uniform."

•

In 1972, Benton returned to Joplin for the first time since 1906. He'd been commissioned to paint a mural commemorating the one hundredth anniversary of the city where he'd begun his career. At the time of the commission, Benton's reputation as the greatest American painter had long since faded, but he was still considered—in the Midwest, anyway—the artist of choice for large mural projects. Hiring Benton was the idea of Mary Curtis Warten, the wife of the longtime Joplin lawyer Henry Warten. To persuade the aging painter and his business-minded wife, Rita, to accept the commission, the Wartens traveled to the Bentons' stone mansion in Kansas City.

"When we drove into the driveway," Henry Warten recalled, "he was standing there with a martini, and he had a black patch on his eye. He looked like a little old pirate."

The two couples discussed the project over drinks. Rita initially rejected the proposal on the grounds that her husband, at eighty-three, was too old for such a taxing commission, but a sixty-thousand-dollar payday helped change her mind. Benton later explained that he was attracted to the project for other reasons. "Every old codger likes, now and then, to recall his youth and . . . tell stories about it," he writes. "Here an opportunity was offered to tell some of mine and in a way that would almost compel attention." He also added that the project was feasible because the mural, which didn't have to be so big as to require "ladder climbing," could be executed in the comfort of his Kansas City studio.

Benton worked seven hours a day on the mural. He had decided on a subject almost immediately after receiving the commission: the mural would depict "the young booming city of Joplin, but also . . . what made it boom." Working from memory and with the aid of old photographs, Benton, as was his custom, began by molding clay models to get a sense of the scale and proportions of the mural; then he made sketches on a grid from which he would paint the scene. The center of the mural shows the influx of immigrants to the booming city: a laden horse-drawn wagon steered by an exhausted patriarch and festooned with a quaint banner reading "Joplin or Bust" crests a hill overlooking the city's bustling main drag. The wagon is contrasted with an electric streetcar, visible in the background, which testifies to Joplin's status as a modern city. Just opposite the streetcar is the House of Lords. Benton, it turns out, agonized over his decision to include the saloon. One of his first sketches for the mural represented two men at the bar conferring in front of the painting of the incestuous siblings. Benton quickly abandoned this subject, however, and it doesn't appear in the finished mural. A Kansas City friend of the artist's, Sidney Larson, explains that Benton "worried that with Joplin in the Bible Belt and with church people and schoolchildren raising money to finance the painting, there could be an unwelcome 'stink'" if the House of Lords appeared too prominently in the painting. It's for this reason that Benton painted into the mural an awkward detail: in the center foreground a Gideon Bible sits on a small table. Whatever his motivation for including the Bible, he wasn't committed to the symbol; his own disinterest in the book's subject is disclosed by the fact that no one notices it, casting doubt on his insistence that whatever the weaknesses of the mural, "at least" its meanings "are not phony."

Benton did include some symbols of the city's dependence on shadier forms of commerce. In the left foreground, just next to the Bible, two older gentlemen play a game of five-card draw. Our suspicion that these aren't upright businessmen is confirmed by their anonymity: we can't see their faces. The vignette was undoubtedly influenced by the French and American traditions of genre painting. For instance, one detail—a pair of disembodied hands, holding an aces-high full house, that seem to come from underneath the table—recalls the deft grifters in the works of the seventeenth-century French painter Georges de La Tour. Nineteenth-century American genre painters also represented card-sharps and confidence men, typically as allusions to enterprising Wall Street tricksters. Benton was particularly fond of George Caleb Bingham, a Missouri genre painter who moonlighted as a politician, and wrote appreciative prefaces for two books on him. What he admired so much about Bingham was how he transformed the "obscure" dystopian complications of capitalist society into "plainer and more matter of fact" representations. Benton includes a self-portrait in the Joplin mural; he sits right next to the gamblers, making an ink sketch—a clear illustration of the artist as an overseer alert to sleight and subterfuge.

The labor that "made [Joplin] boom" is also here. The right side of the mural shows, as he described it, "the different kinds of powers exercised in Joplin's early mining operations": two muscular miners crank a bucket of sludge up from a hole in the earth. But the labor, upon examination, looks like an afterthought. Typical of Benton's figures, the men are full-bodied, and even their clothes—rippling and bulging—are rendered as flesh, yet they hardly seem subjugated to the laws of gravity; rather, they appear to float, light-footed, just above the ground on which they toil. Benton had a habit, for which he was criticized, of paying more attention to design (two men here, a wagon there . . .) than to hard reality. This is why his scenes often look more mythological, or sentimental, than authentic. Regardless of how tired the men were in the photographs that Benton studied while working on the mural, looking at *Joplin at the Turn of the Century*, we can't forget that these two miners are fictional players in a designed space. It's this aspect of Benton's work that John Canaday, the art critic for *The New York Times* in the 1960s and 1970s, remarked upon a few years before he traveled to Joplin to report on the unveiling of the centenary mural. Canaday was himself an antimodernist suspicious of abstract expressionists and ideological art professors, but he was also an astute observer who had as good a sense of Benton's art as anyone of the time. Reviewing a 1969 exhibition of Benton's lithographs at the Associated American Artists Gallery in New York, Canaday commented on the odd disjunction between the artist's mannered style and "everyday" topics: "Mr. Benton's weak spot has always been that the sophistications of his style are out of kilter with the folksiness of his subject matter. The misalliance between Huck Finn and El Greco is as bothersome as ever."

It was likely this criticism that put Benton on edge when he learned that Canaday was coming to Joplin, in April 1973, to interview him. According to Larson, after Tom and Rita settled into a suite (on the doors of which hung new brass plaques engraved with their names) in the best hotel in town, Tom had a "few snorts and already was getting belligerent at the prospect of meeting another hostile Eastern critic." Again, Benton was paranoid: Canaday put him at ease and proved a gracious inquisitor. His piece remarked that "neither Mr. Benton nor his painting style has lost the old zip" and reported on a remarkable scene:

> [T]he sweetest sight of the entire forty-eight hours of the celebration was that of the youngsters who came to shake [his] hand in awed delight as if it had been the hand of George Washington.

By one measure this could be pure Norman Rockwell, but by a better one it indicates a degree of identification between an artist and his countrymen so rare as to merit the risk of calling it unique—at least in our century of divorce between art and daily life.

If the obsequious article pleased Benton, he didn't say so, but he got off easy, as his late paintings are far from his best, and *Joplin at the Turn of the Century*, for reasons above and beyond its timidity, is a sad painting. It's a shame, for instance, that he kowtowed before his patrons. He pretended otherwise, of course, writing to Mary Warten, "Remember, we sign our contract on the theme—NOT ON HOW I HANDLE IT." But in the end what the mural demonstrates is how far Benton drifted in his late years from his "voice," from his vital and impious paintings and his terse, laconic prose. What happened to the Joplin remembered in *An Artist in America*, the one of "soliciting preachers," "decorated girls," "glittering swank," and paintings that could make one "hot with embarrassment"? He lost this Joplin forever when, in the same letter to Warten, he implored, "I am still open to suggestions for the whole thematic concept."

Before hanging the mural for the first time, Benton discovered that its frame was bowing, so he asked for a minute alone and then walked over it to set it straight. With this in mind, one wonders how Benton would have reacted to the news, in March 2005, that when conservators prepared to move the mural from the old Municipal Building to the new city hall, they discovered that it had been splattered with black paint and insect droppings.

In the autumn of 1906, Tom enrolled in the Western Military Academy in Alton, Illinois, twenty-five miles north of St. Louis, just above the Mississippi River. The school, previously known as the Wyman Institute, a boarding school for boys, became a military academy in 1892 and enrolled about 125 cadets when Benton showed up. It was an odd choice for Tom, who left behind no clues as to why the Colonel preferred a military education for him, but he arrived in late September, and it was likely the only school that would accept him so late in the school year. Naturally, Benton hated it. After Joplin, where he'd barhopped, flirted, and made a salary, any school was a step back, and he resisted the arrangement, explaining to his parents that the "academic harness was abhorrent" to him.

Soon after his arrival, he wrote to his mother and complained, "The restriction of this life is something awful." He confessed to getting punched in the stomach and slapped on the face as punishment for his poor posture and conditioning. In order to prove himself, he told Lizzie, he almost knocked out a cadet with a strike to the head; after that, the other boys loosened up on him. After a few days, however, he settled down, pledged to make it work, and arranged his classes—Latin, geometry, literature, and history. Being more mature than the other boys suited Benton well, and he grew into playing the part of an outsider. "There are a lot of awkward boys up here," he wrote to his mother, "and the way some of them stand is enough to make anyone die with laughter."

The football field was one arena where Benton tested himself and sought out some new skills; it quickly became a proving ground, another place for him to demonstrate to the other boys his superiority. In October, as cold winds started to sweep off the Mississippi over the bare campus, the older cadets devised cruel hazing rituals for the new boys; in one instance they abducted several lowerclassmen, tied them down in the woods near the lake, and compelled them to sing "Sweet Adeline" for two hours at the top of their lungs. "Of course they don't bother me," Tom wrote home, "because I have made the first team and am well on my way to making a 'W' to put on my sweater." Benton had always been attracted to contact sports—wrestling at the Force School, boxing in Neosho, and now football. He made no secret of the reason for this: he hated that he was short, and hated even more appearing weak or submissive, so he relished any opportunity to surprise an opponent, actual or perceived. His letters home indicate that he was remarkably serious about football; he treated it not as a diversion but as a way to hone the strength and guile he deemed necessary for getting ahead in a hostile world.

He played end on both offense and defense, positions ill suited to his size but indicative of his guts. His letters home that fall were decorated with sketches of football players and colored by descriptions of amazing feats of athleticism in matches against Smith Academy, East St. Louis High, and Central—hard tackles, recovered fumbles, and game-ending blows to his legs and ribs. In a letter dated December 2, he told of how, in the final game of the season, he would have scored had he not stepped out of bounds a yard shy of the goal line, a humiliation eased by the fact that he'd earned his letter sweater, which he described as being expertly sewn and a fair reward for his hard work.

Though he was never an eager student, fortunately an English teacher took an interest in him and was able to pique his curiosity enough that he maintained a B-plus average. She introduced him to poems by Browning, Shelley, Keats, and Rossetti and taught him that there was more to life than cartooning; out there, she showed him, was "a world of serious painting, the study of nature . . . and the great values of a life of art." He didn't try to hide from his parents that he was doing a lot of drawing at school: his letters were covered with caricatures of teachers and cadets; he was listed on the masthead of the school paper, *The Reveille*, as "illustrator"; and in late November he told Lizzie that the family could expect "posters" for Christmas. Her gift, he said, would be new wallpaper of his design for Oak Hill. Moreover, he informed his father that he'd sent some drawings to the Art Institute of Chicago, which responded by sending him lots of literature on the school. "So my little sketches have caused some little sensation anyhow," he wrote.

What the family talked about over Christmas break is a mystery, but surely Tom begged to be released from his servitude at Western. His mind was made up, and all he was waiting for was the go-ahead from his parents. He must have received good news sometime in late January 1907, for on the twenty-fourth he wrote to Lizzie and M.E. a long, breathless letter:

> I rec'd Mama's letter a few hours ago and never in all my life have I been so much elated. I believe at last that you have come to realize the greatness of the gift which Providence has thrust upon me. I don't believe that you ever thought of it as more than a pastime, to be lightly dabbled with and thrust aside, and I don't believe that I thought much more before Professor Calhoun of Carthage looked at my work and praised it, but since then my mind has been positively made up as regards my profession, and now I believe that you too begin to recognize the value of my gift.
>
> I wish I could see you and tell you how I feel. I can't express myself. I have a continual longing to paint and draw. My mind is continually full of pictures.

The poet John Keats, who was apprenticed to a surgeon says that when he should have been listening to a surgical lecture "a sunbeam would come into the room, and with it a whole troupe of little creatures floating in the ray; and I was off with them to Oberon and fairyland"; and like the poet when I should be listening to some geometrical preparation my mind wanders off and I find myself gazing at some picture, of the imagination, the lesson altogether forgotten. Thus it goes.

These are the very years of my life which should be devoted to the training of my eye and hand and as I have said before it is a waste of money . . . to send me here to learn the inns [sic] and outs of military science.

This school runs in a channel, whose course is directly opposite the artist's nature, yet I have made a success here and the major lately told me that I was as good a man as he ever had, so then, think what I will be able to do in an environment more suitable to my nature.

I am bound to be successful. I have the fullest confidence in myself. Ask anyone capable of judging my work what he thinks of my genius. He will tell you that the greater artists work done in their boyhood does not equal mine . . .

I want you to come up as soon as possible and let me talk with you. I will do my best to learn other things, but what is science and mathematics when compared to nature and I know that I have a touch of nature. So send me to study that which is to be my life work and I shall do that which will never make you regret it.

This brave exhortation was accompanied by a self-portrait of Tom at an easel, brush in hand, and a postscript: "I would rather go to New York or Chicago."

4

CHICAGO

Even though Benton chafed under the regimented curriculum at the Art Institute, and even though he would dream again of a bigger arena for his self-proclaimed genius, living in Chicago, an unrestrained city scaled to its vast surrounding plains, finally unhooked him from his family. It was a good match: surly, belligerent Benton and muscular, brawling Chicago. Gilded Age Chicago was massive and diverse—two million people scattered amid German, Irish, Polish, and Italian neighborhoods—but also infamously dissolute. In 1903, Lincoln Steffens reported on Chicago's reform efforts for *McClure's Magazine* and found a place that was "first in violence; deepest in dirt; loud, lawless, unlovely, ill-smelling, irreverent, new; an overgrown gawk of a village, the 'tough' among cities." Chicago reigned in the popular imagination as the country's wickedest city, and though it was a haven for hoodlums, drunks, and exiles from the small Protestant towns of the Midwest, its culture had been emboldened by the spectacular success of the 1893 World's Columbian Exposition. It's not surprising, therefore, that there was a renaissance in Chicago around the time Benton lived there, from 1906 to 1907: architects designed awesomely high skyscrapers, and a generation of writers with ties to the city—Floyd Dell, Carl Sandburg, Theodore Dreiser, Sherwood Anderson, Upton Sinclair—developed a new literature of realism. Nor is it surprising that these writers described the city's seamy underbelly—its laborers, foibles, and filth.

Benton, too, noticed Chicago's gloom. He arrived in the city in February, during a bitter winter, and in his first letters home he described the "great big cold icy looking" lake and a spectacular blizzard:

> I am looking out of my window now at the storm, raging & tearing like some fierce old bear, made furious by the sting of a bullet which wounds and fails to kill . . . On the corner beneath

my room the street lamp beams like some weird firefly, blue & green in the all pervading mistiness of flurrying snow, and farther down the street another thrusts itself out, indistinct & uncertain as if half afraid of the darkness and the storm, but beside this there is nothing . . . the rolling, restless mysteriousness of the wind and the snow and the darkness.

Picturing Benton, alone and cold in his rented room, one thinks of a passing image of Chicago from Henry Blake Fuller's *The Cliff-Dwellers*: "Here is a town full to overflowing with single young men. They come from everywhere, for all reasons."

Benton came to study illustration, but he got as much from the city's rush and bustle as from his classes. His first Chicago address was on the South Side, where he rented a room—for five dollars a month, in a brownstone overlooking the lake—from Mr. Sidway, an acquaintance of the Colonel's. Sidway and his son Harry, who lived at home, were in business together as real estate agents, and though Benton was under the impression that they were very well-off, he describes them both as dull and frugal. Sidway was a widower, and since none of the three could cook, they ate every meal out at cheap diners and coffee shops, laying down quarters for chops and hot pie. Miser that he was, Sidway never offered to buy the young man a meal, insisting even that Harry pay his own way. Soon Benton took to skipping meals to save money. He often complained to his mother about being hungry and reminisced about home cooking; he was especially tormented by memories of "sausage & hominy & corncakes." "It has never occurred to me before," he added, "that this may be the reason why I never become homesick, for whenever I think of home, the picture is so distinct and real that I truly feel as if I were there. I can hear everybody talking, and smell the ham cooking in the kitchen, and hear old Nat tending the furnace in the basement, just as it is in reality."

Initially Benton hoped to find work as an illustrator, but soon abandoned the idea and was forced to live off money left to him by his uncle Sam. Meant for his education, the money was doled out by the Colonel, who oversaw the trust ungenerously. Tom was always asking for more, explaining in his letters that Chicago was expensive. Living so far south of the Art Institute, he was forced to ride a streetcar back and forth each day; moreover, he had to buy art supplies—paper, lead, charcoal, ink, and paint.

Despite his financial circumstances, Benton enjoyed the city. Many years later, he told an interviewer that it was an exhilarating, if lonely, period for him. In Chicago, he explained, "something was always coming up that you didn't know how to do, that you didn't know anything about; so you had to go after it." In one particularly ironic letter to Lizzie, he mentioned longing for fried chicken and the warmth of the library fire yet bragged about his new wardrobe—a three-piece suit and bowler hat. In his new clothes, Tom set about exploring the city. In late March, for example, he took a sketching excursion to Little Italy, where he observed close-up a kind of urban crowding he had never seen in Washington or Joplin. It is, he said, a "dirty, slovenly, dilapidated" neighborhood; the Italians he described as looking like "one of our hams when just taken out of the charcoal box." As he set up his sketching station, curious onlookers crowded and pushed, overwhelming him with "the smell of garlic, vile tobacco and sweat." But he told the Colonel not to worry.

His greatest pleasure was attending concerts in the great venues of the city. He constantly boasted to Lizzie about these superb concerts, hoping that his description, for example, of Wagner's *Tannhäuser* at Louis Sullivan's Auditorium Theatre would elicit more generous disbursements from the trust. He grew so fond of the Auditorium Theatre, in fact, that he tolerated the sermons of the minister Frank W. Gunsaulus, a beloved Chicago philanthropist and Art Institute trustee, in order to bask in its aura. "In all my life," he wrote to his mother, "I have never seen or heard anything so inspiring, so grand and magnificent as . . . the vast theatre":

> It is impossible to conceive, until you have seen it, the largeness of the house. Great massive architecture, somewhat of the Egyptian style, with gallery after gallery, reaching away up to where the electric lights seem but little stars. A house capable of seating over 6,000 people. Think of a single room that large, what an atmosphere of strength there is in it . . . But I have omitted to mention the grandest part about it, that wonderful organ, its

deep rolling, magnificent tones, which under the hand of man, I should judge possessed of marvelous talent, go straight into the souls of the masses who come to hear.

When spring finally arrived, Tom cheered up and took long walks through the many amusement parks modeled on the Midway of the World's Columbian Exposition. The Midway Plaisance, as it was called, was a narrow, mile-long road lined with concessions and amusements that connected Washington Park and Frederick Law Olmsted's Jackson Park during the fair. Moralizing commentators wrung their hands over the corrupting influence of the lowbrow Midway, which included a greased pole, the Irish Village, and the Street in Cairo, an exhibition featuring exotic and titillating dancing. Critics were dismayed that "amusement[s], of cheap and vulgar sorts," were more popular than educational exhibits; "such pleasing novelties," another writer lamented, "are converting the Exposition . . . into a huge circus."

Benton preferred one park, Sans Souci, which opened in 1899. The park's entrance at Sixtieth and Cottage Grove, adjacent to the Midway, resembled the exterior of a German beer hall, and the interior featured a large open-air eatery, spectacular fountains, glittering lights at night, and ornamental gardens. That first spring, Benton would walk here, often alone, to sketch and listen to the public performances of orchestras led by Giuseppe Creatore, Oreste Vessella, and Don Philippini. Creatore was an especially flamboyant conductor, and in the Chicago chapter of his unpublished memoir Benton describes what it was like to attend one of his concerts:

> In the center of the garden was an enormous bandstand and on it the biggest band I had ever seen. Every instrument that could be applied to band music was there in duplicate or triplicate. It was led by a flamboyant bandmaster of great fame in Chicago, an Italian maestro, who wore his hair long . . . When he would lead his band to a crescendo he would bob and twist and shake his head until his hair flew out in all directions making a sort of tornadic black halo about his face.

He also took to the more lowbrow amusements at these new parks, frequenting the many beer gardens that sprinkled Chicago's public places. In the summer of 1907, just when Benton discovered them, the *Chicago Daily Tribune* ran a story reporting on the temperance movement's attempts to slow the flow of "demon rum" at the gardens. In response to the crisis, the author added, temperance unions had resorted to posting "lurid billboard portraits depicting drunkards in horrible stages of degradation and saloonkeepers as criminals of the deepest dye."

One of Benton's few friends in Chicago was Bob Everhardt, a "compassionate" and "thick set, stocky German student" who was a couple of years older than he. Bob, who was from Iowa, was "a voracious eater and capacious beer drinker," and since he knew Chicago well, he had a knack for dining on the cheap. One afternoon he led Benton to a saloon a few blocks from the Art Institute where there was "an enormous long table full of hams, sides of beef, sausages, beet and potato salads and even tureens of hot bean soup . . . There were hard boiled eggs, cheese, rolls, crackers, and open cans of sardines." For a ten-cent mug of beer, Benton recalled, one could gorge all day on this bounty.

Perhaps to make up for his father's lack of interest in what he cared most about, Benton gravitated toward older men for conversation and advice. In Neosho there was the anonymous law student; in Chicago there was Hudspeth, or Hud. Like so many figures who appear in Benton's memoirs, Hud remains a mysterious apparition—surely real but uncorroborated, as he only emerges in a dreamy unpublished account. Mr. Sidway, Benton explains, had another tenant in his building whom he refused to introduce to Tom. For weeks, Benton passed the door to the tenant's apartment without ever seeing him, but eventually they bumped into each other in the hallway, where they had a conversation. Hud was a banker and had business in Canada and Chicago; he was also smart and curious and perked up when Tom told him he was an artist. Hungry for conversation with someone other than the Sidways, Benton began visiting Hud after dinner. The man had an elegant apartment, decorated with Turkish carpets, heavy drapes, and leather-bound books, a refreshing change from Sidway's "plain and cold" rooms. Before long, Hud was enticing Benton to stay late into the night by offering him scotch and soda and lessons in English literature; a shared favorite was Oscar Wilde's *Picture of Dorian Gray*, which Benton found "perverse" but "irresistible." By his eighteenth birthday, Benton recalled, Hud had become his closest companion in Chicago and had advanced his education "in all directions." The Sidways disliked Hud and urged Tom to leave him alone, explaining that "older men can have bad influences," an admonition they based on Hud's "English accent and . . . superior cultivation," which insulted their own "plain[ness]."

Hud occasionally invited his young companion to a South Side beer garden that Benton describes as being the hangout of an odd crowd. Walking among the tables were groups of "arrogant and superior" men; most were middle-aged, he explains, but some were "young with blond curls about their ears . . . Both young and old walked erectly with a sort of military bearing." These men often stopped by their table, and Hud would join them for a circuit around the garden, whispering secretly. Having learned a thing or two since his encounter with Mr. Calhoun in Joplin, Benton suspected the men were "queer." He pressed Hud about this and was relieved to hear, "They're the German crowd, not *our* kind at all."

But his relief was short-lived. After returning home for the summer and moving into a new apartment the following fall, Benton called on the Sidways—at his father's insistence—to thank them for their stingy hospitality. Afterward, he dropped in on Hud, who greeted him warmly and immediately mixed two scotch and sodas for "old time's sake." He pressed Tom for details on his friends and teachers at the Art Institute, refreshing their drinks whenever the conversation ebbed. Benton rose to leave but was drunk and could hardly stand. He caught Hud staring at him. "I looked at him in a dazed sort of way," he recalled. "Somehow he did not seem like the Hud I had known. His eyes had an unusual expression, vaguely familiar, but not identifiable with Hud, the friend and mentor of last season. Had I been sober I would probably have sensed the meaning of the look but all I could now think was, 'Old Hud's drunk too.'"

Benton certainly leads us to believe that *he* was drunk when Hud persuaded him to stay the night and then coaxed him into bed. Whatever his condition, he describes soberly what happened next: Hud stripped naked, turned off the light, got into bed, and reached over Tom's torso to grab his penis. "Still the only thought that came to me," Benton writes, "was that he was drunk and did not know what he was doing so I turned over to my other side. Then, all of a sudden he stuck a greased finger up my rectum. He'd probably stuck it in a pot of Vaseline because it went way up. I jumped, like a hot poker had been shoved in me and leaped clear out of bed." Disgusted and ashamed, Benton fumbled with his clothes in the dim light from the streetlamps and, amazingly, conjured a gentle excuse. "I can't sleep tonight," he said. "I guess I'll be going."

Hud called after him, sadly, "Shut the door tight."

What to say? First, Benton was assaulted by a friend, and no matter how tersely he managed to tell the story later, it traumatized him (he finishes the story with an addendum, explaining how when he got home that night, he was overcome by diarrhea). But what a strange telling. One is bewildered by elements of this recital: its deadpan delivery; the fact that Benton was suspicious of Hud but got into his bed nevertheless; that he rolled over, showing his backside, after Hud first fondled him; how he expresses more pity than rage. Some have speculated that Benton was attracted to men. In their biography of Jackson Pollock, Steven Naifeh and Gregory White Smith breathed new life into what had been casual speculations about Benton's sexuality when they wrote, "Eventually, not only his sister but his son, several of his close friends, and his biographer began to believe that, all along, Tom Benton had been fighting a losing battle with his own homosexual urges." Though it doesn't preclude his being homosexual, that Benton had sex with prostitutes, lived with a mistress in Paris, had a long and basically happy marriage, and never had a known erotic relationship with a man makes such charges only speculative.

What isn't disputable is that Benton articulated what Mildred recognized as homophobia during and after his departure from New York City. These views evolved from his reaction against the Stieglitz Circle and museums and were espoused in essays, reviews, and interviews. While some attribute this attitude to his being "a macho bastard," others have identified in Benton's odious gay-bashing a "shrill" defensiveness born of self-hatred. No one, however, has suggested that his homophobia grew out of the incidents with Mr. Calhoun and Hud. Not even Benton himself, who had reason and opportunity to justify his views, traced his antipathy back to these two men; all he did was tell the stories, and, interestingly, he told them with barely a hint of anger.

At first Benton was annoyed by the studio work required of him at school. "I was put to drawing casts of Greek statues in the usual conventional ways of art schools," he recalls in *An Artist in America*. "This was humiliating for me, for after the *Joplin American* I regarded myself as a professional artist and above such drudgery." He hated the casts, which struck him as nothing more than sad tokens of a dead civilization. "The beautiful solutions of the Greek figures," he argues, "shining through mutilation and dead plaster, can only be apprehended after one has known the living body. Learning to copy them before such knowledge has been acquired ends only in a thoughtless imitation of their appearance—in a copy, pure and simple." Benton's attitude toward learning from antiquity made his first months at the Art Institute frustrating. "I revolted from the casts within a week after I had begun," he writes.

The School of the Art Institute of Chicago, known today as one of the finest art schools in the world, originated just after the Civil War. In 1866, thirty-five Chicago artists, with the intention of establishing a free school for life and antique drawing, formed the Chicago Academy of Design. After financial collapses, ruinous fires, and several changes in mission, the academy became the School of the Art Institute in 1882 and moved into its current building, erected on rubble from the Great Chicago Fire of 1871 at Michigan Avenue and Adams Street. From the beginning, the school was associated with a gallery of art objects, and by 1880 the institution had two purposes, to educate and to collect. Not surprisingly, plaster casts made up the bulk of the early collection.

Just as Benton enrolled, in 1907, the Art Institute was becoming a major force in the cultural life of the city, enrolling just under five thousand students. During his time there, the school's curriculum emphasized "practical ability," or "a capacity to deal with actual problems." It was likely the Art Institute's reputation as a place to learn marketable skills that convinced the Colonel to allow his son to enroll. In addition, one could get an approximation of a liberal arts education at the school, or so Benton claimed to his parents in a letter informing them he was studying "life, history, religion and [the] customs of Ancient Egypt at the Institute library." A few weeks later, apparently in response to a letter from his parents urging him to enroll in Chicago's Columbia College, he boasted that he could get history, literature, and science on his own: "I am very confident I will be able to talk with intellectual people far better than any college graduate." The boy was to be believed, apparently, for in May he complained that he was losing his eyesight because he was reading Tennyson, Plutarch, and the Psalms late into the night, a claim that Mr. Sidway confirmed, telling the Colonel, "As to working, I never saw his equal in a person of his age." Benton's eyes grew so weary, in fact, that Sidway had to treat them with a solution of boracic acid. The Colonel continued to protest the cost of the Art Institute tuition, but Benton told his father, "If necessary I will show you that I can make my own education. On this matter I would rather see Nat and Mamie and Mido come before me, because I have a gift, some talent, maybe a little genius."

After escaping the tedium of the cast drawing class, Benton found his way into a life drawing class taught by Allen E. Philbrick, a young painter and instructor. Benton struggled to make the switch from pen and ink, with which he was familiar, to charcoal, and in his frustration he became a divisive presence in the class. One day Philbrick was walking among his students' easels offering criticisms; he stopped at Benton's and told him that his drawing wasn't "artistic." As usual, Benton resisted, asking, "Why isn't it artistic, Mr. Philbrick?" The man's pink cheeks flushed with anger. "Because it isn't," he answered harshly and walked away, causing a "faint murmur" in the classroom. In his unpublished memoir, Benton recalls that he became the center of attention in the life drawing studio. Those who admired his work did so more than they needed, he explained, and those who disliked it protested too much: "It was thus at the very outset of my career as an artist that I found myself generating those divisions of opinion . . . which were to follow me through life."

Philbrick never warmed up to Benton, who was eager to move on again. His opportunity came when Frederick Oswald introduced himself and invited Benton to stop by his watercolor class. Oswald was a popular teacher at the Art Institute, and besides his watercolor class he offered instruction in the theory of composition. Benton recalled in an interview that Oswald "was one of those artists who . . . never does anything," then added, "But he was a lucky find for me." During his first visit to Oswald's class, Benton was seduced by color. A pretty girl was posing in the front of the classroom, he remembered, "dressed up in a kind of Spanish dancing costume, bright yellow and pink flowered, with a black velvet bodice. Her flamboyance excited me." He was also beguiled that day by Oswald's attention. When the teacher inspected his first go at the model, he tore up the drawing, only to tell him that he'd make a fine painter—"your stroke shows it."

Among the students that day was a big, buxom, gray-haired lady who was expertly representing the floral patterns of the model's costume "by dropping little blobs of wet color on the wet paper . . . so that they stayed within the spaces laid out . . . without disturbing her drawing." Benton stared at her work, prompting her to ask, "Why are you looking at me like that?" "Because I think it's marvelous what you're doing there," he said. This was Martha Moline, a Chicago socialite, and as Benton explained, "I would soon need her."

Benton decided to drop Philbrick's class but was told by the administration that he'd have to wait until the end of the semester; desperate, he appealed to Moline for help, and she took the matter up with Oswald. When Philbrick learned of this runaround, he confronted Oswald in the hallway, shouting so everyone could hear, and accused him of stealing his best student. "Oh, look at the precious boy," a classmate who overheard this exchange teased. "Oh, the little Jesus." It wasn't the last time he would be ridiculed like this, but it was worth it. "For some reason or other," he told his parents, "the artists lately have been giving me quite a bit of attention. I don't know why unless they see that I mean 'bizness.'"

According to Benton, Oswald believed that learning and doing were inseparable, a theory that shaped Benton's own teaching for decades. Becoming Oswald's pupil transformed Benton—"it made me find myself," he claimed. "Oswald was the perfect teacher for me. He knew how to handle a sort of innate rebelliousness in my character which made me resent instruction from above." Struggling with the technical complexity of watercolor was good medicine for Benton as well; it knocked him off his pedestal by showing him how little he knew about making pictures. Besides assuming the roles of friend and mentor to the immature student, Oswald drilled into him a feel for composition. In *An American in Art*, his "professional and technical" autobiography, Benton writes, "I obtained also in Chicago my first insights into the art of designing—of consciously planning, or composing, pictures before attempting to execute them." In 1908, the students at the Art Institute were treated to a massive exhibition of 650 Japanese prints, which was organized in part by Frank Lloyd Wright, a major lender to the exhibition. Benton points out that "Japanese prints were, very largely because of James McNeill

Whistler's influence, much in favor at this time," and Oswald impressed on his students the compositional genius of the Japanese printmakers, encouraging "continuous study of the way they were put together." As Benton sees it, these prints taught him to arrange his pictures "in definite patterns" and gave him a taste "for flowing lines which lasted all my life." For his part, Oswald distinguished between the "arrangement of objects in a picture," which was a matter of "taste," and composition, which was a "science by which you tied them altogether into one thing." Once Oswald introduced Benton to another foreign style—the incredibly delicate and fine lines of the Spanish illustrator Daniel Vierge, who pioneered new ways to reproduce drawings in print—he finally abandoned the crosshatching style of Clifford Berryman, which had been his model since Washington, and was on his way to becoming a real artist. Years later he would claim that his aspiration to get "rich in a big-time newspaper job" was just a feint to persuade his parents to send him to Chicago; in fact, he was after something "deeper." A classmate of Benton's, Vaclav Vytlacil, claimed that Benton was the "star" of Oswald's class and confirmed his ambition, remembering that he once tellingly remarked, "I want to be as important in art to Americans as the funny papers are."

Surprisingly, Benton never mentions the Art Institute's mural painting classes (a unique curricular offering), and there's no evidence that he was even interested in them. Nevertheless, while he was at the school, mural painting emerged as a medium that conveniently bridged the two elements of art—theory and practice—that institute teachers wanted their students to learn. In 1908, the Art Institute's monthly bulletin reported on this "most satisfactory and remarkable development":

> It is well recognized that there is difficulty in getting the art student to produce actual pictures. Sharing the common human aversion to exerting his mental and inventive faculties, the art student likes best to stand before his living model and reproduce as nearly as he can the forms, tones and colours which he sees. Hence in the art schools of the old world there are found students . . . who are totally unable to put figures together in a composition . . . The solution of the difficulty appears now to be offering itself from . . . the opportunity to execute mural paintings for actual use.

Such an instrumentalist view sounds a lot like Benton's own theories about the social applications of painting during the 1920s and 1930s, when he told anyone who listened that art must have an "actual use" to be of any consequence. Murals, because they are usually public and, architecturally speaking, functional, are especially suited to such a purpose, and Benton understood his own as being utilitarian and practical. At the Art Institute, the opportunity to "design and execute actual murals in high schools and park houses gave students the incentive to create full-blown compositions," and student murals were installed all over the city, at sites like the Crippled Children's Home and Highland Park High School. Regardless of what he knew about the mural program, Benton was surely exposed to the school's open discussions about utilitarian art.

His stated interest, however, was easel painting, which he began to study with Bob Everhardt's encouragement. Though it didn't come easy—the "slippery, buttery" oil resisted his urge to draw—he realized immediately that it was a grander medium, one suited to his ambition. "From the moment I first stuck my brush in a fat gob of color," he recalls wistfully, "I gave up the idea of newspaper cartooning. I made up my mind that I was going to be a painter. The rich, sensual joy of smearing streaks of color . . . was too much for me." In fact, Benton learned to paint at first in drab colors modeled on the palettes of Dutch and Spanish masters, whose works could be studied in reproductions plastered on the walls of Louis Betts's studio. Betts was a renowned impressionist who made a living painting moody portraits of society figures. He studied at the Art Institute in the 1890s before becoming an apprentice to William Merritt Chase, who taught an influential class on plein air painting at Shinnecock Hills on Long Island. Before returning to teach at the Art Institute, Betts traveled to Holland and Spain, where, under the spell of Frans Hals and Diego Velázquez, he added to his repertoire a darker palette for his portraits. Lizzie was overjoyed to learn that Tom was studying with Betts, for she imagined that her son intended to become a portraitist of midwestern elites. But he saw it differently, of course, telling Paul Cummings many years later that Betts "was a standard society portrait painter following Chase and Sargent. But not as good as either one of them."

Regardless of what he thought of Betts's talent, Benton was prohibited from enrolling formally in his painting class. The Art Institute curriculum was loose enough for him to drop by the painting studios, but a more formal arrangement, Benton feared, would not have been tolerated by the Colonel, who kept asking when the cartooning career was going to take off. So to maintain his cover, Benton stayed in Oswald's watercolor class, painted by himself on weekends, and joined an extracurricular painting group that met on Saturdays in Bob's room. "Some of the fellows in this crowd," Benton wrote later, "would get red in the face and cuss and yell at each other over minute differences of opinion," but the disputes, especially the vehemence with which they were fought, thrilled him. "In spirit," he explained, "I had become a young bohemian. One glimpse of the life had captured me."

The Art Institute fostered an amiable atmosphere: male and female students of all ages mingled in studios, hallways, and cafeterias and, like most art students, were eager to shed whatever bourgeois proprieties they had learned at home and inclined to sympathize with each other's idiosyncrasies. For his part, Benton longed to escape the expectations that were his birthright, at one point telling his parents, "You all who don't know much about the artistic can't understand it, you can't appreciate the fact that it is more than play." He said again and again that he wasn't sensible, like his father, but of a different "class and kind." "Every artist in a world of 'practical' men shares somewhat the uneasiness I describe," he explains in *An Artist in America*, "but those who came out of the Middle West at the beginning of the century, I imagine, have had a larger dose than all others." Special to his place, he adds, "the great valley of the Mississippi," there was "the most complete denial of aesthetic sensibility that has probably ever been known." This Benton blames on what he calls a "parvenu spirit," or the "enthronement . . . of the ideals and practices of the go-getter." The Colonel and his "entourage," he argues, "accepted the pattern of the parvenu society . . . and worked within it." In this milieu, Chicago called out to "the radical protestants, the philosophers, artists, writers, [and] musicians," seducing them with the prospect of an intellectual and sensitive community of peers. This, he claims, is what he longed for when he moved to Chicago, and though it was there for him, it wouldn't be enough.

Art Institute students threw lavish parties for any reason at all. Most famous was the annual Mardi Gras celebration, which was organized around different exotic themes. One year the motif was Benton's old favorite, "The Arabian Nights," and a live camel roamed the studios, mingling with intoxicated and masked students. Even rowdier were the initiation ceremonies for new members of the required life drawing class, which often devolved into good-natured hazing rituals. Benton described these "secret" and "most horrible of initiations" to the Colonel, explaining how the new students were stripped to their underclothes, painted, and made to march down Michigan Avenue carrying a coffin with a skeleton in it. Afterward, everyone congregated in the dining hall for "a big feed."

Benton took a break from his studies and returned to Neosho for several weeks in July and August 1907. Happy to be back in a small town, he took it easy and played at being a boy again. He swam in his favorite holes, attended picnics and dances, boxed in the gym, and with a local buddy, Phil Ratcliff, picked fresh mint at the springs, which they brought to a saloon where the bartender mixed them mint juleps. He also brought his easel and paints with him and spent hours sketching and painting outdoors; Lizzie, "nursing probably a romantic view of the artist's life," was pleased. The Colonel, though, was "indifferent," and while they managed to be "cordial," father and son gave each other a wide berth. This small taste of home, relaxing as it was, did nothing to bump Benton off course, and when he returned to Chicago in September, he abandoned the Sidways ("they are *all* business and I am just the opposite") and moved uptown closer to the Art Institute, where he rented an apartment on Michigan Avenue with his acquaintances Bob Levett, Bill York, and Rolf Armstrong (who became a celebrated illustrator of glamorous pinup girls for calendars, posters, and magazines). Benton, because he was the smallest, took the couch and rarely slept through the night as the apartment soon became a "forum for mighty debate" and penny-ante poker. The young men often went as a group to the South Side to hear black musicians from New Orleans play ragtime; afterward, they went to chop suey joints, where they could gorge cheaply, and then to whorehouses, where Benton claims to have behaved. Only "one of our crowd ever went upstairs," he said later, "and the result of his experience was such as to scare the rest of us from tempting it."

Such high jinks exasperated Benton, who fell back into his usual pattern of aloofness and superiority, and after a month he moved back to the South Side, to a small room on Vincennes Avenue, so that he "could be alone and nurse conceptions of [himself] without interference." He was starting to suffer again from the awkwardness he'd experienced around his father's cronies—the ones he felt like hitting "with a rock." In his memoirs, Benton describes being teased on the streets of Chicago for being short and dressing oddly—in corduroy trousers, a black flannel shirt, and a red tie. Also, by this time he was wearing his hair long; he'd stuff it under his derby hat so it looked like a mop. When he called on his new landlady to look at the room, she promptly asked, "Are you a religious man?"

"No Mam," he replied. "I'm an artist."

This explanation didn't put others at ease, however. On the way back to his new building one day, Benton, walking with his customary scowl and swagger, passed a gauntlet of familiar girls sitting on stoops. "Look at that crazy freak," one of them yelled, eliciting a "mounting, hilarious feminine laughter" that humiliated him. He describes these days in *An Artist in America* with his customary taciturn glumness:

> Though I was among "artistic" companions, among young men who like myself were probably regarded in their midwest home towns as a little nutty, a little off-color, and who should have been, therefore, perfect associates for my temperament, I began nevertheless to have recurrences of my old spells of uneasiness. As I became known around artistic circles in Chicago, I again confronted, particularly with the more advanced young men, the same quizzical, skeptical, questioning surveys that I had encountered in my home country . . . The shrewd practicality I had more or less consciously fled from at home was here again, though in different form.

Benton wasn't interested in searching his soul to discover whatever it was about him that turned off these companions; instead, he went on the defensive and found a gym where he started boxing again. The gym rats, who dubbed him Kid Benton, were impressed by the lethal temper he packed into his small frame, a rage that he eventually unleashed on one of his enemies.

A tall classmate, "a gangling six footer," had what Benton describes as a "marked antipathy" toward him and since his first spring at school had publicly ridiculed him in the hallways, calling him Oswald's pet, an

insult that surely tapped into Benton's sexual paranoia. Their size difference, Benton says, prevented him from retaliating, but when the "needler"
got to him again one day in the fall of 1907, he reached "a boiling point
of anger." Entering the men's room at the Art Institute, Benton encountered the classmate smoking a cigarette. After a brief face-off, the bully
turned to his friends and asked, "Hey, boys, do they let little pricks like
that piss in a man's trough?"

Benton laughed (or so he says) and left the room, "but the boil had
started." When the needler returned to the corridor, Tom tripped him,
sending him to the floor, hard.

"I'll shake your guts out," the bully yelled.

And he would have if Bob Everhardt hadn't been there to help. Bob
pushed him to the floor again, and then he and Tom grabbed the guy by
his legs and dropped him down the chute of a coal shaft in the hallway.
Benton admits this was stupid and that he easily could have killed him,
but as it was, the man fell into a bed of powdered coal and was discovered
"crying with humiliation." For two days Benton and Everhardt lived
through the agony of being expelled and facing the prospect of telling
their parents the bad news. Oswald, meanwhile, lobbied the administration on their behalf and won their reinstatement. The needler, Benton
claims, was too mortified to show his face at the school again.

Though he had Everhardt on his side, this fight was just a sensational
example of a bigger problem for Benton: he had a hard time making,
and keeping, friends. Reading his memoirs and youthful letters, one is
struck by the utter lack of references to intimate friends; besides a few
childhood companions in Neosho, some social acquaintances in Joplin,
and Everhardt, he was largely a loner until he moved to Paris and met
Stanton Macdonald-Wright. And when Benton does reminisce about
others, such as Everhardt, he rarely shows them affection. Even his
memories of his Paris mistress, Jeanette, are distressingly unsympa-
thetic. Certainly his compulsive drive and brash confidence explain a
good deal of this; engrossed as he was in developing his "genius," Benton couldn't bother with romance or close friendship. In *An Artist in
America*, for instance, he describes his attitude in early 1907 this way:
"By the time I went to Chicago there were moments when my uneasiness
was intolerable. As the spells came on, the desire to submerge myself in
the loneliness of strange places and peoples bit like a hot flame. The

intimacies of military school burned me up, and though I controlled my inner rages there, sitting alone secretively chewing tobacco, I dived into Chicago as into a cool bath."

Much later in life, he would enjoy the company of many close friends, and even build a kind of commune with his wife on Martha's Vineyard, but in Chicago he was consumed by the question of his destiny—and occasionally by careerism—and this exasperated his classmates. Benton's memoirs and letters demonstrate genuine arrogance, and one imagines that Rolf Armstrong, for instance, believed his roommate was a charlatan. "The majority of the young men of art in Chicago aimed to be illustrators for the great magazines," Benton recalls thinking, "and, after sowing a few wild oats of rebellion, they settled down to taking the kind of training at hand . . . I took no training . . . [A]lthough I didn't judge my work, nor esteem any of it enough to save it, I did like the idea of being a genius and grew resentful of those who questioned it." This from a man who had publicly declared his ambition to be just such an illustrator!

Thomas Craven—art critic, art historian, intimate friend of Benton's, and an outspoken advocate of objective painting during the 1920s and 1930s—also commented on Benton's "genius-pose" during this period. "He had a high opinion of himself," Craven writes, and "dressed like a hoodlum esthete . . . Benton, for all his coarseness and his backwoods buffoonery, was excruciatingly serious. He withdrew from the vulgar herd of docile cast-copiers and illustrators, worked alone far into the night, and in a year's time was acknowledged to be the most promising watercolorist in the history of the Institute." He would sustain his cockiness in Paris, where it often seemed quaintly idiosyncratic to the other oddballs there, but once he arrived in Manhattan, it ran afoul of bigger egos and talents, and finally he would be defied, even humiliated.

Early on Benton complained that he had yet to find an "unoccupied pedestal in the 'hall of fame'" and therefore would have to "make my own." That a special place was reserved for him was never in doubt; days after settling in Chicago, he confessed to his parents, "As each day goes by I become more and more conscious that in me lies some unexplainable power, which sometime in the future, I will be able to chain and which will make me rise above the level of the ordinary mortal. This is not an over confident boyish conceit, I really *feel* that of which I write and am sure of it." Exactly a year later, he was even more confident and articulate about his calling:

> Just the other night I was crossing the Chicago River and was so impressed with the marvelous coloring, as the day drew to a close, that I stood and watched for a long time, saw the sky and the buildings turn from gold, to rose, and from rose to a most delicate blue from which the masts of the ships rose into the sky like vast spider webs. It was divine, and looking at the soft harmony of the whole, I could feel the power of the Infinite, and I could rejoice that I was one of the few who can hear the music that comes from a harmony of colors as well as from a harmony of sound. For me color is music and music is color, and the more that these things grow on me the nearer I come to what I aim for. My art is not to be the art of realism; I am not to put things as they are, but more beautiful than they are.

Chicago's great skyscrapers aroused Benton; he was bowled over by their thrust and scale. Clearly, the massive buildings awakened in him an ambition that hadn't been dormant so much as devoid of context, and they also supplied him with the rhetoric with which to describe his aspirations. When he arrived in the city, there was lots of construction going on, and he remembers "watching the donkey engines manipulate the great steel beams" and says that he "got the first touch of that mania for fire and steel and soaring height which was to dominate America for the next twenty-five years." He adds:

> I am aware of all the false logic that lies behind the skyscraper, of its foundation in deviously manipulated land values and brutal standards of living, but it stands, nevertheless, as the first effort of the American spirit to give itself an original monumental expression . . . Only one utterly blinded by the self-conscious moralities of uplift and reformist pretensions can fail to see the beauty of these great structures, lifted above the dirt and squalor at their feet into our bright American sky.

In the skyscraper Benton found an analogue to his own desire to rise above the average and achieve something grand, and upon his return to

Chicago after his summer visit to Neosho his bluster remained. "I am excited and restless," he wrote to his mother. "I can just feel the power in my hands and brain . . . Is there any reason why I cannot be great?" He thought not:

> I feel in my very soul that I was born to be great, born to do things in which other men have failed. Those men here who call me "promising" know not the magnitude of the "promise" which the gods have given [me] in the late hours of the night, when the hum of the city is hushed in stillness and the winds are dead, and Thought and I commune alone. They know not the greatness that has come upon me at these times, when the mind has leapt beyond the real and soars unrestrained in the mysteries of the infinite.

Benton's greatest successes at the Art Institute came toward the end of his time there. In November 1907, the school invited Ernest Peixotto to campus as a visiting teacher. Peixotto, a San Francisco–born Sephardic Jew, was a jack-of-all-trades—a peripatetic writer, illustrator, and painter who professed peace and humanism. In a letter to his father, Benton boasted that of more than two hundred applicants, he was one of twenty-five chosen to study with Peixotto. Later he opened up more to his mother, explaining that Peixotto had stopped him during class one day to tell him that he was working on much too small a scale, that his drawings couldn't be reproduced as he was doing them. Just the idea of having his work reproduced appealed to him, of course, and he now felt on the verge of something spectacular. More important, perhaps, was that Peixotto had recently studied in Paris at the Académie Julian, an art school popular among American artists, and he told Benton about it.

In addition to attending exhibitions where he viewed paintings by some of America's most renowned painters (Whistler and Sargent, for example) and reading translations of Arabic and Persian poems, Benton continued to study with Frederick Oswald, who believed his student had genuine talent. "I've always felt . . . sort of grateful," Benton said, "to have had the luck to have run into that kind of guy when I was just starting. Rather than some drillmaster." Oswald also got Benton thinking about going abroad. He was critical of Chicago, which he believed was a crude city, and when he overheard Benton complaining about all the distractions keeping him from his work, he suggested Paris as an alternative. Benton raised the issue with his mother in December 1907, but she brushed off the idea, reasoning that he wouldn't make it with his poor French. But the itch to move on again was too strong, and his resentment for his fellow students, those illiterate, small-time illustrators, intensified. He wanted to go and so started writing petulant letters to his parents. In January 1908, he told his mother, "I feel the pull of the world's art center, and my mind is set, and sometime in the future, very soon, I am going." He said that he could no longer fight off the draw of the "great ideas which are continually surging up in the great pot of intellectual genius bounded by the walls of the Latin Quarter." A week later, he added, "There [Paris] the almighty dollar loses his title and Apollo and the Muses take his throne," and mocked Americans' "idolatry of hard silver," a taunt that surely burned the Colonel.

Luckily for Benton, Oswald intervened and told Lizzie and the Colonel that their boy was driven enough to benefit from a trip to Paris. Finally, after Benton appeased Lizzie's last fears—telling her not to be frightened by Balzac's tales of the Latin Quarter—the Colonel capitulated and agreed to free up the last of Uncle Sam's money for the journey, but not before unleashing one more cruel critique: he told his son, just eighteen, that he was "a lizard that changes colors" and yields "to too many influences to get anywhere."

By May he'd had enough and begged his parents to be more enthusiastic about his trip. Whatever their private feelings about the turn of events, they had eased up enough by July to manage a party—an "Oak Hill Hop"—in his honor, and Benton was gracious enough to tell his mother that his time in Chicago had been "the best . . . of my life." And there was another reason for him to exult that summer: he was smitten. Fay Clark's name doesn't appear in any of his memoirs. All that remains of their romance are the letters he sent to her, some of them distinguished by a breathless charm:

> The pink dress was more than a dream, it was divine, truly sweetheart, you were the loveliest, sweetest, most darlingly, dazzling, delicious, charming thing Sat. night that I have ever seen, a real Queen of the Fairies, come to earth and bringing with her all

the streams and soft, caressing, amorous, fragrant breezes, of fairy arms, and fairy eyes, fairy lives and fairy kisses, and more than all memories of the divinely, glorious sweetness of a fairy love.

"Fairy" Fay's response is lost, but in August Benton was on a boat to Paris, fantasizing about Whistler, about genius, and about buying a black walking stick.

5

PARIS

Belle Époque Paris had many attractions for American artists. The city's art academies, especially the ateliers of Jean-Léon Gérôme, Thomas Couture, and Marc-Charles-Gabriel Gleyre, had been luring American painters since the Civil War—Thomas Eakins, Childe Hassam, John Singer Sargent, Edward Hopper, and Robert Henri, to name a few, studied with these teachers—and by 1887 Henry James could remark, "It sounds like a paradox, but it's a very simple truth, that when to-day we look for 'American art' we find it mainly in Paris. When we find it out of Paris, we at least find a great deal of Paris in it." The stories of these artists may not be as sensational as those of the Lost Generation novelists (Hemingway, Fitzgerald, Dos Passos), but they were seminal in that they established Paris in the American imagination as a city with an enticing bohemian social scene and a professional destination full of possibilities. Eakins certainly benefited from studying with Gérôme at the École des Beaux-Arts—it gave his grave realism the imprimatur of academic art—and Childe Hassam, who studied at the Académie Julian, was one painter who helped popularize impressionism in the United States. Robert Henri, as a writer and a teacher—at the New York School of Art, his own Henri School of Art, and eventually the Art Students League, where Benton would teach—revolutionized art training in America by rejecting the precepts and methods of the traditional New York academies, encouraging instead self-determination. But Henri would never have taught Hopper, Stuart Davis, Rockwell Kent, or the gritty realists of the Ashcan school had he not first immersed himself, from 1888 to 1891, in Paris's art academies, which, depending on his motives, he either emulated or criticized.

Gertrude Stein was the most conspicuous American in Paris before World War I. She arrived in 1903, five years ahead of Benton, and moved in with her brother Leo at 27, rue de Fleurus, on the Left Bank. A lot happened in the apartment before the Lost Generation found it and Ezra Pound broke that antique chair: Picassos, Matisses, and Cézannes festooned its walls; Guillaume Apollinaire and Max Jacob stopped by for extended conversation; Alice Toklas moved in, Leo moved out. And though the famous salons at "27" didn't take off until later, Gertrude and Alice, neither of them café-goers, were accustomed to greeting anxious and supplicant Americans by the time Benton arrived, in August 1908. One acolyte was Alfred Maurer, a painter of fauvist landscapes and a moderately successful modernist in New York, and another was Marsden Hartley, who quickly befriended Stein and shared with her an admiration for the philosophy of William James. And arriving in Paris the same year as Benton was Morgan Russell, a well-connected artist who had been a student of Henri's in New York. Russell and Leo Stein grew especially close, and Leo, "with incredible patience," listened to Russell grouse and lent him money; Gertrude, meanwhile, studied him for one of her equivocal verbal portraits: "One was quite certain that he would be one succeeding in living and then that one was quite certain that he would not be one succeeding in living."

Russell introduced Stanton Macdonald-Wright, Paris's most eccentric American, to the Steins. Macdonald-Wright deemed the Steins an "ill-assorted pair"—a fair assessment considering their falling-out—but admired Leo's "retiring but authoritative presence." In a 1971 letter to the writer James R. Mellow, Macdonald-Wright recalled a visit he and Russell made to rue de Fleurus to view some Cézanne drawings Leo had just purchased. Gertrude, he remembered, was "standing in front of [the drawings] dressed in a long brown corduroy kimono . . . pontificating as usual. Her summation of their artistic value was 'they seem to float.' Whereupon, suddenly, she levitated, cigarette and all, and alighted in the pose of Ingres' 'Odalisque' on a couch with a beatific smile. The whole episode struck Morgan and me as highly ludicrous as G was no sylph." Macdonald-Wright explained that he, too, had just bought some Cézanne drawings and saw in them "something vastly more than their lighter than air qualities."

In his memoirs, Benton recalls that at the Café du Dôme in Montparnasse, for years the site of informal salons, he met, among others, George Grosz, Wyndham Lewis, Diego Rivera, John Marin, Arthur Lee, and the Steins. "These people were all around the Quarter," he writes, "but I shied away from them for I soon discovered they were all more talented and capable than I." He admits to being "stubborn" and having an "uneasy defiance" around this group—"there was no difference between the shrewd, canny lawyers of Missouri and the aesthetes of Paris"—but these attitudes were the consequence of his sudden realization that the genius he ascribed to himself in Chicago was, in fact, "purely an imaginary affair." Later he explained to Thomas Craven, "The Quarter was overrun with geniuses . . . I was no good anywhere. In the company of such hardened internationalists . . . and that Stein woman, I was merely a roughneck with a talent for fighting, perhaps, but not for painting, as it was cultivated in Paris."

Benton wasn't the only American painter in Paris around this time who was nonplussed by the Steins. Hopper, who arrived in the autumn of 1906, was unmotivated to socialize with them. "Whom did I meet?" Hopper asked. "Nobody. I'd heard of Gertrude Stein, but I don't remember having heard of Picasso at all. I used to go to the cafés at night and sit and watch. I went to the theatre a little. Paris had no great or immediate impact on me." Like Hopper, Benton wasn't all that interested in the scene at rue de Fleurus, an attitude that had less to do with any particular dislike for the Steins, who they were or what they stood for, than with the fact that he was still an immature and self-absorbed young artist who had practical things to worry about, such as learning how to paint. When he arrived in New York, in 1912, Benton would socialize and work with a coterie of modernists, but in Paris he was content to move in a small, relatively safe circle of peers that included Abel Warshawsky, John Thompson, and later Macdonald-Wright, all of whom were working on the fundamentals of their technique. Before he got to know these artists, however, Benton's only friend in the city was a Turk named Ali.

Benton sailed from New York to Le Havre in late August 1908, on board the French Line's *La Lorraine*, a sleek vessel that carried over a thousand passengers and had sumptuous first-class cabins. Despite his exhilaration, Benton felt utterly alone as he stood in line waiting to board the ship; no one was there to send him off, and he envied those passengers who had family and friends at the dock. "I was very uneasy," Benton remembers. "Everybody was speaking French and I didn't know a word of the language. I was nineteen years old and while I had had a couple of years of independent, family free, experience . . . and felt myself fully grown up, the strange new world of the French ship undermined all my self confidence."

A purser led Benton to his second-class cabin, which struck him as dismal. Once the steamship got under way, Benton went on deck and watched as the skyline of New York City disappeared. As they sailed out of Lower New York Bay and passed Sandy Hook, New Jersey, he felt the first ocean swells and was violently seasick. He ran below and vomited into a grim urinal. As he tried to regain his balance, he felt a hand under his armpit and heard "a kindly voice," first in French, then in English: "It's nothing. It will pass." He turned and saw a squat man with a smile and "large curling mustachios, waxed at the ends." The man led Benton back to the deck, offered him a chair, and introduced himself as Ali, his cabinmate. "I'm going to Paris to study art," Tom responded. "I'm an artist."

"Ali the Turk," as Benton calls him in a peculiar little essay he published in 1971, was thirty-seven and balding. "He was handsome in a way," he adds, "with shiny black eyes and a kind of dark pink skin." A tobacco importer working for New York's cigarette makers, Ali was on his way to Turkey and the Middle East, but not before "a good time" in Paris. He kindly looked after Benton by helping him order food at dinner, work out the language's quirky grammar, and converse with the "voluble" but "exclusive and indifferent" passengers. Much to Benton's liking, Ali always introduced him as "Artist" and, with a cool dispassion, allied with him against brandy-induced attacks on American morals by a peevish French architect. "I have always remembered [the architect's] intense bitterness toward everything American," Benton recalls. "Although in later years I would come across many kindred dislikes among his compatriots I never found any so all enveloping."

When *La Lorraine* docked at Le Havre, Benton readied his luggage for the train to Paris and said goodbye to the Turk, but Ali wouldn't hear of it. He helped Benton tip the porters and jostle his way to a half-decent seat on the train. Once in Paris, Ali led him to a small hotel on the Left Bank's boulevard St. Michel; during his first minute of peace in the city, Benton craned his neck out of the room's miniature window and soaked in the boulevard's panorama—its bustling commuters and ambling flaneurs. But he didn't know anything about Paris yet. "Where all was strange," he ruminates, "a particular strangeness was not noticeable."

That night at dinner he enjoyed his first taste of internationalism. Ali guided him to a café crowded with students from the Middle East, and they joined a group of young men at a table in the middle of the room. Benton panicked, worried that his abysmal French would render him mute, but the students were studying English at the Sorbonne and quickly charmed him with their "friendly and sympathetic manners"; more important, they knew precisely where a young American artist needed to find himself—at the Café du Dôme in Montparnasse. Ali paid, as he did for all the "lunches and dinners, aperitifs and wines" they enjoyed together, and Benton, for the first time in a long while, felt chagrined: here was a group of men who, like him, were eager to learn and were courageous enough to travel abroad to do it; unlike him, however, they were good-natured, generous, and already at home in Paris.

But Ali, eager to steel his American companion for life in the new city, cautioned him to be conservative with his trust. At meals he told Benton long, meandering stories about the spectacular bad luck of acquaintances who were robbed of their life savings, tricked into subsidizing prostitutes, or spiritually ruined—all because they let down their guard in the face of some Parisian seduction. Ali relished telling these fabulous parables; "his eyes sparkled and snapped and he twisted his mustachios vigorously at periods which needed emphasis." Little did Ali know that his companion didn't need to be scared into skepticism; it came to Benton more naturally than happiness.

A few days after arriving in Paris, Benton and Ali made their way to the Café du Dôme. It was after five, and people were just congregating at the sidewalk tables, enclosed within walls of topiary. Their purpose was to find an affordable apartment appropriate for a young American artist, but both were out of their element, and neither screwed up the courage to approach the other customers, who engaged in animated conversation. They did manage to question a waiter, who mentioned a German landlord who frequented the Dôme late at night. For four awkward nights they sat waiting for him. "During the day," Benton writes, "I walked in the Louvre looking at paintings . . . After breakfast I'd walk down the Boulevard St. Michel, wander along the banks of the Seine looking over book stalls and then go into [the museum]. I was still too timid to risk myself in restaurants so I did without lunch." Benton's stomach ached with hunger and fluttered with anxiety.

But on the fifth night the German appeared. "He was completely self-possessed, even arrogantly so," Benton recalls. "He had a small cupid's bow mouth which seemed to pout. His habitual expression, with wrinkles on top of his nose, suggested that he was smelling something putrid. I did not like him, nor did Ali." But the landlord had several renovated artists' studios "for rent to the proper persons." After they visited the unfurnished studios the next day, the German turned to Ali and said, "Your little friend must come with financial recommendations if he proposes to rent." Ali vouched for Benton, who was already brooding: "What annoyed me most was the patronizing word 'petit' which I understood."

Benton paid two months' rent on the spot—sixteen dollars in all—and Ali helped him bargain for the stove. The building was on passage Guibert, a Montparnasse alley leading off a narrow street of low houses and small gardens protected by high walls. "The area appeared rather poor but it had some charm," Benton recalls, "with little flower beds, hedges and sycamore trees glimpsed, here and there, behind tall iron gates." The sculptors' studios were on the ground floor, and the painters occupied studios off a balcony on the second floor. The landlord's mother led the men to one of these rooms, which was about twenty square feet with a large window in the north wall. A small loft for storage or sleeping hung over the room, and the cast-iron coal stove, for cooking and heating, protruded a few feet from the wall; a water tap and two toilets were situated at the end of the outside balcony. "As all was new and bright and the big window filled the studio with light," Benton was pleased. Ali helped Benton furnish the studio that day: in shops near the Gare Montparnasse, they purchased a cot, sheets, a teakettle, a coffeepot, a frying pan, and two sacks of coal.

Before Ali departed, he and Benton had a final supper together and afterward went to the Dôme for coffee. There they ran into a young artist just arrived from New York who was eager for companionship. "He introduced himself with an affable grin," Benton reminisced, "as Abe Warshawsky." Abel G. Warshawsky—born in Sharon, Pennsylvania, in 1883, to an Orthodox Jewish family from Poland, and raised in

Cleveland—was a successful American impressionist who painted breezy, colorful landscapes. Before moving to Paris in the fall of 1908, Warshawsky studied at the Cleveland School of Art and then in New York, at the Art Students League and the National Academy of Design, the country's stodgiest art academy. When he was in New York, Warshawsky somehow finagled a trip to Winslow Homer's studio in Prouts Neck, Maine, and later extolled the American realist's "heroic seascapes replete with power and the tragedy of those who 'go down to the sea in ships.'"

Though they would lose touch after Benton returned to the United States in 1911, Warshawsky, like Benton, struggled to reconcile his preferred style with the precepts of modernism and was harshly critical of abstract art, which he believed sacrificed "beauty" and "ideals" on the altar of "dishonesty" and "showmanship." To escape the "hothouse artistic atmosphere of Paris," Warshawsky retreated to Brittany and the south of France, where he searched for "sanity in the out-of-doors." Unlike Benton, however, Warshawsky "lived on good terms with himself and his art, and it shows in his writing."

When, in 1931, a terrible leg injury had kept him confined to his Paris studio and unable to take his easel outside, Warshawsky passed the time writing a splendid memoir, which wasn't published until 1980. *The Memories of an American Impressionist*, informal and rich with anecdote, serves as a vibrant and revealing account of the daily life of an American artist in Paris. Of the renowned Café du Dôme, for instance, Warshawsky writes, "There was the usual zinc counter, across which drinks would be served direct to standing customers who could thus avoid the tip to the waiter, and a couple of rooms with small marble tables, somewhat dilapidated black leather sofas, and a 'billiard.'" It was, he says, "unpretentious," and unlike at other gathering places for American artists, such as the American Art Club, "absolute and untrammeled liberty prevailed" there. He found the area around the passage Guibert "disconcerting," however: "neglected, bedraggled, even mean and squalid in parts." Nevertheless, he met Benton for the second time at his studio and remembers the evening fondly. It was the night before Thanksgiving, cold and pouring rain. Warshawsky arrived at the studios to meet another companion, Edgar McAdams, an American sculptor, but finding McAdams gone, he knocked on the door of a neighboring studio and was elated to find inside Alfred Rigny, an old friend from

New York, and Benton, who upon hearing that Warshawsky hadn't dined asked him "to pitch in with them":

> A big-bellied iron stove was radiating its cheerful glow from the center of the studio, while the rain, beating against the large glass window, added to the feeling of comfort. A long loaf of delicious tasty bread . . . with a large helping of beef steak smothered in onions and fried potatoes, and a cup of coffee *"a l'Américain"* soon put me in a state of beatitude.
>
> The boys drank red wine during the repast . . . [and] [w]hen asked how I liked the steak, I replied, "Delicious!" So it was, though perhaps a little tough and more sweetish in taste than the beef at home. Roars of laughter greeted my reply. They told me I had been eating horsemeat!

Benton and Warshawsky had much in common. Both were from the Midwest and were stocky and fit—Warshawsky described Benton as a "short, swarthy, compact young fellow"—with a passion for athletics. Warshawsky had supported himself in New York by pitching for a semi-pro baseball team and had a "masculine assertiveness." And like Benton, he was a boxer "who in his quiet, modest way was on virtually every occasion able to outfeint, outfox, and, eventually, flatten every opponent." But their main difference was fundamental: whereas Benton was pugnacious and arrogant, Abe was sweet and reserved. It was this very contrast, however, that drew them together. "Tommy Benton," Warshawsky observed, was "cheerful with a brittle joy that was a veneer for a storm of disquietude within." Many nights during the cold winter of 1908–1909, Warshawsky coaxed Benton outside and "walk[ed] him about for miles, trying to restore him to a normal and cheerful mood." Benton confirms this account, recalling how at the Dôme he'd get drunk on *grog américain* (rum, lemon, and water, served hot), "yell obscenities, senseless shoutings that expressed only an indefinable misery," and take swings at Warshawsky's prominent chin as he chaperoned him back to his studio.

Benton moped around Montparnasse because he couldn't paint yet. The fact is that upon his arrival in Paris, Benton was a novice, unskilled painter; his application was clumsy and heavy—he didn't possess a light or sure touch—and he fretted about where to study and how to get better.

Thirty years later, Craven reflected on this period in Benton's life: detached from the "frontier tradition of the Middle West, from typically American realities, and transported suddenly into the international Bohemianism of the Latin Quarter," he observes, "Benton had the battle of his life . . . lost his assurance and drifted into despondency." Craven exaggerates. He was eager to mythologize Benton as the exemplar of the representational painting he pushed in his dementedly xenophobic criticism. In his own writings Benton also overstated his distaste for French art, but when he was in Paris, he wasn't, in fact, terribly concerned about these so-called American realities or their relation to the new trend in art toward abstraction. Nor was he alone in his unresponsiveness to Picasso: plenty of American artists in Paris at the time were indifferent to cubism.

Craven also didn't know that just after moving into his studio and meeting Warshawsky, Benton experienced a brief moment of poise, even bliss. Abe puffed him up, telling him that his painting was "astonishing" for a nineteen-year-old—a comment that struck the susceptible Benton as authoritative, coming as it did from an experienced painter. "I got a quick reputation," he recalled, "and when I went to the Café du Dôme people looked at me. For a couple of weeks, I walked in an aura of confident genius." But this initial euphoria faded fast and left Benton confronting the limits of his ability: he knew what he knew—which is what he had learned from Oswald in Chicago—but he couldn't build on it. He didn't know how to generate new ideas, experiment with technique, and forge ahead into the "fine" arts. He and Warshawsky hired female models to come to his light-filled studio, but he fumbled with his canvases and failed to analyze the "convolutions" of the women's anatomies. Ambitious but unable to teach himself, he was stuck.

John Thompson, an American who lived in the neighboring studio, suggested that studying at an art academy might inspire him. Thompson was cut from the same cloth as Benton and Warshawsky. Benton describes him as short and sturdy, with "a big chest [and] sloping shoulders," and a "prime bag puncher." "He fitted in with . . . my submerged pugnacity," he adds, "and we got pretty close to each other." Born in Buffalo in 1882, Thompson turned down the opportunity to box professionally in order to study art. Another veteran of the Art Students League in New York, he arrived in Paris in 1902, met the Steins, lived briefly in the same house that George Sand had lived in, and studied classical mosaics, Persian miniatures, the old masters, and Toulouse-Lautrec. But it was the spectacular Cézanne retrospectives, in 1907, at the Galerie Bernheim-Jeune and the Salon d'Automne that most impressed him, and until his death in Colorado, in 1945, he painted analytical, cubistic landscapes.

Thompson had studied at the Académie Julian in Paris and recommended to Benton that he enroll there. Known as Julian's, the academy rivaled the École des Beaux-Arts as the most popular art school in the city for both European and American students. Founded in 1868 by Rodolphe Julian, it was the largest private art academy in Paris and had ateliers throughout the city. The school's reputation was built on its liberalism: it admitted women long before the École des Beaux-Arts; it encouraged students to work on their own interests, at their own pace; it employed enough teachers so that students weren't compelled to apprentice to one master and imitate his style; and it let them study with professors not associated with the academy. Whereas students were required to take "a stiff entry examination" at the École, anyone could enroll at Julian's and "begin his training without delay." The academy offered courses in drawing, painting, and sculpture that were designed to help students gain entry to the École or prepare to become professors. The curriculum, though, was typical—"inspired by Ingres, its program concentrated on drawing, mainly of the human figure, in search for the truth in nature"—and Julian's earned a reputation as a place where artists could study academic technique at their leisure. Celebrated artists who studied at Julian's include John Singer Sargent, Édouard Vuillard, Henri Matisse, Émile Bernard, and Fernand Léger.

But by the time Benton arrived in Paris, Julian's was losing some of its appeal. "The art language was changing with the shifting direction of taste," Warshawsky explains. "'Rhythm,' 'volume,' 'dynamic symmetry' had superseded the old terms 'composition,' 'form,' 'values.' Deftness and sound craftsmanship were at a discount with the *jeunes*, who sneered at such qualities as mere tricks of the art trade." Robert Henri, who had studied at Julian's in 1888, visited the academy in 1901 and perceived stagnancy among its pupils. "These students," he wrote later, "have become masters of the trade of drawing, as some others have become masters of their grammars. And like so many of the latter, brilliant jugglers of words, having nothing worthwhile to say, they remain little else than clever jugglers of the brush."

Benton was critical as well. Though he was drifting, he proved once again too sensitive to authority, and even Julian's loose curriculum irritated him. He enrolled in a life drawing class in the fall of 1908 and struggled right away. Strolling into the atelier, at once arrogant and defensive, he expected big things of himself and the course. But sitting at his easel, set in an arc radiating out from a small stage, he couldn't muster much interest in the apathetic models hired by the school; he said later that what he really craved at the time was some "meaningful subject to fire my interests." He had little sympathy for the students who remained at Julian's year after year and saw mere "exercise" as the "all in all" of art. The "deeply rooted and scrupulously observed" protocols of life drawing at the academy—tacking the light-grained, uniformly sized paper to the easel, jockeying for position within the semicircle, periodically measuring the model with a plumb line, and constantly erasing and redrafting—were eagerly performed by his classmates but struck Benton as pointless. He wrestled above all with charcoal, which required a technique seemingly antithetical to the line-based sketching he had learned with pen and ink. Much later he would reflect on the principles of the class, especially its objective of purging students of preconceptions, and see in them a semblance of John Ruskin's and William James's notions about the "innocent eye," but at the time he "was certain that such methods would not lead to any kind of art that I wanted to produce." The feeling was mutual, apparently, for he was promptly demoted to a cast drawing class, identical to the one he had loathed so much at the Art Institute. "My pride was assaulted," he says, though by his own admission he was "the most inept practitioner of academic drawing in the school."

Eventually, Benton was reinstated to the life drawing class but still couldn't focus on his course work. He preoccupied himself with various extracurricular exercises—painting somber portraits in his studio, drawing the tiled rooftops visible from his big window, and sketching in the cafés around the Gare Montparnasse. Benton loved to sketch because he was a showman; he thrived on performance and got a rush from working in front of a crowd—after all, art had to be a social activity, not an act of self-expression. Sketching was also a way for him to show his peers that he was productive: people stopped and looked over his shoulder as he executed quick drawings of café patrons and their "flashy lady companions," and his friends on the passage Guibert noticed his drawings and called them "clever" (which he later decided was a disparagement).

At Thompson's urging, Benton also began experimenting with impressionism in the winter of 1909. Thompson took him several times to the Luxembourg Museum, where Monet's *La Gare Saint-Lazare* (1877) and Renoir's *Moulin de la Galette* (1876) were on permanent display; upon their return, Benton would hole up in his studio and paint colorful still lifes of apples and pears or take to the streets and paint *en plein air*. It was the first time that he used a full palette in his painting, but by his own admission he wasn't terribly interested in color at this time. He recalls that at the Luxembourg Museum he was struck most by "a sunlit scene of red tile roofs and backyard gardens by Pissarro." He identified in him a devotion to composition that he felt was lacking in the work of other impressionists: "Perhaps because of the clear-cut exposition of method in this picture, I made myself an ardent disciple of Pissarro and tried to paint as nearly in his manner as I could."

In the spring of 1909, Benton enrolled in a painting class at Julian's. Thompson had convinced him that he'd find the class more satisfying than the drawing classes he'd taken, as the instructors "recognize that some people draw better with a brush than charcoal." Julian's didn't teach impressionism to its students; instead, just as at the Art Institute, the academy emphasized the use of a limited palette and encouraged its students to paint in dark tones. Jean-Paul Laurens, an academic painter of "somber French histories," supervised the class. Benton made a few decent portraits that spring but was disappointed with Laurens, who would show up twice a week and offer only a few opaque remarks to each student. A few months later, Benton was finished for good with "the plodders" at Julian's.

To his admiration of Pissarro, his study of tonal painting at Julian's, and his street sketches, Benton added another obsession in the winter of 1908–1909. Ignacio Zuloaga, a Basque painter born in 1870, eleven years before Picasso, had moved to Paris in 1890 and settled in Montmartre, where he befriended Toulouse-Lautrec, Degas, and Gauguin, among others. Though he lived and exhibited all over Europe, Zuloaga was most adored in Paris, where he showed his works at small galleries as well as the official salons. Benton never met him, but Zuloaga's work was easy enough to see as he was celebrated among Left Bank artists as an independent painter unbeholden to any school or movement.

But the so-called Generation of '98, a group of Spanish writers and intellectuals who sought to revive their country's native culture following the Spanish-American War, praised Zuloaga's paintings for their Spanish style and content; like El Greco, he often placed his figures in turbulent environments, and like Goya, he often painted obscure subjects from Spanish folklore and depicted his figures in regional costumes. Zuloaga's landscapes, portraits, and genre scenes are blunt and encumbered, and one reason that Benton admired them is that they aren't very French. Here was a painter who wasn't afraid of solid form, who could beef up his canvases with realism even as he designed and decorated them. Added to this was Benton's sense, however erroneous, that Zuloaga was an outsider in Paris. Benton gushed about the Spaniard in a letter to his father and for a time imitated his "broad brushing manner." More important, perhaps, is that Zuloaga prompted Benton to go to the Louvre and hunt down paintings by El Greco and Goya, the two artists, it can be argued, who influenced him the most: the elastic, mannered figures and hectic coloring in Benton's mature works bear the unmistakable imprint of El Greco, while his fondness for satire, in both his genre paintings and his historical murals, is Goyaesque. It's fair to say, in fact, that what Benton brought home from France was a Spanish aesthetic.

Benton's motive for going to Paris was to learn how to paint. Now, after just eight months, he was saturated and confused, torn between what he would call "opposed and contradictory styles of painting": a studied and somber realism on the one hand, and an impromptu modernism on the other. His friends noticed his turmoil, his constant rehearsing of various styles and techniques, and intervened. One day in the summer of 1909, Abe stopped by his studio. After some hemming and hawing, he poked a finger in Benton's chest. "Tommy," he said, "there are a lot of people in the quarter talking about you. They say . . . you are just smearing around like crazy." Benton couldn't argue, and as he so memorably put it: "I wallowed in every cockeyed ism that came along."

It's revealing to reflect back on Benton's state of mind when he decided he wanted to study in Paris, when he wrote to his mother from Chicago about the spell Whistler had cast on him: "The art of James McNeil [sic] Whistler has left an impression on me . . . Tone, colors harmoniously arranged, a certain quality, a certain lightness of line . . . One of the reasons that I must go to Paris, is to see the greater works of the Whistler I speak of." These desires were now long gone, consumed by Pissarro's "clear-cut exposition" and Zuloaga's "broad brushing manner." Benton still had no artistic identity: he knew he wanted to paint, but he didn't know how he wanted to paint. Would he harmonize like Whistler? Would he represent his impressions of nature, turning his back on form? Would he nurture a folkloric realism? And even if he answered these questions, there were plenty more. How could he distinguish himself from similar artists? Whom did he mean to impress?

He had tried, but neither school nor slavish imitation was going to effect a revelation. In *An Artist in America*, Benton slams the door on this chapter of his apprenticeship:

> Because of my revolt against the patterns of the schools, I spent fifteen years on my beam-end, rocked by every wave that came along. I floundered, without a compass, in every direction. Of course, the compasses of the schools were all cockeyed. No course could be charted with them on a modern sea, and had I depended on their services I should have been no better off in the long run. But it was tough never to know where you were and yet, in the face of the world and for your pride's sake, be compelled to pretend that you did.

There's a lot to contradict and parse in this passage; he did "depend" on the services of academies and teachers, for instance, and one wonders whether pride necessarily compels one to "pretend." In addition, despite what he says, by 1909 he possessed essential skills: he was a gifted draftsman, a competent watercolorist, and a beginning painter with a strong sense of composition. Moreover, he possessed one of the finest attributes of the creative person: because he was public-minded, he wanted to share his art. But he was not, it's clear, a natural student, at least in the academy, so what he needed was a new program, a way to let his curiosity lead him to a style.

Before leaving Julian's, Benton had started drawing at the Académie Colarossi, a private atelier in Montparnasse. Colarossi's was even more informal than Julian's: it was cheap, open to women, had no required curriculum, and offered no instruction; it simply hired models for artists to sketch at their leisure. But the studio was crowded and offered local artists a camaraderie they couldn't find elsewhere, so it became a popular hangout (among the famous artists who frequented the atelier at one time or another were Hans Hofmann, Max Weber, and Amedeo Modigliani). Monday mornings in particular were a circus at Colarossi's, when artists milled around ogling all the models who came by looking for work. The models, men, women, and children, were mostly Italian and made a living at Colarossi's posing as beggars, saints, cupids, and angels. "One of the curious sights," according to Warshawsky, "was to see the models of both sexes, of every hue and age, promenading in the classroom stark nude, waiting to be chosen for the various classes in the school." Benton was relieved to find Colarossi's, where he could move freely around the studio and draw the models from any angle he pleased, and before long he was attending every day and sharing his work with the "mature and even famous artists" who sketched there.

As he was leaving Colarossi's one afternoon, a man approached him and shook his hand. "You're Benton," he said. "They say you're the best ever." This was John Carlock, who, like so many of the men Benton claims as early influences, remains a mysterious figure. While all agree that Carlock was a nephew of Elbert Hubbard—the founder of the Roycrofters, whose writings Tom read with the law student back in Neosho—Benton refers to him variously as "John" and a "fellow named Carlock," while Warshawsky calls him "George" and describes him as "a shy, strange boy." Benton didn't care about the particulars because he was thrilled that this Left Bank veteran had heard of him, though his satisfaction turned to anxiety once Carlock invited himself to passage Guibert to view his work. Over the next several days, Benton worked feverishly to prepare a small exhibition for his visitor.

Carlock arrived at the appointed time but wasn't as gracious as before: he stood motionless in the studio doorway until Benton pleaded with him to come in, an invitation to which he replied with a grunt. "He carried his head, topped by a crop of wiry uncombable black hair, thrust forward," Benton recollected. "His eyes were dark with streaks of green and hazel and blue in them . . . He looked very Irish but like those we called 'black Irishmen' in Missouri. There was a swarthiness in his complexion." Benton's nerves were on edge as this strange fellow silently perused the little exhibition of café sketches, impressionist still lifes, and painted portraits he had laid out. "I am completely disillusioned," Carlock eventually responded. "This is awful. You haven't got anything—you don't know anything at all. You haven't even got any integrity." Crushed, Benton asked what he meant by this last remark— "integrity" sounded like something he should have. Carlock explained that artists who work in so many styles and mediums lack dedication and confidence; such artists, he said, have no intent. As a final insult, Carlock said that his drawings might be fit for newspapers but not for galleries.

After recovering from this devastating critique, Benton decided that he had something to gain from Carlock's cranky wisdom, so he tracked him down at Colarossi's and asked how he might go about drawing more serious pictures. Since he later described Carlock as "an erratic, somewhat inarticulate . . . artist," it's surprising that Benton suddenly abandoned his inherent suspicion of instruction and chose him as a mentor, though he might have been impressed by Carlock's association with the Louvre, where he worked in some mysterious capacity with the collection of old-master drawings. Carlock "had become a student of the fifteenth and sixteenth centuries, especially of the drawings of those times," Benton explains. "It was [his] view that more knowledge of drawing could be obtained by studying in the Louvre than in the classes of the academies." Benton was skeptical at first, but standing before Titian's *Entombment of Christ* (ca. 1520) one afternoon, he had an epiphany: "I was not only seeing its surface but seeing into it, inside it . . . I realized that I was up against a very different kind of flow, one that I did not understand . . . It was a flow not only of lines and contours, but of great forms in and out, over and around." His analysis is shrewd. The painting astonishes both because the graceful outlines of the figures, which flow across the canvas, are rendered so harmoniously and because the solid structures of the bodies, which overlap "in and out," give it a spatial dynamism. We can trust Benton when he says that the Titian exposed him to a "different kind of flow"; we can imagine him seeing for the first time how a great painting transcends its physical confines. Such dynamism would become one of the principal appeals of his mature work.

Now intent on winning over Carlock, Benton showed him the sketch he had made of the Titian. Carlock responded that the drawing was "backasswards" but admitted that it showed devotion and so agreed to meet him in the Louvre the next day. He ushered Benton into a room lined with glass cases of old-master drawings and instructed him to choose one to copy; Carlock said that he had a meeting with a curator regarding a Raphael drawing and that he would return to check on Benton's progress. Benton chose to copy a drawing of a nude by one of the Carracci brothers and, by his own admission, struggled mightily with the baroque figure: he couldn't manage to fit the chest and stomach muscles into the body's outlines. When Carlock returned, he was, of course, unimpressed and accused Benton of choosing the work because it resembled the academic drawings he'd copied at Julian's. Fed up with Carlock's litany of criticisms, Benton shoved the pad and pencil at him and demanded, "Show me how you would study this thing."

When Carlock demurred, Benton believed that he'd exposed him and grew suspicious that Carlock's only purpose was to "clinch his ascendancy over me." But Carlock stared back. "Yes, Benton," he admitted, "I'd have to work at it just like you."

To his credit, Benton would acknowledge later that he learned a lesson that day: he realized at that moment that the interior of a figure, not just the contours, has life. But more important, and apparently unbeknownst to him, he had learned how to suspend his ego long enough to accept someone else's counsel; he was now studying art in a way that suited his hunger for argument. After that day together in the Louvre, Benton and Carlock settled down into a less adversarial friendship. They'd stroll home together from Colarossi's and stay up late in Benton's apartment eating salt fish and bread; as they drank bottles of cheap wine, they talked up Cézanne and the Renaissance masters. They admired Cézanne for the same reason everyone else did: he was able to bring a natural classicism to modern art. Benton credited Carlock with teaching him how to use classical forms in his art, and as Henry Adams points out, Benton always thought of himself as a modern classicist— not because he was an academic or conservative painter, but because he was mindful of compositional geometry and symmetry. In *An Artist in America*, Benton sums up Carlock's influence this way: "I feel I owe my first great artistic debt to Carlock, because in all the years of my floundering, he gave me, through his introduction to the values of the classic masterpieces, something to cling to and return to."

By the winter of 1909–1910, Benton was occupying himself by drawing each day at Colarossi's, visiting the Louvre, painting informal portraits and figure compositions, and reading French literature, especially Verlaine and Balzac. It was this latter diversion, however, that prompted his falling-out with Carlock, who called Benton a "book worm," adding, "The only things real for an artist are those you can see or put your hands on. The rest is all imaginary tripe." The comment offended Benton, who'd lost patience with Carlock's criticisms, and the men drifted apart. Years later, in 1916, they ran into each other in New York, at Stieglitz's 291 gallery, and Carlock used the same line he'd seduced him with at Colarossi's: "Well, Benton, I hear you're the best ever. Can I come by your studio?"

"The story of my life in Paris," Benton reminisces in *An Artist in America*, "is the story of all who went there before the Great War—a lady friend to look after you and run you, a studio, some work, and a lot of talk." Benton met his "lady friend" Jeanette in April 1909, just after his twentieth birthday. Abe had taken a mistress, a redheaded Frenchwoman, and he hosted a party in his studio in Montparnasse to introduce her to his friends. Benton got drunk on wine and cognac and advanced on a woman who was standing alone, glancing at him. It happened in a rush: Abe saw them talking and encouraged Benton to invite her to his studio; he explained that taking a mistress was a good way to acquire some furniture and keep from getting the clap from the prostitutes at the cafés. A few nights later, Tom and Jeanette slept together, "uncomfortably," in his small cot, after some awkward conversation. She left early the next morning, only to return hours later with a cart carrying two chamber pots, a bathtub, and some curtains for the big window.

Jeanette had a large influence on Benton's social life in Paris. He had developed the habit of going to bed drunk every night, but she urged him to drink less. Though he managed to escape some nights to meet Thompson or Warshawsky at the Dôme, he was now domesticated. He didn't have much to say about Jeanette in his memoirs, but several years before his death he opened up a little about what attracted him to her, telling an interviewer, "I was too young for the café crowd [and] as I look back on it I don't think it's good psychologically for a young man to be that alone all the time . . . A mistress was generally accepted practice . . . Most of those girls, I guess you could say, were very effective as 'caretakers of the young.'"

Jeanette was an amateur artist—she sketched and painted—and

supported Benton's art by planning working vacations for him. In June, two months after moving into the studio, she sent him off on a brief sojourn to a cottage near the cathedral at Chartres, about an hour by train from Paris. He stayed for two weeks, making impressionist oil sketches *en plein air*. On his walks in the countryside he kept bumping into a young French artist who engaged in the odd habit of peering through tiny squares of colored glass as he painted. Benton approached the man one day and asked him what he was up to. The man responded that the tinted glass, "because it took the color out of his subjects, helped him find 'les valeurs,' the 'tonal' gradations in nature from light to dark." Upon returning to Paris, Benton found some pieces of this glass and spent weeks examining the city through their colors. He felt absurd, but this exercise proved useful, leading him to "a deeper appreciation of the formal patterns underlying the colors of nature, those substantial patterns which persist beneath all changes of appearance." Though he eventually abandoned the glass tiles after coming under the spell of Paul Signac's pointillism, the lessons he learned stayed with him throughout his career; his mature works illustrate his greater devotion to allover patterns than to naturalistic color.

With Jeanette's help, Benton also made several trips to the village of Garches, just west of Paris, where he luxuriated in the "great trees" and "little red roofed houses"; everything there, he wrote to his mother, whom he never told about his mistress, is "rich and glorious in color," especially the cherries and strawberries. Despite these diversions, Benton remained frustrated with the progress of his art. As his trials with the glass squares demonstrate, he continued to dither with all manner of artmaking and with every genre and style in vogue, but he couldn't make a painting that satisfied his ambition. His letters home were mostly cheerful, but as he later explained, they were meant to convince Lizzie and the Colonel that "everything was O.K.," when in fact he was often "depressed." He complained about money periodically, especially after Jeanette moved into the studio, but in one letter in particular, postmarked July 20, 1909, Benton exposed the tangle he'd gotten himself into. Apparently, the Colonel had sent a letter accusing him of indulging himself in Paris, because Benton's response was a long-winded *principia philosophiae* longer on ideas than concrete plans.

It opens with an admission—"To begin with I want again to impress upon you the fact that I am perfectly aware of my youth and of the foolishness that is generally connected therewith"—but quickly moves on to a pedantic counterattack. "A young man," he writes, "is accredited with a boy's view and nothing more, while it is quite forgotten that John Keats wrote all his around his twentieth year." Imagine the Colonel's exasperation upon reading his boy's proposition that, when judging a man, it would be "better if we pass the years of his animal life and try [to] judge him by the strength of his infinite soul." Despite this initial immature maneuvering, Benton warmed to the task and managed to make a few adroit arguments. "As for the 'Amenities due to others,'" he responded, presumably to the Colonel's charge that he was self-centered, "I have an open heart and hand for every man that will give me friendship, whether he digs ditches, writes poems or paints great pictures. I put myself in no manner above any man, ignorant or learned, if he puts himself below me it is his own affair. I cannot brook arrogance in any form." He also got close to something that sounds like a pragmatic doctrine, which he would realize more fully in the years to come, when he wrote, "I want powerful technique moving in rhythm with great thought. I want the dream and the reality, the motive and the paint."

The letter ends with another appeal to his father to try to understand painting as a profound art. "You have admired Byron, who put his strong passionate soul, at times, into such powerful form, and have derived strength from this," he exhorted. "But the painter poet you have missed and that naturally too, for America and America's artists are just waking up . . . My work is the one serious thing to me, I cannot pass it, it is life."

The very same day, Benton addressed a letter to his mother, and as is so often the case after one sends a passionate confession, he used the intervening minutes to distill his message. "That I have succeeded in making myself plain [to the Colonel] I hardly think probable," he told Lizzie, adding that he had no choice but to employ "bravado" in making his case. All he really wanted to say, he concluded, was "I have chosen my path, trust me to myself."

But Benton's sense of well-being was badly shaken during the second half of 1909. That summer, Jeanette's mother began making regular visits to the studio, and frequently he'd return from the Louvre or Colarossi's to find the two women engaged in earnest conversation. He pressed Jeanette, and she eventually confessed that she was pregnant.

Benton was floored and ran in terror to the kindly Abe for advice. He understood he was in real trouble when even Abe was struck dumb by the news. Apparently, there was no discussion about an abortion, but Benton knew for sure that he couldn't marry Jeanette: everything he had worked for, all the wisdom he had tried to pass off on the Colonel, would crumble under the humiliation of returning from Paris with a working-class wife and a bastard child.

Benton escaped from his anxiety by painting. He had grown fonder of Cézanne and Matisse and tried his hand at modernist still lifes and landscapes. He also painted a self-portrait around this time that his sister Mildred described as a "brown gravy" picture in the vein of Emil Nolde, a German Expressionist painter. When Benton decided that he had a large enough body of work to photograph, he planned to send the images home to appease his parents; he also hoped that they would show the photographs to Mr. Calhoun, who would then arrange an exhibition for him in Joplin. But the day after Christmas, in 1909, Benton studied the photographs closely as he arranged them to send home. Somehow the reproductions showed him what he couldn't see before, and he was devastated. In the letter he included with the package, he berated himself. "These pictures are bad," he wrote, "not only bad but miserable . . . [They] have brought me face to face . . . with the utter lack of sincerity in my work." To make matters worse, Abe stopped by the studio to warn him that Americans on the Right Bank were gossiping about his predicament with Jeanette and that the news might even reach Missouri.

Late one night in January, Jeanette went into labor. Her screams woke Thompson and his mistress, who came running in. Benton asked the couple to stay behind as he ran to get Dr. Chevalarius, a physician who had been checking on them regularly. When they returned, Thompson was gone, and his mistress was on her knees between Jeanette's legs. Benton was "paralyzed" by what he saw: "a small protruding human foot." Dr. Chevalarius tried valiantly, but Jeanette delivered a dead baby. He departed, grabbing a small canvas as payment, and left the couple to spend the night with "a small corpse in the studio." The next day the police arrived, asked a few questions, and discreetly carried the body away.

•

One distraction for Benton from these tragic events was his developing friendship with Stanton Macdonald-Wright, though he didn't tell him about the baby until a few months after the stillbirth. "Funniest God damned thing I ever heard of," Stanton roared. "God damn crazy funny." The response was typical of Macdonald-Wright, whose tactless wit was legendary. Benton first met him late in the fall of 1909, when Jeanette was nearing the end of her pregnancy. He noticed a strange fellow sitting by himself at the Dôme, and hearing him speak English to a waiter, Benton approached his table and asked to sit down. At first, he found Macdonald-Wright's appearance "repellent": he looked sickly, with pale skin, hunched shoulders, and "bilious" eyes—"there was something wrong about his whole physical make up," Benton recalled. But Macdonald-Wright was also dapper, dressed in well-tailored clothes, and as they talked, Benton succumbed to his irreverent humor; it was a relief to laugh again about the inanity of the artist's life in the quarter, and he vowed to seek out Macdonald-Wright again.

Macdonald-Wright was born in Charlottesville, Virginia, in 1890, a year after Benton. From the beginning, he and his older brother Willard Huntington Wright, who became an important ally of Benton's in New York, believed they were blessed with superiority in all things, and Stanton's ego was stupendous; it either charmed or outraged those who encountered it. He is reputed to have said, late in life, "There have been four great American painters, Whistler, Ryder, [Morgan] Russell, and Wright." He was hardly that, but his achievements and transgressions were always noteworthy: beginning in 1912, for instance, he and Russell cultivated a colorful abstract style they called synchromism, so called to suggest an analogy between musical and visual rhythms; he proposed preposterous social philosophies based on elitism, racism, and misogyny; he was the regional director of the Federal Art Project in Southern California from 1935 to 1940; and he became one of California's most famous painters and teachers. The boys' parents were famously indulgent; they hired servants to attend to their personal needs and paid private tutors to educate them in languages, art, and literature. In 1900, the family moved to Santa Monica, where Stanton became a precocious artist—painting competent landscapes by the age of thirteen—and, along with his brother, an avid reader of Oscar Wilde, whom they held up as the supreme artiste. After studying painting at the Art Students League of Los Angeles, getting expelled from private schools, frequenting a Chinatown brothel, botching an attempt to run away from home (Nagasaki was the destination), and getting married—to Ida Wyman—at the age of seventeen, Macdonald-Wright moved to Paris in 1909, accompanied by his bewildered wife and mother-in-law.

Macdonald-Wright had money, something that eluded the other American painters at the Dôme, and this allowed him to rent a studio away from the apartment he shared with his new family and to study painting any way he saw fit. He began at Julian's, but being even more contemptuous of authority than Benton, he couldn't tolerate the academic precepts of Laurens and ended up taking classes, informally, at the Sorbonne. It didn't take long for Macdonald-Wright to discover the modernism of Matisse and Cézanne and, with Russell's help, to begin experimenting with abstract, color-based compositions. One man who knew him well after he returned to Los Angeles, in 1918, was Henry Clausen, a dealer of rare books. Clausen described him many years later as a captivating and droll conversationalist. He "was very much on his toes mentally," Clausen writes, "and could summon Machiavellian cunning on short notice, and also at times, an alarming display of sophistry . . . [H]e crawled out of many a trap in such a manner to be dubbed by Jack Wells, a close friend of both Wright brothers, an 'intellectual inkfish.'"

Despite Macdonald-Wright's eccentricities, it's no mystery why the two got along so well; because Benton longed for new friends, because Macdonald-Wright was eager for an equally uninhibited compadre, and because both men believed themselves superior to the academic hacks at Julian's, they flattered each other constantly. Benton likely decided to keep Macdonald-Wright in the dark about Jeanette at first because he believed a married man would disapprove of his situation, but upon visiting Benton's studio for the first time, Macdonald-Wright sniffed the air with his pointy nose and declared, "There's a woman here." The remark irritated Benton, but once Macdonald-Wright praised his paintings, all was forgiven. Soon they were spending their days together at the Louvre, Colarossi's, and the Dôme.

Benton describes Macdonald-Wright as a savior who rescued him from himself: "This one was to be the only artist in all my life who, as an individual, was able to get past my suspicions of bright and clever people and to have an influence on my ways . . . [He] was the most gifted all-around fellow I ever knew." A dandy who "attitudinized constantly, and had the assured manners of a young lady-killer," Macdonald-Wright managed to loosen up the edgy Benton and even encouraged him to buy some new clothes; now wearing a beret and strolling the boulevards with a walking stick, Benton was dubbed "*le petit Balzac*" by his comrades at the Dôme. One reason for Macdonald-Wright's influence was his dissimilarity to Benton. "He was as brilliant and open as I was confused and devious," Benton admits. "He was outspoken, where I was secretive. While I was losing the physical cockiness of boyhood, he was entering into the intellectual cockiness of young manhood. Paris had shorn me of my outward assurance. It added to his." In addition to their own eminence, the two men spent most of their time discussing books. Benton had learned to read French well enough to get through Baudelaire, but he still spoke the language with a terrible accent and often amused Macdonald-Wright when he'd stand to "ham out the French poets."

But the books they chose to read also revealed their considerable philosophical differences. Macdonald-Wright admired Nietzsche, for example, and got from him racist views based on half-baked theories of eugenics. After Macdonald-Wright visited Gertrude Stein at rue de Fleurus and listened to her ideas about Cézanne, he remarked in his journal, "Steinitis: the Disease of Paris," and allegedly told Benton that she was a "fat-assed kike." (For what it's worth, Stein thought Macdonald-Wright was an arrogant fool.) In a 1995 interview, Clinton Adams, a California painter and colleague of Macdonald-Wright's at UCLA, admitted that Macdonald-Wright "made a lot of anti-Semitic remarks," some of which "were just plain traditional anti-Semitism along all the stereotypical lines."

Macdonald-Wright's opinions, including his argument that Germany should invade France to give it back a "noble soul," outraged Benton. In his view, Macdonald-Wright fancied himself an old-school aristocrat and sustained his claims about Germany on the "wildest assumptions" about Europe and an "invariably fictionalized" history. Whereas Macdonald-Wright was a "California Huntington" (he was related to the prestigious railroad family), "[I was] a Missouri Democrat leaning toward socialist theories." On all subjects excepting their own superiority, Benton explains, "we could not talk for five minutes without violent disagreement. Wright would frequently leave me in disgust and I would wish him to hell, as he went."

Benton got his socialist theories from George Bernard Shaw, John Ruskin, and Hippolyte Taine, whose books Carlock had called "imaginary tripe." Ruskin, whom he read before Taine, was something of an odd choice, as his popularity was at a low point during the late nineteenth and early twentieth centuries, when new aestheticians sneered at his moral high-handedness. Ruskin held that art was instructive and relevant, not distinct from social life; even the intricate buildings of Venice, he believed, should be read as windows into the souls of those who built them. Moreover, he maintained that the rough work of the artisan, as evidenced in Gothic architecture, was infinitely more worthy than the polished work of the Renaissance or the nineteenth century. Benton was likely attracted to Ruskin's skepticism, especially his hatred of moral and intellectual corruption, and one can imagine the Missourian's populist sensibility warming up to Ruskin's attacks on economic injustice, like that from *The Crown of Wild Olive*, in which he professes that there are "two races: one of workers, and the other of players—one tilling the ground, manufacturing, building, and otherwise providing for the necessities of life; the other part proudly idle, and continually therefore needing recreation, in which they use the productive and laborious orders partly as their cattle, and partly as their puppets or pieces in the game of death."

Taine was more in favor than Ruskin when Benton was in Paris. From 1864 to 1884, Taine had served as a professor of art history and aesthetics at the École des Beaux-Arts, where he enthralled students with analytical and erudite lectures based on the arguments about art's role in society that he articulated in his *Philosophie de l'Art*, a book Benton cited many times as a major influence. Taine's view of the world was adamantly determinist; he had little use for theories of art that gave more weight to individual genius or art for art's sake than to the social factors that decided an object's appearance. His dictum, "*race, milieu et moment*," illustrates his scientific approach to art and literary history: Taine believed that an artist's place and time, and to a lesser degree his race—by which he meant his socially conditioned ideology—are what determines his product. For one thing, Taine showed that traditional precepts about artistic quality then prevalent in the academies were elitist and that art history could be studied by anyone, so long as he or she approached the subject analytically. This philosophy, naturally, was amenable to politically minded artists, and Benton, ever scornful of academic authority, claims that "it made a deep impression." He recalls the influence of Taine on his thinking in *An American in Art*, writing, "In the artistic milieus to which I had adapted myself, it was generally assumed that art had its own separate existence, its own special problems and disciplines, and that these bore only a chance and unimportant relation to time and place. This was the Whistlerian view, as it had been expounded to me in Chicago, and something similar to it was accepted by artists everywhere." That Taine's philosophy managed to make Benton rethink his old hero Whistler testifies to its influence on him. "Though I . . . often 'respond' to works of art purely for their color or structure," Benton admits, "I still do not believe they can be separated from their social origins without ignoring the place of meaning in the creative act."

In late 1909, Benton wrote his parents a letter that demonstrates how these readings had begun to shape his political conscience and aesthetic principles. He described the class divisions in Paris, expressing sympathy for the poor and disenfranchised, and predicted an "eruption" among anarchist university students, one radical group among many in the city that opposed the political complacency of the Belle Époque. Benton compared these conditions to shifts occurring in the art world as well. In reference to the rise of cubism and futurism, he proclaimed the division between "the old and the new" to be complete, and though he was not an avant-garde artist, he told his parents, "I am not at all a follower of the academics."

Benton himself recognized that "years later the trends of thought germinated here would mature into [my] Americanist environmentalism." Though his later diatribes against theory and close-minded Marxists, as well as his choice of friends, make it easy to forget, for many years— roughly from 1910 until the mid-1920s—his politics were grounded in the liberal traditions of midwestern populism and mainstream socialism. He was never a radical or a revolutionary, but from Shaw, Ruskin, and Taine he learned a particularly analytical kind of history—and a *people's* history at that. Ironically, he would later cite these writers, Taine especially, in his attacks on French modernism, which he saw as hopelessly inattentive to sociocultural realities and common experience. Abstraction, he would argue, was at odds with art's real-world applications.

Even as he was first reading Ruskin and Taine, in 1909 and 1910, and beginning to realize lucid aesthetic and social philosophies, their writings caused his assessments of modern painting to grow increasingly irresolute. At the time, he explains, "the literature circulating about the new movements gave them a persuasive aura of 'progressiveness' which it was hard for a young artist to ignore." His "dilemma," he says, was that he couldn't reconcile Taine's lessons with Parisian painting, which was "obviously moving . . . further and further away from any recognizable representation of either nature or society . . . [P]aintings were growing out of paintings rather than out of any discernible cultural situations."

His friendship with Macdonald-Wright only exacerbated this dilemma, for Stanton had retrograde social views but a decidedly modern aesthetic; though he had no use for Taine, he immersed himself in the study of impressionism and the aestheticism of Oscar Wilde. Paradoxically, then, Benton grew suspicious of the new styles even as, with Macdonald-Wright's assistance, he assiduously copied them. In the winter of 1910, for instance, the friends were impressed by an exhibition of paintings by the pointillist Paul Signac, and later that year, Benton recalls, they would sit in the Bois de Boulogne "under the great spreading trees . . . daubing spots of paint on canvas." Macdonald-Wright was a much more instinctive painter than Benton; even before he met Russell and began making synchromist paintings, he "loved the rich, sensuous qualities of paint" and "responded . . . to the open, fluid, and diffused surfaces" of the postimpressionists. Under his influence, Benton engrossed himself for the first time "in abstract problems which could not be solved by what I saw before me." After Signac, they turned their admiration on the "'ultramodern' experimenters," such as the fauvists and cubists. Benton, again, was thrown off course. After flirting with impressionism, he pulled back, working again with a tonal palette; after copying Zuloaga, he was led by Carlock to the old masters; after wrestling with Cézanne, he found in his work more classicism than modernism; and now he was studying the postimpressionists. "The pattern of my Parisian experience," Benton later wrote, "was a most illogical zig-zag."

Not surprisingly, none of Benton's friends liked Macdonald-Wright: Jeanette thought he was slick, Carlock cringed at his jokes, and Thompson reputedly referred to him as "that pasty-faced prick." In the late summer of 1910, to get Benton away from Macdonald-Wright for a while, Jeanette suggested that they travel south. She had a friend, Madeleine, whose sister was married to a ceramist named Gabriel Bernadou, an "exuberant, laughing fellow" who made vases and bowls decorated with butterflies. Bernadou's kilns were in Saint-Augustin—a village near the small city of Tulle in the green hills of the Limousin region, near the center of the country—and he encouraged the couple to visit. He explained that Paris artists had yet to discover the idyllic region and that they could stay cheaply at a hospitable auberge that served good peasant food. Using money his parents sent from Missouri, Tom and Jeanette caught an overnight train, escaping the city without telling anyone. At the station in Tulle, Benton was struck by the perfect puffy clouds floating over the hills, the luscious light, the smells of the countryside, and the town's stucco houses. That very afternoon the couple met Bernadou and his wife at the auberge and dined on lamb, black bread, hard cheese, and local wine. This became routine: they painted in the morning, ate an abundant lunch, always napping afterward, and painted again in the afternoon. They stayed until November, when the cold drove them away.

In his eulogy at Benton's funeral, Lyman Field quoted from his friend's memories of life in Tulle. "The poets say there is no occupation so good for your soul as the contemplation of nature," Benton had said. "However, its benefits are heightened, intensified and expanded when you at the same time try to record your findings with images . . . While under the spell of this two fold good, [the artist] is likely to be the happiest of men. This was my case during the late summer and autumn of 1910." The rugged region was ideal for a painter looking for authentic scenery; Benton describes it as having "landscape 'motifs'" everywhere—meandering brooks and picturesque waterfalls. On his sojourns in the countryside, he forgot about his lessons in Paris and strove instead to distill what he had learned over the past two years into an original style. Most of the dozen or so canvases he finished during the trip were done in a pointillist manner, but he claims to have relinquished "all conscious theorizing" in favor of a naturalistic color scheme. Just one work from this period, a painting of a chestnut tree, survived a fire at Oak Hill, and as Henry Adams points out, the canvas, though darkened by a coat of varnish, is less a "direct imitation" than a "symbolic" equivalent of nature: rather than represent the actual colors of the chestnut tree, Adams explains, Benton used orange and vermilion to describe light values and blue to render darker values. Despite his claims to the contrary, the painting shows that even in the hills around Saint-Augustin, Benton wasn't willing to abandon totally the modernism he grew to despise.

Benton had plans for the paintings he completed on the trip: he was confident enough in their quality to decide to exhibit them once he returned to Paris. The idea was to show them in the winter at his studio, which would serve two purposes: if successful, the exhibition would appease the Colonel, who, now that Uncle Sam's money was running out, was pressing harder for evidence of his son's progress; and it would invite expert opinions from the other artists about which works to submit to the spring Salon (having work selected for the Salon, he believed, would also take care of the former problem). Macdonald-Wright told him it was a stupid idea, that it would just attract unwanted attention, but he planned his *atelier thé* with gusto, sending invitations to all of his acquaintances and distributing others at the Dôme. Tom and Jeanette spent precious cash on new clothes and on the day of the *thé* cleaned the studio and set out cakes and tea.

"This effort at self-promotion," Benton recollected, "proved a complete flop." The appointed time came, and nobody showed up. Too nervous to see how it played out, Jeanette fled the studio, leaving Benton alone to pace and smoke cigarettes. When the day was done, only three visitors had shown up: Thompson, who was unimpressed with Benton's turn to postimpressionism; Carlock, who was interested only in insulting Thompson; and Macdonald-Wright, who breezed into the studio decked out in his dandy's regalia and managed, within minutes, to antagonize both Thompson and Carlock. Macdonald-Wright praised the paintings, though, and told Benton not to worry about what all "the fat heads" thought. But it was no use: Benton was humiliated. For the next two months, he brooded, believing himself to be a mediocre artist, an opinion that was upheld by the Salon jury, which rejected his submissions. Judging by the canvas of the chestnut tree, Benton had certainly become a competent painter: the color is rich, the composition achieves a basic harmony, and the pointillist dots quiver and pulse. But the Salon judges obviously discerned what the painting lacks, which is spontaneity, an ease of execution, or what Benton himself had desired in Chicago—"a certain lightness of line." In fact, there's no linearity to speak of in the painting, and Benton clearly suppressed it consciously, for his drawings depended on line for their dynamism. His Tulle oils, if the painting of the chestnut tree is any indication, were too clunky, too heavy, to deserve critical recognition. Benton claims that he sensed this at the time, and though he doesn't mention linearity specifically, he explains that the failure of his *thé* and the Salon rejection backed him into a corner: "Either I would paint in the realistic tradition of Western art with some kind of identification with the natural world, and thus risk being 'unprogressive,' or I would follow the new movements toward an unknown goal, a goal which a number of farsighted critics were already saying might turn out to be an empty square of paint."

One shouldn't underestimate the agony that such a dilemma can inflict on the creative mind. Benton was smart and ambitious and had spent the last four years disparaging academic precepts, so being perceived as traditional was a great fear. Moreover, this problem arose at a time when he was developing a political identity closely tied to aesthetic philosophies; Taine was teaching him that vital art must be conscious of its place and time rather than hackneyed conventions. Benton's relationship with his father had made him particularly sensitive, and his greatest desire was to demonstrate how an artist could be a relevant participant in social and political discourses: it simply wouldn't do to be "unprogressive." So what to do if one felt this way but didn't have a natural affinity for modernism? How could he communicate his progressivism with a traditional style? He wouldn't make a final decision for another ten years or so, and during the intervening period he struggled mightily to reckon with these questions. According to Robert Motherwell, "It may be that the deep necessity of art is the examination of self-deception." Benton intuited as much, and even as a young man experimenting with myriad styles and attitudes, he knew that he'd have to be honest with himself if he wanted to become an authentic painter.

Benton's final months in France were torture; compounding his anxiety about his painting were a host of exasperating personal problems. For one, he and Jeanette began to drift apart. In response, she invited more and more friends to the studio, and he often came home to find her whispering with one companion or another; he grew paranoid that they were persuading her that he was too young to take seriously. Jeanette, meanwhile, was worried that Tom was about to abandon her and return to America. She even asked at one point if she could go with him, a request that sent him into a panic. Macdonald-Wright, ever the sinister meddler, made matters worse by confiding in his friend that he believed Jeanette was cheating on him. He explained that he'd been visiting an apartment to carry on an affair with a Frenchwoman, whom he'd gotten to pose for him in a floppy hat and high heels, and on several occasions he'd seen Jeanette entering the building, where several single men lived.

After Macdonald-Wright's accusation, Benton headed home to passage Guibert to confront Jeanette. When he entered the studio, he found it was arranged for a fancy dinner: the table was set with silverware and fine bottles of wine. Jeanette had guests, two cheery women who he quickly realized were a lesbian couple. Benton later explained that he and Abe had been to a lesbian café a few times and he was not surprised that Jeanette was friendly with such people, but later that night he lay awake wondering what he'd gotten himself into. "What was the son of a Missouri populist politician and a Washington society woman . . . doing in a Parisien Bohemia?" he asked himself. "I was there because I had a passion, a passion for painting, which my own conventional environment could not satisfy." But he also believed that he'd been drawn into a relationship with Jeanette by chance, "not because of love or sexual passion but because it was convenient." He also wondered that night how well he knew Jeanette sexually. Was she a lesbian? Had he missed this because he'd been so consumed by his art? All he knew for sure was that he was starting to have doubts about the relationship.

Even though Macdonald-Wright had precipitated Benton's apprehension, he wasn't any help; he'd just met Morgan Russell, and they were spending most of their time together. Russell, who was from New York, had arrived in Paris in 1906; three years later he met the Steins and through them Matisse and Picasso. As an artist, he was something of a chameleon: he'd trained as an architect, worked as a sculptor in Paris, and ended up a painter—and was "a man of great intelligence," according to Macdonald-Wright. "I have yet to meet a man of greater mental capacity than Russell in any line of endeavor," he said. "His was an astounding mind." Even though the two men dined together, boxed together, played cards, and were professional partners, Macdonald-Wright claimed years later, after the two had a falling-out regarding who invented synchromism, that he "never cared for him at all" and that "neither one of us ever claimed that we were each other's friend." His only explanation for this was that Russell was a hard man "to become too intimate with."

Though Benton didn't see much of Russell in Paris, he did visit his studio one day and was impressed by the substantial clay torsos on view there, which embodied the sculptor's reverence for the old masters. But Benton didn't like Russell, in part because he interfered in his relationship with Macdonald-Wright and also, Adams speculates, because Russell "was soon living off Wright's largesse," which apparently struck Benton as unseemly. Nevertheless, in the spring of 1911, it was through Russell that Benton met Leo Stein and a number of artists acquainted with him and his sister, such as Diego Rivera, whom he would meet again in New York.

Whatever frustration Benton felt regarding Macdonald-Wright's new friend was quickly forgotten when, on March 1, he picked up a letter from Lizzie informing him that she was coming to Paris. He hadn't been to the post office for two weeks and was stunned to learn that she would be arriving at the Gare du Nord in two days, with his sisters, Mamie and Mildred, in tow. The news made him nauseated. "It tore me apart," Benton recalled.

It got worse. He was frozen and incapable of breaking the news to Jeanette gently. He was also panicked about money and thought he'd be cut off if the truth came out, so he deigned to ask Jeanette what they should do. "We will go together to meet your people," she responded. It was an honorable plan, but he couldn't stomach it. "The door to Hell was opened," he remembered thinking, and all he could muster was a clumsy rejection of her: he tried explaining that she wasn't fit to meet his family. Jeanette refused to let him off the hook and responded by suggesting Lizzie and his sisters "kiss my ass."

Mildred was fourteen when she arrived in Paris, and at some point she jotted down a memoir of the dramatic trip. She remembered stepping off the train with Lizzie and Mamie and thinking that her brother looked "spiderish" as he "ran towards us and waved both arms." He struck his family as "an odd little foreigner, dressed strangely and speaking in an unknown tongue. His clothes were exotic in the extreme." Benton spoke idiomatic French, "with an execrable accent," and showed off by haggling with cabdrivers and retail clerks, which the women thought "vulgar." More vulgar, of course, was what they learned the next day. That morning Benton tried once more to reason with Jeanette and somehow persuaded her to visit Madeleine for the day; after he frantically tidied up the studio, Lizzie and the girls arrived. Mildred and Mamie were shocked by the studio, which they thought was pitiful, and began whispering about it behind his back; Lizzie, meanwhile, didn't even glance at his paintings and proceeded to sniff the air and snoop in the closets and drawers. Apparently, she suspected something was afoot and after a few awkward minutes brushed aside a curtain hiding an alcove beneath the loft and saw Jeanette's cosmetics and a primitive douche, a bucket with a hose.

"Oh, Tom, it's true," she cried, collapsing in a chair.

Benton hustled them out of the studio and back to the apartment he'd found for them near the place de l'Étoile.

In the interim, Jeanette had come to her senses; she now realized that she would be better off without Benton. When they met at the studio that night, they had a teary conversation and agreed to part ways, though Jeanette demanded money as a kind of alimony. Benton confessed to his mother everything except the stillbirth, and asked for help. He explained that Jeanette had taken care of him, furnished his apartment, and was being reasonable about the situation, but when he asked Lizzie for three hundred dollars, she threw a tantrum. "She flatly refused to let me have a penny," Benton told Mildred some time later. Desperate, he was forced to beg Macdonald-Wright for money. "Why give the bitch so much?" Macdonald-Wright demanded coldly before handing over the cash, which he specified was a loan. A few days later, Benton and Jeanette parted amicably. He helped her move her belongings into a new apartment, and she promptly adorned it with her own paintings from their idyll in Tulle—a gesture that concluded their affair.

Despite all that had happened, Benton behaved warmly toward his family during the rest of their stay abroad. "It was plain he was glad to see us," Mildred recollected. "He teased all three of us, separately and together, in ways that were delightfully young." Absent their "dour father," she remarked, they were all at ease. But Mildred was surprised by her brother's kindness, which she hadn't witnessed before:

> I don't want to imply that my brother was *un*pleasant at all other periods of his life. He was this-way, that-way—one never knew what to expect . . . He had had (I discovered years later)

a well-trained dichotomy of behavior, even different manners of speech for "ladies and gentlemen" in certain social situations on the one hand and for coarser people in more Bohemian gatherings on the other. It may be that he learned early the usefulness of cultivating this two-sided self when he went as a small boy with Father on political campaigns and hunting-camping parties.

Benton admitted to an interviewer many years later that he was embarrassed by his mother and sisters, who he thought were hopelessly bourgeois. "I had gotten myself accustomed to French life and almost taking a French viewpoint of things," he said, "[and] to have rather . . . middle class American morality coming into it was annoying." Benton phrased it even more harshly in the Paris chapter of "The Intimate Story": remembering how Lizzie spent lavishly on clothes and treated him like a little boy, he wrote, "Her affectionate acts disgust me." Nevertheless, he remained outwardly pleasant and ushered them through the museums, taking care to steer them away from the mediocre works. He also arranged for them to see a production of Ibsen's *Ghosts* (though one wonders about his motives for choosing this particular tragedy, wherein Oswald, an artist, returns from Paris to visit his mother, widow of the profligate Captain Alving, and reveals he has syphilis); took them to Easter services at Notre Dame, where Lizzie wept, overwhelmed by the music, the boys' choir, and the architecture; and invited them on a picnic to St. Cloud with Macdonald-Wright and his wife ("it was *Dejeuner sur l'Herbe* except that no one was nude among us," Mildred remembered). Stanton turned on his charm, and his wife, Ida, delighted to have company, got along splendidly with Lizzie and the girls.

By Benton's twenty-second birthday, on April 15, 1911, Lizzie had recovered enough from the crisis to buy her son a coveted gift—a particular walking stick, "ebony with a round head of elaborately chased silver," that he'd been eyeing in a shopwindow. She accompanied him to the shop one day, and they returned with the prized accoutrement. Benton was "cocky," Mildred said, "strutting around our drawing room, twirling his cane—a little inexpertly." He even demonstrated, for the benefit of his naive sisters, how one tucked the object snugly under an arm when both hands were necessary for browsing books at the stalls along the Seine. (Legend has it that when, about a dozen years later, Benton was illustrating sets for the movie industry in New York, the walking stick made such an impression on Rudolph Valentino that he used it as a prop in a picture.) According to Mildred, her mother delighted in spoiling Benton, in part because he'd gotten rid of Jeanette but mainly because he impressed her with boasts about his work: "That year Mother built 'castles in Spain' founded on Tom's future success, castles in which she would dwell. Probably she expected an immediate financial success."

By summer Benton knew that his time in Paris was coming to an end and that his mother meant to bring him home. Moreover, Uncle Sam's money was gone, and the Colonel wasn't going to finance his dalliances with modern art any longer. In July, after four months in the apartment at place de l'Étoile, Lizzie wearied of Paris, and the family, Tom included, left the city, accompanying Stanton and Ida to London, where they took some time to admire Turner's paintings; the Bentons then continued on to Liverpool to board their ship home. After so long in Paris, Benton was shocked by their abrupt departure, and after four months with Lizzie and the girls he was tired of their company; he recalled that they were embarrassingly snobby and teased him about an eastern European acrobat he befriended on board. By his estimation, he'd grown apart from his family and was anxious about returning to Neosho, where they arrived after a brief layover in Boston during which Benton visited the Boston Public Library to view the murals by Puvis de Chavannes, which he admired at the time but described later as being too inert for his taste.

Benton had spent three years in Paris, where he'd begun to develop a philosophy about the social function of art and had immersed himself in the culture of the new art. He had been exposed to avant-garde experimentation, to masterpieces in the Louvre, to Spanish art, and to a variety of other young artists. Still, he wasn't any nearer to a style than he'd been in Chicago. Craven is unduly harsh about the influence of Paris on his development: he called the atmosphere in the city "romantic" and "irresponsible," and in one of his books he claims that when he first met Benton, "he had enormous energy and determination, but his productions were not his own—nor were they frankly of any school. He made his bow to the current isms, but without grace or that ease of mind which lends the illusion of conviction to imitation." Sadly, Benton said as much himself, belittling Paris in his memoirs. Mildred astutely described his disavowal of the city as disingenuous: recalling the enthusiasm with which he guided her around the Louvre and their tranquil picnic in the Parc de St. Cloud, she explained that "it has always been hard for me to believe that he cast out that love onto the dung-heap of fettering emotions." She might have said the same about his rejection of New York City twenty-four years later.

PART TWO

IN NEW YORK

6

EXPERIMENTS

When Benton returned to Neosho with his mother and sisters, in July 1911, he had no plans. Although the Colonel had given up on his son's being a lawyer, he continued to belittle his art, telling him that the paintings he brought home from Paris were smeared with "streaks and spots" and "lunatic." In a hostile environment and missing his artist friends, Benton grew depressed. He claimed later that he "was glad, in a way, to be released from the constant theorizing of the artistic circles of the Quartier Montparnasse" but also admitted to feeling "very much disoriented." That summer and fall he was listless and irritable.

One quandary was that he didn't know what to paint. Hippolyte Taine's philosophy encouraged him to look around Neosho for subjects, but he didn't yet see how "the Missouri environment could generate much in the way of painting." In order to appear busy, he produced uninspired portraits of anyone who would sit for him. Benton understood that this was a regression and that he was at a critical juncture in his career: if he didn't want to stall his progress, he'd have to find a more hospitable milieu for his creativity. An opportunity presented itself just before Christmas, when he and Lizzie traveled to Kansas City to shop for clothes and presents and bumped into Frank J. Zimmerer, an acquaintance from Chicago. Zimmerer—whose greatest achievement came in the 1950s, when he painted a mural for the Otoe County Courthouse in Nebraska City—had just been hired as head of the Kansas City Art Institute and, upon hearing about Benton's experiences in Paris, invited him to join the faculty.

Hopeful that this would work out, Benton moved to Kansas City in January 1912. He settled into a studio at Fortieth Street and Pennsylvania Avenue, in the Westport section of town, and *The Kansas City Star,* having learned that a bona fide bohemian artist was in its midst, sent a reporter there to meet him. Benton, whom the writer described as "an agile, nervous little man," dressed up for the meeting in a "soft negligee shirt" and "a long black silk tie"; his black hair spilled out from under a "rakish, baggy velvet cap." "It sounds like the beginning of a Leonard Merrick story, doesn't it," the reporter wrote, "and as if a French phrase might be sprung at any time, or an offhand allusion to the Latin quarter? Well, it isn't, and it wasn't even in the Bohemian quarter of New York that the little man was holding forth, but right here in Kansas City, out in a well to do residence neighborhood." The reporter explained that Benton had been studying impressionism in Paris—that he was "lavish with his colors" and "sometimes sees different colors than the rest of us do"—and admitted to being mystified by a painting in the studio of a "blue-haired woman, with a russet skin." Benton assured him, however, that "realism is not an exact copy of any part of Nature but an effort to reproduce in paint a replica of the sensation received":

> But Mr. Benton paints other things besides blue-haired women; because, if the truth were known, the market for them is rather restricted in this part of the world. Therefore he turns his facile brush to landscapes, now and again, and for these he generally goes to Neosho, where the landscape is extensive and blue-haired women exceedingly rare.
>
> However, Neosho does not interest Mr. Benton very much. In fact, he left there about as soon as he was able to . . . "My art," he says, "so far as it has developed, has been an effort toward the presentment of life. I believe that this can be truly given only through the passionate massing of line and color, especially color. Color is the only quality within the realm of painting capable of producing sensation. Life is all sensation and the painting productive of the greater amount of sensation comes nearer [to] being life."

At this point, Benton lit a "cigarette at the candle that flickered in the big draughty room, and shook a vagrant lock of black hair back from his face. 'Wouldn't you like some tea?' he asked the ignorant person."

One senses from the article that Benton's sojourn to Kansas City was ill-timed. He was full of himself and of ideas that appeared out of place. His notions about color, for instance, were influenced by Stanton Macdonald-Wright, who remained in Paris and was still developing synchromism with Morgan Russell. After the Bentons left Stanton and his wife in London, Macdonald-Wright traveled through northern Europe and, upon returning to Paris, visited the studio of the Canadian painter Percyval Tudor-Hart with Russell. Tudor-Hart was teaching in Paris and refining a theory which posited that color and sound were perceived in *"psychologically equivalent terms"*: he wrote about abstract concepts such as "luminosity octaves," the similar "vibrations" produced by color and sound, and color scales. These insights would influence the development of synchromism, and while in Cassis, in August 1911, Macdonald-Wright sent a letter to Benton, then in Neosho, that expounded in quixotic terms on the special properties of color and that clearly influenced Benton's conversation with the reporter. "When the colors are *right*," Macdonald-Wright wrote, "you awaken to find it . . . showing a plasticity of . . . light & form, which when you compare with the things you have done by drawing an outline first will make you faint with joy . . . Color must express *form* in space before it has a raison d'être."

Benton fled Kansas City a week or so after the article appeared in the *Star*. What drove him away, he claimed, wasn't the sneering reception of his theories but what he perceived as the rampant homosexuality at the Kansas City Art Institute. Soon after his arrival, he told an interviewer, the faculty and students threw a party for him, and they all showed up wearing "women's underwear and all that stuff"; he added that Kansas City was "a vaudeville and carnival exchange center, and it was a place where the chorus boys would be stranded for weeks at a time." The city and the school had become a "homosexual center," and, apparently forgetting about his experiences with Mr. Calhoun and Hud, or what he may have seen in Paris, Benton later claimed that he'd never encountered anything like this before—"it shocked the hell out of me." As it turned out, Benton never received a job from Zimmerer, likely because of his critical comments about the Art Institute, and in a twist of fate it was his comments about homosexuals, among other things, that prompted the trustees of the school to fire him from his teaching post in 1941.

Once back in Neosho, Benton spent the rest of the winter painting dark tonal portraits of family and friends. One of these is a somber self-portrait. Except for a blob of blue-purple paint representing a flower on his lapel, the painting is brooding and intense; he seems to recoil from his own gaze and, backed against a dark wall and clutching a hat, stares back at us skeptically. This is a portrait of a man who feels trapped, and not long after he painted it, Benton resolved to move to New York. The decision relieved him of some of his angst, and before going, he managed to enjoy a few months of spring by getting outdoors and painting some colorful landscapes. Some of these paintings, such as *The Fish Hatchery, Neosho* (1912), feature a female figure, most likely Fay Clark. When he returned from Paris, Benton and Clark had renewed their courtship but the relationship fizzled, and Benton moved on.

Benton missed two major New York art exhibitions: he arrived in the city in June 1912, two years after the Exhibition of Independent Artists—a major exhibition of painters, including George Bellows, Everett Shin, and John Sloan, who'd grown weary of the stodgy terms imposed by the National Academy of Design—and that fall he returned to Neosho to attend to Lizzie, who'd suffered a breakdown, and so missed the legendary Armory Show, which featured works by Marcel Duchamp, Henri Matisse, and Pablo Picasso. For a young artist in search of foundational principles, either of these shows might have been revelatory, but as it happened, Benton had to learn what he could from the colorful artists living in the Lincoln Square Arcade, where he rented a room.

The Arcade, located at Sixty-fifth and Broadway, was a sort of artists' commune: Robert Henri opened a school there in 1909; Bellows lived there when he discovered, just across the street, Tom Sharkey's Athletic Club, the venue featured in some of his bravura paintings of boxing matches; Rockwell Kent occasionally slept on Bellows's cot; Eugene O'Neill, who shared a room with Bellows and others, set scenes from one of his first full-length plays, *Bread and Butter* (1914), in the building's studios; and the elusive dadaist poet and muse Elsa von Freytag-Loringhoven visited Duchamp in the Arcade when he was a tenant in 1915. In his biography of John Sloan, Van Wyck Brooks describes the Arcade as the "Latin Quarter in itself," a "rookery of half-fed students, astrologers, prostitutes, actors, models, prize-fighters, quacks, and dancers." "The doors of its long dark halls opened on every known sort of profession," Benton recalls. "Signs tacked on its walls told of Mme. So-and-so, Astrologer from the Court of his Hindu Majesty Shah

So-and-so, or of Dr. So-and-so, King of the Muscle Builders, or of Mme. Minnie who guaranteed Beauty and sure Love Power through her treatments." There were also bedbugs and cockroaches.

Benton chose the Lincoln Arcade because it was cheap and some acquaintances from the Art Institute of Chicago had recommended it. One was Ralph Barton, who lived in the building and was doing advertising work. Later, Barton, as the country's most revered illustrator, contributed to *The New Yorker*, *Puck*, and *Vanity Fair*. The two men, who briefly roomed together, had much in common: Barton was from Kansas City; had studied at the Art Institute; frequently visited Paris, always making sure to stop by the Café du Dôme; and had a taste for French fashion. Thomas Craven described Benton, whom he met at the Arcade, "that nest of youthful genius and dying failure," as "a sight, with his tight French clothes, his flat French hat, and his Balzac stick—the antithesis of everything American." And though Benton was only twenty-three, Craven observed that "he looked old and sad: his face was deeply lined and drawn, and I cannot remember that he ever laughed. He was, I felt, the victim of some strange irregularity of development." Only the causes of their depressions distinguished Barton and Benton: Benton was frustrated with art, Barton with love. Barton confessed to having "been in love ninety-two times" and was married four times (his third wife, the actress Carlotta Monterey, became O'Neill's third as well). In May 1931, a month after his fourth divorce became final, Barton laid out a copy of *Gray's Anatomy* on his bed and shot himself in the right temple.

Though Craven and Macdonald-Wright, his closest friends during these early years in New York, disliked Barton, Benton admired him. "Underneath the pretensions of his vanity," he writes, "it was plain to see that he suffered." And despite a coincidence of history—Barton's grandfather, Joshua Barton, served as Charles Lucas's second when Senator Benton shot and killed Lucas on Bloody Island in 1817—Barton was generous to Benton. "He had a fancy for me," Benton recalls, "and carried me through many tough moments. He was clever, made money easily, and spent it—no small amount on me." Barton also introduced Benton to some other Missourians living in and around the Arcade, including William Powell, who later acted in the Thin Man films, and Raeburn Van Buren, the illustrator for the long-running *Abbie an' Slats* comic strip.

The journalist Frazier Hunt remembered that Benton was "denned up in a miserable little studio painting away desperately at strangely distorted and discolored figures and scenes." He was alluding to the paintings that Benton produced under the influence of Samuel Halpert, a Russian-born painter whom he first met in Paris. Before running into Halpert again in New York, Benton was adrift and struggling to appease the Colonel, who again had grown impatient with his son's solicitations. At first, Benton trudged up and down the avenues with a portfolio of drawings from Paris meant to impress gallery owners; when this failed, he apprenticed to a woman, Mrs. O'Hara, to learn the technique for applying vitrifiable paint and enamel to ceramic bowls and plates, which he then sold for walking-around money.

Halpert also arrived in New York during the summer of 1912, bringing with him from Paris paintings—"decorative adaptations" of Cézanne—that impressed Benton. Along with Max Weber, who brought cubism to America, Halpert took classes at the Ferrer Center and Modern School in Greenwich Village, and they, like many artists and critics in Paris, traced cubism to Cézanne; one Halpert painting from this period, a clunky still life, ended up in the Armory Show. Burying his commercial ambitions once again, Benton studied photographic reproductions of Cézanne's work and began painting fractured planes of color. These studies occupied him for the rest of that summer, but ultimately he abandoned them, claiming that the style was ill suited to painting from living models: "The general 'pull' of my painting interests went toward a greater concern with line and chiaroscuro than a Cézannesque style permitted."

Halpert also played a role in Benton's first social gaffe in New York. They had adjoining studios in the Lincoln Arcade and often visited each other to reminisce about France; their shared experience in Paris induced in them "a sort of snobbery," and when Benton dropped in on Halpert one day, he observed a young man boasting about a group of drawings strewn across the floor. This was Stuart Davis, an acolyte of Henri's and an associate of the Ashcan painters. Davis was visiting Halpert to show off his latest charcoal drawings and, Benton recalls, "was very full of himself, proud of his abilities, and very aggressive." Unleashing whatever authority he believed he'd earned, Benton responded to the presumptuous young artist by telling him that he should "go to Paris and try to learn something." Davis flushed, and Benton saw right away that he'd made a mistake. Davis would become Benton's most vehement critic and, during the 1930s, repeatedly accused him of making racist and fascist paintings.

Benton got in other feuds during these first months in New York, often over romantic entanglements. (In one instance, a woman stabbed him.) His letters to Lizzie and the Colonel failed to mention any of these misadventures, emphasizing instead, as was customary, his twin conditions: precocity and, now that Uncle Sam's money was gone, poverty. One typical letter from that summer announced that he and his friends were living on salad and beer and hinted at his increasing political engagement. "I would be more willing to consider America a civilized country," he explained, "if less attention was given to these howling [political] conventions . . . and a little more bestowed [upon] the poor people in the cities."

Benton was called home in the fall of 1912 to help the family attend to Lizzie, who'd suffered a nervous collapse and was bedridden. Her isolation had become too much to bear: she still missed Washington, and her ache was exacerbated by the Colonel's heavy drinking and increasing sourness, not to mention her son's letters from New York, which were filled with spirited descriptions of city life. Lizzie fretted as well about the futures of her other children. It must have struck Mamie, Nat, and Mildred as unfair that Tom got to indulge his every whim while they wasted away in Neosho, attending to a neurasthenic mother, and the plan was to bring him home to help the family. Though Lizzie recovered quickly, Benton stayed put for seven months. They must have been a terrible seven months, for no one in the family ever cared to recall them. One imagines Tom sulking around Oak Hill while the Colonel and Lizzie argued about the family's future.

Though Benton would claim that missing the Armory Show was no big deal, that he would have been unimpressed by the modernist works on display there, he eventually admitted, begrudgingly, that it was a "good" thing that "these new idioms were injected into the American scene." Officially known as the International Exhibition of Modern Art, the show opened on February 15, 1913, at an armory on Lexington Avenue between Twenty-fifth and Twenty-sixth Streets belonging to the New York National Guard. The exhibition, which lasted just one month and then traveled to Boston and Chicago, included over one thousand paintings, sculptures, and decorative works by American and European artists. Organized by the Association of American Painters and Sculptors, the exhibition was originally intended to showcase American artists, but under the guidance of the association's president, Arthur B. Davies, who was sympathetic to European avant-garde art, the exhibition took on an international flavor and became a forum for comparing and contrasting artists from Germany and France with those from the United States.

Much of the public's reaction to the Armory Show was reserved for Duchamp's now-iconic *Nude Descending a Staircase, No. 2* (1912). The painting, which deigns to represent a single figure at several points in space and time, confounded and angered critics. Former president Theodore Roosevelt reviewed the exhibition in the guise of a "layman" and compared Duchamp's painting unfavorably with the Navajo rug that hung on his bathroom wall; another critic memorably described the painting as an "explosion in a shingle factory." Other European paintings struck one visitor as "the most hideous monstrosities ever perpetrated in the name of long suffering art."

The American organizers of the Armory Show were intent on developing an analogy between the country's war for independence and its new art. Most of the printed material accompanying the exhibition, such as posters and postcards, included an illustration of a pine tree that closely resembled the symbol adorning many New England flags during the Revolutionary War. Benton's comments regarding the Armory Show demonstrate that he was unaware of the degree of American patriotism implicit in the exhibition and that, like so many critics, he viewed the show as an assault on American sensibilities. What he and others overlooked was that the American works in the exhibition illustrated how artists in the United States had already come to terms with European stylistic innovations. Painters such as Halpert, Maurice Prendergast, and Marsden Hartley, for example, exhibited works that reflected principles of postimpressionism.

Whatever the precise nature of his attitudes regarding the show, Benton clearly sensed that he was missing out on something big and so returned to New York in June 1913, settling again in the Lincoln Arcade. A few months later, Lizzie left the Colonel and moved to the city, bringing the kids—Mamie, now twenty-two, Nat, twenty, and Mildred, seventeen—with her. They settled in an elegant apartment building, the Poinciana, on the Upper West Side, and soon after, Mildred enrolled in extension classes at Barnard, and Nat started studying law at Columbia. Benton, who was not earning any money, was soon lodging and eating at the Poinciana with his mother, an arrangement that lasted off and on even as she moved to another apartment on the Upper West Side.

Any chance of Lizzie and the Colonel reconciling literally went up in flames when, in 1917, Oak Hill burned to the ground. The cause of the fire is unknown, though Mildred recalled that the Colonel stood in the woods and watched in horror as flames consumed the house. "It must have been the top emotion of his life," she said. The misfortune devastated Benton as well. The blaze not only destroyed many of his early paintings and cherished boyhood possessions; it also robbed him of a familiar place to get together with family and, perhaps, to mend festering wounds that afflicted his relationship with his father. After the fire, the Benton clan drifted apart. Lizzie moved to Great Neck, Long Island, where she bought a house with her share of the insurance money. The Colonel came east to ask her to return to Neosho, but Mamie had married Henry Briggs, a navy officer, and was pregnant. Lizzie explained to her husband that she couldn't force her daughter to leave New York, and so the Colonel retreated to Neosho, where he spent the rest of his life in rented rooms.

When Benton stayed with his mother or stopped by for meals, he usually brought Thomas Craven, an intimate friend who at times proved a burden (most of the vitriol aimed at Benton during the 1930s accused him of sharing Craven's crude nativism, an indictment he found hard to deflect). Benton had met Craven in the Lincoln Arcade during the summer of 1912, and in early July he explained to his parents that in Craven and Macdonald-Wright, who was writing him letters from France, he had "two very sympathetic and sure friends, two men that I can count on for the defense of my Art from the non-aesthetic vulgarity of the common painting and litterateur." Born in 1889, the same year as Benton, Craven grew up in Salina, Kansas; also like Benton, Craven was raised in the shadow of an overbearing and chauvinistic father, a "grave, high-tempered, sensitive" lawyer with a "will of iron." Mr. Craven made much of his frontier background and told his son stories about Mark Twain's friendship with his grandfather, whose house had been raided by Jesse James and his gang. Craven graduated from Kansas Wesleyan University in 1908, but, he recalls, "the pioneer spirit was in me, and I was soon off and away." He traveled throughout the American West, working as a reporter in Denver, a clerk for the Santa Fe Railway in Las Vegas, and a Greek and Latin teacher in California. All the while, he wanted to be an artist, a profession his father despised as much as the Colonel did. Nevertheless, in 1910, Craven sailed for Paris, where he spent a year painting, composing poetry, and studying art (but never running into Benton). He ended up in Greenwich Village in 1911, writing unpublishable poetry and fiction.

Benton and Craven lived frugally in their Lincoln Arcade studio, often begging food and beer from neighbors. Craven cooked and Benton washed the dishes, an arrangement that struck some as suspiciously intimate. "They used to think we were a couple of homosexuals because we were always together," Benton recalled. "But," he added, in order to put the rumor to rest, "it was for the convenience." Craven periodically traveled far afield—to Mobile, Alabama, or Puerto Rico—to earn money teaching Greek and Latin in high schools, but when he was in New York, he lived with Benton and lazed about in a worn bathrobe reading books. Meanwhile, Benton, according to Craven, "begged, borrowed, sponged, and stole." In *Modern Art: The Men, the Movements, the Meaning* (1934), an analysis of twentieth-century art, Craven reflects on the deprivations of life in the Lincoln Arcade with an upbeat romanticism; in his telling, the various unlucky inhabitants of the building shared poverty and professional disgraces that bred a camaraderie. As Craven remembers it, "We were very young, and we pooled our miseries in a common fund of forced jocularity and hard work. A blow for one was a blow for all, and we laughed it off together; and good luck for one was food for many."

Considering the difficulty Benton had making and keeping friends, and considering his predilection for argument, it's remarkable that he liked Craven. Polly Burroughs, who knew both men, remarked on the improbability of their bond: Benton, she observed, was pugnacious and strong; Craven was shy and frail. Benton spoke in a gruff voice; Craven whined. Benton was a slob; Craven was "neat as an old-maid school teacher." Naturally, their common backgrounds drew them together—

both were midwestern Democrats, both took their art seriously but struggled to find their styles—but more essential to their relationship in these first years in New York was that they spoke plainly to each other: they offered each other encouragement, as well as unvarnished criticism.

Benton's written memories of Craven are for the most part thin and impersonal. He remarks here and there on their bohemian life in the Arcade but leaves the rest alone. Craven, however, thought deeply about the artist's psychology in general, and Benton's specifically. He documented his impressions of Benton in a novel, *Paint*, which he published in 1923. Lewis Mumford reviewed *Paint* in *The New Republic* and lauded Craven's criticism as "keen and indefatigable" and praised the novel as a "first rate piece of fiction."

The novel tells the story of an artist named Carlock, a character obviously modeled on Benton, and opens in 1911, when, fresh from Paris, he is living in poverty in New York. Carlock, a boxer, lives in the Lincoln Arcade, which Craven describes as "infested with grubbers in the several arts." The building was free from "moral surveillance," and life there "bumped along with irresponsible rapidity." It was "the home of beginners and the grave of incompetents." Mumford admired the novel's vividness: "Mr. Craven has given us . . . a sharp glimpse of the real thing, in outlines as dexterous and unrelenting as his hero's pictures: indeed, the very stench of the studio seeps through the narrative, as if the manuscript had lain around until it was spattered with color and impregnated with turpentine and stale tobacco smoke." It is, Mumford argues, a "rogue's tale, with the adventure befalling the hero not on the highroad but within the confines of an inexorable tunnel." If Craven was able to represent the exuberant starts and tragic stops of a painter in early-twentieth-century New York, it was because he witnessed them firsthand (Benton doesn't seem to have minded that his friend dramatized elements of his life), and Mumford particularly admired the book's honest depiction of artistic aspiration.

It wasn't until 1934, however, that Craven directly addressed Benton's fitful search, during his first years in New York, for an identity:

> The nostalgia of Verlaine, the perverse sadness of Baudelaire, the attenuated dreams of the Symbolists—those neurasthenic imaginings of the French genius of the period which today no one would associate with Benton's life and thought, seemed to

compose the fabric of his being . . . He was capable of the most
infantile behavior, of an impossible naïveté that stood out, I soon
discovered, in sharp opposition to his sturdy common sense,
and to the true nature of his thought which, even at that time,
showed considerable integration and logical power.

Craven adds that from 1912 to 1922, Benton was an awkward painter:
"For ten years his painting was so labored and unpromising that most of
his confreres were secretly of the opinion that he was outside his field."

In his letters to his parents, Benton continued to proclaim his genius and anticipate his fame, but for several years after his return to
New York he "tried everything" to make a dollar—ceramics, illustration,
and painting portraits, pinups, decorative panels, and abstract, synchromist canvases. He made a little money selling vases that he painted
with flat floral and figure compositions inspired by the decorative work
of Georges Braque, which was popular in New York after the Armory
Show, and upon learning that Rolf Armstrong, with whom Benton had
shared a room in Chicago, was making a good living executing pastel
bust portraits of pretty girls for magazines and calendar houses, Benton
tried his hand at painting "straight realistic portraits" of female models,
a venture that earned him just a single payday. He remembers portrai-
ture as a competitive field occupied by artists "much more skillful than
I at making flattering pictures." One early success was a commission to
paint five floral panels for a Coney Island dancing pavilion, which came
just as Joseph Stella was producing electrifying futurist paintings of
Coney Island lights and amusements. Unfortunately, the pavilion soon
burned down, so there's no telling how "modern" these compositions
were, but Benton earned almost two hundred dollars for the work. Another early success, in 1913, was a large Whistleresque portrait of Mildred, which was rejected by the National Academy of Design but
eventually reproduced in *Collier's*. Despite these accomplishments,
Benton continued to brood. He blasted the "half-witted, talentless imbeciles" who turned out "vapid" illustrations of the "American pretty
girl" and recalled later that his "tendencies toward a straight visual realism . . . conflicted with equally strong tendencies toward various kinds
of coloristic painting." What bothered Benton most during this time
was the apparent distinction between what he was creating and what

was coming out of Paris: "It was obvious . . . that I belonged to none of the 'progressive' schools."

While Benton fretted about whether his art was modern enough and the degradation of his "artistic ideals," Craven began to detect at least some potential in his friend's approach. For the most part, Craven was critical of the work Benton turned out during his first ten years in New York. "He hung around gymnasiums and prize rings and slowly regained his athletic youthfulness," Craven wrote in 1937, "but . . . so persistent was the French hang-over" that his art was "all symbols and abstractions—something between the classical past and the cubes of modernism—hacked together by brute strength and fierce resolution." On the other hand, three years earlier, Craven offered this summary:

> Every time I returned to New York, after one of my periodic ex-cursions into the provinces, I found him more American—less retiring and better equipped for an active life. I saw him shed the worn-out rags and fripperies of French culture; I watched with amusement the animosity he aroused in contemporaries who clung to the Bohemian idealism of the Left Bank—his wide reading in psychology made him skeptical of the fragile theories upon which Modernism fluttered, and his critical manners were distasteful . . . [H]is . . . own work was technically uncertain and experimental rather than expressive. He had not found himself as an artist, but it was plain that he was beginning to find himself as an American.

Craven clearly betrays his nationalism in this analysis, but reading between the lines, one surmises that Benton's emergent ornery Americanism was a default response to his inability to recognize in his work at the time anything that he called "progressive," meaning French. Benton's ideas about abstract and representational art only became more convoluted once he viewed the synchromist paintings of Macdonald-Wright and Morgan Russell.

Macdonald-Wright arrived in New York in early 1914, and his breezy and irreverent entrance into Manhattan resuscitated Benton's devotion to high-art principles and lifted him out of his creative and psychological funk. As Benton remembers it, Macdonald-Wright was intent on taking the city by storm, and "when the city failed to capitulate he wandered around . . . full of picturesque blasphemy." His blustery impertinence was emboldened by his outlandish brother Willard, who had been in New York since 1911, working as the editor of the clever monthly magazine *The Smart Set*. In 1913, Wright had traveled to Europe to attend an exhibition of synchromist paintings by his brother and Russell. He had already begun to philosophize about modern art, having attended the Armory Show and made the acquaintance of Stieglitz at his influential 291 gallery. Wright's intense curiosity was roused by the new art, and he was primed to admire the paintings that his brother and Russell exhibited at a gallery in Munich.

Synchromism did not arise from a manifesto, or even a clear sense of purpose. The painter Sonia Delaunay claimed that she and her husband, Robert, also a painter, were the first to use the term "synchrome." Around 1912, the Delaunays, along with Duchamp, Fernand Léger, and others, worked in a lyrical abstract style, noted for its colorful and interlocking planar forms, that they compared to music and that Guillaume Apollinaire called "Orphism," after the Greek singer and poet Orpheus. Macdonald-Wright and Russell were not always in agreement as to what theories underlay their work: sometimes they cited Tudor-Hart as an influence; other times they acknowledged the Orphist roots of their movement. Simply put, synchromist paintings required that viewers abandon any notion of content and give themselves over to the experience of color. As Russell said of one of his early synchromist paintings, its "subject is deep blue." Though a familiar enough principle today, this consecration of color, at the expense of not just narrative but line as well, was innovative in 1913. Even more avant-garde was their intention to correlate dynamic patterns of form and color on a canvas with musical rhythms and thus emphasize the synesthetic capabilities of painting: Macdonald-Wright, for instance, thought of color triads as chords that, when combined, would become symphonic. Wassily Kandinsky and other members of the German Expressionist group known as Der Blaue Reiter (The Blue Rider) were more intense in their expositions on the primacy of color and the expressiveness of music (Kandinsky, for instance, espoused the spiritual power of the color blue), but Macdonald-Wright and Russell wanted to transcend improvisation and systematize, even rationalize, abstraction. This quixotic aspiration was destined to fade rapidly—as so many attempts to regulate abstract impulses do— but this didn't dampen the enthusiasm of many American viewers for synchromist paintings.

Once Macdonald-Wright returned to New York, he and Willard began scheming to organize an exhibition. As Macdonald-Wright was broke, this was a matter of necessity. He badgered Benton for the money he had loaned him in Paris, but Benton couldn't repay it. The awkward- ness of the situation almost spoiled their reunion, with Macdonald- Wright threatening a lawsuit against the Colonel and claiming that Benton was "playing poor." Knowing how important it was that his brother be exposed and sell some work, Wright had written an essay titled "Im- pressionism to Synchromism" for *The Forum*, the magazine he would later work for as an art critic. His first piece of art criticism, the essay examines the relationship between synchromism and music, concluding that the synchromists "hold their art superior to music because it is more intimately attached to reality." His point was that even when paint- ers abandon the representation of nature, color always serves as a bridge back to it. Wright seems to have been concerned that the abstract na- ture of synchromism would be off-putting to New York galleries, so he made every effort to ground it in some fundamental relation to reality. In doing so, he hurled a few insults at cubism—a "craze for the static . . . the immovable and the geometric"—and more particularly at Picasso, whom he called "an amateur metaphysician on the loose."

Whether despite or because of this inflated rhetoric, Harriet Bry- ant, who had just expanded her decorating business on East Forty- fourth Street into the Carroll Galleries, caught the buzz and, in March 1914, hosted the first synchromist exhibition in the United States. *The New York Times* was unkind: until synchromism is a great deal more "intelligible" than it is, the paper remarked, "it will be futile art." Wright continued to be the most praising critic of synchromism, arguing in his 1915 book *Modern Painting*—an important if often outrageous survey of modernism—that the synchromists completed what the postimpres- sionists had initiated: synchromism, he writes, "marked a revolution in formal construction." Most important was his claim that synchromism reached far back and was an extension of Renaissance classicism: Macdonald-Wright and Russell, he maintains, "desired to express, by means of colour, form which would be as complete and as simple as a

Michelangelo drawing, and which would give subjectively the same emotion of form that the Renaissance master gives objectively." Craven, years later, was far less kind. He grouped synchromism with cubism, futurism, and vorticism, movements that existed only because of an "agony of effort, of rampant conceit, of swollen sensitivity!" Any writer who was able to explain their "special mysteries," Craven adds, "was esteemed as a critic of enviable penetration." Not surprisingly, Willard and Stanton were not especially fond of Craven.

For his part, Benton believed that the old and the new came together most successfully in Cézanne, in whose work he observed a regulating structuralism: Cézanne, he says, "used . . . abstract properties in the interest of a better representation of nature—for a human purpose, that is." Though he eventually abandoned Cézannism in his painting, Benton saw him not as an "idealist" or "introvert": "For all his talk about his 'little sensation' and the intense turning in on the self . . . , it is plain that he cherished it not for itself, but for what it revealed about something else." Benton, then, took both Wright's and Craven's positions. He wasn't entirely satisfied with Macdonald-Wright's explanation of the synchromist system, but he agreed with Wright that of the Parisian schools the style represented the most "logical connection" between the compositional rationality of the past and the colorism of the present. "What most captured my interest," Benton writes, "was the Synchromists' use of Baroque rhythms"—that is, dynamic rhythms—"derived . . . from the more basic source of Michelangelo's sculptures." Because he remained impressed with the vigorous forms of the old masters that he'd studied in the Louvre—Titian, for instance—even as he explored "the spectral coloration" of postimpressionism, he claimed to be especially sympathetic to synchromism. His analysis of Cézanne, however, shows him also agreeing with Craven, who abhorred modern art's cultish self-referentiality. In sum, Craven and Benton had different opinions about synchromism, but these opinions were based on a shared belief that good painting was painting based on something outside of itself. Benton saw synchromism as referencing past, or public, visual experiences; Craven saw it as referencing nothing more than special, or elitist, visual experiences. So in his response to synchromism, Benton began to formulate what would become his chief artistic philosophy: art is obliged to engage or enact common experience.

Impressed with synchromism's dual allegiance to tradition and abstraction, he visited the Carroll Galleries exhibition each day to study the colorful paintings. Macdonald-Wright had returned to Paris after the exhibition, but he came back to New York in the autumn of 1915, and, renewing his friendships with the brothers, Benton, with what he calls his "usual enthusiasm for a new painting theory," experimented with synchromism. These experiments took two forms—abstract paintings and figure compositions. These latter paintings, which were exhibited in 1916 at the Forum Exhibition, were dynamic representations of contorted Michelangelesque figures writhing in nondescript spaces. Of the abstract paintings, *Bubbles* is virtually the only extant example, though it's a fine one. Taking his cue from Macdonald-Wright's abstractions, Benton arranged colorful circles and curving blocks as if on a fan, radiating out from a central black hole. Benton recalls being content to paint abstractly at this time: "If one admitted, and we all then did, that the procedures of art were sufficient unto and for themselves and that the progress of art toward 'purification' led away from representation toward the more abstract forms of music, then Synchromism was a persuasive conception." But in practice Benton couldn't reconcile synchromism's formulas with his taste and by 1917 had abandoned it altogether. Synchromism was over anyway. Russell continued to paint abstractly but dropped the style's systems, and Macdonald-Wright, tired of the New York art scene, moved to California a few years after the exhibition.

During these years, from 1914 to 1916, Benton moved around the city, shifting between the Lincoln Arcade, the Poinciana, the Bronx, and a house on Arden Street, near the northern tip of Manhattan, that he shared with Craven and Benton's brother Nat. He also bunked for a few weeks with Stanton and Willard, who quarreled incessantly. Though Benton obviously had an unhealthy tolerance for the boorish behavior of the brothers and Craven, he likely stuck with Wright because his literary successes led to opportunities for him as well. In 1914, for instance, Wright asked Benton to illustrate a book he was writing with H. L. Mencken and the drama critic George Jean Nathan. The book, *Europe After 8:15*, is a slim volume of observations on the nightlife of Vienna, Munich, Berlin, London, and Paris. "Its purpose," Mencken explains in a humorous essay, "is to depict, in a suave and ingratiating manner, the postprandial divertissements of five European capitals."

And the subtext, he adds, is to ridicule "the Americanos who snout through Europe" looking for illicit entertainments. Benton's loose and light drawings are the most alluring element of the book; done in ink with an art-nouveau sensibility, they're composed of attenuated figures drinking at outdoor cafés, and at the very least they demonstrate Benton's ability to dash off graphically appealing work.

As he was painting *Bubbles* and mulling over the principles of Cézanne and synchromism, Benton started to work for Rex Ingram, a friend from the Lincoln Arcade. Ingram was born in Dublin as Reginald Hitchcock; in 1911, he immigrated to the United States and studied sculpture at the Yale School of Art. When Benton met him, he was still making sculptures, but soon after he found employment in the city's film industry, signing on with Edison Studios in the Bronx as an actor, scriptwriter, and handyman. He was stunningly handsome and by 1914 was working as a contract actor for Vitagraph in Brooklyn, appearing in such films as *Her Great Scoop* and *The Spirit and the Clay*. He proved a poor actor, however, and by the following year he was working—now as Rex Ingram—behind the camera writing scripts for the vampish Theda Bara and others. Ingram eventually became a master director of silent films in Los Angeles, directing Rudolph Valentino in *The Four Horsemen of the Apocalypse* in 1921. He was "full of theatrical romance" and always trying out his script scenarios on Benton. "He used to get me in a corner," Benton recalls, "mess his hair up, roll his eyes, and recite his concoctions in the most dramatic manner he could think of." By this time, Benton had started to box again and hang around gymnasiums. Ingram, noticing Benton's pugnaciousness, invited him to play a bit role in a barroom scene that also featured Paddy Sullivan, a boxer who appeared in a few films in 1916. Apparently, when the Colonel got wind of his son's film role, he was outraged and sent him an excoriating letter reminding him of his ambition to be a serious artist.

More fruitful for Benton was the job Ingram found him—for the sum of seven dollars a day—as a scene painter at the studios. It was entertaining and informal work. Benton met some of the stars of the day, including Valentino, and painted quick portraits of sexy leading ladies like Bara and Clara Kimball Young. One night at a party he managed to get into a "great knockdown and drag-out fight" with the actor Stuart Holmes over who should control the player piano that was entertaining the female guests. The art crews worked casually, designing sets and backdrops at the last minute, often over a long dinner at Lüchow's, a comfortable German restaurant on Fourteenth Street. The next morning, with a general scheme in mind, Benton would head to the New York Public Library to research landscapes or architectural details relevant to whatever was filming, a Western or melodrama set in the Far East, and then with sketches in hand he'd return to the studio to paint a "black and white thing" on a massive backdrop.

In his later memoir, *An American in Art*, Benton remarks that he learned from the more accomplished scene painters at the studios the process of painting with distemper, a technique whereby glue or gum is mixed with pigments for rapid drying. This, he also acknowledged, led to his use in the 1930s of egg tempera, which also dried quickly and so facilitated the timely completion of his murals. Erika Doss sees in Benton's studio work much more than just a technical influence on his murals, however. She argues that he also learned the "parlance of popular culture" during his experiences in the New York film industry and applied them to his later regionalist aesthetic and content. The movies, she explains, showed Benton how a modern public art might function and what it might look like. The movies were both of this world and dynamic, and "the way the movies looked—flickering black and white scenes full of pantomimed theatrics embroidered in the dramatic camera action and editing of such art-conscious directors as Ingram and D. W. Griffith—emerged in Benton's public murals."

Benton would have been less inclined to be moved by the public aspects of cinema had he not met John Weichsel. When he was hanging around the Carroll Galleries during the synchromism exhibition, in 1916, Benton met many of the city's most prominent artists and critics, including the Ashcan painters Henri, Sloan, and Bellows. But the man whom he found most invigorating and inspiring was Weichsel, who, he commented later, was "more important in my life than probably anybody in New York in [terms of an] economic foundation." Weichsel was a Polish Jew who left Europe in 1890 and settled in New York, where he worked as a mechanic and completed his studies at New York University. Eventually, he headed the Department of Mechanics and Drafting at New York's Hebrew Technical Institute, but in addition to his professional work he was active in artistic circles, speaking, for instance, on the principles of art in Henri's art class at the Ferrer Center, an institution that instructed working-class artists with a secular, liberal, and class-conscious curriculum.

Weichsel's philosophy of art was socialist; his basic premise was that art could be both modern and available, literally and figuratively, to the people, and his views were rooted in social justice; he understood art to be in service of "the revolutionary path of the worker." In a piece for Stieglitz's journal *Camera Work*, Weichsel elucidated the anti-elitism at the heart of his aesthetics: "There is a feeling strongly alive in us, that we, laymen, are not entitled to another position in this matter as long as art is . . . a special manifestation of a number of privileged men, of a sort of aesthetic brotherhood . . . Art itself is [therefore] degenerating into a form essentially technical . . . rather than spiritual." Artists and "laymen," he urged, must come together to awaken the "creative springs of people's souls . . . for an era of truly universal art-life."

Weichsel set these socialist ideas into action when he established, in 1915, the People's Art Guild. The guild was run exclusively by artists, and its purpose was to sell art directly to New York's poorer citizens at exhibitions mounted in settlement houses and public buildings. His dream was to help modern artists by giving them an opportunity to avoid doing business with profit-minded commercial dealers; at the same time, of course, their art would reach a wider audience and thereby offer spiritual (and aesthetic) relief to the urban disenfranchised. In a letter soliciting financial support for the venture, Weichsel summarized the guild's goals: he lamented the poverty of New York artists and noted that "the prevailing detachment of our artists from popular life, leads unmistakably to the impoverishment of the content of art and to a detrimental copying of foreign hobbies . . . WE TEACH THE PUBLIC TO BUY GOOD ART AND TO KNOW GOOD ART." For about three years, this democratized and classless means of exhibiting art was successful: the guild boasted about sixty artist members and sponsored more than fifty exhibitions, and *The New York Times* noted its "'socialization' of art and 'consequent broadening of its scope and patronage.'"

Already conscious of social theories of art, which he learned first from reading Taine and Ruskin when he was in France, and wary of the tendency of American modernists to copy "foreign hobbies," Benton was impressed by Weichsel, whom he described in a letter as "quite as important as Alfred Stieglitz or Willard Wright and vastly more learned about aesthetic theory than either." Weichsel, he says, maintained "a rival station" to Stieglitz's 291 in the Bronx, where he lived and ran the People's Art Guild. In Benton's eyes, Weichsel was a "learned man with Utopian urges about an abstraction called 'the people' which he believed would support art if given a chance"; he also "was a man of sound sense who held the run of conversation and discussion in his place on a saner level than was maintained downtown." Under the tutelage of Weichsel, Benton expanded his reading beyond Taine and dug into Marx, the pragmatist philosophers William James and John Dewey, and the historian Charles Beard, all of whom shaped his philosophy of art. Weichsel also introduced him to various union organizers, whom he was recruiting to support the People's Art Guild. Though Benton chose not to become involved with the unions, which were also organizing workers in the film industry in New York, on the grounds that he "didn't want to be under the rule of any organization"—a plausible explanation considering his dislike of authority—he claimed to approve of unions and, after meeting Weichsel, became a more committed anticapitalist. Recalling these years in an interview conducted toward the end of his life, Benton acknowledged that he "voted socialist and was a quite convinced Marxist."

While under Weichsel's influence, Benton worked in a makeshift style pieced together from numerous sources. His primary subject was the bathing figure, borrowed, he admitted, from Cézanne, but the aesthetic was a mixture of synchromist color, bold, Michelangelesque forms, and baroque rhythm. What's most striking about the bathing pictures of 1916–1917, however, is not so much the aesthetic striving as the appearance in them of a particular kind of human figure. One recurring theme in Benton's career was his tendency to develop boiled-down interpretations of complex aesthetic and social theories; he took from these ideas only what he wanted. So from Weichsel's theories he seems to have arrived at a kind of art he could justify as non-elitist because, first, it was figural and, second, it represented the figure as determined by a struggle to break free from form and engage and experience natural environments. It's not incidental that these figures sit on the water's edge, for swimming was one of Benton's preferred exercises, something he'd come to see as a supreme example of the integration of the body with its locale.

Weichsel's influence on Benton's politics, meanwhile, was even more pronounced than it might seem, for Benton worked out his socialist views not by fixating on the economic circumstances of "the people" living around him in the city but by observing the economic life of the artists in his circle and examining his own psychological conundrums. Just as Weichsel couched his views in terms of aesthetics and exhibitions, Benton first comprehended the consequences of capitalism by watching how it controlled the cultural and emotional affairs of those he knew— how it compelled artists to steal food, scheme for exhibition space and press notices, and, worst of all, make art that offended their own sensibilities, art that had commercial but no social function. Again and again, Benton beat this drum as he reckoned with his own painting. His artistic identity depended less on asking himself whether he was an abstract painter or a representational painter; it had become about asking himself whether he wanted to address art or society with his paintings, and if "society" was the answer, then how to address it? With formalist rhetoric? In a popular idiom?

Benton couldn't answer these questions just yet, but the conversations he had at Weichsel's house in the Bronx did teach him that these weren't just intellectual problems but political and economic ones as well; he was learning to believe that it was too easy for artists to shrink in on themselves, to become obsessed with the juvenile question of whether or not they had "genius." The danger of this, Benton said later, is that "when the artist concentrates upon finding himself as an individual, the attitude toward the arts become[s] quite different than when he thinks of making things which will communicate ideas to the public." This notion later became a cliché, but in 1915 it was a potent revelation to Benton.

It was on these grounds that Benton claimed moral superiority over Stieglitz, who he believed was more "narrowly 'aesthetic'" and more "tied . . . to personalities" than Weichsel was. "There is no real function in such a [capitalist] society" for an artist like Stieglitz, Benton said in an interview, "so he's forced to retire, if he's going to go on at all, into a world that he makes of his own." Nevertheless, in 1916, Benton, Weichsel, and Stieglitz, under the guidance of Wright, cooperated with one another and many others to pull off the Forum Exhibition of Modern American Painters.

•

One common critique of the Armory Show among American modernists was that the exhibition reinforced the prevailing belief that American artists were mere copyists, taking their cues from European trends. The Forum Exhibition can be understood as one attempt to correct this view: the show's catalog, for instance, stated that the exhibition was designed "to turn public attention for the moment from European art and concentrate it on the excellent work being done in America." The exhibition grew out of discussions between Willard and Stanton, who wanted to mount a second synchromism show in New York. In late 1915 or early 1916, Macdonald-Wright wrote to Morgan Russell, who was still in Paris, to announce that he and his brother were planning an exhibition that would feature their synchromist paintings. It "will run a month," Macdonald-Wright explained, "and we, you and I, because of our reputation will sell every thing. Of course, we will hang ourselves in the best space there!" However, upon sensing that there was still some lingering animosity over the Wrights' knocking of other schools during the exhibition at the Carroll Galleries, the planners realized that the Forum Exhibition would have to include a variety of painters, and in order to guarantee that the exhibition would be inclusive, Wright appointed an organizing committee, whose members included Stieglitz, Weichsel, and Henri. Moreover, Mitchell Kennerley—the president of the Anderson Galleries (where the show would be held) and the owner of *The Forum* (the magazine for which Wright worked as an art critic)— played a prominent role in the planning.

In the end, the "excellent work being done in America" was illustrated by 193 canvases painted by seventeen different artists, including Macdonald-Wright and Benton and, significantly, many artists associated with Stieglitz, such as Marsden Hartley, John Marin, and Arthur Dove. Though these artists worked in various styles, they all used at least some abstract elements in their work, and the Forum Exhibition, though not a success financially speaking, consecrated this first wave of American abstract painting. For instance, one of Hartley's contributions to the exhibition was *Movements* (1913), a large oil painting that arranges fundamental geometric shapes into flat patterns. The painting illustrates how one might modify one's experience of the material world into personal, imaginative, and pictorial forms, and in his brief statement for the exhibition catalog Hartley remarks, "It will be seen that my personal wishes lie in the strictly pictural notion, having observed much to this idea in the kinetic and the kaleidoscopic principles. Objects are incidents: an apple does not for long remain an apple if one has the concept." In other words, objects, according to Hartley, limit our experience of nature; it's the conception of an object that is fresh and poignant. Such a theory, attractive insofar as its relativism empowers any individual consciousness, proved remarkably seductive until the end of abstract expressionism in the 1950s. Similarly, Dove believed that the impressions one gathered from nature were more provocative than its mere material presence. One of his paintings in the exhibition, *Nature Symbolized, No. 2* (ca. 1911), illustrates his desire "to give in form and color the reaction that plastic objects and sensations of light from within and without have reflected from my inner consciousness." Wright, who was becoming an exemplary formalist critic, was acutely conscious of the theories of the painters in the exhibition, and in his contribution to the catalog, titled "What Is Modern Painting?" he elevates abstraction over the representation of recognizable objects: what matters, he argues, are "the inherent aesthetic qualities of order, rhythm, composition, and form."

Benton wasn't able to celebrate his inclusion in the exhibition as a personal milestone, as a first vindication after years of toil, because his participation both ignited a small controversy and cast a light on the debate that would characterize American modernism for the next thirty years. The controversy had to do, in part, with the appearance of favoritism: some artists believed Benton was selected for the exhibition only because he was close to Willard and Stanton. Though this may have been true, many of the artists were exhibited only because they knew Stieglitz. The other charge, Benton admitted later, had "just enough plausibility to . . . make it sting." There was a sense that the paintings Benton exhibited were derivative of the early synchromist works shown in Munich in 1913. Benton, for instance, exhibited one of his bathing subjects, *Figure Organization No. 3* (ca. 1916, now lost), a representation of heroic, Michelangelesque figures that resembled that work in content and in how it handled tone, rhythm, and the distribution of volume and weight. The painting is a sort of copy of Michelangelo's marble *Battle of the Centaurs* (ca. 1492) and as such marks the beginning of his interest in sculpture, both in the making and in the illustration of it. "In speaking of the works of Michelangelo as 'models,'" Benton writes, "I do not mean that they were in any way copied. Quite the opposite, they were studied, their formal structures analyzed, and then reconstructed, often in utterly different patterns." But whatever his motivation might have been, Benton goes on to explain that even before the Forum Exhibition opened, "it was bruited about that I had taken up the synchromist palette only to get myself exhibited." Many years later, Benton was still sore about this episode, remarking to an interviewer, "I was interested; it wasn't a venal thing at all."

The more profound problem that the inclusion of Benton's representational painting in the show elucidated was that the organizers of the exhibition disagreed about the basis and function of modern art. Whereas Stieglitz and his artists understood the Forum Exhibition as a testament to the ascendancy of formalism and idea-based expression, Weichsel and others saw it as an opportunity to advocate for a materialist art that sprang from and attended to the universal human condition. In a review of the exhibition he helped to mount, Weichsel examines the latter mode: It "is more than a search for this or that aesthetic incarnation. It is an all-inclusive renascence . . . an initiation of a search for a living truth that is above factional strife . . . above either academic or secessionist doctrine" and is instead "a token of a liberating affirmation." The reference to "secessionist doctrine" appears to be a swipe at Stieglitz—whose 291 gallery was founded as the Little Galleries of the Photo-Secession—and his apparent elitism. Benton's *Figure Organization No. 3*, meanwhile, suggested to Weichsel "the irascible dynamism of our epoch" and the ability of humanity to transcend conventions as it struggled to create a new and better society. But as far as the Stieglitz Circle was concerned, Benton's paintings, with their corporeal figures, had no aesthetic value, for the Circle preferred what Marcia Brennan describes as "nonbodily bodies," or nonfigural forms, on their surfaces.

Though he was more interested in Weichsel's notions than Stieglitz's, Benton was not prepared to advocate with any conviction one position or another. His statement in the Forum Exhibition catalog demonstrates just how turned around he was on these matters: on the one hand, he claims to be skeptical of "intellectualist formulas" and interested mainly in the force of "alternate bulgings and recessions." On the other hand, he concludes with this formalist statement: "I believe the representation of objective forms and the presentation of abstract ideas of form to be of equal artistic value." Benton later claimed that he added this statement to his catalog essay at the urging of Wright so that "it would appear that I was 'in harmony' with the thinking of my fellow exhibitors."

As Dennis Raverty explains, the exchanges between Wright and Robert J. Coady, the owner of the Washington Square Gallery, best illustrate the terms of the discourse engendered by the Forum Exhibition. On March 12, 1916, the day before the exhibition opened, the New York *Sun* reported on the discussions that the show had already given rise to. "One thing that will surely impress the public more than any other," the paper remarked, "is the struggle that the various committees and individuals are making to swing the movement into different channels." On the one hand there was Wright, whose formalism had been spelled out in *Modern Painting* and his criticism for *The Forum*. He had come to see art as determined by an inevitable evolution toward "abstract purity." The article in *The Sun* was followed by a letter submitted by Coady, who made his case for a more grounded art, to be expressed in works based on observations of the American scene. He accused the Forum Exhibition organizers of being "blind to the big spirit here [in America] that has grown out of the soil" and failing to understand that American art "is not a refined granulation nor a delicate disease" but an "expression of life—a complicated life—American life." The call-and-response between Wright and Coady would echo for decades.

So the Forum Exhibition has two legacies. As noteworthy as the avant-garde paintings on display was the degree to which some organizers and reviewers of the exhibition struck the chord of American exceptionalism: the exhibition was a model of a political idea, one that was nationalist and that sought to wrestle away American art from petty bourgeois interests and from capitalist promoters of European culture. Nor was this nationalist rhetoric limited to painters; novelists, poets, and essayists of the period, such as William Carlos Williams, Lewis Mumford, and Waldo Frank, expressed a similar devotion to regionalism. Carl Sandburg, for instance, in his book *Chicago Poems*, published in 1916, celebrated the average American citizen living in cities, and a year earlier the literary historian Van Wyck Brooks, a nationalist member of the Stieglitz Circle (indeed, nationalism was one theme that united some members of the Stieglitz camp with some members of Weichsel's group), spoke of the need to identify in America a usable past and to adopt an artistic expression that sought high ideas in the nation's everyday life. So the exhibition generated the debate that would shape Benton's life and art for years to come: Would modernism be driven by ideas or by experience?

Benton soon was compelled to reason through his response to such a question. In the months following the Forum Exhibition, from December 1916 until March 1917, Stieglitz staged shows for three *Forum* exhibitors—Abraham Walkowitz, John Marin, and Macdonald-Wright. Benton, however, was not invited to show at 291. During Macdonald-Wright's exhibition, sensing once and for all that he was being forced to take a position, Benton wrote Weichsel a letter in which he griped about Stieglitz, whom he now viewed as an elitist and egomaniacal formalist. He noted that while Macdonald-Wright was "quite in vogue," there was "no use" for his own work. He added that Stieglitz "has respect only for those who care enough about him to tolerate his loquacity" and that "he knows nothing about what I myself am trying to do." Benton would admit to admiring aspects of Stieglitz and his circle, and to a "sort of regret" about his exclusion from this coterie of artists—"it had a kind of glamorous character which I never expect to find again," he writes—but again and again he returned to the subject of Stieglitz's long-windedness as a barrier between them. Benton acknowledged that he, too, talked too much, and the noise that each man generated obviously prevented the one from ever hearing the other. But, he concluded, "I thought he was a pain in the neck. He talked all the time. You never could get a word in." At Weichsel's, at least the "social as well as the artistic questions were discussed."

Besides Weichsel and Craven, one friend of Benton's during these hard days was Charles Daniel, who'd gone from a café and hotel operator to a gallery owner in 1913. Daniel was impressed by Stieglitz and admired modernists like Marsden Hartley and Charles Demuth (whom he represented from 1914 to 1925). Though his gallery, on the tenth floor of a building at 2 West Forty-seventh Street, was "a hot house of artistic quarreling" plagued by "suspicions and enmities," all the artists admired Daniel. After the Forum Exhibition, Benton continued producing his heroic figure compositions, canvases based on classical and Renaissance models, and though Daniel seemed not to like them very much, he showed them in his gallery—an arrangement that earned Benton a little money and, as he was now twenty-seven years old, a respite from having to ask the Colonel for support.

In the early spring of 1917, Benton followed the movie studios across the Hudson River to Fort Lee, New Jersey, where he set up a work space in an old house. Fort Lee was cheap, and the surrounding Palisades offered dramatic perspectives from which to paint views of the river and the Manhattan skyline. Sometimes in the company of George "Pop" Hart, a vivacious artist who also painted scenes for the studios, Benton ascended the Palisades and made watercolor drawings of the river tugs and cityscape beyond. Hart socialized with a cadre of progressive artists that included Walt Kuhn and Arthur B. Davies, who were primary organizers of the Armory Show, and this group confirmed Benton's sense that New York artists were clannish and aggrieved. Kuhn—who "considered himself . . . more responsible than either Alfred Stieglitz or Willard Wright for the introduction of modern idioms to America"—was miffed at being excluded from the Forum Exhibition planning committee and in retaliation set up an informal school in Fort Lee to rival Stieglitz's studio. Though Kuhn's resentment and "pretensions" made Benton uneasy—like Stieglitz, Benton explains, Kuhn tended "to make art revolve around personalities"—he occasionally joined this group and their city friends for weekend meals at Albig's, a German restaurant in Fort Lee.

But Benton returned to the city that summer. Through the People's Art Guild, Weichsel had established connections with various city organizations to establish "people's" galleries, meant to foster popular appreciation of the arts, and he arranged for Benton to work as a general caretaker and occasional curator at the Henry Street Settlement, located on the southeast end of Manhattan. (The Henry Street Settlement, established in 1893 by Lillian Wald, a service-minded nurse, attended to the Lower East Side's sick and poor, and is still in operation today.) Benton took the ferry from Fort Lee each day to open the gallery and show visitors the art on display. Shortly after, he assumed a similar position as director of a gallery run by the Chelsea Neighborhood Association, located on Ninth Avenue near Twenty-eighth Street, for which he was paid fifty dollars a month. The association had been established in 1913 to influence zoning laws and keep the buildings in the neighborhood from falling into any more disrepair and believed an art gallery would help rehabilitate Chelsea. Benton also took on a job teaching drawing classes at night to adults in a Chelsea public school, and to be closer to work, he moved from Fort Lee into an unheated flat on Twenty-third Street and Seventh Avenue.

By all accounts, Benton enjoyed teaching and working at the Chelsea gallery. He met interesting and humble artists; taught a diverse group of immigrants, mostly Jews and Italians; and had time for painting. In May 1917, Benton showed his own work at the gallery, mostly his heroic bathing figures, and received his first piece of serious criticism, a review of the exhibition written by Wright, who pointed out that Benton was not a member of any clique and so was a neglected artist "treated with the injustice of silence." "Those reviewers who pretend to look with favour upon the new art no doubt missed the strange surface aspects in his works, and concluded that he was not 'modern,'" Wright explains, "while the avowedly conservative reviewers were probably shocked by the rugged vitality of his drawing and by his unusually bright colouring." He admired Benton's "classical *élan* toward the complexities of profound composition" and his striving for "visual unity" but was less impressed by his distribution of color, which he describes as "not always sensitive" and occasionally showing "signs of crudity." Benton likely agreed with this assessment. In retrospect, he admitted that his painting of this period was an "eclectic combination of classic and ultramodern ways." He claimed to see "in those Renaissance masters I loved so much, nothing but geometrical orders," and added, "I was full of *principle*. And yet, at bottom, I didn't believe in my own logic."

Even the abstract constructions he was making out of wood, wire, and colored paper—what might be called exercises in synthetic cubism—had an odd pedigree; he claimed these were more influenced by the sixteenth-century Italian artist Luca Cambiaso than by Braque and Picasso. It's clear that by 1917 Benton still didn't possess a coherent principle of art: he was inclined to paint active compositions but wasn't sure whether the dynamism he was after came from the masters or the moderns, or whether it was best achieved through abstraction or representation. At the time, this was not a matter to be trifled with: serious artists knew one way or the other. To not know whether one was a figurative or abstract painter was to not know the most fundamental thing about oneself. This was the period of Benton's career that Craven describes as a "trying interval," the period before he figured out how to use "the human stuff of his New York experiences in his painting." A few years before he died, Benton explained in a letter to Matthew Baigell, who was writing a biography of the artist, "There is really not much ground for setting me up as an 'important modernist' in the years just before and after World War I—much less an influential one . . . As I look back at the period previous to 1919 I see myself as reacting to others rather than acting upon them."

In 1918, just shy of thirty, Benton stopped working at the Chelsea gallery, probably because the association could no longer pay him, and was forced to move into his mother's house in Great Neck. All he had was his friendship with Craven; Macdonald-Wright left New York that year and moved to California, announcing, "I'm tired of chasing art up the back alleys of New York." In a letter to Weichsel from the previous year Benton had already painted a sad picture of his circumstances. He explained, matter-of-factly, that he'd gone "flat broke about the middle of May"; claimed that Daniel hinted to him that "a man with classic aspirations has no claim to respect as a modern artist"; and concluded, "I am in good physical condition and am perfectly indifferent about the future." He also mentioned that he might enter the navy.

7

EXPERIENCES

Benton did not join the navy out of a sense of patriotic duty. Like other leftists, he believed that World War I was a struggle "between big capitalists for control of the resources of the world." But he didn't exactly join out of desperation, either. Military service was for him an escape from the posturing that he'd come to find so enervating during his first six years in New York, and *The New York Times* went so far as to describe his time in the navy, in 1918, as "a cubist's holiday." In truth, neither Benton nor Craven "relished the idea of stopping bullets," and they considered various options for dodging service, including declaring a pacifist stance and fleeing to Mexico, but the navy, they concluded, offered "the safest and least troublesome asylum," and so Benton schemed to use his father's influence by persuading Alexander Dockery, who'd been the governor of Missouri when the Colonel represented the state in Congress and by the war was the third assistant postmaster general, to help him get a plum position on a base. Benton spelled out his desires in Dockery's Washington office, and the man, though greatly amused by the request, agreed to do what he could and handed him a letter of introduction. What Benton fails to mention, according to Henry Adams, is that Lizzie accompanied him on this trip and was the one who spoke to Dockery. Either way, Dockery's intervention worked, and in late June 1918, Benton was summoned to Norfolk, Virginia.

Immediately after his arrival on the Norfolk naval base, Benton was sent about thirty miles across Chesapeake Bay to little Cherrystone Island off Cape Charles. His arrival on the island was inopportune, however, as it coincided with the landing of a barge piled with coal that had to be loaded, by his shovel, onto waiting ships. In a letter to his mother written during his first days of service, Benton grumbled about blisters but was quick to point out, "I have landed in the softest spot in the Navy . . . There is plenty of time for swimming and the water . . . is wonderful." Craven was less fortunate. He remained in New York, on reserve and dirt-poor. In late July, Benton sent him a letter. "Well Craven, old top," he wrote, "I have fallen in to a much softer dump than yours." He proceeded to describe leisurely days spent swimming, sailing, and rowing around Chesapeake Bay's inlets. "You can sit on the sand and smoke if it pleases you," he added. "And the nights here are the real kind, white moon and cool breeze." Finding that his body responded well to the rowing, Benton learned that he could skip the coal shoveling if he signed up to fight in weekly boxing matches on the island, a diversion that he paid for "by taking a beating every Saturday night, for the entertainment of the sailors." His defeats, he explained later, had less to do with his physical skills than his "poor ring psychology."

In September, Benton—tan, strong, and cocky—was sent back to Norfolk, where his superiors promptly ascertained that he qualified to work as a draftsman. He started making freehand watercolors, for the purpose of documenting activity on the base, of buildings, airplanes, and blimps—work, he told his mother, that "must be more accurate than artistic" but that was not "unpleasant." Still, he wanted to work on subjects and in styles of his own choosing and expressed his intention to ask Dockery for help persuading his superiors to let him paint for his "own purposes." Though he didn't receive such permission, he was promoted to the position of "camofleur." Twice a week he accompanied another young artist aboard a forty-foot motorboat on cruises around Norfolk harbor during which they painted and photographed camouflage ships, producing illustrations that could aid in the identification of vessels sunk by torpedoes. "I have not time to be very critical and cannot judge the real worth of these things I make down here," he wrote to his mother. "For that reason I save all of them. Those which have no artistic value will at least serve as a record of my experience."

Much has been made of the influence this six-month navy excursion had on Benton's career: Benton's biographers mark this period as one of the crucial turning points—along with his father's death, in 1924, and his travels through the Ozarks and the South soon after—in his artistic philosophy. Before the navy, the story goes, Benton was undisciplined; he flittered about and experimented with this and that, failing to comprehend how his roots connected to his practice. According to Craven, the first to describe this professional arc, "the last vestiges of French influence disappeared" from Benton's work during his navy service. His "career since the War," Craven pronounced in 1934, "is the story of the reciprocal effects of extraordinary experience and extraordinary technical knowledge." Three years later, Benton echoed his friend's observations by attributing his initial skepticism about the "art-for-art's-sake world" to the authentic experiences he had in Virginia "among boys who had never been subjected to any aesthetic virus." The boys he swam and sailed with, Benton explains, were from Tennessee and the Carolinas, and "their egos were not of the frigid, touchy sort developed by brooding much on the importance of the self . . . They were objective." Benton claims that once immersed in such a pragmatic society, he learned how to see again: "My interests became, in a flash, of an objective nature." The matériel on the Norfolk base—"the airplanes, the blimps, the dredges, the ships"—transfixed him; they "tore me away from all my grooved habits, from my play with colored cubes and classic attenuations, from my aesthetic drivelings and morbid self-concerns."

Returning to New York in November 1918, Benton arranged an exhibition of his navy illustrations at Charles Daniel's gallery in December. A reviewer for *The New York Herald* praised the works and emphasized their grounding in "experience." "The strenuous life lived by the painter," the author writes, "has cleared his eye, chastened his imagination and made his power of selection much more sure than before." Naturally, Benton agreed with this analysis. He explains that his navy bosses "did not care *how* I did things but how accurately I *described* them. The subject became, rather suddenly, a very important factor." But in a review of the same exhibition, a *New York Times* critic disagrees. Benton's blimps, the author observes, "betray" a penchant for formal experimentation rather than close observation. "In their sinister invertebrate bodies, soft and distended," the critic explains, "he finds his chance to get in the peculiar vice of a large class of modernist painters, a glorification of swollen substances and forms that hint at Chinese gods and fungus growths. The soaring majesty of the balloon in action apparently has no charm for him." There are enchanting vignettes in Benton's navy illustrations—his representations of the various kinds of boats that crowded Norfolk harbor, for example, and a pen-and-ink drawing of sailors in a mess hall—but *The New York Times*'s reviewer is right that in general, the pictures are typical of much machine-age art: their compositions tend to revolve around swirling vortices or geometric patterns.

Benton may have grown sensitive to experience during his navy service, but his pictures from that summer, like those from the previous six years, filter his experiences of the world around him through a modernist sensibility.

Perhaps a more telling emblem of the changes Benton underwent during these months is Jesse Ames Spencer's *History of the United States*, which was published in four volumes between 1858 and 1866. In the fall of 1918, when Benton was boarding at a Norfolk lodging house, he came across Spencer's volumes in the parlor library. He studied them at night and, as with the historical texts he came across when he was a boy, was struck by the book's engravings, which were produced from drawings by the nineteenth-century artist Alonzo Chappel, a successful painter of subjects from American history. The frontispiece of Spencer's first volume, for instance, depicts Christopher Columbus standing on the terra firma of the New World surrounded by conquistadores and a genuflecting Indian woman. Another typical illustration from Spencer's volumes depicts a beautiful young Pocahontas saving Captain John Smith from the club of a fierce executioner. Benton claims to have been moved by these pictures not because they were visually compelling but because they suggested to him a series of provocative and ultimately transformative questions. "Why," he asks, "could not such subject pictures dealing with the meanings of American history possess aesthetically interesting properties, deliverable along with their meanings?" And, "Why not look into [history painting] again . . . and try to fill the contextual void of my own painting, give it some kind of meaning?"

Released from the navy and aware that "things existed in the world outside myself and that it made no difference whether I had any 'genius' or not," Benton "proclaimed heresies around New York." Benton says "heresies" because what he decried that winter was Stieglitz's 291 gallery, which many artists and intellectuals perceived as a holy place. Just after the war, for example, Waldo Frank, the novelist, historian, and critic, declared 291 "a religious fact." "It is an altar," Frank explains in *Our America*, "where no lie and no compromise could live . . . '291' was a candle that did not go out, since it alone was the truth." Upon returning to New York, Benton sought out John Weichsel but found that the People's Art Guild was defunct; in search of some companionship, he then visited 291 and showed Stieglitz his navy watercolors. The meeting did not go well. Stieglitz criticized Benton's work, denouncing his hard lines and asking him why he didn't try to paint like John Marin, whose watercolors were looser and more abstract. Benton attributes Stieglitz's slight to the "rigid taboos among the aesthetic elite." After the war, he recalls, he finally broke free from the "prewar crowd" and their "sickly rationalizations" and "God-awful self-cultivations." To varying degrees, but evermore, Benton saw himself as a *people's artist*—as the last line of defense against the introspective, detached theories of Stieglitz and his allies.

By his own admission, however, Benton took Stieglitz's criticisms to heart at first and, briefly, tried to paint without making preliminary drawings. He produced expressionistic landscapes similar to those he'd made at the Palisades near Fort Lee but quickly grew frustrated and complained in a letter to Stieglitz that his focus on "spontaneity" was leading to a "structural loss" in his drawing. For a while, Benton earned his only money from sales arranged by Alfred Raabe, a Bronx physician from the Ukraine whom Benton had met several years earlier at one of Weichsel's gatherings. Raabe was left-leaning and had an appreciation for the arts; he was also curious, which appealed to Benton, and they became friends. He would visit Benton and take away several small paintings and drawings, which he'd then place in frames he built in his basement as a hobby. He purchased some pieces himself, but mostly he sold them to his wealthier Jewish patients, an enterprise that earned Benton as much as three thousand dollars one year. Years later Benton expressed amusement and satisfaction that so many of his works made it up to the Bronx this way and boasted, "Never, even when I became well-known and my pictures started bringing good prices, never have those paintings come on the market. I consider that quite a tribute."

In the fall of 1919, Benton read an article on Tintoretto that described how the artist had made preparatory sculptures for some of his paintings, a process that appealed to him as he'd been contemplating the representation of volume ever since he'd studied Michelangelo's *Battle of the Centaurs* while preparing for the Forum Exhibition. For several months Benton experimented with forming clay and plasticine dioramas modeled on Ghiberti's masterful doors for the Florence baptistery and the carvings he'd seen at cathedrals in France. Once he perfected the modeling process, the dioramas proved so beneficial—because they offered him lively approximations of real-world material relations—that he continued to make them for the remainder of his career. What

Benton realized was that he needed to paint from what he called "concrete references." When he was making a portrait or studying a scene in nature, these references were right there before him, but when trying to arrange multiple figures in an imagined composition or historical scene, Benton struggled to represent spatial and formal relationships. But when producing a painting after a diorama, Benton explains, "the *actual* forms of sculptured figures, projected in a real, even though miniature, space, would possess the same tangibility as objects in the space of the natural world." There were several interesting consequences of Benton's new procedure. First, he finally felt connected to a practical tradition, which he believed instilled in his art a legitimacy that was authorized by history, because he never trusted that aesthetic innovation legitimized itself. Second, the sculptural method distinguished Benton once and for all from the abstractionists—"pallid abstractionists," Craven called them, in his inimitable way—of the Stieglitz Circle. He now had his own method, one, in his words, that "would arouse sharp animosities among artists and critics and catapult me into twenty-five years of controversy"—controversy that he came to relish. Finally, in short order the new method led to his first masterpiece, *People of Chilmark* (1921–1922), a large oil painting depicting a group of figures on Martha's Vineyard.

Benton visited Martha's Vineyard for the first time in the summer of 1920, when he followed a young woman there. This was Rita Piacenza, an iron-willed Italian beauty whom he'd taught in Chelsea. Rita had come to America in 1912 from Lombardy with her two brothers, Louis and Santo, and moved in with her uncle and aunt, who was a successful dressmaker and taught Rita to fashion hats. After Mr. and Mrs. Piacenza arrived in New York, the family settled in an apartment on Twenty-ninth Street on the West Side, and Rita enrolled in nighttime classes at the Chelsea Neighborhood Association to improve her design sense. In a 1973 interview, Rita recalled the first time she met her husband. She brought sketches that she'd made of museum paintings to the first class, and Benton promptly remarked, "These are no damn good," before proceeding to set up a still life for her to draw. Rita remembered that she'd heard criticisms of Benton's work—Robert Henri told her that his work was "too Michelangelese"—but she persevered, taking classes with him until he left for the navy and then, after the war, becoming his model. Benton's memories of their initial flirtation are as unsentimental as Rita's. "She was slim, dark-eyed, and beautiful," he recalls. "She wore a red hat and was disposed to be friendly. We commenced going around together." When Benton returned to New York after the war had ended, he and Craven got in the habit of visiting the Piacenzas for Sunday dinner: "We'd sit in silence and stuff ourselves with great Italian courses, get in a stupor with wine, and then rise silently and go away." Though Rita's parents spoke no English, they expressed their doubts about the relationship to Rita. Santo recalled that the family didn't approve: "We thought that he didn't have a job; the things that he was painting he couldn't sell; and Rita had to support him. You know, the Italians, they have a very funny way about that."

In the fall of 1919, Benton and Craven, who were sharing a bleak three-room flat above a saloon, received a visit from some friends who'd just returned from Martha's Vineyard with tales about "delicious beach plums" and "handouts of fish." So the next summer, when Rita invited them to accompany her and Lillian Hoffman to the island, the men jumped at the opportunity to escape the heat of Manhattan. The group—which also included Rollin Crampton, who would become a color-field painter praised by Clement Greenberg—departed the city in July. It was a long journey. They boarded a night boat to New Bedford and then a steamer to Oak Bluffs, where they hired a Model T to drive them the bumpy eighteen miles to the village of Chilmark. Rita had arranged to rent a weathered, shingled barn from Ella Brug for twenty-five dollars for the summer, but she and Hoffman ended up staying in a nearby bungalow, and the three men settled in the barn, sleeping on the floor. Describing his first encounter with the island, during the summer of 1927, Lewis Mumford recalls "drenching in the nakedness of natural scenes, natural forces, natural acts." Polly Burroughs, herself a Vineyarder, describes the place as blissful: "Situated on the western slope of a hill, the barn embraced a striking view of the ocean, Menemsha Pond, and the Elizabeth Islands across the western entrance to Vineyard Sound." It was surrounded by wild roses and set near a cistern and a freshwater spring; paths cut down the hills to private dune beaches where the men could dig for clams at low tide. The land was marked by "undulating gray stone walls rolling over the moors . . . sheep grazing everywhere . . . and scattered clumps of scrub oak and pine sculpted close to the ground by the relentless winds." Benton was moved. He recalled that "getting out of the damn city and living an open life . . . on the beaches and doing work" had a salubrious effect on him. "The relaxing sea air, the hot sand on the beaches where we loafed naked, the great continuous drone of the surf," he explains in *An Artist in America*, "broke down most of the tenseness which life in the cities had given me." Benton's portrayal of the island as a Whitmanesque arcadia was partly a gambit designed to emphasize the narrative of his rebirth as a populist—a narrative that Craven contributed to by describing Benton's "resplendent physical condition" during these months.

Chilmark was a genuine Jeffersonian village: one walked the hilly town, which was populated by fishermen and sheep farmers, and one got by without electricity. Rita would meet the catboats at the docks and pick up fish—mackerel, haddock, flounder, and lobster—and on her way back to the bungalow she'd stop by Frank Tilton's place for an armful of fresh vegetables. She also picked berries on the moors and mushrooms in the stunted pine forests. The group would swim at Stonewall Beach and picnic at Menemsha Pond or Gay Head. Craven wrote to Lizzie to tell her that "all goes well here . . . the out-of-doors is irresistibly seductive and everyone around is on vacation." He also mentioned that Tom had "made a beautiful pencil drawing of a segment of seacoast," probably a sketch of Wequobsque Cliffs.

The idyll, though, was contrasted by the hard work performed by the impressive Chilmark Yankees. It was the Vineyard, in fact, just as much as it was the Midwest that shaped Benton's interest in agrarian labor. The islanders were friendly to these interlopers—especially to Rita, whom they saw as one of their own—but were decidedly exotic. Chilmark was home to a large number of deaf-mutes, mostly stoic farmers, whom Benton sketched and painted on several occasions. His famous 1926 double portrait, *The Lord Is My Shepherd*, is based on a sketch he made during the summer of 1922 of George and Sabrina West, who lived down the hill from the Brug barn at Beetlebung Corner. George West was a deaf-mute, and so were two of his sons. Burroughs portrays the Wests as "hard workers" who lived a "sparse existence without amenities" and tells a story about when Cyril Norton, another Chilmark native, saw Josie West "kill his old horse by braining it over the head with an ax, instead of shooting it." She also describes how Norton observed Josie's brother "out alone at Abel's Hill cemetery on a cold, bleak winter's day with a raw wind coming off the ocean, digging his wife's grave." Whatever his time in the navy had taught Benton about labor and physical exertion was doubly reinforced by what he observed in Chilmark, and though he apparently had a harder time getting to know the Vineyarders than Craven and Rita did, he explains that "for all their crotchety ways," they "had the nobility of medieval saints." It was on the island, he claims, that he first began his "intimate study of the American environment and its people."

In 1919, Benton completed *Garden Scene*, the first painting he produced employing his new procedure of making clay sculptures based on drawings. The painting depicts four figures and a dog arranged in a cubistic landscape and, typical of his early work, is compressed and clunky; the heavy figures are crammed into the frame and seem to have turned to stone in the middle of their picnic. Working from a preparatory maquette clearly helped him represent figural volume, but his painting still lacked grace or delicacy. Nevertheless, Benton was encouraged by the sale of the painting to the collectors Tom and Sarah Kelly, Philadelphia patrons who'd moved to New York. In Chilmark that first summer, Benton made drawings in the same vein and produced from them a much stronger work, *The Beach* (1920–1921), which better testifies to what Craven calls "the uncanny palpability of his forms, and his realization of great spatial depth." Though the individual bodies portrayed in the painting are inelegant, contorted, and broad shouldered, there's an organic flow to the overall distribution of forms that demonstrates his nascent philosophy of environmental determinism. The six figures are bent into complementary crescents and interlock in a circle, as if the concave cliffs and undulating shoreline are what determine their rhythmic postures. Seen in this light, the painting appears to diagram how an environment can shape the forms and activities of the people who experience it.

In the spring of 1921, Dr. Albert C. Barnes, the legendary Philadelphia collector, admired the painting at the Pennsylvania Academy of the Fine Arts, where it hung in the Exhibition of Paintings and Drawings Showing the Later Tendencies in Art. Organized by Arthur Carles, the exhibition included almost three hundred works by such progressive artists as Charles Demuth, John Marin, Georgia O'Keeffe, and Marguerite and William Zorach. Craven reviewed the exhibition in *The Dial*, the leading literary and arts journal of the day that was guided by a crack editorial board that included Randolph Bourne, John Dewey, and Mumford. Craven, beating Benton to a steady paycheck, started writing essays and reviews for the journal the year before. At this time Craven's criticism was decidedly formalist—he defended the modernists' search for a venerable purity—and it wasn't until the mid-1920s that he turned on modernism and argued for a more experiential approach to artmaking and criticism, thus earning his reputation as a reactionary. But Craven recalls that in his early pieces for *The Dial* he "defended Modernism against all comers, hammering home the truth that the movement was a salutary return to first principles," a position that "delighted" Scofield Thayer, the journal's editor. Craven's review of the Philadelphia exhibition makes just one brief reference to Benton; he praises his fusion of "classical composition" and the "objective and dispersed facts of experience" as both an antiquated and an avant-garde mode of expression. What intrigued Craven most was that the conservative Pennsylvania Academy of the Fine Arts had opened its doors to the moderns at all, an invitation that he interpreted as proof that "our younger artists . . . have been victorious over Philistine resentment."

A reviewer for *The New York Times* also remarks on Benton's obvious study of Renaissance composition and admires the painting's "opulent design" and "strong lines . . . made with the sweeping power of which the Chinese calligrapher was master," but worries that it possesses "the lassitude of youth" and some "laziness." But Barnes, who by this time had amassed in his gallery (located in Merion, Pennsylvania) a stunning collection of Tintorettos, Cézannes, Matisses, and Picassos, saw something in *The Beach*, one of just a handful of paintings he purchased at the exhibition. Barnes liked Benton—he was impressed by his intelligence and his enthusiasm for the technical aspects of painting—and admired his compositions. Later that year, he invited Benton and Craven to his house, even paying their rail fare from New York. The formidable Barnes told the men about a book idea—a technical examination of painting—and asked Craven to write it and Benton to supply some compositional diagrams. Many years later, Benton recalled that Barnes had a more sincere fascination with painting than other collectors. "I think he did have this kind of sensuous interest," he said, "interest in the object itself, not in what anybody said about it or even what it meant. It was just a sensuous interest in its color and form, chiefly its color."

But Barnes was volatile. A 1928 *New Yorker* profile characterized him as "inexhaustible" and "nervous": "His square determined jaw, large head, and piercing blue eyes, which take in everything about him with quick, suspicious glances, top off a solid beefiness that would suggest an Irish police captain if it were not for that seething, restless energy." And Barnes liked to fight, which Benton discovered soon enough. During a follow-up visit to Merion, Benton blundered when he argued that it would be pointless to diagram the paintings of the impressionists because they were totally inept at composition. Barnes recoiled, sensing that the remark was an attack on his taste, and later sent Benton a scathing letter exclaiming, as Benton paraphrased it, that "my cockiness with regard to the arts derived from the fact that I was only a runt anyhow, and runts like me are always combative." "He was a vicious bastard," Benton concluded, "but he did love art."

Needless to say, the book wasn't written, though Benton did make use of the diagrams in an important series of essays, "The Mechanics of Form Organization in Painting," published in *The Arts* in the winter of 1926–1927. The essays mark Benton's most sustained effort to explain his theories of composition and, generally speaking, attempt to articulate the fundamental importance of formal rhythms. On this score Benton was heavily influenced by Willard Huntington Wright, who had argued in *Modern Painting* that "significant form must move in depth—backward and forward, as well as from side to side." The essays and their accompanying illustrations demonstrate how Benton achieved unified patterns from the foreground and background forms of his compositions, patterns that were dynamic yet harmonious—"the parts . . . must be held in a state of balance," he argues. These complementary convexities and concavities, according to Benton, should operate on a large scale (in the composition as a whole) and on a small scale (in the representation, for instance, of a muscular arm). "There are here," he writes, referring to two illustrations of such an arm, "a series of masses which bulge and hollows which recede." Much has been made about how these theories shaped Benton's teaching and the compositional strategies of Jackson Pollock, his most famous student, but it's important to understand as well that the essays were a culmination, an articulation at last of the systematic approach Benton had taken to painting for the previous six years.

During their second summer on Martha's Vineyard, in 1921, Benton helped Craven prepare an article on his career and work so far. Published in *Shadowland*, a short-lived magazine covering the arts and film, the essay observes that Benton's basic interest was in "design," in the construction of "an object in which all the parts were precisely and harmoniously related." "Mr. Benton," Craven adds, "has a predilection for models of unusual muscular development; and to attain greater bulk and solidity, to make his work richer and more rugged, and to increase its power and momentum, he paints these figures beyond naturalism . . . [and] strives for final unity." Having experimented with this manner in his bathing pictures and, later, in *Garden Scene* and *The Beach*, he finally was prepared to illustrate it more clearly in *People of Chilmark*, which Benton likely began just as Craven was writing the essay and completed the next year.

The assiduous figures in the large, strenuous painting, who twist and turn as they frolic in the surf, are not, as the title says, the "people" of Chilmark. They were modeled, again, on those friends who were in close contact that second summer on the island—Craven, Rita, and her brother Louis, among them—and embody the baroque grandeur of a common experience in the water off Chilmark. The people engage in common seaside rituals—launching a boat, holding a beach ball, and rowing—and are in active commerce with their environment. The "bumps and hollows" do their work here, animating the surface, which is painted with a sharp chiaroscuro. In September, Craven wrote to Lizzie to inform her that Benton was at work on an "enormous picture." It is "easily the most complex and mighty work he has yet undertaken," he said.

People of Chilmark, at about five and a half by six and a half feet, was the largest painting Benton had executed to date, and in designing it, he called upon all he'd learned about baroque composition. The intention behind the work is more ambitious than it is in the earlier ones, for it illustrates his evolving theories about the relationship between what he called, in a 1924 essay, "form and the subject," which he then contrasts with "form and feeling"—something he identifies with the Stieglitz Circle and calls the "indispensable shields behind which the modern artist conducts his defense against the inquisitive layman." He argues that "the most highly emotional response to some fact of experience" is typical of modern artists and not a "really true expression of experience"; form, rather, must be instrumental—that is, it must derive

from "some conception of purpose and definite ideas of sequence" before it can approximate experience, an argument that reveals the influence on Benton of Weichsel's writings. In other words, form results
from arranging objects with an eye to clarifying how they were initially
experienced, not from mere "feelings" about the objects. *People of Chilmark* achieves this insofar as it isn't an expressionistic painting, recording
Benton's emotional response to a place, but one that attempts to prag-
matically represent, by downplaying his figure's emotions and emphasizing their postures, how he and his cohort physically inhabited a space
as they experienced it.

As he worked on the painting, Benton was developing a philosophy
about how a particular geography affects the people who dwell in it,
and there's some truth, in fact, to his claim that he was the first to advocate a turn to "environmental experience for American artists." What
Benton called "environmentalism" was derived, in part, from notions
that Dewey expressed in essays such as "Americanism and Localism,"
published in *The Dial* in 1920. In the essay, Dewey demands a literature that portrays how "a locality exists in three dimensions," states
that "the locality is the only universal," and maintains that when we
explore our immediate domain, "its forces and not just its characters
and colors, we shall find what we sought." Five years later, Dewey
turned to aesthetics—in an essay that appeared in a journal published
by Barnes and that introduces some of the key concepts he would treat
more fully in the 1930s—and claimed, "The 'eternal' quality of great art
is its renewed instrumentality for further consummatory experiences."
In other words, we ought to value art because it can objectify and represent for us the chief attribute of complete experiences, which Dewey
describes as the synthesis of people and their locale. *People of Chilmark* achieves this on both formal and symbolic levels. Formally, the
painting resolves an oversupply of visual information—oars, waves, sails,
torsos, and clouds—into an integrated surface, one made dynamic by
"bumps and hollows" but held together by graceful rhythms. As symbol,
the painting illustrates the key components of Deweyan experience:
"that interaction of organism and environment which, when it is carried
to the full, is a transformation of interaction into participation and communication." So at home in their environment are these people on the
Chilmark shore that they have no need to speak to one another; their
communication occurs naturally.

Matthew Baigell suggests that Dewey's ideas might have reached Benton through the writing of William Carlos Williams—not his poems so much as the content of the magazine *Contact*, which Williams edited. Williams was far more comfortable in the Stieglitz Circle than Benton but was intrigued by the concept of experience and borrowed heavily from Dewey, and so might have suggested to Benton a way of moving modernism closer to what would eventually be called regionalism. "Contact" was Williams's word for the coming together of place and language, and in the inaugural issue of the magazine he states that it was "issued in the conviction that art which attains is indigenous of experience and relations"; in a later issue he maintains that it's in the "taking on of certain colors from the locality by the experience" of it that America is realized. Williams's arguments would have appealed to Benton not just because he was developing his own theory of localism but also because Williams urged American artists to temper their enthusiasm for European aesthetics: "If Americans are to be blessed with important work it will be through intelligent, informed contact with the locality which alone can infuse it with reality." "We are here," Williams stated earlier, "because of our faith in the existence of native artists who are capable of having, comprehending and recording extraordinary experience," artists "who deal with our situations." The notion of contact for Williams was a way of moving beyond Emerson's self-reliance and arguing instead for an "interdependent individualism" and social awareness. As one literary historian puts it, Williams "attempt[ed] to *humanize* knowledge by stressing the fact that, to be truly useful to us . . . knowledge must be seen as having a body, an immediate concreteness which we apprehend sensorily before we can usefully assimilate it." Williams was a paradox: an avant-garde poet who held the position that modernism dislocated one from time and space. His sense of locality began with "a somatic awareness, a physiological presence in time and space."

Another major influence on Benton's environmental aesthetics was Mumford, who maintained that "the region provides a common background: the air we breathe, the water we drink, the food we eat, the landscape we see, the accumulation of experience and custom peculiar to the setting, tend to unify the inhabitants." As Mumford's biographer Donald L. Miller explains, he advised against "sweeping national crusades for change" and urged one to "start immediately in your own region and locale to lay the basis for the renewal of life"; Mumford preferred what he called, in *The Story of Utopias*, published in 1922, "definite, verifiable, localized knowledge." More than most, however, Mumford clarified the role of the artist in the process of social renewal. "Art in its social setting," he writes, "is neither a personal cathartic for the artist, nor a salve to quiet the itching vanity of the community, it is essentially a means by which people who have had a strange diversity of experiences have their activities emotionally [fit] into patterns and molds which they are able to share pretty completely with each other."

Again, the people in *People of Chilmark* are not "the people," but there's no doubt that island fishermen and farmers inspired it. Of the local Vineyarders that Benton was meeting at this time, Burroughs writes, "They never spoke of a love for the Island, they lived it; close to the soil and the sea whose moods and secrets they experienced daily, so sensitive to the slightest shift in wind it would be casually mentioned while they were in the kitchen eating supper." Benton observed these people at work and through surrogate figures represented their vigor, gallantry, and moral superiority to the bourgeoisie. Twenty years later, recalling his impression of these people, Benton remarked:

> You learned things about people who had been on whaling ships and had swum miles at sea holding onto their boots, who had walked across miles of Arctic ice and had had their teeth pulled by the village blacksmith with all the local heavyweights sitting on their arms and legs. Listening, you shared not only the adventures, but the spirits of the talkers. Keeping your mouth shut, you came to know the Island folks and what they and the Island stood for. You got in touch with what was real.

As Benton depicted it, though, Martha's Vineyard was not just a community of white Yankees. Behind the right shoulder of the figure with the beach ball is a conspicuously darkly complected man. Amazingly, until a recent dissertation on Benton and race, not a single critic or art historian has even mentioned the presence of this dark figure. The author of the dissertation speculates that this is an African American man, the first to appear in a Benton painting. There's good reason to believe that she's right, considering that there had been an African American enclave in Oak Bluffs, on the other side of the island from

Chilmark, since the early twentieth century. It's possible that Benton included the figure to appeal to Barnes, who'd purchased *The Beach*. He surely knew of Barnes's interest in and patronage of black artists, as well as his collection of African sculpture, so perhaps he thought that featuring an African American in the painting would make Barnes more likely to purchase it as well.

Another possibility is that the figure is not an African American but rather a Wampanoag Indian. The Wampanoags lived in southeastern Massachusetts and Rhode Island, as well as within a territory that encompassed current-day Martha's Vineyard, Nantucket, and the Elizabeth Islands. When Benton was summering in Chilmark in the 1920s, he would have met Wampanoags, who still live there today. As he was working on the painting, he included a portrait of a Wampanoag sachem in the panel *Palisades* (1921–1922) from *The American Historical Epic* (1919–1928), his first mural series, and while the figure in *People of Chilmark* is considerably darker than the Native American figures in the series, Wampanoag men often shaved their heads, as this mysterious figure has done. Benton's inclusion of the figure illustrates either his sensitivity to the eradication of Native populations— a sensitivity on full display in the panels of *The American Historical Epic*—or his lifelong interest in African American subjects. At the very least, though, the presence of this figure among the people of Chilmark illustrates Benton's view of the place as an integrated community.

In the fall of 1921, Craven moved to Brookhaven, Long Island, and Rita, who was twenty-one, moved into Benton's apartment. He was thirty-two. That winter, Benton received an awkward visit from Rita's father, who expressed his misgivings about their living arrangements, and in February the couple got married at the Church of St. Francis Xavier in New York. They stayed with Lizzie for a few months in Great Neck before Rita located a fifth-floor apartment at 42 Union Square, and, as Benton remembers it, "we lived from hand to mouth, but we lived." He would carry heating coal up the stairs, and they lit the apartment with kerosene. Thomas Craven's son, Dick, recalled a story that his mother, Aileen, told him on occasion: She visited the Bentons in New York one day and, overwhelmed by the "abject squalor and chaos," asked Rita how she could stand it. Without skipping a beat, she responded, "My husband is a genius."

By all accounts, Rita's devotion to her husband was remarkable and constant. She worked at first but quickly abandoned her sewing column to manage Benton's career. Until his death, in fact, she served as his agent, keeping an inventory of his paintings and brokering virtually all of his sales. Jessie Benton, the couple's daughter, born in 1939, was in awe of her mother's commitment to her father's career. "She never faltered from her one purpose," Jessie once commented, "which was: he was a great artist, no matter what. She saved all the money and saved all the paintings . . . Sometimes we were very poor. Sometimes we had lots of money if we sold a painting. But the life of the house never changed, and that was my mother's genius."

In the early years of their marriage, Benton traveled a lot and was often ornery, but according to Rita's brother Santo he understood that he would have gone nowhere without Rita. "If it wasn't for her," Santo recalled Benton telling him, "I would still be a bum and wouldn't have a dime to my name." Benton's first paean to his wife was a modernist bronze bust portrait he made of her in 1918, but his best was *Self-Portrait with Rita* (1922), the double portrait of the couple on a Vineyard beach that punctuates the so-called environmental tendency in *People of Chilmark*: whereas the earlier painting imagines the island as a place to institute healthy communal relations, this portrait reifies that idea by illustrating the island as a locale where Benton and his wife belong.

During the early 1920s, Benton fought, drank, and painted, finally arriving at his mature style, exemplified by *The Yankee Driver* (1923). The driver is identified as Billy Benson, "an infamous character" in Chilmark, who was "a sort of handyman who did odd jobs around the property where Benton stayed" and was known "for stealing sheep and [once] trying to poison his parents with arsenic." Benton appears to have decontextualized Mr. Benson: he shows only a glimpse of land behind him. But his environment is there, in the "bumps and hollows" of his flesh. Benton, in fact, borrowed these terms, which refer to the convexities and concavities so noticeable in his canvases, from the idioms of topographic description in the Ozarks: the undulating copses and so-called hollers of that terrain. As Benton pictures him, Mr. Benson's face has taken on the features of his environment; he has lived his locale into his body, which is bent and crooked and undulates like the hills around Chilmark. Looking at *The Yankee Driver*, we know what Mumford meant when, reviewing a 1927 Benton exhibition in New York, he noted, Benton "draws people out of their soil, like potatoes, with the earth still clinging to them."

Perhaps due to stress over finances, Benton started drinking a lot on Martha's Vineyard, which got him into some infamous scrapes. Prohibition was merely an inconvenience during those island summers; Benton and his friends knew the schedules of the local rumrunners and would meet the boats with their illicit cargo at the shore. "We got down there before their trucks came along and picked it up off the beach," Benton explained. "We used to pick up scotch and rye, good Golden Wedding Canadian Whisky." If that failed, they'd mix up moonshine with water and glycerin. A Vineyard farmer named Craig Kingsbury told Burroughs some fantastic stories about the "hell-raisin' parties" that Benton and his friends attended. They usually started drinking at the Brug barn, where Tom and Rita stayed, and after Rita would throw them out, they'd move on to another party. On one occasion Benton beat up Max Eastman, the progressive writer and editor, and Mumford recalls an incident when a woman burst into his house one night, fleeing from Benton and his friend the artist Boardman Robinson, who'd chased her over the moors: "She wasn't one to mind the passes, but apparently she didn't like the smell of liquor, or at least wanted to keep the initiative in her own hands." The drunken men prowled around the house for hours.

In addition to these antics, though, Benton also got a political education on the Vineyard and started to build on what he'd learned from Weichsel. Before meeting Weichsel, Benton was skeptical of politics; Erika Doss believes that he was especially bitter about his father's generation's failure to modernize republicanism for the twentieth century and so as a young adult rejected "political liberalism as a failed ideology," taking up modernist aesthetics in its place. But under the influence of Weichsel, Benton began to formulate a leftist politics: he read *The Communist Manifesto*, discussed *Das Kapital* with his friends, and, as one living in poverty, grew to resent the wealthy. He recalls, in fact, that into the 1920s he felt invisible—"something less than nothing"— at New York parties, "where easy money, confident gesture, and the displays of quick and questionable success were much in evidence." In New York after the war and flat broke, Benton had also worked briefly as a stevedore on the Hudson River piers, a job he quit when he discovered that he'd been hired as a scab. "Although politically I was a conventional American Democrat," Benton explains, "and voted that way when I took the trouble to vote at all, I entertained ideas about 'capital and labor' much more radical than the Democratic party would have stood for. Thus no matter how much I needed money, I couldn't go on playing the 'scab,' even with what amounted to Union permission." In addition to Marx, Benton immersed himself in more generally leftist literature: through the writings of George Bernard Shaw, for instance, he became acquainted with British Fabianism, an early-twentieth-century socialist doctrine, and read Charles Beard, who reevaluated U.S. history to emphasize economic determinism rather than the heroics of the Founding Fathers.

Beard's faith in reformist politics influenced Benton's support of the New Deal in the 1930s, but Benton met Beard—an eminent historian who'd resigned from a teaching post at Columbia University in 1917 to protest the school's handling of professors opposed to the war— sometime in the early 1920s and frequently discussed art with him then. It was Beard's argument about the role of economics in the shaping of American progress that inspired Benton's mural series *The American Historical Epic*, which he began after his return from the navy. Though Beard did not advocate a proletarian revolution, arguing instead, as Richard Hofstadter puts it, for "an open and pluralistic theory that would have the feeling of Marxism for hard realities without its monolithic implications," Benton fashioned from Beard's arguments something more radical. Recalling this period, Benton writes:

> It seemed to those of us who tried to think in our poverty-stricken studios about what was happening around us that an entirely new world was due . . . [and] that Russian Communism, as the only practically operative form of Marxism, provided the most advanced form of society ever known and the most hopeful for mankind . . . My readings in American history were convincing me that the "people" of America—the simple, hard working, hard fighting people who had poured out over the frontiers and built up this country—were, more often than not, deprived of the fruits of their labors by combinations of politicians and big businessmen.

Whereas Beard observed that "economic elements are the chief factors in the development of political institutions" but didn't mandate a revolutionary reaction to this fact, Benton, in the early 1920s anyway, subscribed to Marxist principles. "I had agreed," he recalls, "that what was needed for 'peace and progress' was a 'people's society,' one where the people, that is, would have control over the instruments of production . . . I was pro-labor, anti–big capitalist, and psychologically ready for large-scale social change."

Within the community of artists and writers on Martha's Vineyard, Benton had ample opportunity to nurture his emergent political philosophy. In the summer of 1921, he and Craven again shared the Brug barn, and Rita stayed in the bungalow, and once again it was a fine summer. Rita earned a little money designing hats and bags for the sewing page of *The Ladies' Home Journal*, Craven worked on his essay for *Shadowland*, and Benton experimented with clay that he'd found at Vineyard cliffs. There was plenty of leisure, too. Craven wrote to Lizzie in June and cataloged the island's myriad delights: "Wild strawberries, sweaters, blankets, fish, lobsters, wind, ice water, swimming . . . washing, lamps . . . Yankees . . . old white clothes, white hats . . . flowers, fish, sea water, freckles, strength, and fish." And parties. The group attended many of the get-togethers at Barn House, a Chilmark summer colony started in 1919 by Stanley King, a Boston businessman, and later president of Amherst College. With a view of the ocean across rolling fields, Barn House was really a compound consisting of an eighteenth-century farmhouse, a barn, and some outbuildings and chicken coops. For a small fee, invited guests summered there, the only requirement being that they subscribe to socialist principles. The locals, Burroughs tells us, called it "that hangout for radicals." Among the many guests at the colony were the writers Max Eastman, Van Wyck Brooks, and Walter Lippmann; Roger Nash Baldwin, the founder of the ACLU; the legalist Felix Frankfurter; and Dorothy Kenyon, the feminist, judge, and civil liberties activist.

"They always had a punch made out of bathtub gin," Benton recalled, "and I got quite drunk on occasion." He did more than that, though, forging friendships based on intellectual and political interests with, for instance, Eastman and Boardman Robinson. Eastman was editor of *The Liberator*, the successor to *The Masses*, a leftist monthly that he'd edited until 1918, when it was closed under the Espionage Act of

1917 (a congressional response to radical criticism of U.S. involvement in World War I). Benton and Eastman had much in common. Though six years older and better educated, Eastman was from a well-to-do family and started kicking around lower Manhattan in 1912, the same year Benton moved into the Lincoln Arcade. Eastman also had a remarkable physique, though whereas Benton was short and strong, he was tall, tan, and Hollywood handsome. Before the war, he wrote poetry, lectured on philosophy at Columbia, edited *The Masses*, supported the feminist movement, and, as one historian puts it, "emerged as the orphic bard of the Left, the eloquent lyricist of liberation." Their deepest connection involved their relationship with the Left, for Eastman also turned against radicalism and infuriated his old allies by denouncing Soviet communism (and Marxism more generally). Like Benton, Eastman spent the years around World War I struggling with a basic tension: on the one hand, he believed in the power of poetry, of aesthetics, to describe "the immediate qualities of things" and to capture intensities of feeling; but, based on his admiration for Dewey ("It was not God but man that Dewey was worried about," he claims in a sketch of the philosopher), he also had a "dispassionate respect for the actual world of fact and experience" and trusted that pragmatism could reconcile poetry with practical knowledge. Marxism attracted Eastman for the same reasons that it attracted Benton: it seemed to suggest a method for linking imaginative ideals with concrete realities.

Benton's deepest connection was with Robinson, "a friend and helper year after year," with whom he likely bonded over a mutual disdain for the Académie Julian, where Robinson had studied in 1898. Robinson, who had a flaming-red mess of hair and a beard and was one of the country's most famous political cartoonists, had worked for Eastman at *The Masses* and *The Liberator,* making bold drawings of heroic workers and scathing antiwar sketches. In 1915, he'd accompanied John Reed, the prominent communist activist, on a tour of Russia to study the eastern front, and though he continued traveling to Europe for another eight years, he started spending summers on the Vineyard in 1917. Robinson probably met Benton for the first time at Barn House in the summer of 1921, when he was cartooning for *The New York Call*, a socialist newspaper with a no-nonsense masthead: "Devoted to the Interests of the Working People." "This was an important meeting for me," Benton declares, because Robinson shared his political views as well as a growing suspicion of the "more esoteric tendencies of the schools of Paris and the influence they were exerting in the United States." Benton was in the habit of waking up early in the summers, and by 1923, after their friendship had ripened, Robinson frequently joined him for dawn strolls to Windy Gates Cliffs or along the misty moors; Burroughs visualizes the men "staring out to sea with the roar of the breakers and the echoing rumble of pebbles churning in the ebbing tide." By this time Robinson was taking up painting, and he and Benton spent hours discussing Renaissance composition and working through the problems of form and subject. "He did the first experimentation that I knew anything about," Robinson said of Benton, and "though [his] technique was not flawless he did work intelligently and I profited by his keen reasoning."

Benton never produced radical or social realist paintings—he depicted productivity, not injustice or alienation, and he'd be accused of belittling radical art by the likes of Stuart Davis and Meyer Schapiro—but he and Robinson thought a lot about how to transform the aestheticism that dominated the 1920s into something tuned in to the experiences of the American people. Recalling his politics of the 1920s, Benton says that he was getting himself in "a psychological condition to face America." He wanted a cultural, economic, and political metamorphosis, and though by the early 1930s he was a pragmatist who believed that the nation already possessed the means—a republican tradition of autonomous producerism—to achieve it, this attitude was preceded by a progressive stance. Benton, for example, urged artists to be "part of the world," and his paintings reveal, according to Doss, "a concern with . . . communal fellowship and common values that could unite the American people."

Benton expressed his political views in *The American Historical Epic*, an ambitious series of narrative paintings. He began work on the project in 1919 and had completed the first five panels by 1925. He was inspired to paint the grandiose and didactic series when he saw Rubens's Marie de' Medici cycle in the Louvre and initially envisioned a series of ten "chapters," each made up of five painted panels, representing American history from discovery to the triumph of modern industry. Though there are various proposals about the sequence of the paintings, Benton quit working on the series in 1928, having finished three chapters totaling fourteen or fifteen panels. Benton is the source of this confusion. In

"My American Epic in Paint," the 1928 essay he wrote to defend the series against a claim that it wasn't really history painting, he implies that he conceived the cycle when he was in the navy and began work on the canvases in 1919. But Benton's memories of his early career are unreliable; he routinely miscalculated dates by a year or more. The fact is that Craven makes no mention of *The American Historical Epic* in his 1921 *Shadowland* article and that a letter Benton received that year from Edward Heyman Pfeiffer, whom he met at the Chelsea Neighborhood Association, implies that he'd just completed the first panel. "I am certainly interested in your plastic and symbolical history of the United States," Pfeiffer wrote, "of which the first is under your hand."

Like *People of Chilmark*, *The American Historical Epic* is difficult to categorize. The panels' style can only be described as modernist realism, and Benton's attitude here is leftist, even though his subject is history, not the present. In *Aggression* (1923) and *Retribution* (1924–1925), for instance, panels from the first chapter, Benton depicts the horrific attacks and counterattacks waged by settlers and Native Americans in their territorial wars. We can say that the panels are modernist because they depict propulsive, shapely forms in abstracted and bare spaces, but politically they adhere to Beard's revisionist thesis. Virtually all of the panels are violent; the brawny paintings feature guns, axes, and spears. The history Benton tells here is inexorable and totally determined by a struggle for resources—and the power and hate that this struggle engenders. The series is distinguished by Benton's trademark dynamism, but this dynamism isn't productive; instead, it results everywhere in wasted hillsides. Benton must have said something about this in his lost letter to Pfeiffer, for in his response his old friend encourages him to go ahead and paint "the organic ever-onward-pressing, changing inner forces that mold a restless agglomeration of peoples." (If Pfeiffer ever saw the panels, though, he was likely taken aback, as he couldn't have anticipated their cynicism and made a point to urge Benton to stay away from the "artificial, transitory concoctions brewed in tea-pots by agitators," meaning his radical friends.) Benton eventually made his intentions for the series as plain as can be:

> My original purpose was to present a peoples' history in contrast to the conventional histories which generally spotlighted great men, political and military events, and successions of ideas.

I wanted to show that the peoples' behaviors, their *action* on the opening land, was the primary reality of American life . . . [I]t was first suggested to me by Marxist-Socialist theory which . . . was very much in my mind when I turned from French-inspired studio art to one of the American environment . . . I had in mind, following this theory, to show that America had been made by the "operations of people" who as civilization and technology advanced became increasingly separated from the benefits thereof.

Between 1925 and 1928, Benton reaped the rewards of his sudden development of an environmentalist philosophy and style. In 1925, for instance, he exhibited panels from *The American Historical Epic* at the Architectural League of New York's annual exhibition at Grand Central Palace. In 1927, he hung nine panels from the series at the New Gallery on Madison Avenue as part of a larger exhibition that also included the six panels that made up his mural series *The History of New York* (1926–1927), which he had made on spec to the precise measurements of empty niches on the third-floor walls of the New York Public Library. *The History of New York* was essentially a compressed version of *The American Historical Epic*: it covered the same themes and history in just four panels and two lunettes. While the library never did acquire the panels and they languished in Benton's possession for years, critics admired them. Most of the reviews of *The American Historical Epic* and *The History of New York* focused on the panels' formal elements; Craven, for instance, remarked that the New Gallery exhibition "proclaimed in downright, unequivocal language what I believe to be the beginning of an epoch in American painting—the emancipation of the American artist from the French tradition." But some critics noted the paintings' political content. A writer for the *New York American* declared, "While these [paintings] sound conventional, they are not, either in point of view (witness the caustic comment on the treatment of the Indians) or in their acceptance of the law of mural painting that a wall must be flat." In a letter to *The Nation*, Boardman Robinson adumbrated the ideological slant of both series, asserting that they would be "shocking" both to "the hundred-percenter who resents an America shown so harshly" and to "the young communist who regards it as capitalist propaganda," thus portending the political imbroglios that would envelop

Benton's 1930s murals. (More recently, Matthew Baigell detected in *The American Historical Epic* a definite leftism: "Although Benton believed in the American Dream," he writes, "good Middle Western populist that he was, he saw no part of it in Wall Street buccaneering and economic exploitation of common people. On the contrary, his mural cycle was to show the embezzlement of the American Dream by predatory capitalism—an ambitious project at any time, let alone in the early 1920s.")

In 1927, before the New Gallery exhibition, Benton corresponded with Mumford, whom he'd met on Martha's Vineyard, and asked a lot from him. Specifically, he wanted Mumford to persuade his architect friends that both series were indeed murals—as opposed to a series of museum pieces—that could hang in a building. Mumford obliged by writing the essay for the exhibition catalog and, a few months later, a review in *The New Republic*. As he'd published books—*The Story of Utopias, Sticks and Stones* (1924), and *The Golden Day* (1926)—that argued for the value to contemporary writers and artists not of European trends but of vital American traditions in architecture and literature, Mumford was inclined to admire Benton's paintings. "Mumford's revisionism," according to the art historian Wanda Corn, was "dismissive of artists popular in their own lifetimes but newly appreciative of figures whose lives could be recounted as struggles against a rapacious American society." *The American Historical Epic* and *The History of New York*, Mumford believed, viewed U.S. history in a useful way. "Mr. Benton," he writes in the New Gallery catalog, "has followed the events from the raw wilderness of Nature to the equally raw and majestic wilderness of the Machine" without "reducing the subject itself to a subjective ghost, which may mean all things to all men because it means nothing precisely to any man." Later, in *The New Republic*, Mumford claims, "The idiom in which Mr. Benton expresses these things is his own; but behind it is a common American quality which we all share and easily understand; something that is both sober and intense, that seizes upon the most drab and forbidding objects—as Sandburg embraces Chicago, hog-butcher of the world—and by a certain naïve energy that makes them loveable, almost fine." He also saw Benton as a kindred spirit in political terms. In the 1960s, the men had a famous feud over the war in Vietnam, but in the 1920s both were unabashed leftists who were growing wary of the rigid ideology of American Marxism. But in his essay for *The New Republic*, Mumford observes that "Mr. Benton holds a nice balance between abstract design and those juicy gobbets of observation that reveal, a little acridly, our American scene."

Besides helping to forge an intellectual and political context for Benton's series, Mumford was the first critic to present Benton as a mural painter. Benton had always envisioned *The American Historical Epic* as a mural, and by 1925, after he hung the five panels of the first chapter at the Architectural League's exhibition, he was hopeful that the series would find a home—and not, he told Mumford, in a museum. But as with *The History of New York*, his wish never came true, and Craven claims that during this time his friend "was often referred to as a mural painter with no walls to decorate"; nevertheless, Mumford continued to insist that the series should be hung in public buildings. "Mr. Benton's major paintings," Mumford argues, "demand a definite place in a definite building," and he wrote a few months later, "If this art does not belong to the age of the Skyscraper, then Spengler is right: such an age has no place for art!"

Craven was always close with Benton's mother, and he announced in the winter of 1923 that he was getting married to Aileen St. John-Brenon, whom he'd met in Maine. Having heard so much about the pastoral appeal of the island and wanting to meet Craven's fiancée, Lizzie rented one of Ella Brug's bungalows, bringing along her daughter Mamie, whose husband was on naval duty, and Mamie's son, Nat. The next summer, Lizzie purchased two acres from George and Sabrina West. The land was adjacent to Brug's and had a view of Menemsha Pond and Vineyard Sound beyond, and by the summer of 1925 she had moved into a simple shingled house with a cathedral ceiling and a fieldstone fireplace.

Lizzie and Rita never got along, though. Both women were amateur artists and decorators, and both tried to manage Benton's career, but the main problem was that Lizzie, according to one Vineyard neighbor, was "vain and snobbish." She retained the haughtiness that she'd picked up in Washington as a congressman's wife and always resented her daughter-in-law's ethnic heritage. According to Jessie Benton, Lizzie "wouldn't let Rita in the house. She thought she was a 'damn foreigner.' But they dealt with it." Benton refused to take sides and visited his mother every day, always taking time to play games with young Nat.

Despite his drinking and the family tensions, Benton made a point of getting up early in the summers and painting each day. He was getting to know the islanders pretty well, and by the mid-1920s, he'd painted numerous portraits of the Wests, Frank Flanders, and Chester Poole, a temperance advocate who, finding bottles stashed on the beach by rumrunners, smashed them with a crowbar. Like *The Yankee Driver*, Benton's portraits of these uncultivated Vineyarders are earthy and colloquial—he depicts Frank Flanders, for instance, as a stolid man with a coarse face and swollen belly—and represent attitudes regarding "localism" that were articulated by Dewey, Williams, and Mumford. Benton, in other words, had absorbed the basic tenets of an "environmental" perspective before he started traveling through the Ozarks and the South, making sketches of the people he found there and practicing what's come to be called regionalism.

The Colonel, who was living alone, was diagnosed with throat cancer in 1923. In March 1924, Benton, apparently hoping to reconcile with his father, left Rita in New York and moved with him into a rented house near a hospital in Springfield, Missouri. For a month and a half, he sat at the Colonel's bedside watching him waste away and listening to fevered reminiscences of his Ozark campaigns. Benton's brother, Nat, who was practicing law in Missouri, stopped by occasionally to sit with them, but Lizzie remained in Great Neck until just a few days before her husband's death. In a letter to his mother written during the final weeks of the Colonel's illness, Benton described his father as "pitiful." "He was sleeping the other afternoon," he told her, "and as I watched him his jaws and hands were continually moving as if . . . intent on something. I watched him a long time. When he awoke he said he had dreamed he was cutting and eating a big steak with mashed potatoes. It was all I could do to keep the tears back."

Benton claimed to be transformed by his father's death. The Colonel's last days coincided with the Missouri Democratic convention, in Springfield, and dozens of delegates, including "Boss Tom" Pendergast, the corrupt political leader, visited their old representative in the hospital to shake his hand one last time. "I listened to old-timers try to revive my father's failing interest in things," Benton recalls, "and I got a renewed sense of the variety and picturesqueness of his life and of the life of the people of my home country which the infatuated artistic vanities of the city had brought me to regard as stale and stuffy." Burroughs believes that Benton exaggerated the degree of estrangement between father and son in order to dramatize the psychological effect of returning to Missouri to watch him die, but Baigell imagines a poignant experience full of Freudian symbolism: "In the conflict between his father's earlier rejection and Benton's desire for retroactive acceptance, Benton began to identify very closely with his father." Either way, he began to think differently about the legacy of his childhood experiences. Observing the Colonel connect with his constituency one last time compelled him to return to the environment—the Springfield Plateau and surrounding Ozark Mountains—that he hadn't visited since his father's campaigns.

He stayed in the area for two or three months, leaving Rita alone in New York, traveling dirt roads and making drawings and watercolors of farmers and their families. "The flavor of a premachine-age past hangs in [the] drawling speech" of Missourians, he explains, along with a "certain contempt for the regulatory claims of governing bodies . . . a heritage from our pioneer fathers." If not for the success of the exhibition, titled *In Missoura*, that Benton mounted at the Daniel Gallery in November 1924, he might have made less of his return to rural America. The critic Lloyd Goodrich reviewed the exhibition and admired Benton's ability to bring his figures to life. "He has struck a rich vein," he writes, "and it is to be hoped that he will continue to work it." Curiously, though, Goodrich believed that the artist was making fun of these rural characters. "He evidently has a natural flair for caricature," he observes, "somewhat akin to that of the comic strip artist." The comment foretold one of the principal controversies surrounding Benton's work in the 1930s, for his chief critics—such as Stuart Davis—viewed it as dime-novel history. Benton, of course, saw it differently and would argue that what his critics were really seeing in his art was their own arrogant attitude toward rural America: only "outsiders may laugh at [Missouri's] skeptical slowness," he says.

In the years following his father's death, Benton took numerous excursions into the hinterland, often alone. In the spring of 1926, for instance, he visited northwest Arkansas and southwest Missouri for a walking tour of the Ozarks, followed by a foray into Texas oil country. In the summer and autumn of 1928, he drove with Bill Hayden, a pupil of his at the Art Students League, through the South and out to the Rockies; he sketched in Wyoming in July 1930; and throughout the 1930s he returned periodically, usually in the summer, to the mountains of Virginia, Tennessee, and North Carolina. "All of this poking around the country," Benton reminisces in *An Artist in America*, "was not . . . 'for art's sake' alone. It was 'for fun' and, to no small degree, for release from art, or from the world of art." He adds, "I was moved by a desire to pick up again the threads of my childhood. To my itch for going places there was injected a . . . purpose which, however slight as a far-reaching philosophy, was to make the next ten years of my life a rich texture of varied experience."

Benton's trips were inspired in part by the memory of a grizzled, nomadic Pappy Wise, his mother's father, who, afflicted with a "foot itch," rambled about Kentucky, Tennessee, Missouri, and Texas, thus implanting in his descendants a "nostalgic craving to be up and going." Benton also describes his sojourns as being distinguished by Deweyan kinds of experiences, productive incidents of contact and communion. Though he'd been familiar with Dewey's work since the early 1920s and Dewey was famous enough by 1928 to appear on the cover of *Time* magazine in June of that year, Benton published *An Artist in America* in 1937, after reading Dewey's *Art as Experience* (1934), a seminal analysis of pragmatist aesthetics. According to Dewey, "Experience in the degree in which it *is* experience is heightened vitality. Instead of signifying being shut up within one's own private feelings and sensations, it signifies active and alert commerce with the world; at its height it signifies complete interpenetration of self and the world of objects and events." Another key point of Dewey's philosophy is that experience is widely available and instrumental; one can have an experience in the backwoods of Missouri or in a gallery of modern art, and, more important, one can say truly that one had *an experience* if it contains potential, if it can be used to help us get by in a chaotic world. Some experiences, Dewey understands, are useless: experiences that have "beginnings and cessations, but no genuine initiations and concludings," are "anesthetic." A consummate experience, on the other hand, has communal purpose.

What Benton tries to communicate in *An Artist in America* has something to do with authenticity, with the sort of experience that comes before subject and object are split, before habits of mind spoil perceptions. Having gleaned what he could from Dewey, Benton conceived of experience as what happens between a person and a place (or object) *before* ideology manifests itself; nevertheless, he uses the notion of experience in his memories of these months for ideological purposes. Written after he'd grown accustomed to defending his murals against attacks from the Left, the book attempts again and again to locate the genesis of his artistic philosophy in actual moments. It wouldn't do for Benton to link his ideas about experience to Dewey, or to any other writer for that matter. In order to be persuasive to his more discerning readers, Benton's philosophy of experience had to be seen as growing from experience itself—from the mountains and valleys of the Ozarks— rather than from intellectual discourses. But the experiences themselves were lost, having been transformed into memory, and at times it seems that he recalls them in the book for the sake of argument—to distinguish his development from that of supposedly elitist artists, as if they hadn't any experiences of their own.

But it's fair to say that Benton rubbed up against more of rural America than any artist of his generation. In the mine country of western Pennsylvania in 1928, for instance, he had sketched stooped miners and run afoul of superintendents and security guards. On one occasion, he and Hayden fled from a skeptical sheriff by driving a small dirt road across the state line into Virginia, where they ended up camping for the night by a stream in the hills. As darkness fell, they were visited by a group of "shaggy, unprepossessing toughs"—Benton describes them as "hillbilly protestants against the evils of industrialism"—who entertained them with stories about selling Prohibition whiskey and smut. Sex, oddly, is a featured topic in *An Artist in America*. "The industrial South is a great land for riotous whoredom," he tells us, and "the loudmouthed, Bible-quoting morality of its public citizens is a thin layer of hypocrisy over a lot of sexual filth." Benton was propositioned again and again in cotton-field villages, by white and black women alike, and endured ribald stories about farmers peeping at ladies, with their "paps a-stickin' up," washing in the brush by the river—a memory that surely influenced his scandalous 1939 painting *Persephone*.

He also encountered less friendly citizens in the backwoods. On his 1926 trip to the Ozarks, for example, Benton came across a rambling log house and called out to see if anyone was home. A woman poked her head out a window, said nothing, and disappeared. Just then a man approached him, wearing a black hat pulled low and carrying a rifle; he pointed his thumb toward a trail leading up a hill, and as Benton fled, he could feel the man's eyes "in the middle of my back until the foliage hid me." Another time, traversing the White River country along the Arkansas-Missouri line, Benton came across a ferryman, with a face "fat like a pillow," who refused to carry him across the river. Benton asked the man why he was ignoring him. "Say," he responded, "I c'n tell clever people no matter how they's dressed. I c'n tell 'um by their eyes." Then the man pointed Benton down a trail that disappeared a mile or so into the dense woods.

The principal pastimes in the woods were religion and music. The South, Benton observes, was afflicted with a "peculiar brand of ecstatic religion popularly known as the Holy Roller Faith" that blended a "wild mixture of sex, exhibitionism, and hysteria." Almost every day he stumbled across impromptu religious meetings distinguished by unconventional hymns, baptisms, and exorcisms that left congregants rolling on the ground in spasms and foaming at the mouth. Benton was both impressed and amused by these primitive rituals; they caused him to view the faithful as both ignorant and pure, as deluded but free from egomania, and he claims that their "Dionysiac madness moved me deeply" and caused "my sides [to] split with suppressed laughter." What got to Benton the most, though, was mountain music. Though he claims to have had no ear for music as a child, he was exposed early to Pappy Wise's expert fiddle playing and his mother's passion for the piano. From Virginia to Arkansas, music spilled out of the hills—hymns, bluegrass, and folk—and not surprisingly, Benton admired the authentic sound.

Benton exhibited his travel drawings alongside panels from *The American Historical Epic* at the New Gallery in 1927, which prompted Craven to write a review featuring his newfound nativism. By 1925, Craven had abandoned formalism in favor of "cultural organicism," or a reactionary criticism that denigrated the purification of art, which he saw as dehumanizing for how it set painting apart from experience. "The modern painter is an inferior being," Craven now believed. "Of all the workers in the arts," he explains, "he is the least alive—no man of brains and education could possibly waste his life in performances which are not only paltry and mechanical, but also totally divorced from current affairs." Craven's review of the New Gallery exhibition clearly exemplifies his shift to a criticism based on the adoration of American experience and the rejection of European trends. "In the parade of sentimentalists, merchants of illustration, and purveyors of the latest Gallic fads," the review opens, "the exhibition . . . stood out preponderantly, not only by reason of its rich achievement but as an indication of a new order of things . . . Mr. Benton brings a mind to American painting, but he brings something still better and rarer in this anarchic day—an Americanism which has challenged the modern European tradition with belligerent confidence." Mumford wrote the foreword to a brochure accompanying a later exhibition of travel drawings, and a few paintings, held at the Delphic Studios in late 1929. Though a more controlled analysis than Craven's, Mumford's piece strikes some similar notes, commenting that Benton's pictures, derived "by tough experience," embrace "the crudest humanity" in a refined manner.

Benton, these critics believed, was now a "regionalist," a term designating a frame of mind, even a method of sociology, more than a style of art. Mumford had examined the concept throughout the 1920s. He advocated countering the ill effects of metropolitanism with a "Regional Survey" that would reveal a "non-political grouping of population with respect to soil, climate, vegetation, animal life, industry and historic tradition." Specific areas of land, according to Mumford, must be used not for exploitation and the mere supply of material for the city center but as models of community and culture. Mumford encouraged community planners to build, "region by region," a "humanized" environment "with countryside and city developed together for the purpose of promoting and enhancing the good life." So Mumford's regionalism was built on a philosophy that local customs and common experiences trump political or ideological categories.

Benton's understanding of Mumford shaped his emerging attitudes regarding the value of communities and the hermetic intellectualism of modernism: his travel drawings, for example, were presented as communal and useful where modernism was closed and emotional. Benton transformed his experiences on the road into a Jeffersonian brand of populism. He became a chimera, half nineteenth-century idealist, half modern populist. As the historian Michael Kazin has shown, progressives who subscribed to socialist theories, and even to producerism, "were caught in a linguistic bind" and often employed a Marxist rhetoric, regardless of whether or not they supported revolutionary politics. "Using the Marxist vocabulary of their more powerful counterparts on the Continent bolstered their conviction of how the class struggle would end," he explains. "But talk of 'proletarians' toppling 'bourgeois rule' also offended Americans' reverential [attitude] about their political heritage, capitalist though it was." So while Benton would toss away Marxism, on the grounds that it was inflexible, in the 1920s he didn't yet see a contradition between his faith in a Jeffersonian producerism and radicalism. And Jefferson himself, it's worth pointing out, provides us with a "democratic critique of U.S. democracy" even as he provides us with a sense of democracy's possibilities. Not incidentally, Senator Thomas Hart Benton advocated for both the "productive and [the] burden-bearing classes," a position passed on by the Colonel. By the late 1920s, then, Benton had gotten from Dewey and Mumford several principles: a devotion to experience, an anti-elitist concept of art, and a confirmation that centralized intellectual and political power was contrary to democracy, the only political model that was practical for America. This, Doss says, was the foundation for Benton's republican liberalism; others say it was the basis for an American exceptionalism that resulted in a crude nationalism and xenophobia.

Benton's career was in full swing by 1926, the year his son, T.P., was born. He started to sell paintings based on his travel drawings and to publish more regularly. In December, for instance, he wrote a review for *The Arts* of a Constantin Brancusi exhibition at the Brummer Gallery. As an example of pure, essentialist art, the exhibition was an opportunity for Benton to express his ideas about the importance of subject and experience. He lauds Brancusi as "ingenious" and, in terms of craft, "nearly impeccable." "But," he adds, "these are academic virtues of the school, the studio, the cloister. They are the virtues that naturally result, the only virtues that could possibly come from the scholastic quest for 'essences,' for 'essential realities,' and they are comparable to those fine webs of strictly verbal logic spun by theologians about the qualities of God, perfect—and meaningless." Though his critique of Brancusi's formalism comes as no surprise, his belittling of the academy and the studio is odd considering that earlier that year he'd started his first regular teaching job—a post at the Art Students League secured for him by Boardman Robinson.

Founded in 1875 as an alternative to the genteel National Academy of Design, the Art Students League had more liberal enrollment, curriculum, and hiring policies. Early on, the school thrived under the oversight of William Merritt Chase, its chief instructor, and the influence of Robert Henri and John Sloan. In 1891, the spirit of the league was described in *Harper's* as practical and democratic. "Culture is not bought with French pictures and peach blow-vases," the author argues, adding, "[T]he aim of the Art Students' League . . . is not to make poets in paint, nor to transform stupidity into genius, but to make thorough craftsmen, good workmen, people who, when they have thrust a thumb through a palette, know what to do with the other hand." At the same time, the league, because of its progressive policies, was known as "a sort of Left Bank for young people," and some of its famous students included George Bellows, Georgia O'Keeffe, and Stuart Davis. The social realist painter Raphael Soyer studied there as well and deemed it "livelier, freer, noisier, and less orderly" than the National Academy.

The Art Students League was a social place; there were frequent parties and costume balls, and abstractionists and social realists, men and women, all painted together and gathered around easels for intense discussions about method and content. The league had no rigid pedagogical philosophy when Benton started teaching there, and instructors were "permitted complete freedom of method." But by most accounts, Benton was, at first anyway, a stiff teacher. Using "The Mechanics of Form Organization in Painting," his essays published in *The Arts* in 1926 and 1927, as a treatise, he arrogantly required his students to concentrate on bulging and recessive forms rather than light when working from live models. Stewart Klonis, who served as the league's president and executive director, remembered him as "pugnacious" and "very independent." Benton would walk up to his fifth-floor studio and stand at the door, calling out, "Anybody ready for a criticism?"

"What I taught was what I knew," Benton once said. "I taught what I was trying to learn," which he described as updating Renaissance and baroque composition based on a "semi-Cubistic" process. At least one student chafed under this regimen. Fairfield Porter, the painter and art critic, told an interviewer that "Benton's style as a man was that there is a body of knowledge and that it is three feet wide and one foot thick and that's it." Porter and Benton were quite close, in fact, and Porter, like several students, visited him on Martha's Vineyard, but later he grew annoyed with Benton's anti-intellectualism and critiques of Stieglitz. But Benton made up for his pedagogical shortcomings by breaking down the barriers between teacher and student. "I didn't treat them like the rest of the teachers did," he said. "Or like Mike [Boardman] Robinson did. He never let them get near him; he kept aloof, the great master stuff, you know. I never did that with them." And he took them traveling, too.

Hayden, for instance, and a student named Slim joined Benton on his journeys to the South and the West.

Jackson Pollock started studying with him at the league in the fall of 1930, at the suggestion of his older brother Charles, one of Benton's first students. Charles developed an interest in art at an early age, and many who knew him believed he would be the great artist in the family, but even as his brother surpassed him in skill and fame, he continued to aspire to greatness. Charles was well dressed and wore his hair long, and when, in 1922, he enrolled at the Otis Art Institute in Los Angeles, he became engrossed by *The Dial*, a seminal literary magazine of the modernist movement. But, he recalls, "whatever talent I had when I came to New York was nonexistent," adding, "I had only enthusiasm, excitement, and a burning desire to study with" Benton. He had read Craven's article on Benton in *Shadowland* and moved to New York in 1926 to enroll in the Art Students League. He lived a few floors below the Bentons on Eighth Avenue and frequently babysat T.P., and while he described Tom as "genial" and "very dynamic," he was closer to Rita, who adored all the Pollock boys and believed, at first, that Charles would surpass her husband as a painter. A refined and self-possessed young man, Charles was received warmly by the Bentons, once recalling that he "was almost a member of the family"; in return for babysitting T.P., for instance, he was invited to the Vineyard and well fed by Rita. He recognized Benton's imperfections—and, like his brother, would later try to shed his influence—but admired his mind: "He was highly intelligent, well read in certain areas and wrote highly competent prose articles in the early twenties." Without any pretensions about his own excellence, Charles enjoyed Benton's class; he was content to study technique and develop his skills, working in a regionalist style until the 1940s, when he turned to abstraction. (Charles would serve as the supervisor of mural painting and graphic arts for the Federal Art Project in Michigan from 1938 to 1942, and went on to teach printing at Michigan State University.) Frank Pollock, the third son, moved to New York in 1928 to be near Charles, and he too relied on the Bentons. Immediately after he arrived, Frank's first stop was the couple's apartment; flat broke, he asked for money. "Rita," he says, "took care of the Pollocks, see; she really loved us all."

Benton's salary at the Art Students League was over one hundred dollars a month, but he and Rita remained poor. His travels, their rental costs on Martha's Vineyard, and the arrival of T.P. stretched their budget. His teaching was going well enough, however, that in the late 1920s he was hired to give lectures at Bryn Mawr, Smith, and Dartmouth, opportunities that earned the family a little extra money. Benton asked Rita to find them a new apartment, one with heat and hot water, but she proposed that they instead purchase Wampum, the bungalow where Lizzie first stayed on the island. Rita wrote to Ella Brug with an offer, and they ended up buying Wampum for two thousand dollars. Benton remained, as ever, very productive, spending his summer days in a barn on the property that he'd set up as a studio. He painted images based on his travel drawings and developed a keen interest in the Mexican artists Diego Rivera and José Clemente Orozco, whose "humanistic" leanings appealed to him. He also "looked with envy" on the public mural commissions these artists received and decided that he, too, "must find walls."

8

EXPRESSIONS

An exhibition of drawings, watercolors, and a few paintings, which opened on October 14, 1929, at Alma Reed's Delphic Studios on East Fifty-seventh Street, solidified Benton's reputation as a painter of the contemporary American scene. Reed had a colorful but tragic past. On assignment in Mexico for *The New York Times*, she became engaged to the Yucatán's radical governor Felipe Carrillo Puerto, but in 1924, before the wedding, opposition forces assassinated Carrillo Puerto. Reed ended up in New York and in 1928 opened Delphic Studios, a gallery primarily intended to promote the work of her new lover, the Mexican muralist José Clemente Orozco, whom she first met in 1923. Before long, though, the gallery became a major venue for modern artists, including Ansel Adams, Edward Weston, and Georgia O'Keeffe.

For the exhibition, which documented his trip to the South the previous year, Benton divided his work into four subject groups—"King Cotton," "The Lumber Camp," "Holy Roller Camp Meeting," and "Coal Mines." Compared with his travel drawings from 1926, they are much more contextual; they manage to illustrate the "operations" and "processes" that Benton hoped *The American Historical Epic* would show. A painting of a Louisiana rice field, for instance, and a drawing of miners going to work are anecdotal and descriptive; we see the materials and procedures of particular kinds of labor in particular places and know that one force or another—desire, necessity, greed—compels these figures to convert rugged terrain into productive fields and mountain factories. This shift in Benton's style caught the eye of collectors and critics alike. Frank Jewett Mather Jr., a prominent professor of art history at Princeton, purchased a drawing of a mountain baptism. Lloyd Goodrich, writing for *The New York Times*, argued, "As an artist, Mr. Benton is a strangely contradictory temperament. The theoretical side of his nature is so strongly developed that his paintings seem mere demonstrations of his theories about form. And yet in these drawings all this side of his character is submerged; he has gone direct to reality and created work that has the true breath of life." In a different review of the exhibition, Goodrich added, "[The drawings] are comparatively free from the obvious forced rhythms of his earlier style . . . Their strength lies in their downright, matter-of-fact vigor. Everything in them can be touched and grasped, and what cannot be submitted to that test is apt to be ignored."

The 1928 painting *Boomtown*, which was featured in the Delphic Studios exhibition, illustrates Benton's turn toward analytical observation and anecdotal narrative, which were influenced by Frederick Jackson Turner's frontier thesis. Benton studied *The Significance of the Frontier in American History* (1893) in 1927 or 1928, and Turner's arguments, more than Marx's, corresponded to his memories of rural Missouri and, more crucially, the experiences he had on the American frontiers he'd just visited. This is one of the reasons that in the late 1920s he started to focus on more contemporary history. Based on a sketch made in Borger, Texas, where the Dixon Creek Oil Company had struck it rich in January 1926, the painting depicts the bustling, dusty town as seen from a window of Dilley's American Beauty Bakery. The town of Bolger had been banged together in the days immediately following the oil strike; an uninhabited barren plain became a town of thirty thousand with a frontier economy in just three months. Benton remembers the town as devious, totally slapdash, and stinking of gas. "Slot machines banged in drugstores which were hung with all the gaudy signs of medicinal chicanery and cosmetic tomfoolery," he writes, adding that whores, gamblers, and bootleggers were regularly run out of town by a ragtag group of Texas Rangers. The painting generally conforms to the historical evidence; Benton shows the cars, the pedestrians, the teetering buildings, and the seediness of opportunism. But he also shows a giant plume of black smoke rising from the oil well just beyond the town limits. This is the key detail of the painting, for the dense plume holds the overall design together but also, as Matthew Baigell puts it, "demonstrates the waste and pollution [Benton] has always deplored. The responsibilities to art are respected, but simultaneously an American quality of turmoil is communicated."

In a long, insightful essay on the painting, Karal Ann Marling argues that it is a "calculated mixture of documentary fact and epic drama," for it takes a few crucial liberties with the historical record. For one, Benton increases the relative height of many of the buildings. He also rearranges some of the town's commercial buildings, choosing, for instance, to paint a movie theater in the place where a drugstore stood. The first alteration transforms a flat expanse into a symbol of surging aspiration, while the second illustrates Benton's affection for populist entertainments. Marling even suggests that *Boomtown* exhibits a tawdry Americanism in order to insult modernism's more precious conceits. Though it's doubtful that the painting represents a deliberate attack on "the hermetic integrity of modernism"—as Benton still believed there was common ground between regionalism, modernism, and social realism—the painting annoys some present-day art historians for many of the same reasons that his 1930s murals would infuriate Stuart Davis and other critics.

Marling points out that the art historian James Dennis, in his book on Grant Wood, disputes the sincerity of Benton's regionalism. Dennis writes, "In lieu of familiar aspects of daily existence within a particular locale . . . immediately observed and drawn upon from memory, Benton favored remnants of the legendary past." He reiterated this position in a later book, critiquing Benton's "caricatured . . . cartoony images of working-poor folks" and accusing him of distracting "traumatized urbanites" from Depression-era anxieties. *Boomtown*, Dennis concludes, "speaks to the jackpot mentality of the American Dream: strike it rich and watch the money roll in."

Such arguments—that Benton dramatized and sentimentalized complex political and economic interactions that are best examined through analysis—have appeared again and again since Davis started publishing letters and essays demonizing Benton. In fact, one of the most fascinating aspects of Benton's legacy is that scholars continually reconstitute the rhetoric of his feuds with Davis and others. Henry Adams, who curated Benton's centennial exhibition (1989) at the Nelson-Atkins Museum of Art in Kansas City, and published his biography of the artist the same year, plays Benton to Dennis's Davis. Adams's analyses of Benton often come across as brash boosterism, which has annoyed many art historians, including Robert Hughes, who titled his review of the centennial exhibition "Tarted Up till the Eye Cries Uncle: Reviving the Vulgarity of Thomas Hart Benton." Whereas Adams reads *Boomtown* as great fun (and Benton as a heroic slayer of pretense), Dennis reads it as fraudulent. The painting really does mark a beginning for Benton, then; it's his earliest painting that continues to spark controversy.

Marling does the hard work of synthesizing these two arguments. In her final analysis, *Boomtown* is neither absurd mythology nor unpretentious documentary; it's a bit of both. On the one hand, the painting reifies Benton's new regionalist ideology—America is out there, not in Manhattan—and on the other it proves Turner's thesis: frontiers shape American character. And how did Benton know this? Not only because he saw as much in the shambolic spirit of Borger, but also because he himself had changed on the journey to Texas and become a different kind of artist while standing at the window of Dilley's American Beauty Bakery. He *experienced* transformation firsthand in that dusty town, and "new experiences," Turner maintains, are what the frontier gives us. So he knew he was telling the truth, only, as Marling points out, he told it artfully. Benton composed the very book in which he describes his trip to Bolger, *An Artist in America*, with great care, in such a way that he shows us how the "flight westward from an expiring Old World civilization" induced his rebirth as a regionalist. In a letter to Baigell, written in 1967, Benton admitted that he never believed an artist could actually illustrate Turner's thesis, explaining, "Turner's 'Frontierism' lent support, however, to my own more paintable conceptions of the development of our American culture—development through 'action of the people' as they moved west with the advancing frontier. This *action* I took to be more generative than *ideas* as our American culture took form. It was certainly more paintable." And it was "action," his trip to Borger, rather than an "idea" that led directly to his success (the Delphic Studios exhibition), so Turner's arguments seemed to corroborate his own experience of accomplishment. In the end, Benton decided that when it came to theories of determinism, Turner's thesis made for more interesting pictures than Marx's. Awkwardly for him, though, he made this decision just before the Depression and the retrenchment of the urban Left toward doctrinaire Marxism, and he'd pay dearly for provoking the ire of radical artists and critics.

•

On October 8, 1917, Charles Beard—whose historical analyses had influenced Benton's vision for *The American Historical Epic*—announced to his history class at Columbia that he was resigning from the university. Addressing the administration that same day, Beard claimed that the university had been infiltrated by activist trustees "who have no standing in the world of education, who are reactionary and visionless in politics, [and] narrow and medieval in religion." Beard resigned to protest the university's authoritarian president, who had fired two professors for expressing dissident views regarding U.S. intervention in World War I. In May 1919, James Harvey Robinson, also a professor of history at Columbia, resigned as well. Both men were progressive "new historians," and Robinson in particular drew on John Dewey's philosophy to formulate an instrumental social science. In his book *The New History* (1912), for instance, Robinson encouraged his fellow historians and teachers to relate the past to the present in such a way that their students could integrate history into their appraisals of and prescriptions for the current moment. "I have no reforms to recommend," Robinson states in his book *The Mind in the Making* (1921), "except the liberation of Intelligence."

Beard and Robinson quickly found a stimulating camaraderie within the circle of intellectuals associated with *The New Republic*. Herbert Croly, who founded the magazine in 1914, sympathized with the men and organized weekly meetings at his offices so they could discuss the formation of a truly liberated social science institute for the instruction of adult students. Participating in these sessions were such men as Dewey, the economist Thorstein Veblen, the publisher George Putnam, and Alvin Johnson, an associate editor of *The New Republic*. More quickly than any of the men could have hoped, Dorothy Straight, heiress to the Whitney fortune, pledged $100,000 to the project, and the New School for Social Research was an imminent reality. The school opened in February 1919, with Beard and Robinson as its quixotic co-directors, and offered a progressive curriculum based on Veblen's and Dewey's educational theories, which viewed learning as a continual process and a moral responsibility. In contrast to Columbia, which its president, Nicholas Murray Butler, maintained could ill afford "either political or religious controversy" due to its traditionalist and Christian roots, the New School founders insisted on exposing the moral and political ideologies that shaped social science. Upon its opening, on West Twenty-third Street in Chelsea, the New School invited "intelligent men and women" to study the "grave social, political, economic, and educational problems of the day" and to prepare for careers in journalism, labor organization, and teaching.

In part because the school's campus, which comprised six Victorian mansions, reinforced the institution's "clubiness [*sic*]," Alvin Johnson, who'd become director in 1922, initiated a capital campaign in 1927 with the aim of finding a new location. Insisting on a modern edifice in the International Style, Johnson hired the Austrian architect Joseph Urban to construct the school's main building on Twelfth Street in Greenwich Village. Urban had been a member of the Viennese Secession before moving to New York to become a set designer for the Metropolitan Opera, and he jumped at the chance to build a modern educational structure in the bohemian Village. The resulting building fulfilled Urban's goal to "house an idea"—an idea, in this case, of functional newness. The structure's facade, with its alternating, horizontal bands of brick and glass, resembles much International Style architecture; it's minimalist but practical. In its original state, however, the interior was more decorative, even expressive, than one might expect. Urban insisted that the walls and ceilings be painted with warm, cheerful colors— yellow, red, and green—and designed an organic, oval-shaped auditorium. In the end, Urban's building encapsulated two equally important principles of the New School: its faith in the contemporary and its emphasis on education as a progressive experience. Johnson was thrilled with the structure, describing it as "straightforward, rational and unafraid"; like the New School itself, he added, "it seeks to win a realistic understanding of the spirit of the past, but it lives in the present."

Many aspects of the New School appealed to Benton. Most obvious was the association that intellectuals whom he admired—Beard, Dewey, and Mumford, for instance—developed with the institution. Like Benton, these men were critical of capitalism—Beard, for instance, saw much of U.S. history as determined by conflicts between northern industrialists and southern and midwestern agrarians—but also skeptical of the cynicism of American communists. Benton agreed with all three that industrialism and technology had taken over the national economy but that social progress was still feasible within a republican system. By 1930, Benton had abandoned Marxism, disillusioned, as many others were, by Stalin's totalitarian society. Dewey agreed and, in the words of one historian, believed that "modern technology, communication, and scientific inquiry could be mastered and used to re-create the public." Benton was also sympathetic to Johnson's rhetoric about the intermingling of the past and the present; by 1926, Benton says, he was "stumped by the Marxist picture of history as a 'dialectic' progression," an argument he came to see as a mere "intellectual feat." Johnson's notion that liberation was possible, so long as a modern social scientific method was brought to bear on the past, meshed with Benton's attitude that the means for transformation were already in place. Benton had already illustrated these ideas in *The History of New York*, the mural series he'd hoped would be purchased by the New York Public Library in 1927. The second panel in the series, *1653: Pilgrims and Indians*, represents a malicious but familiar episode from American history: unsavory Dutch settlers offer a Native American a barrel of liquor in exchange for furs. Thus begins the nation's often abusive economy of self-interest. But Benton attempts to resolve this legacy in the final panel, *1927: New York Today*, which shows a cooperative force of laborers digging the foundations and maneuvering the steel beams that support the modern structures of the city. History may be ugly, Benton says, but the dynamism of the present—the want-to and the progressive spirit—can buttress a triumphant modernity.

When Johnson assumed control of the New School, he diversified its emphases, orienting it toward modern culture as well as modern social science, and added courses taught by some of the leading critics and artists of the day. In addition, Johnson instructed Urban to design walls that could hold floor-to-ceiling murals in the school's dining room and some of its seminar rooms. When Alma Reed, of the Delphic Studios, learned that Johnson was interested in installing murals in Urban's building, she immediately contacted Mumford and asked to be introduced to Johnson. Reed's motive was to secure wall space for Orozco, and the two worked out a deal whereby Orozco would paint frescoes for the fifth-floor cafeteria: Johnson would pay only for the cost of the materials and in return for such a meager benefit would grant the artist almost total freedom. "Paint me a picture," Johnson instructed. "Paint as you must. I assure you freedom." When Benton heard the news from Ralph

Pearson, a friend who taught art at the New School, he was irritated, believing that Reed had neglected him by only representing Orozco. He had great admiration for the Mexican muralist, whom he saw as a kindred spirit—"the Mexican concern with publicly significant meanings," Benton later explained, "and with the pageant of Mexican national life corresponded perfectly with what I had in mind for art in the United States"—and believed he was up to the same task. Pearson took up Benton's cause and marched into Johnson's office demanding to know why an American muralist had been ignored. Sensing that he could commission another mural series on the same terms, Johnson agreed to include Benton and so secured the services of two top muralists for next to nothing. The specifics of the deal were worked out between Rita and Johnson at a Greenwich Village party: it was agreed that Benton would paint murals for the boardroom in return for the price of the eggs (used in the tempera) and modest recompense for a few lectures at the New School. In the end, Johnson's only instructions for the two painters were that they depict contemporary life and make works so great that "no history book written a hundred years from now could fail to devote a chapter to [them]." Reed was angered by this maneuvering and received the news of Benton's commission "very frigidly"; as Benton remembers it, she believed that he had acted opportunistically, an accusation that was, he claims, "plausible." In retrospect, however, Benton's behavior appears reasonable; his exhibitions at the Delphic Studios had been well reviewed, he'd been working on mural series for ten years, and he took advantage, as any poor artist would, of an opportunity to associate himself with a grand enterprise. At the age of forty but still possessing the combativeness of his youth, Benton finally had the attention of the public he claimed to know so much about.

Johnson rented a loft to serve as Benton's studio. It was just a few blocks from Urban's building, and Johnson visited the studio every day to check on the progress of the murals. Benton painted his scenes on wallboard coated with heavy linen, and though his process was labor-intensive—he covered the panels in gesso, sketched on them with distemper, and finished them with egg tempera (Johnson claims that Benton "bankrupted" him by purchasing "dozens and dozens of eggs")—he worked quickly, completing the *America Today* murals in nine months. According to Johnson, Benton would piece together drawings and then make a "little garden of the needed solids in clay and study it painfully" before making the distemper underpainting. Most of the drawings that he used for inspiration were from his earlier tours of the South and the Midwest, but he also made some new drawings specifically for the murals. For instance, Johnson asked a Wall Street friend to arrange for Benton access to the Bethlehem Steel plant in Sparrows Point, Maryland, and his studies of the facility were the source for the panel *Steel*, which shows strong, determined men laboring with vats of molten metal. As he was working on the panels, the painter Reginald Marsh visited Benton in his studio, where Benton held forth on the benefits of egg tempera, gleaned from an early-fifteenth-century handbook by Cennino Cennini. Benton's use of historical techniques was another way that he rejected modernism as decadent and un-American, and egg tempera (egg yolk mixed with dry pigment and water) was a medium that connected him to the old masters. Tempera has been described as a "draftsman's medium" because it "encourages precise lines and sculptural modeling"; in addition, it is easier to control than oil because it dries faster and is more durable. Marsh's description of his visit serves as the best summary of Benton's working methods:

> When I first got acquainted with him, I called upon him frequently, apparently always in time to help him carry about the studio his 400 lb. murals . . . The time was summer and it was amusing to watch Benton, muscular in his underwear, sit low in his armchair, survey the mural, suddenly load his brush with a lot of tempera goo, crouch like a cat, spring across the room in a flying tackle, scrub the brush around in great circles, catch his breath, and then resume his place in the chair.

The lectures that Benton gave at the New School were titled "Craftsman and Art" and likely emphasized the artisanal methods of art production rather than its more romantic myths. One reason that Benton favored working with the egg tempera, for instance, was its association with the Italian Renaissance, a period he admired as much for its system of training, apprenticeship, and craftsmanship as for its grand manner. Painting, Benton believed, was a manual labor as much as it was an intellectual exercise. This, as well as his various attitudes regarding industrial life, explains the mural's vision of modern America.

In places Benton found it impossible to connect scenes in one panel with those in another, and in these instances Urban was able to help by designing art-deco aluminum-leaf moldings to frame the scenes. All in all, though, Benton's great accomplishment in *America Today* was to integrate each discrete narrative into an overall dynamic scheme; he managed to weave together seemingly incongruous aspects of American life—popular entertainments, for instance, with representations of agricultural and urban labor. As a result, *America Today* functions as both a critical analysis of labor throughout American history and a celebration of popular culture. As in the work of John Dos Passos, these different aspects of life—labor and entertainment—occasionally complement each other and occasionally conflict. In his *U.S.A.* trilogy, published between 1930 and 1936, Dos Passos combined various modes of writing: "Newsreels," "Camera Eyes," biographical portraits, and fictional narratives. This fractured writing confounded the critics; as Michael Denning puts it, they couldn't decide whether Dos Passos was "a Marxist, a Veblenite, a Beardian, a technocrat, a Binghamite, an anarchist, or a Whitmanian democrat." In a "Statement of Belief," published in 1928, Dos Passos himself had said, "The only excuse for a novelist, aside from the entertainment and vicarious living his books give the people who read them, is as a sort of second-class historian of the age he lives in."

The analogy is useful not just because Dos Passos and Benton shared a similar political progression—both were leftists in the 1920s but later turned on Marxism—but also because Benton's critics, those of his time and contemporary art historians alike, have struggled to classify the politics of the mural. The main question seems to be whether *America Today* represents industrial capitalism's destruction of true democracy or the triumph of a producerist ethos despite the nation's industrialization after the Civil War. It turns out that the answer, as is so often the case, is both, which makes sense, considering that when Benton executed the mural he was in the midst of his transformation from a Marxist to a skeptical Democrat.

The mural was unveiled on January 15, 1930, and Benton claims that because it "contained no specifically anticapitalist or revolutionary imagery," radical groups labeled him a "chauvinist" and a "reactionary." Though Johnson sensed that he was "destined for difficulties about those paintings" and acknowledged that one critic complained to him that Benton had "no social philosophy" and "depicted the gigantic, inhuman machinery of industrialism with never a pathetic note for the wage slaves operating it," the vast majority of reviewers lauded the mural, even as they recognized some of its ideological ambiguities. (Most negative criticism of Benton emerged after he completed his second mural, *The Arts of Life in America*, for the Whitney Museum of American Art.) For his part, Johnson was thrilled with Benton's work, and to the tetchy critics he responded, "I too have seen the men in industry operating thousand-horsepower machinery. They look triumphant, they feel triumphant, they *are* triumphant." But the mural's political equivocations flummoxed most reviewers. One writer, for instance, observes that the mural is full of paradoxes, noting that it "reveals the power, strength and harshness of our rapid, hilarious life," and even Craven, Benton's most vocal booster, acknowledged its ironies. "What is chaotic in Benton is his modern America, and who can deny the factual and spiritual truth of this aspect of his work?" he asks. But the mural will be valued, he concludes, "because it is veracious experience and not futile prophecy." Edmund Wilson, reviewing the mural in *The New Republic*, also qualified his conclusions. "These pictures," he writes, "are tangled and jarring: they strain like the life they represent, and their forms can never seem to rise alive out of something basically heavy and hard . . . But they are true images and products of that life." In sum, what these critics agreed upon was that Benton's accomplishment was his refusal to be either wholly cynical or wholly optimistic about America's transformation from an agrarian republic into an industrial society.

Over the past twenty-five years, art historians have worked hard to develop the right terminology to describe the attitudes represented in *America Today*. Indeed, because the ambivalence of the mural's political ideas is representative of Benton's political woolliness more generally, it's fair to say that analyses of *America Today* are some of the most insightful about his work. Emily Braun, in one of the first revisionist studies of the mural, insists that Benton was no backward regionalist but a purveyor of "progressive liberalism," a school of thought articulated best by Beard, who recognized the alienating effects of technology but believed that a true "industrial democracy" could be achieved with pragmatic means rather than "dogma or revolution." This attitude is represented, for instance, by contrasting the heroic workers in the panel *Steel* with the hunched miner in *Coal*, who seems utterly defeated by mechanized labor. Another art historian, Elizabeth Broun, also rejects the easy characterization of Benton as an "escapist" who retreated to a mythical Jeffersonian agrarianism. He was instead a man of his moment and a liberal populist who, like Whitman, saw vitality everywhere: hence the boxers and burlesque girls in the panel *City Activities with Subway*. Erika Doss synthesizes these revisionist analyses of Benton's populism and progressive liberalism. The mural, she concludes, illustrated that "in modern America the producer tradition was not just healthy, it was dominant." Benton, she explains, was not stuck in the past but rather "transferred an older republican ideal of the American worker to a contemporary setting." Like Beard, Benton was wary of industrialization, but the mural "announced human liberation through producerism."

But no matter how persuasive these scholarly analyses are, most viewers—everyday admirers and cultural critics alike—continue to judge *America Today* a nationalist work of art. Conservative critics have remained enraptured by what they perceive as the mural's advocacy for American principles in the face of foreign influence, while critics with different sympathies have remained outraged by Benton's "Populist/Capitalist Realism" and claim that its "synthesis of the national and industrial landscape was used to celebrate American cultural exceptionalism." Even Elizabeth Broun, an admirer of Benton's mural, acquiesces: "In this high-spirited salute to American independence the abstract theory of social order finds no place." By avoiding "the abstract theory of social order"—the political radicalism that was as much a part of urban life as Benton's progressive populism—Benton exposed himself to rebuke. Critics could rightly claim that he had a limited view of the American scene because he failed to represent the vigorous rituals of leftist politics. For instance, whereas he depicted most figures in the mural as dynamically engaged with the environment around them, Benton upset his leftist friend Max Eastman by showing him sitting idly on the subway, distracted by a sexy young woman, rather than participating more meaningfully in the pageantry of American life.

Some of the complexity of the mural's politics stems from the ambiguity of the term "populism," for as students of American history or contemporary politics well know, populism serves the Left and the Right equally well. In 1834, Senator Thomas Hart Benton saw no distinction between producers and "burden-bearing classes" and, according to Michael Kazin, maintained that "having an occupation, doing the necessary work of society, was what entitled 'the people' to have power." Such a theory, which Benton inherited from his family and adapted for the

Depression era, borrows from both liberal and conservative principles: it grants power to the collective "people" but demands that they be productive by conventional standards. As Kazin puts it, "American populism binds even as it divides"; to argue "that most citizens—whatever their occupation or income—are moral, hardworking people denies the rigorous categories of Marxism and the condescension of the traditional Right." It's the populism of *America Today*, then, that explains its equivocal representation of the United States as both a democratic and an exploitative nation. Like populism itself, Benton's mural is a "grand form of rhetorical optimism": it represents a state that is fully prepared to save itself. Benton didn't intend for the mural to represent an attack on Marxism, however; he intended for it to illustrate the essentially hopeful attitudes of the progressive thinkers associated with the New School. Put simply, Benton had good reasons for wanting to please his patron. Doing so meant staying true to his family's political philosophy, satisfying the requirements of a business contract, no matter how disadvantageous to him financially, and therefore, with any luck, earning more commissions. He was successful on all fronts.

Benton lived well for the four months or so following the completion of the New School mural. Rita worked hard to sell his work and received good money for his *America Today* studies. His brand of whiskey improved, and the family hosted many parties, funded in part with money from Rita's sales. "The freedom with which [the whiskey] was served became famous," Benton recalls, "and Rita and I, taking stock one early morning of our more or less inebriated guests, discovered we had never met a damned one of them before." They shut down the parties and escaped to Martha's Vineyard to recuperate, spending the Christmas holiday of 1930 on the island, ice fishing and staying warm near their coal stove. When the Bentons returned to New York after the New Year, Tom was upset by some of the negative comments directed at the mural by various friends, especially Boardman Robinson and Ralph Pearson. Such a bold statement about American national culture was bound to ruffle a few feathers, but Benton bristled at the slightest criticism and fell into a deep funk. In February 1931, he escaped by himself to the Vineyard but fell ill with a bad flu and spent several weeks shivering in the hospital.

Before undertaking his next mural project, Benton received an invitation from the historian Leo Huberman to illustrate his book *We, the People* (1932). Likely he was relieved by the request, as Huberman was an outspoken Marxist writer and educator and his interest in Benton's work vindicated the mural's politics. Based upon his impression of the representation of the laboring classes in the New School mural, Huberman felt that Benton was a good choice to illustrate *We, the People*, a history of America written for an adolescent audience. For his part, Benton claimed later that he was still sympathetic to Marxism and in "intellectual harmony" with Huberman. The book, though light on Marxist rhetoric, is a socialist manifesto; it caricatures capitalists as unfeeling, bottom-line men and describes producers as victims of a cruel calculus: "There was no way out—work or starve." The greatest American invention, the author argues, was not the factory but the union. "Alone they could do nothing," Huberman writes. "Organized together as one group, they could exert pressure on their employers." One reviewer, claiming that Huberman was an heir to Beard's kind of history, concisely summarized the book's accomplishments. "Huberman," he writes, "has pitched out of the window all the lying solemnities with which our school children today are being tricked by the official historians: the high-mindedness of politicians, the righteousness that always characterized American causes, the social usefulness of the private acquisition of wealth, the disinterestedness of the state in class antagonisms."

Marling asserts that Benton's drawings for *We, the People*, which were based on sketches he made during his 1928 trip, demonstrate "how ill-used he was by his critics on the far left." Like Huberman's nononsense prose, Benton's illustrations are blunt and effective. In one titled *The Colonial Social Ladder*, for example, he arranges four bust portraits in ascending order to represent the hierarchy of men during the nation's settlement. A black figure writhes in the lower register, and above him, in order, are a sorrowful Native American, a proud frontiersman wearing a coonskin cap, and, finally, a fat colonist clutching a piece of paper (likely containing empty promises about equality and justice). Most of the drawings are narrative, but others are equally forceful in their symbolism, such as one that compares an early metalsmith with two heroic workers in a modern steel mill—thus connecting industrial work with a more obviously dignified mode of production—

and another that shows striking workers demonstrating before a brutish enforcer.

Besides this small project, Benton kept busy in the years between his first and his second murals by dedicating himself to his teaching at the Art Students League. Though not the most innovative teacher pedagogically, he continued to encourage camaraderie among his pupils and often invited them to his apartment (first on Abingdon Square, later at 8 West Thirteenth Street) to play harmonica and sip from the whiskey jug. In the classroom, Benton depended on Renaissance, mannerist, and baroque greats and emphasized compositional dynamism; he pushed his students to strive for both surface and dimensional vitality. Though Fairfield Porter complained about what he perceived as Benton's ornery anti-intellectualism, he did credit his teacher with stimulating his taste for Tintoretto and Rubens. Joseph Delaney, an African American painter who studied at the Art Students League in the early 1930s, was much more grateful for these lessons on the old masters. As Delaney remembered it, Benton favored Botticelli, Raphael, Michelangelo, Titian, and Cézanne and supplemented his formal lessons with discussions of Taine's theories about the environmental influence on artistic expression. Delaney credited this exposure to Taine with helping him to make sense of his identity as a black artist from the South and concluded, "Benton will be with me always."

Benton attracted, and was attracted to, a certain type of student. Younger artists from more humble backgrounds admired his populism and appreciated his sympathy for the poor and dispossessed. He was undoubtedly skeptical of wealthier and better-educated students such as Porter, who'd gone to Harvard, and was eager to help those who lived through the sort of poverty he experienced during his first years in New York. This preference for students from certain classes was part of Benton's anti-elitism, and whether fair or not it earned him a great deal of admiration and loyalty from a cadre of students. In the words of Steven Naifeh and Gregory White Smith, co-authors of a Pollock biography, it was in "the role of the 'man's man'" that Benton made his mark:

> Such was its power that, despite rejecting his art and denouncing his political views, an entire generation of artists was shaped by Benton's archetypal machismo. What Hemingway was to a

generation of writers, Benton was to a generation of American painters, the ideal against which, consciously or unconsciously, they measured themselves—as drinkers, as fighters, as rebels, as provocateurs, as womanizers, as debunkers, as outsiders, as Americans, and as artists.

Sensational as this portrait may be, Benton's gruff manners and primitive speech alienated some students at the league; in their view, he was inflexible, arrogant, and occasionally cruel. Whitney Darrow Jr., who would become a cartoonist at *The New Yorker*, thought very little of him as either "an artist or a teacher," and Alexander Calder, the famous sculptor, described Benton's classroom dictum—"Even if it's wrong you make it definite"—as a ridiculous precept. Reggie Wilson, another league student, recalls that Benton came into the studio and "was rigorous about drawing the figure—draw, draw, draw—*his* way . . . Tom was the kind of teacher who wasn't very interested in you unless you did things exactly the way he thought they should be done." Benton had no interest in finessing the technique of his students, and he certainly played favorites (which is the likeliest reason for the mixed feelings about his teaching), but one student believed he was simply a blowhard. Edith Simonds, a displeased female student of his at the Art Students League, says that he wore his "hard-boiled, rough-fellow manner the way an artist puts on a cape so he'd seem a hillbilly." But it's also possible that these less admirable qualities of Benton's teaching had less to do with a character flaw than with his inexperience, the lack of pedagogical training at the league, or the simple fact that, in the early 1930s especially, he was preoccupied with his mural commissions and financial insecurity. The reasons for his apparent misogyny, however, are more perplexing. By many accounts, he treated his female pupils poorly and, in the words of a male student, Mervin Jules, lost the respect of the "menopause crowd." Simonds recalls that though she learned about frescoes and egg tempera from Benton, "he never said my work was any good." He "didn't think women should be painters," she says; "he would look at the work of a dear friend of mine . . . and tell her to go down and draw a skeleton," an ironic suggestion considering Benton's distended figures.

A Benton neighbor on the Vineyard claimed that Rita would "tell everyone that Tom hated women because of his mother," who was now

Thomas Hart Benton, *Self-Portrait with Rita*, 1922, oil on canvas.

Benton, *City Activities with Subway,* from *America Today,* 1930, distemper and egg tempera on gessoed linen with oil glaze.

Ferdinand Thomas Lee Boyle, *Senator Thomas Hart Benton, Statesman*, ca. 1861, oil on canvas.

(National Portrait Gallery, Smithsonian Institution. Photo: National Portrait Gallery, Smithsonian Institution/Art Resource, NY)

Maecenas Eason Benton in 1897.

(State Historical Society of Missouri)

Benton, "*. . . The retired artist sat on a barrel in the shade close by . . .*," pen and ink, illustration for *The Adventures of Tom Sawyer*, Mark Twain.

(New York: The Limited Editions Club, 1939. State Historical Society of Missouri. Reproduced with the permission of Easton Press, MBI, Inc.)

Benton, detail of *Politics, Farming, and Law*, from *A Social History of the State of Missouri*, 1936, egg tempera and oil on canvas mounted on panel.

Benton, *Joplin at the Turn of the Century*, 1972, acrylic on canvas mounted on panel.

Stanton Macdonald-Wright, *Self-Portrait*, 1907–1909, oil on canvas.

(The Nelson-Atkins Museum of Art, Kansas City, Missouri. Gift of the Enid and Crosby Kemper Foundation, F89-39. © Estate of Macdonald-Wright, 2012. Photo by Jamison Miller)

Stuart Davis, *Self-Portrait*, 1912, oil on canvas.

(Courtesy of Curtis Galleries, Minneapolis. Art © Estate of Stuart Davis/Licensed by VAGA, NY)

Benton, left, with companions in Neosho, ca. 1912.

(Courtesy of Neosho Historical Society)

Stanton Macdonald-Wright, *Abstraction on Spectrum (Organization 5)*, ca. 1914–1917, oil on canvas.

(Purchased with funds from the Coffin Fine Arts Trust; Nathan Emory Coffin. Collection of the Des Moines Art Center, 1962.21. © Estate of Macdonald-Wright, 2012)

Benton, *Bubbles*, ca. 1916, oil on canvas.

Benton, *Harbor Scene, Norfolk, Virginia*, 1918, watercolor on paper.

Benton, *People of Chilmark*, 1921–1922, oil on canvas.

Benton, *The Yankee Driver,* 1923, oil on canvas.

ABOVE: Benton, *Miners Going to Work*, 1928, pencil, pen, ink, and ink wash on paper.

LEFT: Benton, *Aggression*, from *The American Historical Epic*, 1919–1924, oil on canvas, mounted on aluminum honeycomb panel.

Benton, *Boomtown*, 1928, oil on canvas.

Jackson Pollock, *T.P.'s Boat in Menemsha Pond*, ca. 1934, oil on tin.

(New Britain Museum of American Art. Gift of Thomas P. Benton, 1973.113. Art © 2010 The Pollock-Krasner Foundation/Artists Rights Society (ARS), New York)

T.P., Tom, and Rita playing musical instruments in New York, ca. 1933.

(The Nelson-Atkins Museum of Art, Kansas City, Missouri. Ann Constable Collection)

Alfred Eisentstaedt, *Coburn Gillman, Jackson Pollock, and Rita Benton*, 1937.

(Time & Life Pictures/Getty Images)

Benton, *Arts of the West*, from *The Arts of Life in America*, 1932, egg tempera and oil glaze on linen.

Benton, *Parks, the Circus, the Klan, and the Press,* from *A Social History of the State of Indiana,* 1933, egg tempera and oil on canvas.

Imogen Cunningham, *Alfred Stieglitz at An American Place*, 1934, gelatin silver print.

Benton, *Preparing the Bill*, 1934, oil on canvas.

Benton, *Huck and Jim* (top center), from *A Social History of the State of Missouri*, 1936, egg tempera and oil on canvas mounted on panel.

Benton, *Frankie and Johnny* (top center), from *A Social History of the State of Missouri*, 1936, egg tempera and oil on canvas mounted on panel.

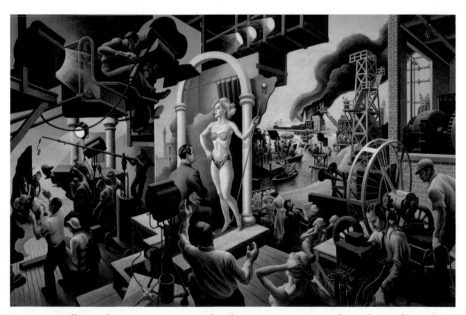

Benton, *Hollywood*, 1937, tempera with oil on canvas, mounted on plywood panel.

Alfred Eisenstaedt, *Thomas Hart Benton
Painting "Persephone,"* 1939.

(Time & Life Pictures/Getty Images)

Benton, *Persephone*, 1939, tempera with oil glazes on canvas, mounted on panel.

Townsend Godsey, *Thomas Hart Benton, Grant Wood, and John Steuart Curry at Benton's house in Kansas City*, ca. 1938.

Benton sketching by a river.

Benton, *Father Hennepin at Niagara Falls*, 1961, oil on canvas.

Advertisement for Lucky Strike cigarettes, *Life*, July 20, 1942, featuring Thomas Hart Benton's *Outside the Curing Barn*, 1942.

Former President Harry S. Truman climbing scaffolding to chat with Benton and inspect the mural *Independence and the Opening of the West* in the lobby of the Harry S. Truman Library in Independence, Missouri, December 18, 1959.

Benton, *Independence and the Opening of the West*, 1958–1961, acrylic polymer on linen mounted on panel.

Benton, *Again*, from *The Year of Peril*, 1941–1942, oil and tempera on canvas mounted on panel.

Benton, *Flight of the Thielens*, 1938, oil and tempera on board.

Benton sketching Henry Look on
Martha's Vineyard, ca. 1941.

Benton, *New England Editor*,
1946, oil and tempera on
gessoed panel.

Benton, *The Sources of Country Music*, 1975, acrylic on canvas mounted on panel.

splitting her time between Long Island and Martha's Vineyard. Rita clearly felt it necessary to justify something that cannot be justified, but what's stranger is that Benton's insufferable ignorance on this score did not upset their marriage. In fact, his tough treatment of women was partly a result of a repartee that he rehearsed every day with his wife. They were fiercely devoted to each other and developed, as all couples do, a banter built on exaggerated versions of themselves: Rita played the tough Italian wife and Benton the profane, insensitive husband. "They were always hollerin' at each other," a neighbor recalls, "and he used words that made a child's hair curl." Maria Piacenza, Rita's niece, describes the couple's back-and-forth bickering as a system of checks and balances, even a kind of intimacy. "Whatever abuse she got from Tom," she says, "he got his back." The problem was that while these theatrical exchanges may have seemed cute in the privacy of their apartment, they lost their charm in public; Benton's machismo simply turned off his female students.

Despite these disturbing shortcomings, Benton could be a demanding teacher, which his students appreciated. His pupils spent fifteen hours a week sketching nude models so that they might be able, in the words of one student, Axel Horn, "to articulate and express the softness, the tensions, the recessions, and the projections of the forms that together make up the human figure." Horn recalls that Benton even demanded that his pupils caress the models' naked bodies "to identify the direction and shape of a particular muscle or bone." He also spent many hours in the library with his students analyzing old-master drawings and philosophizing about Renaissance composition. His particular gift as a teacher was to combine these formal lessons with casual instruction, at hoedowns in his apartment, for instance, which gave his students a sense of how their art studies might pertain to the lives they lived. Though he could come across as merely anachronistic, Benton meant to demonstrate the relevance of tradition—in music, in art, in relationships—to modernity and so he had devotees, especially the Pollock boys: Charles, Frank, and Jackson.

One thing that connected the Pollocks to Benton was drinking. "You know," Frank recalls, "Sande [the second Pollock son] drank, I drank, Charles drank, we all drank." And Benton was there for a lot of it. Charles describes him as a "four-square drinker" but points out that he could hold his alcohol: "He was never out cold, contentious or violent."

Much of the time, in fact, he was performing music. The Pollocks typically went on benders with Benton on Monday nights, during the musical gatherings in his apartment, where bootleg liquor was in abundant supply. Benton didn't drink when he painted or taught, but he swilled plenty during these jam sessions. During his depression after the New School project, he'd picked up T.P.'s toy harmonica and discovered that he had Lizzie's talent for music. He became obsessed with the instrument, calling it "a revelation from heaven," and developed a unique notation system, still used today by commercial music publishers, that's easier for novices to read than a typical scale system (the tablature uses numbers and up and down arrows to indicate the holes a player should inhale or exhale through). Eventually, Benton worked out arrangements for songs such as "House Carpenter," "Casey Jones," and "Poor Ellen Smith," and in 1942 released an album, *Saturday Night at Tom Benton's*. He was interested enough in music before picking up his son's harmonica to have performed some folk songs at the unveiling of *America Today* at the New School. For the occasion Benton put together a string band that set up in front of the mural and played some of the songs he'd learned in the Ozarks. The guitarist was the musicologist Charles Seeger, the father of the folk musician Pete Seeger, and supposedly this was the performance that turned Charles on to folk music. Seeger remembers the evening fondly. "As the music spread out into the other halls, more and more people came in," he recalled. "We finally had to crouch over our instruments, jammed in like sardines, while a couple of hundred people packed themselves in that little room and applauded again and again. We had to play our program over I don't know how many times."

Benton and Seeger, who knew each other slightly in the 1920s, became friends—bonding, for instance, over an appreciation for the Appalachian banjoist and balladeer Dock Boggs—and both avidly collected song lyrics and musical ephemera. In 1935, Seeger moved to Washington, D.C., to become director of music in the Special Skills Division of the Resettlement Administration. For Benton, folk music was a way to become more intimate with the experiences of many of his mural subjects, the steel-driving producers and railroad engineers, for instance, who appear in so many of his paintings. Moreover, folk songs appealed to Benton's sense of narrative structure. As in his murals, these songs present history anecdotally: in folk tunes, colorful characters and scenarios serve more general stories about injustice, labor, or outsider status. While collecting may have schooled Benton in folk legends and types, playing folk music was a way for him to literally become one of his own subjects, for musicians didn't just recite experiences of the folk but lived them as well. Dewey recognized the authenticity of music too, noting that "sounds have the power of direct emotional expression. A sound is itself threatening, whining, soothing, depressing, fierce, tender, soporific, in its own quality." The art historian Leo Mazow argues that Benton partook in what the cultural historian J. M. Mancini calls "anthological modernism," a process of preserving a "musical authenticity" that people like Seeger and Harry Smith "believed was vanishing amid the commercial music and cultural conformity of Cold War America." In a famous passage in *An Artist in America*, Benton laments, "The old music cannot last much longer. I count it a great privilege to have heard it in the sad twang of mountain voices before it died."

In the fall of 1931, Benton formed the Harmonica Rascals, a musical group that rehearsed in his apartment, with Benton and Manuel Tolegian, one of his students, on harmonica; Charles Pollock on mouth harp; Rita and Axel Horn, another student, on guitar; Bernie Steffen, an Art Students League student, on dulcimer; and eventually T.P. on flute. When the group first formed, Jackson Pollock wanted to join and so tried to learn the fiddle. Unable to master it, he gave up, supposedly breaking an instrument in frustration. But when Benton returned to New York from Indiana, where he'd painted a mural, Pollock, who'd learned to play the mouth harp a bit, joined the group as an informal member. The Harmonica Rascals played hard and loud. Naifeh and Smith say that Benton "had an almost comic enthusiasm for making music: he stomped, hooted, and 'danced' through every number," shaking the floor during renditions of "In the Good Old Summertime" or "The Jealous Lover of Lone Green Valley." The group played regularly at Greenwich Village parties and lived up to its name; the Rascals, frequently inebriated, always made a scene.

Jackson Pollock, more than the others, developed a reputation for causing trouble, and his behavior at these performances has become part of his infamy. During the Christmas season of 1933, for example, the Harmonica Rascals performed at the home of Joel Elias Spingarn, a Columbia professor who often hosted gatherings of reform-minded friends. This was a formal party in an elegant apartment on the Upper

West Side; butlers served liquor, passed hors d'oeuvres, and handed out gold-tipped cigarettes. After the performance, Pollock headed directly to the bar and, chafing at the bourgeois company, "muttered" insults to a group of men in tuxedos. In the fight that followed, Professor Spingarn's well-stocked bar was smashed to pieces.

Jackson Pollock had moved to New York in 1930, having been persuaded by Charles and Frank to study with Benton at the Art Students League. Benton famously claimed that "Pollock was a born artist" and "the only thing I taught him was how to drink a fifth a day." Neither is true: Pollock arrived in New York with almost no skills as an artist (he didn't start painting until meeting Benton) and was a heavy drinker before coming to the city. Born in 1912 in Cody, Wyoming, Pollock grew up in a little adobe house in Phoenix, where his father had bought a twenty-acre farm. Roy Pollock was a quiet, hardworking, and strict father, though he was devoted to progressive populist politics and gave his son a lifelong distrust of authority. Stella, Jackson's mother, was also quiet but very protective of her children; her hovering, according to Naifeh and Smith, "produced a family of timid, fearful sons, of such delicate sensibilities that any contact with the outside world produced near panic." By 1921, Roy had abandoned his family, and not long after, when still a boy, Jackson started furtively drinking, a habit his brothers had modeled for him. In 1928, after a period of family turmoil, Jackson enrolled in Manual Arts High School in Los Angeles, where he came under the influence of the art department head and hung out with a cohort of young artists. Two years later, he arrived in New York just as his brother Frank had—penniless—and moved into Charles's small walk-up apartment on Union Square.

Like so many authors, the art critic Carter Ratcliff views Benton's influence on Pollock as wholly negative. Ratcliff admits that Pollock saw in Benton a surrogate for his "weak and absent father" but believes that Benton was a poor father figure: "He didn't want a son so much as a sidekick, a young and manipulable version of himself." Even Rita, in Ratcliff's harsh estimation, was bad for Pollock. Though she saw him as "a fragile creature who needed mothering," she did little to discourage his awkward obsession with her. What's more, in "struggling to draw in Benton's manner," Ratcliff concludes, Pollock "shamed himself."

Benton, to be sure, was not the best role model for the defiant Pollock, but such a portrait of their relationship grossly simplifies the complex affinity they had for each other, ignores the alcoholism and depression that Pollock brought with him to New York, and dismisses all that the Bentons did for their friend. By contrast, George McNeil, a painter who attended the Art Students League in the early 1930s, recognized that Pollock had problems completely unrelated to Benton. "Jackson was very macho from the beginning," he remarked, "drinking being the big thing . . . Yet he was shy, hated crowds . . . There was always an emptiness about Jackson, like living in an abyss; you could feel it in the way he talked, in the way he looked. It was as if he came from nowhere and felt from nowhere." McNeil also acknowledged that the relationship between Benton and Pollock was shaped by a nuanced intensity: "There was a rhythm, a flow, between them from the beginning to the end of their lives. It was a physical, gestural rhythm; teacher and student were *bonded*, you might say."

Benton is always inhibited when writing about his friends or personal matters, and his account of Pollock in *An Artist in America* is no exception. The passage opens with a deadpan description of the moment when he learned about Pollock's death: Benton recalls that he was sitting on the steps of his Martha's Vineyard house when two men approached—Herman Cherry, a student from the Art Students League, and Willem de Kooning, the abstract expressionist painter, whom he barely knew. Benton invited the men inside, where they told him that Pollock had died in a car crash the previous night. Cherry and de Kooning left immediately. "With such news there was nothing to talk about," Benton reasons. His stoic expression of grief upon learning about the accident reveals nothing of the affection that he felt for Pollock. In fact, his loyalty was such that after Pollock publicly rejected him— claiming in a 1944 interview that Benton was important to him "as something against which to react very strongly"—he continued to invite him to his house in Kansas City and give thoughtful analyses of his art.

Benton recalls that Pollock's "personality was such that it elicited immediate sympathy," and Rita and T.P. were drawn to him immediately. Apparently, the quiet and introspective T.P. was never close with his father, who was too busy to give him much attention, and so the boy developed a dependency on Jackson, whom he adored (a professional flute player, T.P. grew apart from his family in the 1950s and lived as a recluse in Massachusetts until his death in 2010). Jackson often babysat T.P., telling him stories about an imaginary hero named Jack Sass who roamed the Wild West and lived among "shadowy white wolves," and Rita compensated him by paying for milk and food to be delivered to the apartment he shared with Charles. For his part, Benton may have questioned Pollock's inexperience as an artist, but he admired the young man's "intense interest" in art and viewed him as a friend, which he badly needed at the time. Though Benton and Thomas Craven were still close, Craven was busy with his books and art criticism; Pollock, by contrast, was enough of an uncultivated outcast to serve as a model for figures in many of Benton's paintings—the harmonica-playing frontiersman in *The Ballad of the Jealous Lover of Lone Green Valley* (1934), for example. Like Benton, Pollock despised authority, questioned conventional wisdom, and was profane. As Joseph Delaney saw it, "Benton was a strange shot, and he was inclined to be a more personal guy with people who were strange shots like he was." And Pollock, Delaney added, "was the strangest shot of all." Though he never said as much, Pollock's creative struggles likely reminded Benton of his own angst-ridden early days in New York. Benton didn't profess that innate talent was a prerequisite for making good art; all that was necessary, he believed, were ambition and authentic experiences to draw from. Finally, Benton was pleased, of course, by Pollock's affection.

Pollock was desperate to prove himself to someone, and Benton, it turns out, was enough like Roy Pollock to become that person. He began to talk and dress like Benton, and just as Benton sold himself as a midwestern artist, Pollock embellished his western identity, assuming the traits of the fictional Jack Sass. He "tailed after Benton like a puppy dog," Harry Holtzman remarked. "Whatever Benton did, he wanted to do too." After his first year at the Art Students League, Pollock, having learned from Benton the importance of getting out and meeting real folk, hitchhiked with Tolegian from New York to Los Angeles and reported to Charles that the country didn't get interesting until he met the wheat farmers in Kansas. Not surprisingly, then, the student started to paint like the teacher. He took Benton's lessons to heart and spent each Tuesday and Friday in an Art Students League studio engrossed in his drawing, sometimes even making direct copies of Benton's work. Benton acknowledges that his student did have "an intuitive sense of rhythmical relations" and that "even as an utter novice, he never made anything ugly." Besides Benton, the greatest influence on Pollock during the early 1930s was Albert Pinkham Ryder, the mysterious nineteenth-century romantic painter whom Benton praised in his classroom. Such Pollock paintings as *Going West* (1934–1935) and *T.P.'s Boat in Menemsha Pond* (1934) bear a strong resemblance to Ryder's dark, rhythmic compositions and demonstrate as well the influence of Benton's mannered representations of the American scene. Like Charles, Jackson was briefly awestruck by his teacher's work and claimed in a letter to his father, "Benton is beginning to be recognized as the foremost American painter today. He has lifted art from the stuffy studio into the world and happenings around him, which has a common meaning to the masses." But as Bentonesque as Pollock's work was in the early 1930s, a higher degree of spontaneity and romantic expressionism distinguishes it from typical American scene painting of the period, and by the late 1930s Pollock was tapping into the collective unconscious and producing expressionist paintings of animals and totemic forms. In addition, Pollock's realism is darker than Benton's; he had a more cynical vision of labor during the Depression, for instance, and while Pollock painted Benton's subjects, he illustrated more "despondency" than his mentor. "Perhaps Pollock's upbringing amidst the actual circumstances of rural poverty," Doss muses, "which Benton observed but never actually lived, influenced his darker outlook, or perhaps his father's fatalism struck deeper than Benton's intonations of producerism."

Much of what Benton knew about Depression-era poverty he learned from observing the Pollock boys struggle to stay afloat. When Jackson finished his last class at the Art Students League, in the spring of 1933, he had to forfeit the school grants that had sustained him. The next year, Benton helped him find a job as a janitor at an elementary school in Greenwich Village, but he was soon obliged to share his meager salary with his brother Sande, who came to New York to monitor Jackson's drinking. Though the brothers squatted in an abandoned building on West Houston Street, they couldn't save anything and ended up on relief; during the winter of 1935, Jackson and Sande scavenged food and fuel from the streets. In a letter to Reuben Kadish, Sande bemoaned their trying circumstances. "Trying to wring a bare existence out of this goddamned city," he explained, "takes most of ones time. The rest of the time is spent holding ones nuts in one hand to keep them from freezing and stealing potatoes with the other." During this difficult time, the Bentons were the Pollocks' chief benefactors. The Pollocks spent much of their summers on Martha's Vineyard—looking after T.P., painting trim, chopping wood—and Jackson cleaned the floors, windows, and carpets in the Bentons' New York apartment. Rita's biggest act of charity was to open an ad hoc gallery in the basement of the Ferargil Galleries, her husband's dealer, to exhibit work by Pollock and other young, struggling artists. With her customary entrepreneurial zeal, Rita enlisted the help of Tolegian and Pollock to clean up the gallery basement in order to display, among other works, small ceramic bowls and plates that Pollock had painted. All of the ceramics sold, and Rita, though having funded the rehabilitation of the exhibition space, paid Pollock for each one. She also purchased some of the objects for herself and paid him to tend to the makeshift gallery.

While Benton was only willing to go so far as to acknowledge that Rita "took to [Pollock] immediately," Naifeh and Smith maintain that she flirted with him shamelessly. Apparently, she had attempted to seduce Frank Pollock in 1928, squeezing his knee at a Harlem nightclub, which Frank believed was more than an innocuous gesture. "I was unused to that sort of thing, and all I can remember is my embarrassment," Frank told the authors. "I couldn't believe it was true." Rita was a sensuous woman with motherly instincts and clearly was affectionate toward the helpless but handsome Pollock boys. Whether her warmth sprang from maternalism or sexual desire is a matter of debate, but there's no doubt that it elicited from Jackson what Ratcliff describes as a "violent and baffling infatuation." Pollock's virginity was a matter of significant frustration for him, and his anxiety about his innocence only grew deeper when he listened to his brothers brag about their escapades in whorehouses, or to Benton boast about sexual adventures during his sketching trips. (There's no direct evidence that Benton cheated on Rita, and a friend, who chose to remain anonymous, stated that though Benton "loved a good party," he never spoke of "another woman in his life." Benton, however, reportedly once said, "You know how dogs are—well—I was like that. When the urge came on me, it came on me, that's all. Nothin' to it.") It wasn't that simple for Pollock, though, as sex and romance were a constant struggle for him. Though he told his brothers and some friends that he "used to fuck" Rita, he later admitted to his wife, Lee Krasner, that "Rita Benton played with me and titillated me and got me all excited, but when it came to the moment of truth, she wouldn't go through with it." His tactless phrasing makes the affair sound awfully sordid, but the sexual energy between Rita and Pollock was not all that illicit or strange; only a prig would have been dismayed by this young man falling for an attractive older woman who cared for him. What's more, Jackson and Rita likely saw each other naked many times.

The Bentons and their guests frequented a beach near their home on the Vineyard where the waves made for ideal bodysurfing; many summer afternoons a crowd gathered there to frolic in the water, and more often than not everyone was unclothed. Benton recalls that this grew into a "cult of nudity and most any time you go down on our shores, you are affronted with some of the most extraordinary sights in the world"; on the beach, Benton writes, were "aggregations of female skin and bone," "bulbous flesh," and "hairy, potbellied, fat-ass male caricatures of the human race." He goes on to explain this exhibitionism as a way for the frustrated "self, unfully realized and checked in modern life," to find release in "a form of the primitive." And as if to justify his wife's taste for such sexual display, and perhaps the games she played with Jackson, Benton concludes that those of his generation who stripped naked on the beach did so "as if they were making a last blind gesture toward youthful sex and strength and beauty, which, though they know to be secretly lost forever to them, cannot quite be given up."

Despite their affection for him, Pollock could annoy the Bentons. He was often unhappy and reticent when he visited them, and his lack of interest in literature and current events exasperated Tom. Though Pollock attended Vineyard parties where he had ample opportunity to join in debates between "John Deweyites, Marxist radicals, and extreme conservatives," he never pitched in. "Though plainly intelligent," Benton recalls, "he seemed to have no intellectual curiosity." Even more frustrating were Pollock's alcoholism and the fiascoes that arose from it, in which Benton often intervened. On one occasion, in the mid-1930s, Pollock took the ferry to Edgartown and started angling for a ride to Chilmark, where the Bentons, who had no idea he was coming, were spending a fine summer afternoon. Bored of waiting for his unsuspecting hosts to get word that he was on the island, Pollock bought a bottle of gin, got drunk, and rented a bicycle to have a look-see about the island. Before crashing the bike and cutting his face, he'd spent the evening riding after girls and hollering like a madman. The Bentons eventually received a call from the sheriff, who demanded that they bail their friend out of jail. Pollock's antics amused the Bentons at first, but it wouldn't be long before he persuaded them once and for all that he suffered from a bona fide psychotic alcoholism.

As Benton's reputation increased during the 1930s, he also became more confrontational, issuing attacks against what he perceived as the obscure theories and meanings of modern art. Despite his stated affection for the public, he didn't address it with much finesse and often took defensive positions before he needed to. For instance, in November 1932, the month before he unveiled his Whitney mural, he was invited to Providence, Rhode Island, to engage in a public conversation with Frank Lloyd Wright on the general topic of "the arts and their role in the daily life of a community." Brown University and the Rhode Island School of Design, which co-sponsored the so-called Community Art Project—a civic program that cultivated dialogue regarding the public role of art—arranged the conversation between the two men. The organizers had already hosted three-day conferences addressing such topics as art education, museum patronage, and modern painting and architecture; the speakers at these events included the art historian and critic Frank Jewett Mather Jr.; William Sloane Coffin, president of the Metropolitan Museum of Art; and Juliana Force, director of the Whitney Museum. Try as they might to tailor their remarks for the Providence public, the speakers, all from specialized and privileged professions, struggled to abandon the argot of their fields. Benton, likely invited to the conference that November 11 on the recommendation of Force, who had commissioned the Whitney mural, was on edge. Though he wanted to live up to the civic spirit of the Community Art Project by demonstrating his difference from the refined elites who'd already participated, he was surely aware that the audience comprised cultural conservatives determined to preserve Providence's "colonial heritage." In other words, Benton—who was wary of elite discourses and stodgy sensibilities—likely felt cornered and so was primed to play the role of the plain-speaking craftsman. As such, his performance that day foreshadowed the tone and substance of his better-known assaults against modernism.

Wright, by contrast, was in the mood for some precise philosophizing. First of all, he disliked murals and believed mural painters should respect the original design of the walls on which they worked. Though he was one of the most respected architects in the country, during the early 1930s, when the Depression reduced his workload, Wright advocated for architecture's co-option of what he called the "allied arts," which included glassware and textiles but also painting and sculpture. Earlier that year, Wright had established the Taliesin Fellowship as a forum for exploring the synthesis of the allied arts and had begun lecturing about his vision for Broadacre City, a never-realized community that he hoped would be self-sufficient and built by cooperative artisans. Moreover, like Benton, Wright was "cantankerous" and "argumentative" and had a "flair for the dramatic," and he appeared at the Providence event with a bandage on his nose, which he'd injured the previous week during a brawl on a New York street. So the stage was set for a provocative debate.

The organizers planned for a formal conversation, with the participants delivering statements in turn, but Benton, who spoke first, promptly announced that he would forgo lecturing, preferring instead to carry on an informal colloquium with the audience. "Therefore, in my case, I am going to ask you to . . . interrupt me whenever you will," he began. "We stand a better chance that way, both of us, of escaping boredom." Dispensing with formalities and bringing the discussion down to earth became a common strategy in Benton's lectures and essays; it may have been transparent, but it was an effective way to establish a rapport with his unprofessional audience and authenticate his populist insights. In truth, however, Benton enjoyed lecturing and in this instance warmed up quickly, jumping right into an appraisal, that dumbfounded the room, of what he believed to be the cultural elite's abstruseness. Artists and critics want us to focus on "process" at the expense of meaning, he explained, but mural painting "indicates that Art may once again have a function—that it may provide something more than studio play dedicated to a small class and for the enjoyment of which you must possess a special key." Here, in the first few minutes of one of his first public performances, Benton introduced the core arguments that obsessed him for the next decade or more: most modern artists, he claimed, are sophists who obscure their purposes behind an esoteric rhetoric that deliberately subverts the common man's desire to find useful value in art. The modern artist, he continued, "has demanded that the lay person get interested in his technique or give up any pretension to love of Art." The key to meaning, he argued, will only be made available to those who are willing to obtain an "aesthetic emotion," which he deemed an invented "special faculty" and a "fetish." The principal danger of this trend, according to Benton, was that meaning no longer was inherent to art precisely at a time when art should be dealing "with subjects which, by having a relation to our modern environment, would provide meaning automatically." The modern artist, he warned the audience, "is shutting himself off from you."

At this point, Wright interrupted Benton to ask why the art of painting doesn't just forgo all of this silliness and "return to 'Mother,'" by which he meant architecture—the "mother of the arts." Benton was prepared, though, and responded, "You want to tie the painter to your apron strings. 'Mother' always wants to do that to her 'boys.' But you know 'boys' that have any vitality, refuse that. They run away and find out something about life, something, maybe, that 'mother' does not know." Wright coolly put the metaphor to rest. "Mr. Benton," he asked, "isn't that the attitude of an unregenerate bad boy?"

Though he had invited Wright's insult, Benton was after a finer point; he wanted to outline a function for art in trying times. His caricature of modern artists was designed to set up the more nuanced argument that vital paintings have instrumentality, which was neither an unusual nor a reactionary claim for the time. By the early 1930s, Dewey, along with pragmatist educators and psychologists, advocated for an instrumental culture, and virtually any modern artist would have agreed that paintings should be useful for some purpose. What seemed old-fashioned (and what seems all the more so today, in a culture accustomed to postmodern ironies) was Benton's insistence that paintings employ "structures to unify the disparities found in things experienced in life." His belittling of art that resisted explicitly illustrating how experience and emotion fit together was intellectually shortsighted, for it denied, erroneously, that esoteric art could be instrumental, relevant, or engaged.

Benton unveiled the Whitney mural a month after his appearance in Providence, and Paul Rosenfeld, a critic associated with the Stieglitz Circle, accused the "unregenerate bad boy" of producing "another tiresome expression of the childish lack of respect for the identity of things." Rosenfeld and Benton had a history: in 1921, Rosenfeld had published an essay in *The Dial* that belittled his work. The critic hit Benton where it hurt, taking aim at his writhing figures ("they do protest too much") and his method of mimesis ("it is as though the artist himself were not using his body properly"). An incensed Benton blamed Stieglitz, who was a friend and mentor of Rosenfeld's, and sent him a churlish letter. "I have done a lot of God damned hard work and absolutely original investigation and experiment developing a process to further me," he exhorted. "I do not believe it is altogether petty that my pride should revolt at having that fact publicly slighted every time I show a canvas." In his defense Benton explained that while "so many of the moderns" were intent on formal experimentation, he was interested in "extended sculptural form." Theoretically, Benton had a good point—what, he wanted to know, was inherently inferior about his kind of experimentation?— but he simply couldn't persuade his critics that his paintings were formally appealing. Twelve years later, when Benton's "extended sculptural form" and claims to authenticity were on full display in *The Arts of Life in America*, Rosenfeld attacked again.

Benton had conceived the mural in early 1932, after Rita, ever the diligent businesswoman, reminded Juliana Force of her husband's meager recompense for the *America Today* mural. Force, who'd become Gertrude Vanderbilt's assistant in 1907 and the first director of the Whitney Museum when it opened in 1931, had a reputation as a fearless advocate for the well-being of artists and had commiserated with the Bentons about how little the New School paid for the mural. Throughout her career with the Whitney Studio, the Whitney Studio Club, the Whitney Studio Galleries, and eventually the Whitney Museum of American Art, she tended to the financial needs of artists: she found them jobs, money, and studios, and she gave them food, drink, and emotional encouragement. She also bought their art. Believing that Force would be sympathetic to their financial condition, Rita approached her and confessed that she and Tom were losing their Vineyard house because they couldn't make the mortgage payments. Force had only a tiny acquisitions budget but agreed to loan the couple three thousand dollars without interest. When it became apparent that the Bentons couldn't pay her back in cash, Tom suggested that she take paintings instead. Force balked at this solution, as it was a careless way to set a value on art and she wanted murals "specially made" for the museum instead. So they agreed, in January 1932, that he would paint a mural for the library in the Whitney building on West Eighth Street.

Benton worked on the mural during the spring and summer of 1932, while Franklin Delano Roosevelt campaigned for his first term as president and introduced America to his New Deal. To get inspiration for his investigation into the nation's popular arts, Benton also hit the road, observing fiddle players and ecstatic worshippers, including an entranced "Appalachian Oread," in the coal regions of Virginia and backwoods of Georgia. Upon his return, he asked Force to reimburse his travel expenses and finance his summer work in the library; she reminded him of the three-thousand-dollar loan and explained that she'd rather he quit the project than pay him again, but somehow Benton persuaded her to pay him another thousand dollars, plus six hundred dollars in material expenses, upon completion of the mural.

The hyped-up panels transformed the intimate library into a showcase for American spectacles. Once again it was a Deweyan notion that Benton illustrated. "The arts which today have most vitality for the average person," Dewey writes, "are things he does not take to be arts: for instance, the movie, jazzed music, the comic strip, and, too frequently, newspaper accounts of love-nests, murders, and exploits of bandits . . . and all the rhythmic crises that punctuate the stream of living." Above all, it's this rhythm that Benton was after in the mural: the way he painted the figures, with a brawny physicality and zeal, was an attempt to bring everyday culture to immanence. The first panel, which depicts the "Indian arts," features activities typically associated with Native Americans: ritual dancing, basket weaving, hunting, and the preparation of animal skins. The second panel, *Arts of the West*, includes vignettes of two couples dancing to musicians playing "Swing 'Em Round and Come Down the Middle," a group of men playing horseshoes, broncobusters, a poker match, and a man shooting a rifle, all set in a frontier environment. The so-called arts of the city in the third panel are more illicit: sexy women dance for aroused men, a woman bartender mixes drinks, children read the comics, and a jazz orchestra belts out a song. In *Arts of the South,* a mixed-race crowd of Holy Rollers experience spiritual ecstasy, three young black men shoot craps on the dirt, and in the background a man sits on a mule wagon and a small crowd gathers in front of a wooden chapel. Benton also included three narrow vertical panels that illustrate the lyrics of popular songs, agitated labor protesters, and speed, symbolized by a racing car, an airplane, and a train barreling down the tracks with a blazing headlight. Stimulating as they are, these unintegrated vignettes—the strapping figures, gyrating dancers, rearing stallions, and hunting Indians were splashed across the walls of a tiny room with sloping ceilings—contain none of the structural harmony Benton advocated for during the conversation with Wright in Providence.

In his essay for the mural brochure, Benton says that he means to set up a contrast between "popular outpourings" and "those specialized arts which the museum harbors and which are the outcome of special conditioning and professional direction." He cautions against reading too much into the title, however, explaining that naming a thing isn't the same as knowing it and that "the arts of life" are by nature "undisciplined." As such, he adds, the panels take some liberties with the life they purport to represent. "In the process of correlating things directly known," he explains, "needs arise which cannot be met with logical devices of the past . . . Experience is not of a logical nature—all integration involves distortion of some sort." Whether or not Benton recognized that such an argument contradicted his avowed preference for unifying the disparities of experience, Paul Rosenfeld certainly did and scolded the artist for his impure design. The panels, Rosenfeld chides, "are evidently giving an exhibition of shadow-boxing: lunging, ducking, delivering uppercuts and body-blows; and never for an instant letting us forget . . . the muscularity involved in them . . . Benton has exhibited the ugliness of his human subjects in an ugly fashion." Rosenfeld also expresses disgust with the mural's presentation of the popular arts, calling them "thoroughly crude, gross, and ungracious," and, betraying his elitism, quips that Benton's "super-life-sized" figures attribute to the American folk "importance which they actually have not got."

Though this likely didn't bother Benton a bit—his brochure essay targets what he calls, in contradiction to his avowal of structural unity, the Stieglitz Circle's "fetish of purity"—the mural falls short of his own demands for good art by exaggerating his own experiences of "life in America" to such a degree that few could recognize them as being like their own experiences. Therefore the mural's instrumentality was cast in doubt, for critics wondered what aspects of the nation Benton was trying to represent and how these representations might be useful. The fact of the matter is that not everyone who saw the mural comprehended how a folk ethos, illustrated as it was with sweeping generalizations about particular regions, amounted to a practical solution to Depression-era problems.

But Benton had faith in the ability of art to transform society, and his purpose in the Whitney mural was to restore republicanism "through the rejuvenation of American folk traditions and values," such as those depicted in *Arts of the West* and *Arts of the South*. "In the Whitney panels," Doss maintains, "Benton submitted that folk culture could unite the American people and thus strengthen their fight against corporate hegemony and the alienation of modern life." On the surface, such a position seems to correspond to the arguments that FDR made on the campaign trail that year. "The welfare and the soundness of a Nation," he said in his nomination acceptance speech at the Democratic convention in Chicago in July 1932, "depend first upon what the great mass of the people wish and need." And Roosevelt believed that what the people of America wanted above all else was to be productive and to preserve their customs: these "are the spiritual values, the true goal toward which our efforts of reconstruction should lead." A few months later, however, Roosevelt delivered a radio address that outlined a far more aggressive and interventionist program that was at odds with Benton's romantic glorification of regional culture, which had little use for radical reform. Roosevelt reiterated his belief that local communities ought to fight unemployment but maintained that such a duty was hopeless without radical government intervention. "I am very certain that the obligation extends beyond the states and to the federal government itself," he said, "if and when it becomes apparent that states and communities are unable to take care of the necessary relief work." Charles Beard also rejected the revitalization of Jeffersonian parables as a pragmatic response to the Depression. In his 1931 essay "The Myth of Rugged American Individualism," Beard declares, "The cold truth is that the individualist creed . . . is principally responsible for the distress in which Western civilization finds itself," and he concludes that "severe restraints" must be placed "on the anarchy celebrated in the name of individualism. The task before us, then, is not to furbish up an old slogan, but to get rid of it."

It wasn't Benton's class loyalties that came under attack—though Henry McBride, a stodgy formalist critic who disdained the hybridization of popular and fine arts, scoffed at the mural's "vulgarity" and deemed it appropriate only for "restless illiterates"—but his political tone. Just when leftists were making their case for either federal intervention or total ideological reform, he appeared, in their eyes anyway, to promote the American region as a utopian cure-all. He may have intended to illustrate how time-honored rituals could contribute to the nation's recovery, by reminding his viewers of all that past generations and rural folk had accomplished with their plain-speaking gumption, but critics saw on the Whitney's walls an awkwardly nostalgic, antimodern, and hopelessly adulterated social scene that obscured their forward view of a transformed society. What, these critics wondered, did old-time religion or a game of craps have to do with the economic welfare of America's citizens?

Writing several years after the mural was completed, Stuart Davis complained that Benton was unable to perceive his "environment, not in isolation, but in relation to the whole . . . Benton's sketches may be from life, but their co-ordination in mural form is conditioned by sketchy ideas as to their political, social and economic significance." In 1938, Meyer Schapiro, writing in *Partisan Review*, expressed it as bluntly as can be: he accused Benton of concocting "an escape from the demands of the crisis" and providing a "pitiful and inept" alternative to "realism guided by radical values." What Rosenfeld, Davis, and Schapiro imply, then, is that the mural is sentimental; they object to its overbearing optimism, to the way it occasionally descends into a generic form of civic boosterism. In other words, the mural's sentimentality results from Benton's peremptory insistence that one should identify in his figures clichéd sorts of American productivity and know-how. The stereotypical characteristics of Benton's Americans were his bugaboo; criticisms of this aspect of his paintings didn't stop hounding him until his death. Davis, for instance, argued that Benton "should have no trouble in selling his wares to any Fascist or semi-fascist type of government . . . [His] qualifications would be, in general, his social cynicism, which allows him to depict social events without regard to their meaning." What Davis meant was that Benton, because his figures appeared hackneyed, was incapable of offering a critical or progressive picture of American life. Benton, he believed, served up an America that played into dominant and therefore conservative attitudes about the nation's citizens.

Davis and others, though, were particularly outraged by the mural's lunette, titled *Political Business and Intellectual Ballyhoo*, which includes crude stereotypes of readers of the leftist magazines *New Masses, The Nation*, and *The New Republic*. Davis points to the "vicious caricature" of a Jew in this lunette—the figure holding *New Masses*—as evidence of a nativism that Hitler "would love." Indeed, the caricature is a pathetic attempt at humor that totally poisons an otherwise legitimate effort to critique dogmatism and "pure" thinking of any stripe. In his brochure essay, Benton writes, "In life, the claim to purity is practically a declaration of impotence. It is a compensatory value, born of and reared in some kind of frustration." Like so many engaged intellectuals of the era—Dewey, Lionel Trilling, Edmund Wilson, Dos Passos—Benton grew wary of absolutist thinking and cautioned against hard ideologies of all kinds. "This mural," he explains, "is certainly not a pure work." Marcia Brennan analyzes the formal fracture evident in the Whitney panels and offers an astute reading of the disorientation they cause the viewer: the forms pull us in and push us out, and as a result "the viewer is not so much absorbed in Benton's murals as entangled in them." Benton intended for this dynamism to symbolize the busy goings-on of America, which he believed contrasted with the rigid worldview of hard-line radicals, represented by the Jew. But his meaning backfired, as the caricature reveals his narrowness of mind rather than an appreciation of the myriad cultures that make up America.

To his dismay, Benton paid a price for the mural's shortcomings above and beyond the negative reviews. On December 7, at a Whitney party celebrating the unveiling of *The Arts of Life in America*, Force handed Benton a check. Benton was drunk—"tight as a jay bird in blackberry season," he recalls—and didn't examine the check until after he vomited in the street. He was shocked to see that it was for a thousand dollars, less than he had anticipated. The next morning, Benton sent the check back to Force. She insisted that he take the money, which he did, but over the next several years the two exchanged bitter letters regarding the financing of the mural, and Benton remained dissatisfied with the commission until his death. Even worse, Davis rallied teachers and students at the Art Students League to sign a petition demanding that the mural be destroyed, on the grounds that it contained racist caricatures of blacks and Jews. As a result, some of Benton's minority students withdrew from his courses. The stage was now set for Benton's melodramatic exodus from New York.

•

The 1933 World's Fair in Chicago was to open in late May, but just seven months earlier, what Colonel Richard Lieber called the "lead-ass" committee in charge of the Indiana display for the exposition still had not decided on a plan for the state's exhibition space. The committee finally met on December 19, 1932, to hear a proposal by Lieber, head of Indiana's Department of Conservation, about commissioning Benton to produce a 250-foot mural depicting that state's history, and the members accepted the proposal on the grounds that Benton could work quickly and on a large scale. Lieber had tested the waters before the meeting, sending Thomas Hibben, an Indiana architect, to Benton's New York apartment in November. Hibben knew Benton and made an attractive offer: the artist would have total control over the mural plan and was free, as Benton put it, to indulge his interest in doing "a social history . . . showing the changes brought about by . . . mechanization." Three days later, Benton signed a contract in Chicago.

A short time after, Benton was in Indiana, lying in a hotel bed with a cold and a pile of books on the state's history. During the day, he devoured the books and talked with anyone he could about Indiana history; in the evenings, he drank Brown County whiskey with Hibben and some new friends before getting back to work on his plan. Benton toured the state for a few months, making about six hundred preparatory drawings on ordinary paper stained with his own tobacco spit. He sketched people, buildings, and machinery—water mills, a cannonball stove, and an 1830s printing press. It was a daunting task, but the gusto with which Benton attacked the project testifies to his confidence in his powers of observation and ability to get down to the business of experiencing a place and its folk. Remarking on Benton's fantastic work ethic, one local reporter asked, "How does an artist set about so enormous a task? Does he sit down and wait for the art spirit to move him? Does he try to induce this curious thing called genius and wait for the creative fervor?" No, the author observed, "he sets about his job just the way a great engineer or a manufacturer sets about his," a comparison that surely pleased Benton. Indeed, the drawings helped Benton piece together the overall flow of rhythms in the finished mural as much as they familiarized him with the Indiana landscape and its inhabitants.

In his rented Indianapolis studio, he produced a high-relief clay model of each vignette while assistants applied gesso to the panels. Various Hoosiers stopped by to model for the figures, and he constantly altered his plan as he worked. Eventually, he started on the panels, splashing on the egg tempera in fits of activity. "I hardly know how I did it," he recalls, adding, "A mural for me is a kind of emotional spree . . . [that] puts me in an exalted state of mind." It's fair to say that Benton wrote and talked too much about the ambitions behind his murals. His drive to explain has the same melodramatic quality of the works themselves, which demand that we see the country through a very particular lens. For instance, in "A Dream Fulfilled," his statement accompanying the mural, Benton insists that his purpose is to "unroll progressively the social and environmental changes of the country from the savage Indian to the present days of our machine culture." Taking aim once again at the "neurotic 'purities'" of "modern" art, he claims to seek a "grip on the life of men and . . . an art that would have meaning for men." "History," he adds, "was not a scholarly study for me but a drama. I saw it not as a succession of events but as a continuous flow of action having its climax in my own immediate experience." Benton knew he would get "a critical whaling" for his heavy-handedness but didn't care; he was sure that he'd produced his best work so far.

The Century of Progress exposition opened in Chicago on May 27, and as it turned out, Benton took his "whaling" from the Hoosier press. The main objection was to the depiction of a Ku Klux Klan rally in the panel *Parks, the Circus, the Klan, the Press.* Several months earlier, Benton had shown some of his preparatory drawings to Lieber, who approved the general scheme but objected to the inclusion of the Klan meeting. Benton responded by inviting Lieber, Hibben, and a group of Democratic legislators to discuss the panel's content over a bottle of whiskey. The legislators agreed that the Klan's role in Indiana politics was too important to ignore, and Lieber acquiesced.

In the end, Benton crowded over a dozen vignettes into the panel, and while they are independent in terms of narrative, most of them depict everyday heroics. In the lower right corner, for instance, Lieber plants a tree; in the upper left, firefighters douse a blazing building; and in the middle foreground, a reporter taps at his typewriter and a nurse tends to a sick black child. In the background, serving as a narrative foil to these humble protagonists, a group of robed Klansmen hold a rally in front of a burning cross.

Benton didn't have to fictionalize the influence of the Klan on Indiana's history, for between 1921 and 1928, 40 percent of the state's white men paid dues to the organization, and when the group's Indiana leader was jailed, in 1925, for brutally raping and poisoning a state employee, his testimony led to indictments of the mayor of Indianapolis and the governor of the state for complicity in Klan corruption. Benton maintained, therefore, that his inclusion of racism in an otherwise uplifting panel "was merely realism." His depiction of the newspaper reporter at a typewriter backs up his claim, as it was the investigative reporting of *The Indianapolis Times* that had exposed the corrupt influence of the KKK on state politics. Nevertheless, Benton understood that his juxtaposition of nurses and firefighters with Klansmen was bound to provoke; in fact, he meant the offensive scene to be interpreted as a warning that the "just civic sphere" described elsewhere in the panel must be protected from a threatening backwardness embedded in the state's history.

Ultimately, two kinds of critics were riled by the Klan vignette: liberals who believed that Benton was either racist or ignorant of the true character of most Hoosiers, and conservatives who felt that the scene was further evidence, along with his depictions of striking workers in the panel *Coal, Gas, Oil, Brick*, of the artist's "socialist tendencies." All in all, though, the mural was viewed as a tough but triumphant characterization of the state. Wallace Richards, the exhibition's publicist, monitored viewer responses to the mural and reported to Lieber that "we have been extremely successful in having won over half the visitors to an understanding of an exhibit modern in atmosphere and often brutally truthful in content." Richards, in fact, worked hard to downplay the controversial elements of the panel, telling, for instance, the Daughters of Indiana, a group of Chicago women who had been born in the state, that "not all that is shown in this mural is pretty, but it is real. The Klan was active in Indiana, whether we like to admit or not."

Benton was exhausted when he returned to New York. He'd been working flat out for two years, and as he puts it, "I had milked every emotional possibility out of myself and was good for nothing." He didn't touch a paintbrush for months, and his only joy was playing harmonica. In addition to working out new folk tunes, Benton learned some Bach suites: "I loved to squeak them out note by note and I'd keep it up for hours, beating time with my foot." When he did get back to work, good things came to him. In 1934, for instance, Benton produced two of his more popular paintings, *Lord, Heal the Child* and *The Ballad of the Jealous Lover of Lone Green Valley*, wrote an essay on the Ozark Mountains for the magazine *Travel*, and held exhibitions at Ferargil Galleries that received mixed reviews but solidified his reputation as the premier regionalist painter. He was rewarded for this hard work when asked to join a commercial enterprise developed by Reeves Lewenthal, a former reporter for the *Chicago Tribune*. In July 1934, Lewenthal met with twenty-three artists in Benton's New York studio and pitched his scheme: he would pay the artists two hundred dollars to produce etchings and lithographs that he would then sell at department stores frequented by U.S. consumers. The prints, each retailing for five dollars, would be produced in editions of two hundred impressions. Benton and other artists, including John Steuart Curry, Doris Lee, and Grant Wood, joined the enterprise, called Associated American Artists, likely because, in contrast to the Federal Art Project (the visual arts division of the Works Progress Administration), it had the potential to reward them with a decent profit. By October, over fifty department stores were selling the prints.

Tapping into New Deal attitudes, Lewenthal promoted the prints as populist depictions of the American scene. After several months, however, sales dropped off, and he developed a new plan—to sell the prints by mail. The price remained the same, but now he advertised directly to consumers. After this change in strategy, sales jumped by $80,000, and by 1941 the enterprise was making $500,000 each year and operating galleries in major cities. The success of Associated American Artists testifies to the appeal of regionalist art in the 1930s and 1940s, and in particular to the popularity of Benton's work, which sold better than that by any other artist, likely owing to his media exposure and treatment of recognizable subject matter. Many years later, Lewenthal recalled, "I knew the regionalists were popular because their names were in the art magazines all the time. But they weren't popular enough, and they weren't making any money. Why, when I first went to Tom Benton's New York apartment he was living in utter squalor. I more or less rescued him."

Benton's public exposure reached its zenith in December 1934, when *Time* magazine ran a feature on the regionalists and put a Benton self-portrait on the cover. Titled "U.S. Scene," the article opens with an analysis of the art market during the previous year, which was particularly robust despite the economic turmoil. Sales of contemporary American paintings were notably high, which the magazine attributes to a growing skepticism about the value of "the crazy parade of Cubism, Futurism, Dadaism, [and] Surrealism." In a gross simplification, the article traces the "opposition to such outlandish art" to the Midwest, to the art of Benton, Curry, and Wood. "To them," the feature explains, "what could be seen in their own land—streets, fields, shipyards, factories and those who people such places—became more important than what could be felt about far off places." Benton, the author decides, "is the most virile of U.S. painters of the U.S. Scene."

The *Time* story reflected a refrain that critics and artists had been sounding in relative obscurity for some time: in the article, as one historian puts it, "regionalism became the triumphal moment in an epic struggle between French modernism and good old American common sense." Such reasoning was largely the work of Maynard Walker, a Kansas-born journalist who became a partner at Ferargil Galleries in the early 1930s and promoted to *Time*'s editors the idea for the story on American scene painters. In 1933, the entrepreneurial Walker organized the first exhibition, held at the Kansas City Art Institute, to feature works by the regionalist triumvirate of Benton, Grant Wood, and John Steuart Curry. After that he became a tireless advocate of a "most vital modern art" that he believed was centered on "our long backward Middle West" and that would reveal the art coming from Paris to be "rubbish." Two years later, Walker established an eponymous gallery in New York that became the exclusive dealer of work by Benton, Wood, and Curry. Though he helped publicize and sell Benton's paintings, Benton never mentions Walker's name in his books, essays, or interviews, which causes one to speculate that despite their professional relationship the men were not friends.

But no one contributed more overblown rhetoric to the consideration of an American art in opposition to European modernism than Benton's old friend Thomas Craven. Busy as both men were, they saw each other less frequently now, though Craven's tendentious criticism, which crudely attacked foreign modernism and celebrated native artists, contributed as much to Benton's success as anything else. In the 1920s he wrote book reviews and essays for *The Dial* and *The New Republic*, pieces that offered essentially formalist critiques of art history but that also contain contextual—or what one historian calls "experience-based"—attitudes about art. On the one hand, Craven argued that art is not "inevitably linked to its environment" and is instead "above temporary circumstances"; on the other hand, he professed that "the context of art is peculiar to its time." The competition between experience and form as the driving forces of artistic creation would polarize Craven and Benton from their peers in the late 1920s and the 1930s, but early on Craven was ambivalent about this issue and so suggested, plausibly, that both played their parts. But in later articles such as "The Curse of French Culture," "The Bohemians of Paris," and "Our Art Becomes American," he excoriated the "fetish" of the "emotional tendency" in French culture and defended America's instrumentalism and "hard facts"; the bohemianism of Paris, he adds, "is the artificial prolongation of youth—youth extended beyond its brief romantic span, youth corrupted by that dreadful infirmity of mind which consents to no development and no maturity."

Craven declared that Benton and other American painters had given rise to a new spirit because of their "insistence on the superior value of directly perceived facts," which "has made it possible for any artist to get at the roots of his original self" and, presumably, purge himself of any impurities. Benton would eventually attempt to downplay his association with Craven, calling him a "highly controversial art critic" and explaining that he "never went quite as far as Tom Craven did" in his attacks on modern art, but his efforts to distance himself from Craven's reactionary criticism were weakened by Craven's constant praise of his art. In 1937, for instance, Craven described Benton as a "vivid exponent of . . . American civilization" and predicted that "no superlatives would be too extravagant for his attainments"; Benton, he explained three years earlier, was able "to build an art of and for the American people." Such tributes gave Benton's detractors, such as Davis and Schapiro, the rhetorical edge in their negative appraisals of his art, which they deemed too optimistic, especially in its portrayal of the American laborer.

Davis, proving yet again to be Benton's nemesis, was disgusted by the *Time* article, and a few months after it appeared, he published an attack on the ethos of American scene painting in *Art Front*, a leftist periodical that, like Davis himself, who was a founding editor, negotiated the common ground between radical politics and modernist aesthetics. He reserved much of his vitriol for Craven and what he calls his "vicious and windy chauvinistic ballyhoo"; Craven's essays, Davis explains, "bring art values to the plane of a Rotarian luncheon and are a particularly repellent form of petty opportunism." The U.S. scene in general, he adds, is nothing more than a "slight burp" in American art. Reversing the terms of contrast developed by Benton and Craven, Davis asks, "Is the well-fed farm hand under the New Deal, as painted by Grant Wood, a direct representation or is it an introspective abstraction?" This harsh review prompted a sensational war of words between Benton and Davis that they waged in the pages of *Art Front* and *Art Digest*. Neither man took the high road. Benton, for example, responded to one Davis reproach, "No verbiage can disguise the squawks of the defeated and impotent." He also demanded that the editors of *Art Front* pose ten questions to him so that he could clarify his positions. He received the questions but published his answers in *Art Digest* instead. In dense, defensive prose, Benton reaffirmed his belief that "'aesthetic' values" are inseparable "from human ways of perceiving and doing," to which Davis responded, "It is now clear that the disorganization, the bad color, the unpleasant surface and the social Nihilism of his work are not, as he himself boasts, the crudities of a man of the soil and of the pioneer stock, but rather the logical result of an innate inability to think straight and realistically."

Truth be told, few of the artists who published letters and essays on these topics wrote with remarkable analytic clarity; much of the ink spilled in these debates was impenetrable and conflicted, and art historians have long parsed loaded terms such as "experience," "liberal," and "authentic" in an attempt to determine precisely where Benton and Davis stood. For instance, Edward Alden Jewell, the *New York Times* art critic who would become an outspoken opponent of American abstract art when it reemerged in the 1940s, opened a 1935 article on Benton by exhorting him and Davis to refrain from their "frenetic and sometimes heavy-footed bombardment[s]" of each other. "If only artists would resist the temptation to wrangle and would stick instead to their paint," he argues, "there would be less general befuddlement and there might also be more progress in art itself." Though Jewell was mistaken when he predicted that readers would soon grow "too sick of the whole mess to read another line," he earns our sympathy when he writes, "The result of my reading [of the feud] . . . is a sense of sadness over so much wasted time and the generation of so much hindering animosity."

Persuasive as some of Davis's critiques are, he was wrong to draw no distinction between Benton and Craven: both could be crude, but Benton's prose was more nuanced and less partisan than Craven's. Whereas Craven only promoted American-born realists, Benton felt obliged to critique "the fictions of political nationalism," insisting, for instance, that "the notion that there is such a thing as a common humanity must be abandoned . . . There are humanities, but not *a* humanity in the world in which we now live." And later, Benton admitted that while Craven's criticism helped his career, "Craven never minced words and often in the interests of strong statement would go clear overboard." Moreover, one of the ironies of the Benton-Davis feud is that both men appealed to a Deweyan rhetoric to make their cases. Since the beginning of his career, Davis had defended the instrumentality of art, and in August 1935, just a few months after attacking Benton, he struck a familiar refrain, writing, "A work of art is a public act, or, as John Dewey says, an 'experience.' By definition, then, it is not an isolated phenomenon, having meaning for the artist and his friends alone. Rather it is the result of the whole life experience of the artist as a social being." It would appear, then, that the main point of contention between Benton and Davis was aesthetic rather than philosophical; they couldn't agree on whether representational or abstract art was best suited to illustrating common experience. Whereas Benton believed that authentic experience ought to be represented realistically, Davis maintained that abstractions contained "life's dynamic nature" and modeled "future understanding." The two men might have left it at that had they not so rigidly conflated aesthetics with ethics and politics, though in fairness to them both that was easier said than done during the heady 1930s. As Schapiro explains, their moment was one of genuine crisis, and to many artists and critics it seemed to demand a response, even if such niggling, in Benton's case, occasionally conflicted with his stated ambition to address the real-world concerns of "the people" rather than the apprehensions of intellectuals.

When Benton returned to Manhattan from Indiana in 1933, he still believed that his political philosophy was compatible with that of the city's Left. "I thought it possible an exchange between us might forward an understanding," he explained later. "I thought I could make it clear that what separated us was not our basic attitudes toward the depression-ridden people of America, or even the morality of the Capitalist system, but only a theory about what should be done to improve the situations of these." The "exchange" that Benton refers to was actually a series of conversations that he had with members of the John Reed Club in 1934 and 1935. The New York John Reed Club—one chapter of about thirty that were established in American cities and aligned with the Communist Party U.S.A.—banded together in 1929 under the aegis of *New Masses* and proclaimed that membership was open to any "writer, artist, and worker in any one of the cultural fields, subscribing to the declaration of purposes and the ultimate triumph of the working class." Among other things, the club's stated goals were to cooperate with artists and writers in defense of the revolutionary labor movement and "to struggle against all art and literature rooted in bourgeois ideology." Though there's some debate about how organized and committed the New York club's members were, they fomented a radical subculture, grew to dominate the editorial principles of several leftist journals, and enlisted the likes of Lewis Mumford and Meyer Schapiro to lecture at the John Reed Club School of Art.

In February 1933, Benton contributed four works to a John Reed Club exhibition titled *The Social Viewpoint in Art*. But when Schapiro reprimanded the club for including him in the show, Benton responded impetuously, deriding club artists for their dogmatism and refusal to experience the actual culture of America. In the spring of 1934, Benton decided to address the club in a speech titled "Art and Nationalism," the main purpose of which was to parse the differences between radical art and his brand of American scene painting. The organizers anticipated a small audience, but after a large contingent of John Reed Club members crowded the room, they moved the event to a larger space. "You make good priests in the road you are going," Benton boldly told the club members in the audience, "but unless you are able to subordinate your doctrines and realize that the actualities of direct experience are of more value for art than the promised land, you will not make artists."

Benton also used the opportunity to speak about the controversy surrounding Diego Rivera's mural for the lobby of the RCA Building in New York. Rivera had been commissioned in October 1932 by the Rockefeller family to paint a mural titled *Man at the Crossroads Looking with Hope and High Vision to the Choosing of a New and Better Future* for the building in Rockefeller Center. Considering the contrasting politics of the arch-capitalist Rockefellers and the Marxist Rivera, it was an odd commission from the beginning, but controversy arose in April once Rivera added a portrait of Lenin to the wall. When members of the press learned about the portrait, they attacked the Rockefellers, who responded by asking Rivera to remove the face of Lenin. Rather than capitulate to censorship, Rivera refused and so was dismissed from the project, and on February 10 and 11, 1934, the mural was destroyed.

The episode caused a firestorm, and John Reed Club members were especially outraged. Rivera and other Mexican muralists were greatly admired by American artists: radical artists were impressed by their ability to marry populist ideology with avant-garde styles, while Benton admired their use of Renaissance materials, such as fresco, and envied their lucrative commissions. But when Benton refused to officially protest the Rockefellers' handling of the affair, he was criticized by his more radical peers. So in his speech, he defended his position. "To conclude—and in answer to some persistent questioning—I have not joined those who have been protesting the indignity put upon Diego Rivera's work in Rockefeller Center," he said, "because I do not feel, in view of the seriously decadent condition of our own art, that what happens to a Mexican art is of great importance."

As Benton remembers it, the event devolved into an angry fracas, with one furious youth yelling in his face, "I always knew you were a dirty anti-Semite, Benton." "This remark," he recalls, "without rhyme or reason, crude, deliberately offensive, knocked me off balance with anger." Before a league janitor cleared the stage, someone—an "enraged Commie," according to Benton—threw a chair at him.

Benton never again pretended to stand on common ground with the radical Left, though he did feel compelled to contemplate his rejection of Marxism. In 1937, more than a decade before Lionel Trilling bemoaned "the dark and bloody crossroads where literature and politics meet," Benton denounced the intrusion of ideology into life (albeit disingenuously, as his art was profoundly ideological). "Why I Don't Like Marxism" is the first of three essays in a series, titled "Confessions of an American," that analyzes the nation's inhospitality to dogma. "Life for the vital is to be lived," he begins, "and for most of us it is with a sense of frustration and some unwillingness that we set deliberately about thinking." Such sentiments, expressed in disdainful tones, opened Benton to charges of anti-intellectualism, and indeed the essays, which are nothing if not deliberate and dogmatic, are a bit absurd. "I am an amateur thinker," Benton feigns, "and one who thinks on the side, mostly in the privy. But I'm going to give some of my findings just the same." His thesis is that the logic of Marxism is merely a feeble representation of life as it's actually lived. "Truth, manhandled and stripped of some of its parts," he explains, "becomes readily a mere instrument of purpose." It is "the entrance of the *will*" into thinking, he maintains, that foils pragmatic thinking and "suppresses the urge to check and re-check in the field of experience." Benton expresses less skepticism about Marxism's declared ends than with its "intellectual methods," which strike him as "absolutist" and "programmatic." In 1935, when asked about his political viewpoint, he had offered this brief précis of his philosophy: "I believe in the collective control of the essential productive means and resources, but as a pragmatist I believe actual, not theoretical, interests do check and test the field of social change."

In an unpublished essay titled "Philosophy," Benton claimed that the intellectual paradigm that most appealed to him is the "relatively illogical and unsystematic body of comments called Pragmatism." To call pragmatism "unsystematic" seems fair, but the illogic of it, to Benton's mind anyway, seems to arise from the dense discourse that Dewey drew from in formulating his philosophy. Dewey, I imagine, is not easy for anyone, but Benton admits that others "would scorn the conclusions I draw from" him because "who ever completely understands a Philosopher?" That the amateur philosopher is able to draw conclusions from Dewey at all is because he has a way of writing about the relation between thinking and nature, about the organic and practical aspects of thoughts and ideas, that makes that relation appear utterly logical— thoughts that work are true. This is easy to read as an argument for action over reflection, and so it's not surprising that it was on these grounds that Benton attacked the intellectualism of Stieglitz. That Benton often spoke of Stieglitz as a religious figure, as a mystic with his own cabal, also isn't unexpected considering that Dewey cited William James's evaluation of the pragmatic turn as "an alteration in the 'seat of authority' that reminds one almost of the protestant reformation."

Benton's voluble negation of radical politics, in this and earlier writings and lectures, only confirmed what his leftist foes had always believed, that he was hopelessly backward—reactionary at best, and at worst, according to Davis, semi-fascist. For instance, the communist artist Jacob Burck excoriated him in a 1935 *Art Front* critique, suggesting that he was paranoid, haunted by a Stalinist "spectre," and nothing more than a failed modernist. But while Benton could be obstinately confrontational, he was not delusional; his anticommunism, in fact, was part of a larger trend among Popular Front intellectuals—Dewey, Dos Passos, and Edmund Wilson, for example—to bail on dogmatic radicalism during the mid- to late 1930s.

Dewey was never a communist, but he certainly rejected traditional liberalism's emphasis on individuality and advocated certain Soviet principles. In fact, his political philosophy was enmeshed enough with certain Marxist ideas that he felt compelled to distance himself from communism. As he so often did, Benton borrowed from Dewey when he titled his *Common Sense* essay "Why I Don't Like Marxism," for Dewey had published "Why I Am Not a Communist" three years earlier. In the essay, Dewey sounds a familiar refrain among non-Marxian reformers: "Particularly unacceptable to me in the ideology of official Communism is its monistic and one-way philosophy of history." He rejects dialectical materialism as illogical; its "uniform theory of revolutionary strategy and tactics," he concludes, fails in particular to account for the realities of American history and the American present.

Dos Passos, by contrast, had joined the Left in 1926, when he became a member of the executive board of *New Masses* and the Sacco-Vanzetti Defense Committee. He was, according to Michael Denning, a "rightful heir of John Reed" and even joined the picket lines of a textile workers' strike in Passaic, New Jersey. But Dos Passos would shift course, and because he satirized the Communist Party in his novels of the 1940s and 1950s, he suffered, in many ways, a similar fate to Benton's: just as critics forgot Benton and he was supplanted by Pollock, they ignored Dos Passos, who was surpassed by William Faulkner. Another similarity between the two was their admiration for distinct moments in American political history. Whereas Benton linked himself to Jeffersonianism, Dos Passos, according to Denning, told the tale of the decline of the Lincoln republic. In "The Use of the Past," his introductory essay to *The Ground We Stand On* (1941), Dos Passos insisted that there must be, somewhere in the American past, a non-Marxian model for reform. As further proof of the similar political trajectories of the two men, Benton's "Why I Don't Like Marxism" immediately preceded Dos

Passos's *Common Sense* essay "Farewell to Europe!" in which the author critiqued communist dogma.

"It was not easy," in the words of the literary historian Louis Filler, "to balance the desire for continuity and belonging with the need to dissent." We'd do well to keep this in mind as we consider Benton's place in 1930s political discourse. The prevailing view on his art and prose of the period is that they illuminate the tensions between, first, industrial progressivism and class struggle and, second, pragmatist and formalist aesthetics. In either case, Benton is the reactionary skeptic, opposing revolutionary politics or modern art criticism. No one can deny that he baited the Left with false dichotomies, or that he occasionally expressed misogynistic and homophobic attitudes, but his role in 1930s debates was not simply that of the contrarian. If we can trust his advocacy for "experience" and active commerce with the world at all, then we ought to be able to judge him as one who "lived" his heady political moment. What's often lost in sketches of Benton is the genuine anxiety one feels when compelled to choose between kinds of absolutism. The compulsion of Benton, and of his peers and enemies, was to always express themselves with finality and to construct foundational principles. This can be exaggerated and dangerous work, for it often obscures the ambivalences that determine character and belief. Having a chair thrown at him by an angry communist, or being called a fascist, had as much to do with Benton's reaction to radical leftism as did his pragmatism. Is this a revisionist view? Only insofar as biography is a revisionist methodology—and it seems silly to say so. In this case, what biography gives us is less a "new" Benton than "a man in full"—one who lived in his moment rather than one who merely observed it. The political portrait is a portrait of one's exterior; the political portrait, because it ignores human inconsistency, is usually a caricature. Biography works against caricature; it's a search for interiority, or what Leon Edel terms "habitual disorder"—the ironic, abrupt, and occasionally unreliable ways that humans express their experiences.

PART THREE

AFTER NEW YORK

9

AT WORK

When Benton was invited, in the winter of 1935, to join the faculty of the Kansas City Art Institute and to paint a mural in the Missouri State Capitol, he saw an opportunity to make some money and drive home a point or two. The offers allowed him to leave New York on his own terms and were attractive enough to persuade him that he was leaving for bigger and better things; a triumphant return to his native Missouri, he felt, would demonstrate his conviction that the nation's cultural vitality was centered on its middle states and that New York had become unhinged. Naturally, his public and distressing feuds with Stuart Davis and the John Reed Club made the decision easier, but, in addition, during the months prior to his departure Benton had finally sought his revenge against Alfred Stieglitz in a now infamous critique of the older man's legacy, which prompted an exchange of juvenile letters. Even before the dust had settled on these disputes, Benton understood that his life in New York was coming to an end.

On New Year's Day 1934, Stieglitz turned seventy. For three decades he had run galleries, mentored fellow artists, and served as vicar of "Spiritual America"—an America revitalized by a modern cultural idealism. In a portrait from that year by the photographer Imogen Cunningham, Stieglitz stands in front of *Black Iris* (1926), a painting by his wife, Georgia O'Keeffe, that's representative of much that he believed in: its expressiveness, formal elegance, and supposed objectification of feminine identity make it an icon of American modernism. Posing in front of the painting, Stieglitz is cerebral but regal: sharply dressed in a crisp white shirt, gray suit, and dark overcoat, he peers through a pair of delicate spectacles, the perfect complement to his wispy white hair. Stieglitz is the master of his universe: a patriarch, a seer, and, in a time of economic depression, a giver—of money and motivation. And so to celebrate his birthday and triumphs, and the ascendancy of modernism more generally, Stieglitz's friends and admirers apotheosized him in a lavish tribute, a Festschrift titled *America and Alfred Stieglitz*.

The book, published in late 1934, is an example of the occasionally absurd idolatries upon which some modern art depended. Biblical epigraphs ("And a man shall be as an hiding place from the wind, and a covert from the tempest; as rivers of water in a dry place, as the shadow of a great rock in a weary land") are followed by accolades from Lewis Mumford, John Marin, and Charles Demuth. William Carlos Williams sets the tone in an introductory essay that places Stieglitz in a Manichaean relation between Old World culture and American pragmatism. But, Williams concludes, he "carried the fullest load forward." Gertrude Stein contributed a poem titled "Stieglitz": "If anything is done and something is done then somebody has / to do it." A meditation by Sherwood Anderson, "City Plowman," closes the book. Anderson compares Stieglitz to the imaginary "Uncle Jim," a nurturing Ohio farmer. "And so Stieglitz to me," he muses. "He in the city releasing the men about him, turning the imaginations of other men loose in his city." The book's conceit isn't so much that the wise Stieglitz *is* America as that the man and the nation were shaped simultaneously by the inevitabilities—triumph over adversity, the hand of man in progress—of modernism.

The book was well received. The populist Literary Guild, run at the time by Carl Van Doren, chose it as its December selection, and *The Nation*, though admitting that the book was an "unusual experiment" and dogmatic, judged it a "success." But the elderly Stieglitz and his grandiloquent devotees were easy targets for those critics who believed that esoteric formalist credos had been usurped by Depression-era realities. These commentators objected on ideological grounds to nearly everything Stieglitz represented: elitism, chimerical intellectualism, and abstraction. They allowed that Stieglitz had had his day, namely in the years immediately preceding and just after the Armory Show, when he exhibited the work of European modernists at his 291 gallery and secured his position as the arbiter of modernism in America. Stieglitz's critics acknowledged that his exuberance helped revolutionize art in this country, only they believed that the revolution was over, and had been for some years before his seventieth birthday. In a review of *America and Alfred Stieglitz*, Edward Alden Jewell remarked that Stieglitz's mission "has fostered a sort of half-idolatrous worship, an atmosphere of incantation and pseudo-mystical brooding upon the thisness and that-ness of life and the human soul; a cult—it really seems to amount to that—befogged by clouds of incense and bemused by an endless flow of words." Frank Jewett Mather Jr. commented that inclusion in Stieglitz's circle required "idiosyncrasy rather than individuality."

The most relentless Stieglitz foe was Thomas Craven, who as early as 1924 had accused Stieglitz of hiding a lack of talent as a photographer behind an elaborate rhetoric. "I think that Stieglitz feels unconsciously the meager success of his intentions," Craven wrote in *The Nation*, "and for this reason discovers symbolical meanings and curious psychic values in what are only" photographs. In the same year that *America and Alfred Stieglitz* was published, Craven released *Modern Art*, a celebration of the regional painters he was friendly with. Perhaps Craven was aware that the Stieglitz book was due to be published, because his survey, by taking direct aim at the elderly photographer, reads more like a polemical manifesto than a critical analysis. "Art is not a philosophical system embracing the whole world," he comments, "it is the expression of the adventures and discoveries of the human organism reacting to environment, of the perpetual readjustment of habit to the procession of changing facts." Good art, according to Craven, is local, and he deprecates Stieglitz's foreignness; to his mind, American modernism is an abomination practiced by "every Jean, Jacques, or Judas," and Stieglitz's art in particular "had no possible bearing on American life." He portrays the 291 gallery as the hideout where this treacherous clique exchanged "half-baked philosophies and cockeyed visions." "Stieglitz," Craven concludes, "a Hoboken Jew without knowledge of, or interest in, the historical American background, was—quite apart from the doses of purified art he had swallowed—hardly equipped for the leadership of a genuine American expression; and it is a matter of record that none of the artists whose names and work he has exploited has been noticeably American in flavor."

Craven's caricature of Stieglitz was particularly nasty, especially considering that Stieglitz took considerable pride in his Hoboken roots. In a guide to a 1921 exhibition of his photographs at the Anderson Galleries, Stieglitz had written: "I was born in Hoboken. I am an American. Photography is my passion. The search for Truth my obsession." An "American" from Hoboken, according to Stieglitz; a "Hoboken Jew" in Craven's eyes. Stieglitz's trespass wasn't so much his aesthetic program as his insistence on being understood as essentially American. But Stieglitz was a smart man, and he took Craven's mean-spirited attacks for what they were. He never replied to Craven directly, choosing instead to dismiss him in letters to other people. Shortly after *Modern Art* was published, Stieglitz wrote to the critic Sheldon Cheney: "I suppose you have seen Craven's book. Ye gads I wonder does he recognize *art* when he is in front of it. I doubt it." For emphasis, Stieglitz directed Cheney to a review of Craven's book by Mumford that had run in a recent *New Yorker* issue. Mumford claimed that "Craven's attack on the abstractionists . . . would probably stir up the animals," meaning, perhaps, Stuart Davis and Benton.

Benton's reaction to his old mentor's commemorative was not so obviously racist as Craven's, but it was no less vulgar, and the vehemence of Benton's assault on the book, and modernism in general, upset Stieglitz. The cruel review, just as much a character assassination as a piece of cultural criticism, marked the end of another friendship for Benton. In addition to finally repulsing the patient Stieglitz, he insulted his own past. Though Benton had already published statements denigrating Stieglitz and his circle—in 1928, for instance, he recalled how "lonely" he used to feel at 291, adding, "I was deeply antagonized to discover that cryptic significances were being attached to . . . modern abstractions," and "[T]he horse sense that remained in this Missouri lawyer's son . . . revolted, and I began to wonder why, logic or no logic, I should continue to try getting representative meanings out of my art if I was going to put mystical ones in"—he had also admitted that his exposure to the 291 artists was an epochal episode in his life. But he always used the people he knew best, friend or foe, to advance his own interests. He couldn't imagine another way to behave. His review appeared in the journal *Common Sense* under the smug title "America and/or Alfred Stieglitz." Edited by Alfred M. Bingham and Selden Rodman, *Common Sense* (1932–1946), a left-wing monthly, encouraged a pseudo-socialist alternative to capitalism. Under the slogan "Production for use and not for profit," the editors of the journal, whose contributors included Upton Sinclair, John Dos Passos, Theodore Dreiser, and James Agee, called for a social and economic transformation driven not by a proletarian revolution but by middle-class dismay with the "ever-dwindling elite that was coming to own most of the property."

Benton probably gravitated toward *Common Sense* because of

Dewey's association with its editors and because the journal also sought out a middle ground between capitalism and communism. But whatever the exact nature of Benton's politics in 1935, he determined that *Common Sense* was the ideal venue for labeling Stieglitz an elitist, and he seemed to relish dismissing New York's art-world patriarch. "For the benefit of readers unacquainted with its subject," Benton writes, "let me say that I can testify to Stieglitz' existence in the flesh." The man, he acquiesces, is "lovable." But Benton quickly dispatched with the pleasantries. Stieglitz "has a mania for self aggrandizement and his mouth is never shut," he exclaims, adding, his "once potent" influence "is now dead"—his "illusory promise of achievement through 'mood cultivation,'" or emotional expression, was, Benton believed, a thing of the past. Of 291 Fifth Avenue, the gallery where Benton once had sought friendship and patronage, he quips, "I am certain that no place in the world ever produced more idiotic gable [*sic*] . . . The contagion of intellectual idiocy there rose to unbelievable heights." Writing about the contributors to the book, and about Stieglitz's disciples more generally, Benton claims, "Knowledge of life and of reality becomes for them . . . discoverable only in their egos." They are hedonists, he concludes, and "like boys addicted to bad habits." "Can you imagine [them] . . . throwing a baseball straight?"

While this issue of *Common Sense* was still on the newsstand, a hurt Stieglitz sent Benton a letter. "And ye Gods didn't I chuckle," he wrote, "as . . . I shared the good time you had while writing" the review. Stieglitz compared the criticisms in the review to the "contortions" in Benton's murals and reminded him that at one time he had begged to have his work shown at 291. Benton responded a few days later and dug in his heels, insisting that he had never asked to exhibit at the gallery. He also reflected, combatively but indelibly, on the tribulations of an artist's work, which he called a "battle royal":

> And, believe me, that [painting] exercises your ingenuity and enlarges your acquaintance of many, many things that you'll never read about. And that you can't write about. It's one "desperate situation" after another, but, By God, let me live desperately—I'll let the literary gigolos do the "thinking" if I can keep tangled up in situations. I am an American and when I have a theory, it's a tool and not a God.

Benton never wrote so emotionally about his work, in particular the psychological trauma a painter suffers in the working out of relevant experiences and political expressions, what he calls "situations." One may cringe when reading these letters, especially their petty jabs, but they're remarkable documents for how they articulate the co-dependence of modernism and regionalism—for each requires the rejection of the other—and the doubts that haunted each man.

Stieglitz had the last word, replying to Benton's letter before he'd even finished reading it. He asked for Benton's sympathy, explaining that his duties at An American Place, his latest gallery, required him to meet with thousands of people, many "foolish," but some "intelligent," each month. He dispatched with Craven easily—"blind as a bat and as prejudiced as anyone I have ever met"—but admitted that Benton's review had upset him: "What I can't understand is the animus which prompted you to pour slops over my head just because some people insisted on writing a book about me because I happened to be seventy years old and in service for fifty years without ever having received any remuneration personally in any form for all this service." In closing, Stieglitz invited Tom and Rita to have dinner with Georgia and him, "to have a good laugh," but their correspondence ends there. Just a month before Benton's *Common Sense* review appeared, one critic had commented presciently on Stieglitz's monumentality, pointing out that other artists' egos "break upon him, but he lets them engineer the collision. He does not bruise them; they bruise themselves."

By April 1935, Benton had had enough of such skirmishing and announced that he was leaving New York and returning to Missouri. The announcement came just when his reputation had reached its height in New York: the *Time* article had appeared three and a half months earlier, he was contributing regularly to journals and magazines (that were well-known in downtown Manhattan at least), and during the first two weeks of April he had a successful exhibition at the Ferargil Galleries. Full-blown regionalist paintings such as *Lord, Heal the Child* and *Preparing the Bill* received both plenty of criticism and high praise, and Mumford used the occasion to write a lengthy review for *The New Yorker*. He identifies three Bentons: "a man with a great appetite for facts," evidenced in his travel sketches; an ambitious and reaching artist with a weakness for sentimentality; and a "more human" and "more profound . . . observer and poet" whose smaller oils were often "sweet and poignant."

Though Mumford believed that to find an artist equal to Benton's journalistic images of plain life one had to go back to Winslow Homer, he also felt that Benton strove too hard to strike an earthy tone: "Afraid of being highbrow, he takes refuge in puerility." It was a fair review, and likely a sign of Mumford's willingness to remain friendly with his old acquaintance, but nothing could hold Benton back from dishonoring the city that had given him so much. Before departing, he gave an interview to the New York *Sun* in which he hurled some final insults at the city he had called home for over twenty years. He was going to Kansas City, he explained, because this "place has lost its masculinity . . . You can't go to any cocktail party or sidle up to any bar without having somebody grab you by the coat lapel and deliver you a body of principles . . . Do I think I'm going to escape stupidity in the Middle West?" he concluded. "Of course not. Wherever people talk, idiocy thrives." In another interview, Benton blamed doctrinaire Marxism for his disillusionment with New York. "Don't get the idea," he said, "that I have any hatred for Communists—I used to be one of them myself ten years ago, and I still am a collectivist . . . If the radical movement is to get anywhere in this country it has to drop Marxism as an outworn historical and economic notion and rely wholly on a pragmatic observance of developing facts."

These assertions illustrated his adherence to an "ethic of responsibility," which Max Weber differentiates, in "Politics as a Vocation" (1919), an influential essay for American pragmatists, from an "ethic of ultimate ends." The latter appeals to radicals, the former requires one to account for the foreseeable results of one's action. An ethic of ultimate ends, as Weber defines it, has only "exemplary value"—what Benton described again and again as a verbal appeal—while an ethic of responsibility emphasizes consequences over principles. Such political arguments are emblematic of a larger cultural discourse that emerged in the early 1930s. In the days before his move to Missouri, Benton worked hard to authenticate his grassroots pragmatism; to do so, he tapped into a rhetoric of regionalism that was aggressively antimodern in its back-to-the-land campaign. In 1929, for instance, the journalist and commentator Walter Lippmann had intoned against the "acids of modernity"—which he understood as inhospitable to any kinds of basic assumptions, or "orthodoxies"—and built the foundation for a philosophy that was articulated more emotionally in the first regionalist manifesto, *I'll Take My Stand* (1930), a book of twelve essays by leading southern agrarians. In his essay "The Hind Tit," Andrew Nelson Lytle issued the book's most vociferous credos. "To be caught unwittingly in this unhappy condition" of false prosperity, he argues, "is calamitous; but to make obeisance before it, after learning how barren is its rule, is to be eunuched." Lytle goes on to advocate doing "what we did after the war and after the Reconstruction: return to our looms, our handcrafts, our reproducing stock. Throw out the radio and take down the fiddle from the wall."

Artists and writers obliged: that same year Grant Wood painted *American Gothic*, and in the next Pearl Buck published *The Good Earth*, a bestseller. The regionalist revolt was under way, and its charge was to stem the nation's decay and redirect the course of empire away from material and intellectual excess—away from cosmopolitan consumption and back toward a hearty folk ethos. Occasionally, tactless attacks on intellectuals and modernists, such as Benton's on Stieglitz, indicated what Robert L. Dorman, in his history of the regionalist movement, called the "siege mentality" adopted by many regionalists who feared that modernization would totally disintegrate familiar ideals. According to another *I'll Take My Stand* essayist, Lyle H. Lanier, who believed that magazines, radios, and billboards spouted the false promise of progress, "The conviction that our noisy social ferment portends progressive development toward some highly desired, but always undesignated, goal is perhaps the central psychological factor in the maintenance of our top-heavy industrial superstructure."

But if these were some of the basic tenets of orthodox regionalism, then Benton certainly had *not* been a regionalist during the early 1930s, for his murals were full of the modern symbols these writers deplore (subways, popular entertainments, skyscrapers, and technological forms of labor), which are presented right alongside more rural behaviors, as vital aspects of contemporary experience. But as Dorman explains, regionalism did profess some modish impulses, including a desire "to make a democratic politics out of the essentially modernist faith in the ordering, integrative 'power of art,'" a high degree of idealism, and a fervent pursuit of a national aesthetic.

In 1951, almost a decade after regionalism lost its charm and hold on the popular imagination, Benton reflected on the nature of the movement's art, which he said represented a "home-grown, grass-roots artistry which damned 'furrin' influence and which knew nothing about and cared nothing for the traditions of art as cultivated city snobs, dudes, and assthetes knew them." But sixteen years earlier, as the movers were emptying his New York apartment, he sat down and composed a farewell essay to New York City that exposes the cosmopolitan spirit underneath his regionalist persona. He calls Manhattan "provincial" and intellectuals "dogmatic, self-righteous, and humorless" but also acknowledges his affection for both, noting that the "warring cliques of the city have provided a constant accompaniment to my doings." He offers a warmhearted goodbye to "people I learned to like," among them shopgirls, burlesque dancers, "actors and pugs, homos and skirt chasers, radicals and conservatives," and his students. "I wouldn't have missed living in New York," he concludes, "even if I am now through with it forever."

In the winter of 1934–1935, before he left New York, Benton traveled to the Midwest on a lecture tour arranged by Audrey McMahon, the head of the Federal Art Project in New York City, who recruited him to promote New Deal arts projects to midwestern politicians. "My known attitudes," Benton recalls, "might offset the belief, aroused by the vociferousness of New York's young communist artists, that art had become a disloyal enterprise." Benton got a six-week leave from the Art Students League and headed out to stump for McMahon, visiting auditoriums, colleges, and universities from Pittsburgh to Lubbock. In Iowa, he met Grant Wood, who encouraged him to return to the Midwest, and in Jefferson City, Missouri, he met up with the state senator Ed Barbour, an old acquaintance and the subject of a 1934 painting. *Preparing the Bill* depicts Barbour negotiating with two constituents in a hotel room. The men sit around a small desk, talking, smoking cigars, and drinking; they have already finished one bottle and are onto another. A Gideon Bible sits on the edge of the desk and contrasts a stricter kind of law with the closed-door, inebriated dickering taking place in the dark room. Apparently, Barbour was not pleased with the painting, likely because it portrays him as susceptible to seamy influences, but when the painting was shown in New York, it received universal praise, even from the leftist press. A critic for *New Masses*, for instance, praised Benton for getting "below the surface to more significant meanings."

Coincidentally, it was at a hotel-room bender with Barbour and other Democratic politicians, which took place during Benton's visit to Jefferson City, that the idea of a mural for the Missouri capitol was first raised. Everyone was "spinning" from the alcohol when Barbour made the suggestion, so Benton believed it was an empty promise. But a few months later, after he'd returned to New York City, his brother, Nat, prosecuting attorney for Greene County, sent him a copy of a bill that was before the Missouri legislature: it recommended that the state commission him to make a mural for the capitol on the subject of Missouri history. The bill passed on May 28, 1935, and appropriated sixteen thousand dollars to Benton. He was pleased by the money but quibbled with one point in the contract: he refused to work under the authority of the Missouri State Art Commission, which he suspected would resist in his social history of the state the inclusion of lowlife subjects, such as Jesse James and the story of Frankie and Johnny. To Benton's great surprise, his terms were accepted. He later marveled at the deal having been struck, for he'd learned that McMahon had traveled to Missouri to build support for Federal Art Project artists from New York and had offended many state politicians with her "pretensions." These officials, according to Benton, were wary of big-city artists coming to the state and preferred to administer their patronage on their own terms. But his theory as to why he won the commission is a bit far-fetched: he speculated that state Democrats agreed to the terms to honor his father's years of loyal service to the party. True or not, Benton believed that the mural commission was a deferred patrimony, and so he must have been struck by the irony that from beyond the grave the Colonel had facilitated the career that he'd so often criticized when he was alive.

Benton explained to a Missouri reporter that he was returning to Missouri because "this part of the country is going to dominate social change and I want to be here to see what happens, not just hear about it." So on September 23, 1935, after months of bluster, the Bentons moved into their new house at 905 East Forty-seventh Street in Kansas City. From the beginning, Benton envisaged the capitol mural, which he called *A Social History of the State of Missouri*, as a people's history, and almost immediately after arriving in Missouri, he began choosing which Mark Twain characters he would include and traveling throughout the state to sketch local folk, farms, and livestock. But even during these preparatory stages he had to dodge criticism, especially from observers who worried that the new mural would raise the kind of negative press he'd received for his earlier works. But as usual, he was unfazed. "Now get me right," he said, "none of my stuff is propaganda. I'm a realist. I paint what I see. You supply the materials. I can't always be painting pictures of people going around in frock coats and carrying Bibles. They don't act that way."

Benton worked on the mural for over a year, completing it in December 1936. Besides his sketching sojourns and taking time to build a massive fifteen-foot-long clay model, he had to develop a plan for filling a huge amount of wall space in the House lounge of the capitol building. Moreover, he had to reckon with windows, doors, and right angles that interrupted the flow of the walls and presented him with his most difficult technical challenge yet. Still another impediment was the weather; while he painted in the House lounge, the temperatures ran from below zero to above one hundred degrees. Benton took on these challenges with equal parts ingenuity and obstinacy. On the one hand, he worked hard every day; erected an elaborate scaffold; figured out the sequencing, proportions, and illusionistic effects of the mural; and finished the project a month before the contract deadline. On the other hand, for an artist who paid so much lip service to the public and popular taste, he proved remarkably inhospitable to comments and advice about his subjects and execution.

In addition to removing any mention of the Missouri State Art Commission from his contract language, Benton refused to submit preliminary designs to any of the boards that oversaw the decoration and architecture of the capitol building. According to Sidney Larson, a student and close friend of Benton's, once Benton decided on a plan for a painting or mural, he was intractable. "Gee," Larson recalls observing one day, "you don't allow any room for intuition. You don't allow any room for the painting talking back to you." Benton responded, "All those things can happen in the planning." One can understand, perhaps, the necessity for a focused, systematic approach to the mural; Benton was a seasoned professional trying to complete a large project with a firm deadline. He knew what he was doing, and state oversight would only interfere with his progress. More surprising was Benton's refusal to listen to the mural's patrons or constituents, the people who paid him, posed for him, and made up the mural's subject matter and audience. His approach to this group was, ironically, "artist knows best," a Stieglitz Circle principle that he'd obstinately rejected in his many statements and articles advocating populist philosophies.

On one occasion a reporter from the *Kansas City Journal-Post* visited the House lounge and remarked to Benton, "Interesting faces—whom do they belong to? Thinkers, orators, actors, businessmen?" Angered by the perceived criticism, Benton responded that his depiction of these figures was perfectly legitimate: "The average businessman has an absolutely uninteresting face . . . because he has dealt with abstractions for so long that he has ceased to be a realist." He claims that only people "who handle things, objects, actualities" have interesting faces. "Your garage man, your coal man, your farmer," he writes, "they are men with physiognomies which attract and hold attention." Benton's defensiveness was odd, especially considering his willingness to open the House lounge to visitors while he was working. *Time* magazine reported that visitors, many of whom ate while they browsed the lounge, "gaped earnestly at a small, dark, wiry man painting furiously in a faint odor of rotten eggs, while the walls slowly blossomed with mule skinners, Mormons, dancing Negroes and Mississippi boatmen." But though he'd invited them there, Benton claimed that he didn't want to be bothered: "I do not want busybodies fussing with my subject matter—at least until I have finished." In fact, he posted a letter in the lounge asking that guests keep their mouths shut. "The 'realness' of this work," he explained, "depends on a lot of abstract adjustments of lines and planes and gradation of color. These adjustments cannot be disturbed without causing me a lot of work, without, in fact, making me do this thing all over." When he was bothered, he'd stare down the culprits, and on one occasion, when two visitors disturbed some of his paints, he came down from his scaffold and scolded them: "God damn it, keep your fucking hands off my stuff."

Benton acquiesced to outside pressure only once. Missouri's governor, Guy Park, summoned him to his office one day and informed him that an important black politico from St. Louis, Mr. Sharkey, was sitting in the waiting room and had just complained about the depiction of African Americans in the mural. In particular, he was angry about a small vignette on the north wall that showed black slaves being whipped at the lead mines of St. Francois County, an event that Benton had researched. Sitting in the governor's office, trying to reassert his control over the project, Benton had an idea. He asked to see Mr. Sharkey and escorted him into the lounge. He explained to him that he'd been having a hard time with a depiction of an outdoor political rally on the east wall featuring his father. He needed a model for a black figure who is prominently placed, leaning against a dead tree, and listening intently to the Colonel's speech. "Mr. Sharkey," Benton said, "I've been looking for a face of a prominent politician of your race for this figure. I want to show the progress of Missouri's colored people from their unhappy beginnings, shown by the lead mine scene, to their present position of political importance in the State . . . How about my putting your face on that figure?" The man agreed, and the sensitive situation was defused.

The story, which flows across the walls with a boiling energy, begins on the north wall with scenes of pioneers arriving in the state by boat and settling the land. Benton depicts various frontier types on this wall, including a trader and an Osage Indian swapping whiskey for furs, an ax-wielding timberman, and a blacksmith forging a wagon wheel. Directly above the north door is the most famous scene from the mural. The first of three panels illustrating Missouri legends, it shows Huck Finn admiring a trophy catfish caught by his friend Jim. In the background, a paddleboat—the *Sam Clemens*—cruises the Mississippi River. The east wall is composed mostly of scenes that Benton knew directly from childhood experiences, such as the political rally, and from his tours throughout the state—a courtroom vignette, for instance, based on a visit he made to a Springfield courthouse to observe his brother, Nat, prosecute a case. The second legendary scene is placed above the east door and depicts the outlaw James Boys staging bank and train robberies. The south wall describes city life in Missouri and includes scenes of shoe manufacturing and the brewing industry. A lively depiction of the tragedy of Frankie and Johnny, memorialized by many composers in popular songs that tell the story of how Frankie killed her lover, is situated above the south door. In Benton's telling, Frankie discovers her man, Johnny, with another woman in a barroom heated by a potbellied stove; enraged by his indiscretion, she shoots him in the rear, thus taking a violent, sexualized revenge.

The mural, in fact, is full of violence: a lynched slave hangs from a tree, the James Boys shoot innocent victims, and a butcher in rubber boots prepares to kill another cow in a stockyard. Missouri history, Benton shows, was characterized by aggression, revenge, and blood. As

Benton sees it, this history was the foundation for the boisterous, vital present of the state. True to his stated plans for the mural, his social history is unromantic and fulfills his promise to convey what he called the "characteristic aspects of human struggle that was and is Missouri." The occasionally acid tone of *A Social History of the State of Missouri* demonstrates that Benton was no Jeffersonian idealist but, rather, a New Deal reformer who now and then reminded his audience of the "inadequacies of democracy in the past, and in the present." Benton's purpose was to illustrate a faith in modern industrialization "tempered by the values of a reinvigorated producerism." To this end, the numerous vignettes, and the various centuries they depict, hang together insofar as they provide settings for the same kind of purposeful labor.

True though this may be, commentators fixated instead on the mural's exposition of a flawed democracy and its overwrought storytelling. *The Kansas City Star* reviewed the mural favorably, noting that, in Benton's hands, Missouri's history was "sometimes inspiring, sometimes a little ridiculous and even shady, but always intensely human." Many public officials were less kind, however. Lou E. Holland, for instance, a former president of the Kansas City Chamber of Commerce, criticized the mural's depiction of Missouri history. "Missouri is not proud of hangings and Negro honky-tonks," Holland claimed. "She is not proud of the whipping of slaves, the slave block and Jesse James holdups." Another detractor was T. G. Field, who wrote a letter to the *Star* declaiming the "crudeness" of the mural: "The work of true artists, such as Daumier, Rembrandt, and Brueghel, often presents unsavory subjects but does so with beauty and fluency." Field's implication was that the mural was less fine art than sensational entertainment and that its dramatic narrative and baroque forms contaminated the walls of the lounge, transforming its serenity into a spectacle. Considering his affection for the popular arts, however, one suspects that Benton would have been pleased by such a characterization of his mural.

Missouri legislators were equally outraged. "Benton's shown Missouri as nothing but honky-tonk, hillbillies, and robbers," one said. "We're more than a coon dog state!" Another angry legislator exclaimed, "Not a brush mark indicates cultural, moral, or spiritual institutions in the state!" It was the inclusion of a portrait of "Boss Tom" Pendergast, shown at a business dinner on the south wall, that most irritated the critics. Pendergast, the corrupt boss of Kansas City Democrats, was arraigned in 1939 for failing to pay taxes and bribery, but the investigation into his strong-arm tactics had begun in 1936, and many legislators were furious that his was the mural's face of local politics. The uproar over the Pendergast portrait lasted for some time; as early as January 1937, one newspaper accused Benton of libeling his home state ("Shame on you, Thomas Hart Benton, shame on you"), and six years later representatives were still demanding that the governor remove the portrait from the mural. Matthew Murray, the state Works Progress Administration director, put it most succinctly: "I wouldn't hang [Benton] on my shit-house wall."

A few years before his death, Benton casually dismissed the controversy surrounding the Missouri mural, remarking to an interviewer that the general public admired the work. He explained that it was "just a bunch of machine politicians and the polite element of society, mostly Republicans," who protested. In fact, and not surprisingly, he was dismayed by the criticism, which was unforeseen (was this the public he'd so longed for in New York?) and struck him as stupid (since when was history supposed to be beautiful?). Benton made his case in an essay, "The Missouri Mural and Its Critics," written shortly after he completed the project. Sounding a familiar refrain, he argues that while murals historically have been hijacked in the name of political power, "I see mural painting as no different from any other painting in its responsibilities to experience." He adds, "The actions of Frankie and Johnny back on the St. Louis waterfront . . . illustrate better the realities of life as it is actually lived than do anybody's opinions about the Constitution."

As frustrating as it may have been to have to spell out his philosophy for those he'd hoped would get it, 1937 was a good year for Benton: he received assignments from a major magazine and published his autobiography, and an exhibition of his work in Chicago earned some high praise (a *Tribune* critic called the paintings "virile" and "serious"). In July, *Life* magazine hired him to make sketches of a labor war in Michigan: leftist organizers and union busters were facing off in Flint, and bloodshed seemed imminent over the Independence Day weekend. Though the sketches were merely objective descriptions of protesting workers, union men, and the police, *Life*'s editors presented them as satires of proletariats and those who worked on their behalf. Though there's no record of his reaction to this editorial decision, it might have warned Benton, who in fact was ambivalent about unions but always sympathetic to laborers, that magazine work was more trouble than it was worth.

But the next month he received another commission from *Life*, this time to go to Hollywood to paint a picture of the motion picture industry. While in Los Angeles, Benton socialized at the Cock and Bull and made sketches of casting calls, set designs, and stars such as W. C. Fields. Other populist painters had preceded him to Hollywood, most notably Norman Rockwell, whose painting *Movie Starlet and Reporters* appeared on the cover of *The Saturday Evening Post* in March 1936. Whereas Rockwell stereotyped the lure of fame—the painting shows a beautiful blond actress surrounded by slavering reporters—Benton's painting is more perceptive and illustrates how his critical eye distinguished his work from Rockwell's cartoony pictures.

As the editors wanted a large painting, Benton worked on a big scale: the painting is five by seven feet. His imaginative solution to the challenge of working on this scale was, for the first time, to treat the canvas like a mural, breaking the narrative into busy vignettes, each describing an aspect of movie production. The acting is depicted in the center of the painting—where the bombshell, supposedly modeled after Jean Harlow, preens and holds a pearl-tipped scepter and the leading man kneels at her feet, staring at her midriff—and to the left, on a secondary set, where a man rescues a woman from an ax-wielding attacker. Behind the center stage, several actresses wait for their turns with a makeup artist, and beyond them, in the far background, a reconstructed city burns in a smoldering fire during the filming of *In Old Chicago*, starring Tyrone Power. To expose those elements of filmmaking that are unseen in the final product, Benton encircles the starlet on the central set with the workers and machines that actually record the image and sound of her performance; we see the cameraman hovering on a boom above her, the director gesturing next to a spotlight, and two men operating the microphone and recording equipment.

Benton made his intentions very clear when he said that the painting was meant to reveal "the combination of a machine and sex that Hollywood is." One assumes that the *Life* editors were displeased with such an unglamorous message, one, moreover, contained in such a complex composition. Whereas the movies are meant to spirit us away from this world, Benton pulls back the curtains on that trick, showing it to be an illusion made possible by toiling craftspeople. So to put it more directly, what the painting does is portray Hollywood as a machine that produces commodities but that is powered by the hard work of actual laborers. Seen in this light, the painting is a Marxist critique of the desires that drive capitalism, and so it's no surprise that a popular magazine chose not to publish it.

Surely it would have been easier for Benton to depict Hollywood glamour, as this is what his editors desired. They had arranged for him to work out of the luxurious office of Raymond Griffith, a producer for Twentieth Century–Fox, and expected that he'd make sketches and a painting to promote the film industry to the magazine's readers. Though the editors gave no reason for rejecting the painting, Henry Adams speculates that the almost-nude "blond sex bomb" at its center was too "salacious," while Erika Doss argues that the editors were turned off by its emphasis on the labor behind cultural production rather than the enchantments of movies themselves.

In July 1934, Benton had published an article and some sketches describing a trip to Arkansas's hill country in *Travel*, a magazine issued by the McBride publishing company. Based on the success of that article, the New York publishing house commissioned him to write an autobiography, which he worked on after he arrived in Missouri and published in October 1937. Benton had always been quick to the pen, dashing off richly descriptive letters to family and friends and frequently responding to criticism with thoughtful essays and articles, and *An Artist in America* is generally recognized as a classic of its kind: the narrative is terse but vivid, and the sentences are characterized by a pungent vernacular language. The book is part autobiography (offering candid reminiscences of his childhood), part travelogue (describing in abundant detail his various trips to the Ozarks, the rural South, and the mountainous West), and part political manifesto (emphasizing at every turn his liberal pragmatism). It's as good a book about the era as any by an American artist and has been reprinted several times. Sinclair Lewis praised the book in *Newsweek*, writing, "Here is a rare thing, a painter who can write. Here is a rarer [thing]—a man who meditates on beauty and has the sanity to recognize it . . . He has the painter's eye, that perceives the strangeness in everything from the bayous of Louisiana by moonlight to the expert spitting of a Georgia justice of the peace." Clifton Fadiman, writing in *The New Yorker*, exclaimed that the book was "all Missouri and no Compromise," while another popular regionalist painter, Grant Wood, called the book "vigorous and provocative."

Well-written and entertaining as the book may be, it's pure ideology. It's been suggested that Benton wrote the book to justify, to himself and his critics, his moving back to Missouri; certainly the fracas over the capitol mural caused Benton to second-guess the decision, but his autobiography works tirelessly to describe a Missouri that gives birth to authentic men. Benton may have been much more than a reactionary, but *An Artist in America* structures an undeniably conservative story: the young boy, schooled in hard knocks, seeks out the modern world, only to return home, not quite chagrined like the prodigal son, but humbled— and respectful of what he'd abandoned—nevertheless. Benton's parting words for New York intellectuals hadn't been forgotten, and not surprisingly the city's leftists, who felt betrayed by his rejection of the urban scene, attacked the book by claiming that it demonstrated his hackneyed traditionalism.

Reviewing the memoir in *Partisan Review*, Meyer Schapiro argues that "despite his frankness and his admission of doubts, the story of his pivotal decisions and their effects is too much on the surface, too rationalized, to be altogether convincing." Schapiro judges Benton's attitudes toward modern art to be "philistine" and based on personality rather than the "problems posed by the time." But the review takes politics, not aesthetics, as its main topic and summarizes a familiar critique of Benton: Schapiro argues that the book's principal line of reasoning is "If we must not escape from this world, neither should we change it." It may be too soon to consider Benton a "fascist," Schapiro concludes, but the "appeal to the national sentiment should set us on guard, whatever its source." As he did in many of his paintings, Benton obscured his pragmatist politics behind mannered and occasionally mythopoetic imagery—what he himself admitted was perhaps a "romantic view"— and so all but invited leftist criticism.

One irony of the book, however, is that despite its testaments to American democracy, it bears witness as well to the experimentation, doubt, and transformation that distinguish an engaged life. Whatever the precise nature of Benton's stated political philosophy, *An Artist in America* illustrates, alternately with reasoned analysis and what Clarence R.

Decker, the president of the University of Kansas City, called a "puckish zest," the rewards of intellectual exploration and the necessity to question power, both of which can lead to radical metamorphosis. Each of the personal shifts Benton describes in the book comes on the heels of a period of deliberate engagement with a new idea or milieu—with synchromism, for instance, and communism, the folk of Chilmark, John Weichsel's progressivism, and Dewey's theories of experience. Whatever else might be said of Benton, he wasn't complacent or capricious, and his book is the culmination of twenty years of intellectual engagement. Whether he'd agree or not, it speaks to a life of the mind as much as it does to a life determined by experience. The Benton described in the book, while pugnacious and arrogant, remains curious and wide-awake; even if he practiced them heavy-handedly, Benton came by his philosophies honestly.

The rhetoric of experience in Walt Whitman's poetry and prose obviously influenced the book's language, and its Whitmanesque passages in turn influenced Woody Guthrie's beloved autobiography, *Bound for Glory* (1943), which also borrowed heavily from the language and attitude of the poet-troubadour: both Whitman and Guthrie talk of loafing and wandering, and both speak to and on behalf of popular experience—"the main thing," Whitman observes in *Democratic Vistas*, "being the average, the bodily, the concrete, the democratic, the popular." Guthrie's book resembles Benton's in uncanny ways. Though there's no evidence that the two ever met, the art historian Ellen G. Landau finds numerous analogies between the men and their "vernacular" language: one, she observes, was an artist who played folk music; the other was a folk musician who made numerous sketches and drawings, many of which illustrate his book. In addition, during World War II, both expressed a vehement antifascism—Benton in his series *The Year of Peril* and Guthrie in poems and songs.

The books, though, have something even deeper in common: both authors tell stories of how direct engagement with common folk obliged them to break free from the psychic insularity an artistic life can induce. Contrary to popular opinion, the books celebrate not a rural provincialism but, rather, a vast and diverse national geography and culture. For example, reminiscing about an employment opportunity in Oklahoma, Guthrie envisions the vistas that would open for him in the heartland. "The world got twice as big and four times brighter," he writes. "Flowers changed colors, got taller, more of them. The sun talked and the moon sung tenor. Mountains rubbed bellies, and rivers tore loose to have picnics, and the big redwood trees held dances every night."

In January 1939, *Life* magazine sent its best photographer, the German-born Alfred Eisenstaedt, to take pictures of Benton as he worked on his infamous nude *Persephone* (1939). One of the unpublished photographs from the portrait session, which depicts Benton as he puts the finishing touches on the painting, corroborates the popular image of him as a brash, masculine, tobacco-smoking artist: as Benton stares at his model's breasts, he clenches a pipe bit in his teeth. And yet the photograph illuminates much of what is admirable about Benton's art; it shows an artist committed to visceral, sensorial experience. At the moment depicted, he is in contact with the eroticism that is the painting's subject; he experiences the titillation, and even enacts the voyeurism, that *Persephone* illustrates. Observing Benton standing there, between the canvas and the naked model, one literally sees the painting come to life.

The *Life* article profiles two paintings that Benton produced during the late 1930s, *Susanna and the Elders* (1938) and *Persephone*. It explains that he'd been reviewing the Apocrypha and Greek mythology looking for ancient subjects to update and place in a Missouri setting. *Susanna and the Elders* had been shown in 1938 at the Whitney, as part of an exhibition titled *Artists West of the Mississippi*, and received typically mixed reviews, but the painting became infamous when the exhibition was shown the next year at the City Art Museum in St. Louis. The director of the museum, Meyric Rogers, threatened to ban the painting from the show on the grounds that it was "much too nude." Rogers acquiesced, however, and exhibited the painting, though with a rope around it to prevent viewers from taking too prurient an interest in its details, such as Susanna's pubic hair. Nevertheless, some local viewers expressed outrage: Mary Ellis, for instance, a sixty-five-year-old pastor, exclaimed, "The nude is stark naked. It's lewd, immoral, obscene, lascivious, degrading, an insult to womanhood and the lowest expression of pure filth." Benton, though, pretended to be unperturbed; upon hearing about Ellis's comments, he responded, "That's funny as hell."

In fact, he was irritated by the controversy, frustrated yet again that the public (especially the Missouri public) proved more conservative than he anticipated. When a former student of Benton's from the Art Students League, the muralist Archie Musick, slighted the painting—in a review of the exhibition he quipped that "even Benton has achieved better flesh tones . . . in a bar-room nude"—Benton shot Musick a farcical letter:

> You flea-bitten red rock coyote, so you've turned art critic on us have you. The Rocky Mountain assthete. You begin . . . with promise. Quite like the type you start your career by completely disregarding all facts and mislabeling a masterpiece. You have the abandon of a Union Square historian, the malignant and atrocious affrontery of a Fogg graduate and the ignorance of a professor or a Forbes Watson. Bar Room nude! Educate yourself in the simplest distinctions of our craft. Don't you know that bar room nudes do not have hair on their pussys?

The Rape of Persephone, the original title of the second nude, depicts Pluto—who abducts the goddess to the underworld—as an old, horrifyingly lecherous Missouri farmer; he creeps up on Persephone as she daydreams on the banks of a pastoral stream. Benton endows the female figure with all the attributes a goddess of springtime could ever need: black silky hair, full red lips, ample curves, and firm breasts. She's a fruit ripe for picking. Despite the overstated allegory—the art critic Robert Hughes describes it as fit for "the Moscow subway"—the painting is significantly better than *Susanna and the Elders*; it's full of color, lavish natural details, and soft spring light. But the public reacted, of course, to the painting's sexuality, not to its pastoral symbolism or aesthetic qualities. One female critic, for example, described the painting as "cheap and trivial, with the subtlety of a calendar picture," while Karal Ann Marling, a contemporary art historian, claims that *Persephone* is "one of the great works of American pornography." Adams detects a personal iconography in the painting's extravagant salaciousness, suggesting that Benton had in mind the barroom nude that he'd seen at Joplin's House of Lords thirty years earlier, which also featured an assault on a naked woman. In addition, Benton's Persephone resembles the Joplin prostitute to whom he lost his virginity; Persephone, like the prostitute, has black hair and a red kimono. Adams also supposes that the painting illustrates Benton's recollection of his parents' disturbing sexual relationship: Benton recalls being frightened by his mother's "protesting screams when my father entered her room at night." Pluto, like the Colonel, is an ugly brute.

Speculative as such a reading may be, *Persephone* undeniably treats the more general themes of sexual conquest and frustration. For one thing, Benton admitted to being sexually attracted to the model who posed for Persephone. She "was a beautiful girl," he told an interviewer in 1939. "I saw her the other day and she's more beautiful than ever. She's so beautiful that you go away muttering for the rest of the day." Seen in this light, the painting becomes something more provocative than a mere nude, springtime allegory, or autobiographical reference; it becomes a visual record of an experienced arousal, of the artist's desire for the flesh of his model/subject. We can read, then, in Eisenstaedt's photograph a symbolism that mirrors that of the painting: the model becomes Persephone—innocent and prostrate—and Benton assumes the role of the abductor having his way with her body. But whatever Benton's precise intentions with the painting, one is struck by how a painter known for pragmatic expression arrived at an allegorical mode of storytelling in *Susanna and the Elders* and *Persephone*.

One explanation is that he turned to mythological, apocryphal, and personal subjects to express not just sexual desire but, as Doss puts it, "a profound lack of faith in the tradition he had celebrated throughout the thirties." As the decade drew to a close, New Deal reformism petered out, and the nation turned its attention from political transformation to antifascism and other international dilemmas. As a result, Benton was momentarily stuck—he admits, in fact, that as the 1930s came to an end "there came over me now and then a sense of uneasiness," adding, "I was almost completely frustrated" by the "new democratic patterns"—and so sought in the nudes a new mode of expression ("an art of fantasy," according to Doss) that invites psychological readings. Seen in this context, *Persephone* symbolizes anxieties that aren't just sexual but that relate as well to a loss of control over the instrumentality of his art during a disorienting moment of political change.

The Eisenstaedt photograph that did appear in the *Life* article reveals yet something else at work in the painting. Like the unpublished photograph, it captures Benton at work on *Persephone* in his classroom studio at the Kansas City Art Institute, where he began teaching shortly after his return to Missouri. The photograph demonstrates how Benton had come, through his teaching, to view painting as an act of communal fellowship. To be sure, there's an element of performance in his teaching as seen here—he's clearly the master of the studio—but there's also a degree of collaboration occurring in the photograph, as Marguerite "Margot" Peet, one of his female students, stands behind him at work on her own painting of the nude model. In other words, whatever the precise nature of Benton's experience with his nude model, it was an experience he was willing to share with his students and, in the form of the painting, with the public. Despite his frustrations, sexual or professional, painting for him remained a public act, instrumental in every way, even as he shifted from a prosaic to a more allegorical mode of art.

The history of the Kansas City Art Institute dates back to 1885, when the city's population swelled to more than a hundred thousand, its agricultural industries thrived, and William Rockhill Nelson ran the successful *Kansas City Star*. Civic leaders formed a sketch club that year, in order to focus the city's cultural energies, and by 1887 had raised enough capital to establish the Kansas City Art Association and School of Design. In 1933, the William Rockhill Nelson Gallery of Art and Mary Atkins Museum of Fine Arts (later the Nelson-Atkins Museum of Art) opened and established a financial association with the school, thus entrenching it permanently in the cultural identity of Kansas City. When the governors hired Benton in 1935 to head the department of painting, they hoped his presence—he was the country's foremost muralist, a painter who was constantly in the news, and the first artist ever to appear, just the year before, on the cover of *Time* magazine—would secure a national reputation for the academy and allow it to compete with the more illustrious School of the Art Institute of Chicago. In return for an annual salary of three thousand dollars, Benton's impact was felt right away: enrollment rose to 438 students, and W. Rickert Fillmore, the president of the Art Institute's board, stated during his first semester that "more enthusiasm today had been shown in the opening of the Institute than ever before." Just as the board had banked on, many students, having seen Benton in *Time* or *Life*, came to the Art Institute specifically to study with him.

Benton taught his classes in a greenhouse that had been converted into a studio and, as he had in New York, stressed the importance of strong composition—"Grand Design," he called it—and the dynamism of rhythmic bumps and hollows. Artistic tradition was always one of Benton's primary concerns in the classroom, and he thought systematically about the most useful ways to introduce his students to past art. He discussed his philosophy of tradition in the essay "The Dead and the Living" (1941), which made the nervy claim that "environmentalism"—his preferred term for art of the American scene, which he claimed to have originated in the 1920s—had achieved dominance in the United States, but then warned that the popularity of the environmental mode can lead students astray; he worried that "it runs too frequently to a stupid literalism" or a "bum sort of photography." This problem arises when students only look to the end of a chain of influence—to Grant Wood, for instance, rather than, say, a Flemish master. Benton addressed this tendency in his course on compositional analysis by projecting slides on the wall—images of Egyptian and Assyrian reliefs, and by baroque masters such as Rubens and El Greco—and having his students sketch abstractions of the compositions, thus orienting themselves around the beginnings rather than the ends of the chain.

One student, Ed Voegele, recalled that Benton would tell them, "If you have a good composition, hang the painting upside down, down side up, or on either side. The composition will still look good." But while he was dogmatic about what constituted a good picture, Benton behaved informally in the classroom, leading by example. On occasion he would strong-arm his students, pushing them out of the way to fuss with their inexpert daubings, but mostly he let them work. Another student, Duard Marshall, who in 1939 painted a mural for the Neosho centennial celebration after Benton said he was too busy to do it, described him "as a terrier that takes a rat, shakes the hell out of it, and then watches it run."

His two greatest skills as a teacher were speaking plainly to his students and involving them intimately in his own work. "Tom had a wonderful way of expressing things without any clutter," claimed Jack Barber, and Roger Medearis, who became a regionalist painter in Missouri after studying with Benton, remembers his "good-natured growl—direct, blunt, profane." While he was executing the Missouri mural, Benton recruited students to pose for him and invited several to observe him at work in the House lounge, which made a lasting impression. "When all has been said about Benton as a teacher," Medearis says, "I turn again to the hours spent watching him in the act of painting. Talking about how to paint is one thing, of course, and actually seeing the way a painting comes into existence is another."

Benton treated his teaching studio as a living space, welcoming students to regard it as a commune of sorts. He worked closely with his apprentices, frequently asked them to train on his own paintings and murals, and often invited them to his home for Rita's special spaghetti. Benton's students considered him a teacher first and a famous artist second; to them he was less someone to emulate than a paternal figure. Earl Fred Bennett, for instance, a painter who worked under Benton at the Kansas City Art Institute from 1938 to 1941, commented that Benton "was like the sun coming up in the morning to all of us little bastards . . . [H]e was a much better father figure than I ever had, and I'm sure that was the case with a lot of us." Significantly, his lessons extended to beyond the classroom, and he frequently took students on rural sketching trips. In 1940, for instance, he arranged a classroom trip deep into the Ozarks with two cars and nine students, including, much to the embarrassment of the Art Institute board, two women. An article in *The Kansas City Times* detailed the trip's shenanigans. One student lost his pants in a stream, a razorback sow broke into the trunk of a school car and ate the group's steaks, leaving only crackers and sardines, and on the way home Benton drove the car off the road. The purpose of the trip was lost on the school's trustees. Medearis describes Benton as a "corrupt Pied Piper leading his followers into the wilderness— males and females together without proper supervision, using primitive privies and bathing in the rivers, on an unscheduled, unauthorized lark." "Experience," Benton said, "is the only thing that changes form."

Benton had several female students at the Kansas City Art Institute, none of whom were critical of his teaching (as some of his female students at the Art Students League had been). Margot Peet studied with him in 1940 and recalled that he helped her exhibit a still life in New York that year. Peet described him as an equable teacher. "He was just interested in anybody who was really trying to learn something," she said.

While a majority of his students adored him, others turned on him with the same ferocity that a rebellious child turns on a strict father. Benton could be pushy in the classroom, especially when he was working on a painting of his own. He was determined not to let teaching keep him from his work. Voegele, for instance, dropped out of the class in disgust after Benton situated himself between his easel and a model, effectively blocking his students' view. The same happened to Eric James Bransby: "Tom set this [composition] up in the greenhouse and we all went to work on it. And of course we went through all the procedures that he did. We made drawings of each figure. We made tone studies. We made a clay model. And we made color studies. So we had all kinds of references and research. Then Tom decided he was going to paint it himself. He moved in and chose a position that blocked me entirely. So I took my studies home . . . and painted in my room alone."

Another student from the Art Institute, Robert MacDonald Graham Jr., remembered that Benton could be cruelly fickle with his attention and graciousness. At sixteen, Graham was the youngest student in the class and, at first anyway, received encouragement from Benton, who claimed he was one of the strongest students in the course. But years later, when Graham phoned Benton at night to ask for a reference letter for a teaching position at the University of Texas, Benton shouted into the phone, "What the hell do you mean, calling me at this time?" Ultimately, Graham claims, he was merely "bewildered" by Benton and felt compelled to break free from him.

The Art Institute board of governors regarded him as a superb teacher. Rossiter Howard, the school's director when he was there, called him a "great master of design and color and a splendid professor." Nonetheless, a campaign to oust him from his position occurred in 1938. Leading the charge was Howard E. Huselton, a real estate agent, former editor of *The Kansas City Star*, and second director of the Art Institute. Described as an "odd man" and a "lone wolf," Huselton was a stubborn prude, one of the moralists who had spoken against the Missouri mural, calling it a "low type of painting" and "odious." In the summer of 1938, Huselton obtained a copy of Benton's *Artist in America* and took a red pencil to what he deemed its most immoral passages—those discussing mistresses and prostitutes. He then mounted an aggressive campaign to terminate Benton's contract with the Art Institute. In a formal letter to the board, Huselton outlined his charges against the teacher. "I have read quite a bit of the book," he explained, "and its blasphemous, lewd, lascivious, immoral, degrading, sex-perverted contents, can have no other effect on anyone who reads it, except to make them either sorry that they ever did so, or lower their own standards of decency and morals." Though several civic leaders reiterated Huselton's complaints, the board, after protracted debate, elected to reappoint Benton to his position. The campaign roused friends, reporters, students, and fellow teachers to support Benton, but when he ran afoul of the board several years later, these allies were unable to save his job.

Among the many professional accomplishments Benton achieved after returning to Missouri, perhaps none brought him as much pleasure as the publicity he received when returning to New York to mount exhibitions. In 1939, Reeves Lewenthal, director of Associated American Artists, persuaded Benton and Grant Wood to leave Maynard Walker, their New York art dealer. To celebrate, Lewenthal held a big retrospective exhibition of Benton's work, which opened to great fanfare at the Nelson Gallery of Art in Kansas City before moving to New York, where it also got strong reviews and sold well. The next year, Benton arranged a show, again with the Associated American Artists Galleries, located on Fifth Avenue, of his students' best work. Adams maintains that the event was unique. "Never before or since," he writes, "has a teacher from a regional art school held such a nationally reviewed New York exhibition of student work." In his essay for a small catalog, Benton struck the same chords he would a year later in "The Dead and the Living." Apparently aware that critics might comment on the unmistakably Bentonesque qualities of the students' work, he writes, "American Regionalism through a loose application of the term has, in a large part of the critical world come to be synonymous with a mere recording of local fact." But, he adds, "[w]e defy any school in the country to produce anything comparable in the matter of all around technical excellency."

In April 1941, Benton returned to New York to prepare for another exhibition of his work at the Associated American Artists Galleries. Emboldened perhaps by his recent successes there, he foolishly staged a press conference in the back room of the gallery and spoke his mind. Benton clearly had his share of vanities, and a need to be heard was one of them. Publicity was for him a vindication of his aesthetic philosophies, and he likely viewed press coverage as proof that his attacks against the artistic elite had merit. At any rate, smoking a pipe and sipping whiskey at the press conference, he conjured his nastiest self and let rip a foul tirade against homosexuals and museums.

"Do you want to know what's the matter with the art business in America?" he asked. "It's the third sex and the museums. Even in

Missouri we're full of 'em. [Museums are] run by a pretty boy with delicate wrists and a swing in his gait. If it were left to me," he added, "I wouldn't have any museums. I'd have people buy the paintings and hang 'em in privies or anywhere anybody had time to look at 'em . . . I'd like to sell mine in saloons, bawdyhouses, Kiwanis and Rotary clubs, and Chambers of Commerce—even women's clubs." The stupidity of the remarks was explicit: they exposed Benton's absurd homophobia and insulted the very institutions that had sustained his success. But the slurs were more offensive than some reporters might have known, directed as they were at particular administrators, curators, and trustees of the Nelson Gallery, which was intimately associated with the Art Institute. Peyton Boswell—editor, author, and, for a time, admirer of the American scene painters—was just one of the many journalists to swiftly and severely denounce Benton. "He strikes out with all the strength of his pugnacious soul," Boswell points out, "but too often dogmatically condemns whole groups because of his bitterness against an individual."

Once back in Kansas City, Benton made a few feeble attempts to mitigate the fallout. He asked his old friend Thomas Craven, still a conservative art critic, to speak on his behalf and issued a press statement: "All this a little storm in the teapot of aesthetics." For the most part, though, he dug in his heels, telling one reporter, for instance, "And now after six years the Art gang here in Kansas City is after my scalp. And I'm going to get the gate here from the same kind of Art gang that I thought I had shut the gate on when I said good-by to Paris and New York." He added, "It's a small thing. My losing my job doesn't mean much." In another press statement, this one apparently never published, he attacked what he called the "fat men pussyfooting around" and claimed, "Without me the Kansas City Art Institute will drop back to the kind of third rate joint it was before I came."

A little more than three weeks after the remarks appeared in the papers, fifty students from the Art Institute staged a demonstration at the school in support of Benton, but it was too late, and he was fired on May 5. Unfortunately, Benton learned little from the episode. After his firing, for instance, he told the *Art Digest* that "stuffed shirts and sissies have won over the will of my students," comments that were reprinted nationally in *Newsweek*. He did write an essay for *Common Sense*, "Art vs. the Mellon Gallery," that attempted to put his comments in philosophical context. As he had so many times before, he alludes to John

Dewey, who had critiqued museums in *Art as Experience*. "Our present museums and galleries," Dewey writes, "to which works of fine art are removed and stored illustrate some of the causes that have operated to segregate art instead of finding it an attendant of temple, forum, and other forms of associated life." He continues, striking a Marxist vein: "Objects that were in the past valid and significant because of their place in the life of a community now function in isolation from the conditions of their origin. By that fact they are also set apart from common experience, and serve as insignia of taste and certificates of special culture."

But whereas Dewey's critique is a considered assessment of the role of museums in a capitalist economy, Benton's essay reads more like a bitter screed. He admits to having had "a couple of highballs" before making his remarks, and manages to omit overt references to homosexuals, but reiterates his belief that curators do more harm than good for American art. "Museum people," he says, "are a sort of pain in the neck, but they are also dangerous. If they get their fingers into the business of art education, they will kill it." The next month, Benton again expressed resentment, in a letter to John D. Weaver, a Kansas City writer who'd moved to Los Angeles. "If I teach it will not be simply because someone is paying me to do so," he says, "but because there is talent that is worth teaching and that feels that it needs my brand of teaching." He also claims that he's had to put up with a lot of bores in Kansas City and that "any body that gets in my house now and drinks my whiskey gets there because I like them."

Contrary to his claims that he didn't care one way or the other whether he was fired, Benton seems never to have gotten over the episode. In "After," a chapter he wrote in 1951 for a new edition of *An Artist in America*, he argues that he was fired for his political views rather than his rancorous and paranoid remarks. "I was too obviously a damned Roosevelt New Dealer," he asserts. "This meant to respectable Republicans, and Republicans most of the respectable people of Kansas City were, that I was something close to a red-eyed Communist." Benton displays some of his pathologies in this passage, explaining how during the days when his job was in the balance, he played competing Kansas City newspapers against each other, and that he decided to remain in Kansas City only to stick it to his critics, to prove that the job had not been his only source of income and that he was "a pretty successful screwball." At age eighty-three, Benton was still harping on the Art Institute fiasco, telling an interviewer that what he'd said years before was as true as ever—"these homosexuals are quite influential in this particular game I'm in"—and that the "main" reason for his dismissal was that he refused to issue formal grades to his students, which upset the board of governors just as they were seeking accreditation.

Benton not only damaged the reputation he'd worked so hard to build; he also hung his loyal students and co-workers out to dry: at least one professor at the Art Institute resigned to protest the board's decision, and many of his students dropped out of the school, undoubtedly hurting their careers. Benton had gotten far on the goodwill of Kansas Citians, but by embarrassing the city and insulting some of its leaders, he showed his unwillingness to return that goodwill and the limits of his supposed political skills. Doss suspects that he also damaged the American scene movement that he'd once defended so passionately, probably hastening its "swift decline in terms of popular and institutional support." Certainly his infamy made it easier for critics to caricature regionalist artists as ignorant of modern attitudes. She also suggests that his attacks on homosexuals were one way of reasserting his own manliness and "were bitter revelations of his own sense of impotence in the changed world of the 1940s." His remarks, in other words, while intended as an informed critique of the contemporary art business, ended up demonstrating his bitter and parochial social philosophies. Deep down, Benton likely believed that his provocations were interesting. The forbidden had appealed to him for a long time; in the past, he'd successfully used profanity and sex to distinguish himself from elite society, to signal his refreshing unconventionality and outsider status. In this case, though, he missed the mark badly. His maledictions were neither stimulating nor popular, and they continue to haunt his reputation.

Benton did earn a Pyrrhic victory, however. Almost immediately after he made his comments, Billy Rose, the entertainment impresario, contacted him to ask if he meant what he'd said about exhibiting his art in "saloons" and "bawdyhouses." Rose, who began his career as a theatrical lyricist and Broadway producer, opened his infamous Diamond Horseshoe nightclub, situated in the basement of the Paramount Hotel in Times Square, in 1938. The Gay Nineties–themed club, decorated with deep reds and rococo flourishes, was enormously popular, serving a five-course meal nightly to seven hundred patrons and earning one million dollars a year, and Rose attended carefully to the club's reputation, billing its stripteases as wholesome spectacle. It was logical for Rose to be interested in a popular artist like Benton, for both men well understood the lure of nostalgia for American history. The nightclub's bar, for instance, the Silver Dollar, had an Old Western theme; coins were embedded in the bar, and memorabilia hung from the walls. According to one historian, "By linking the nightclub to this version of the past, [Rose] integrated it into Americana. No longer alien, the nightclub . . . became an American institution." Moreover, Rose relished thumbing his nose at propriety; he would try anything to publicize the Diamond Horseshoe, and displaying a sensational nude by a controversial artist seemed a safe bet.

After hearing Benton's comments, Rose publicly invited him to display *Persephone* at the Diamond Horseshoe: "I've got a saloon—perhaps the biggest saloon in this country. You have a great picture, perhaps the greatest yet painted in America, so let's get together." Benton agreed, and on the evening of April 8 the painting, valued by Associated American Artists at twelve thousand dollars, was fitted with a glass cover to protect it from beer and spirits and hung on the red-plush walls at the nightclub's entrance. Benton later commented on the appropriateness of the venue, pointing out that like Pluto, many of the nightclub's male patrons "had also sneaked out from darkness, from the spiritual darkness of the countinghouse or from that maybe of a Puritanical home, where some age-embittered fury ruled the roost, to take their own Plutonic peep at pink breasts and well-turned young asses." In the end, though, the gimmick was less successful than Benton had hoped: Rose never purchased the painting, and the heat from the club's blazing lights cooked the canvas under its protective glass, badly cracking the paint. After a few months, the painting was removed so that it could be restored.

Reminiscing about the "exhilarating years" between his move to Kansas City and the beginning of World War II, Benton notes that they were a period of "much work" and "perhaps the best of my life." Even taking into account his disastrous press conference and ignominious firing from the Art Institute, it's unfair to argue otherwise. During these six years, Benton had performed a small miracle: even as he and Rita settled into a comfortable domesticity, he managed to teach, write, travel, entertain, and, above all, produce art—a mural, easel paintings, drawings, and lithographs—that was marketable. He earned enough money from this work to buy a new house, purchase more land on Martha's Vineyard, modernize the Chilmark house, and even save a little. Certainly his work ethic made an impression on those who knew him. Earl Bennett marveled at his teacher's diligence. "I still can't figure out how Tom could sit out in the bright sunlight with this bright white gessoed panel for hours," he recalled. "I couldn't imagine that he wasn't totally blinded by it, that he could do it all the time."

10

AFIELD

The citizens of Kansas City celebrated Benton's arrival in the autumn of 1935. The Nelson Gallery and the Art Institute both mounted exhibitions of his work, and more than a thousand people attended a reception in his honor, at which students from the Haskell Institute—a trade school for Native Americans in Lawrence, Kansas—performed dances and recited stories. But Benton also bewildered his new neighbors. "Missourians are notoriously skeptical" and "want the facts," observes a 1941 guidebook to the state, published by the Missouri Writers' Project under the auspices of the Works Progress Administration. These skeptics were unsure whether Benton was the genuine rustic he often claimed to be or the rude New York artist he sometimes sounded like. He was, as his good friend Thomas Craven noted, "half-hobo and half-highbrow."

For his part, while he may have been disappointed by the criticism directed at his Jefferson City mural, Benton grew fond of Kansas City and its people and, two years after his arrival, expressed his amusement with them. "They lisp the same tiresome, meaningless aesthetic jargon," he observes. "In their society are to be found the same fairies, the same Marxist fellow travelers, the same 'educated' ladies purring linguistic affectations. The same damned bores that you find in the penthouses and studios of Greenwich Village hang onto the skirts of art in the Middle West." These remarks demonstrate how surprised Benton was to learn that Kansas Citians shared with New Yorkers what he believed were effete views about art. Nevertheless, he adds, "taken as a whole, I like the men and women who make the real Missouri. I get along with them." And even as he was fighting to keep his job at the Art Institute, he told a local reporter, "I like Kansas City. It's a good place to live. Rocks stick out of the ground and you have to look up and down hills to see things. Flowers grow easily and there's a lot of redbud in the spring. There are plenty of regular men and women who live here—men and women you like because you can be yourself with them."

Benton had arrived in Kansas City at an auspicious time. Just two years before he moved there, the city held ceremonies marking the opening of the University of Kansas City (renamed the University of Missouri–Kansas City in 1963), the Nelson Gallery, and the Kansas City Philharmonic Orchestra. And several years later Benton observed the people of Kansas City rise up against "Boss Tom" Pendergast and take back control of state politics and financing. "Here was the city of the future," one historian writes, "dressed in the fabric of its dreams."

The Bentons hosted a lot of guests in Kansas City and stayed in touch with most of their old friends. One notable visitor was Jackson Pollock, who came from New York during the holiday season in 1937. Unfortunately, it proved to be a painful two weeks for everyone, as Pollock spent his time there drunk and depressed. After Benton left New York in the spring of 1935, Pollock had experienced a brief period of good fortune. That summer he rejoiced, as so many struggling New York artists did, upon hearing the news that the government had established the Federal Art Project, which paid unemployed artists to produce work for public buildings. According to May Tabak Rosenberg, the wife of Harold Rosenberg, who became a leading art critic in the 1950s, the morning of August 1, 1935, started with artists spilling into the streets of downtown Manhattan and shouting the news that the federal government was hiring artists. "They were shouting with the excitement of children at a zoo," she recalled later. Pollock got on the Federal Art Project payroll right away, earning ninety-five dollars a month (much more than he was accustomed to) working first in the mural department with Job Goodman, who'd been a student of Benton's at the Art Students League, and then in the easel division, which gave artists more freedom so long as they produced about one painting each month. This initiated a period of relative sanity and creative productivity for Pollock; he lived on Eighth Street with his brother Sande, who looked after him, and exhibited several small paintings in the style of Benton and Ryder. He was still drinking but happier than he'd been in years.

In February 1936, Pollock met a new mentor, the Mexican muralist David Alfaro Siqueiros, who at age thirty-nine came to New York to organize a workshop of artists intended as a collaborative "laboratory for experimentation in modern art techniques" that would "create art for the people." Siqueiros was a bombastic and volatile Stalinist, but most relevant to Pollock's development was his commitment to artistic experimentation, especially to throwing and splattering paint, an outgrowth of surrealist automatism (the practice of bypassing perception and reason so that the subconscious can spontaneously express itself). According to Axel Horn, an artist friend of Pollock's, Siqueiros showed Pollock "a way out of his lack of technical facility." It was under Siqueiros's influence that Pollock, in 1936, first lay a canvas on a floor and dripped paint on it directly, though it would be about eleven years before he developed the technique into his signature method of action painting. The workshops came to a sudden end, however, in early 1937, when Siqueiros left New York to fight for the Republican army in the Spanish Civil War.

It was that summer that Pollock alarmed Tom and Rita by getting arrested on Martha's Vineyard, after getting drunk and chasing girls on his bicycle. They bailed him out of jail and worried in a general way about his behavior but still didn't comprehend the seriousness of his alcoholism or mental illness. If they had recognized that episode for what it was, or if they had known that that fall Pollock descended again into a sorry state, Benton likely would not have invited him to Kansas City. As it happened, though, Pollock took a leave from the Federal Art Project and boarded a Greyhound bus at Port Authority, riding it thirty-eight hours to Kansas City.

The Pollock biographers Steven Naifeh and Gregory White Smith describe the visit as a disaster. Benton was distracted by his duties at the Kansas City Art Institute, and Pollock, though he spent his days at the Bentons' house, was apparently too agitated to pay any mind to T.P., who later claimed to have no memory of the visit. At night Pollock spent his time with Benton's students, drinking at holiday parties. One night Pollock, emboldened by booze, confessed his love to Rita and, after seven years of "forbidden longings and private looks," asked her to marry him. She turned him down, and, according to Naifeh and Smith, Pollock took out his anger on Benton, yelling, "God-damn you, I'm going to become more famous than you." Pollock then fled the house and drank so much whiskey that upon his return Rita drove him to a doctor, who promptly diagnosed his alcoholism. Pollock returned to New York and continued his bender. On June 12, panicked after Jackson disappeared for four days to drink, his brother Sande drove him to New York Hospital in White Plains, known as Bloomingdale's, and checked him in for psychiatric evaluation. He remained in treatment for over three months, finally leaving the hospital on September 30.

Neither Tom nor Rita seemed to care much about sexual indiscretion or drunken boorishness, and both were typically tolerant of Pollock's behavior and sent him letters expressing their sympathy for him. In fact, Benton continued to support Pollock, by visiting him in New York and sending a letter of recommendation on his behalf to the Guggenheim Foundation. But the last time they saw each other was in 1944. Three years later, when Pollock was making his drip paintings and abstract expressionism was ascending as the most vital mode of American artistic expression, Benton started to reveal his true disdain for the new art, which constituted a direct threat to his realism.

Besides the occasional cocktail party or night out at the orchestra, in the years after Pollock's visit Tom and Rita stuck close to home and remained contentedly married. Benton had made enough money in the late 1930s for Rita to surprise him in 1939 by buying an impressive stone house at 3616 Belleview Avenue in wooded Roanoke Park (now a state historic park). They often spent their evenings listening to T.P., who turned thirteen that year, play the flute. They also had a grand piano in their living room, and on Saturday nights a gang of musicians, including members of the orchestra, gathered there for jam sessions. It must have been an uncanny place to play, as Rita maintained an immaculate gallery of her husband's artworks in the room; she also painted the walls in neutral tones and draped the furniture with beige slipcovers to accentuate the paintings' vibrant colors. When he wasn't traveling, teaching, or entertaining, Benton spent most of his time in the carriage house studio adjacent to the house. (Frank Lloyd Wright, whom Benton hadn't seen since their forum in Providence, was working on a house next door and offered to design the studio, but Benton turned him down, explaining that he wanted a roof that "didn't leak.")

The Bentons' domestic routine remained unchanged for the rest of their lives. Sidney Larson, a muralist and art conservator who first met Benton in 1949 and moved into the house in 1959 to help Benton—who, owing to years of hard work and rugged travel, was ailing from bursitis—plan a mural for the Harry S. Truman Library, describes social evenings at the Bentons' as "fascinating" and recalls Rita's superb cooking, their huge Japanese police dog, Joto, and the "lively" conversation among the art-world celebrities who frequently visited. One such visitor was the poet Robert Bly, who stopped in on the Bentons one damp November day in the early 1970s. Subsequently, Bly wrote a prose poem about the visit, describing Benton as a "short tractor." "On his face there is labor," he continues, "this is not the carefree poet typing his poems twenty minutes a day, but the cattle driver walking through snow, the wrestler wrestling with the angel lifting him and driving him down to earth again and again, the joy of hard work, the thresher defeated by dusk by the weight of the bundles." Rita, meanwhile, is "strong, radiant, pure, triumphant, having survived the flesh, like the ship that has returned from the moon, and splashed down in some Russian meadow." During the intervening years, Rita had grown even more maternal and was apparently perfectly content raising their children (daughter Jessie was born in 1939), tending to the house, cooking dinner for guests, and caring for her husband. One Kansas City acquaintance of the Bentons' recalls her typical response to Tom's staying up late to drink: *"Tom! Come to bed!"* she would yell, and he would run upstairs.

Among the Bentons' close friends in the late 1930s and early 1940s were Grant Wood and John Steuart Curry, the other renowned regionalist painters of the time. Though Benton met Curry in 1926, the two didn't become friends until the early 1930s, and he met Wood in Iowa City, where Benton had stopped during a 1934–1935 lecture tour. Because by 1936 all three were living in the Midwest—Wood taught at the University of Iowa, Curry at the University of Wisconsin—they found it easy to see each other on weekends. Wood, in particular, was a frequent guest and drove to Kansas City regularly to escape a bitter marriage and terrible academic bickering at the University of Iowa.

The most publicized rendezvous of the three occurred on March 5, 1938, when Wood and Curry joined Benton as judges of the Art Institute's annual Beaux-Arts Ball, a spring costume party. The theme that year was "Arabian Nights," and juiced up on liquor, the three men, much to the outrage of Howard Huselton, flirted with the young female students and awarded a first prize—a case of whiskey—to a young man in pajamas. Benton greatly admired both men and wrote tributes to them after they died—Wood in 1942 and Curry in 1946. "We were different in our temperaments and many of our ideas," he remarks about his friendships with Wood and Curry, "but we were alike in that we were all in revolt against the unhappy effects which the Armory show of 1913 had had on American painting . . . [W]e had for all our differences developed a close personal friendship."

But during the forty years that he lived in Kansas City, Benton was happiest when he was afield, traveling in rural Missouri and throughout the United States on personal or professional trips. "From where I live I can take my car and in a few minutes run past the junk heaps and gaudy signs of Kansas City into deep country," he writes in *An Artist in America*. "In a few hours I can be in the utter backwoods." The ability to escape the city, he explains, was crucial for his work and peace of mind:

> There is a high rugged bluff above the Missouri River a few miles from Kansas City. I drive out when I get bored and sit on that bluff. The river makes a great curve in the valley below and you can see for miles up and down the running yellow water . . . Either I am just a slobbery sentimentalist or there is something to this stuff about your native land, for when I sit above the waters of the Missouri, I feel they belong to me, and I to them.
>
> As a matter of fact, I feel I belong all over my state. There is about the Missouri landscape something intimate and known to me. While I drive around the curve of a country road, I seem to know what is going to be there, what the creek beds and the sycamores and walnuts lining them will look like, and what the color of the bluffs will be.

The very chapter titles of *An Artist in America*—"On Going Places," "The Mountains," "The Rivers," "The South," "The West"—demonstrate how much Benton identified various regions with his personal growth. Perhaps his greatest passion, though, was the nation's waterways, and he frequently visited western and midwestern rivers. "River tradition runs toward toughness," Benton observes, and so it was to rivers that he went to authenticate his own fortitude and intimacy with the flow of American life.

Benton modeled his love of rivers on his fellow Missourian Mark Twain, and his illustrations for editions of *Tom Sawyer, Huckleberry*

Finn, and *Life on the Mississippi*, made between 1939 and 1944, capture the mysterious lure of moving water. As the art historian Leo Mazow explains, "The river and atmospheric perspective suggest an ethereal neverland into which Huck seems to dissolve." For Twain, he explains, "rivers are refuges for children facing 'real world,' adult problems." For Benton, though, they were more than apt symbols with which to explore Twain's themes of inequality and innocence lost; they were just the right place to venture a reconnection with the supposedly uncorrupted experiences of youth, to observe and illustrate the inexorable action of a fluid subject (water, humanity) on a fixed object (land, the world). Benton understood, though, that such an attitude was "pure romance and . . . untenable." On rivers, just as in life, flow isn't inexorable but fraught with danger; rocks, shoals, and rapids trouble our journey, occasionally spilling us into cold water. Just as Twain's boys were bygone, so was the unimpeded river in Benton's day. In the river chapter in *An Artist in America*, he mentions an old, rusted river steamer stuck in a mudflat on the Ohio River. In a typically evocative personification, he describes the decrepit vessel as "some proud but bedraggled and improvident old woman, who after passing a glittering and gay life" has died alone.

Benton had a keen interest in river tragedies, in fact, and on two occasions documented the tragic consequences of floods in Missouri. In February 1937, just as he was finishing his autobiography, heavy rains caused severe flooding along the Mississippi River and its tributaries. Benton traveled on assignment for *The Kansas City Star* and the *St. Louis Post-Dispatch* to report on and sketch the damage and relief efforts along the St. Francis River in southeast Missouri and northern Arkansas. He was horrified by what he observed: "Description can give no sense of the dread realities of flood misery—the cold mud, the lost goods, the homeless animals, the dreary standing around of destitute people." "The conditions themselves," he adds, "all humane measures notwithstanding, were such as to make one wonder whether civilization had at all improved the status of the region's inhabitants above that of its aboriginal occupants." Mazow points out that Benton's commentary "ironically pitted the flood against the supposedly progressive nation itself," for while he admired the Red Cross's efforts, he was devastated by the "little knots of somber-faced women" he observed "looking at their rooftops out in the water."

Then, in 1951, Benton interrupted his summer on Martha's Vineyard to return home and report on the flooding of the Kansas River, also known as the Kaw River, which meets the Missouri at Kansas City. After a few days of intense storms, on July 13 ("Black Friday" to some) the Kaw overtopped its levees, inundated the region with up to thirty feet of water, destroyed the Kansas City Stockyards, and caused $840 million in damage. Benton illustrated the flood in a lithograph titled *Homecoming—Kaw Valley*, and in October he used his prestige by sending signed copies to each member of the U.S. Congress to encourage passage of a federal flood rehabilitation bill. The next month, outraged by the inadequacy of the passed bill and a suspicion that most of his lithographs "went into the waste baskets of the Capitol," he published an essay in *The New Republic* describing the tragedy. He mentions houses "smashed, splintered, overturned and uprooted by the swirling mud and water" and editorializes, as he would again later, on the incompetence of the Army Corps of Engineers, with which he'd grown familiar during his reporting on the flood. "Hadn't Congress and the Army Engineers spent millions of dollars building levees, current blocks and containment basins to protect . . . from the river?" he asked. "And hadn't a solid number of . . . Senators and Representatives shown, by speeches and votes, that they believed further engineering protection a waste of money? Was there any sign of uneasiness among the river engineers themselves about too much country water on the upper Kaw and its tributaries?"

Mazow discusses how Benton again exercised his considerable influence with the press to advocate for environmental stewardship of the region's rivers. In two trips—one in 1965, the other in 1970—Benton arranged for reporters and photographers to accompany him on floats down the Missouri and Buffalo Rivers. "As I've said lots of times," Benton remarked, "I like rivers. I especially like those clear free flowing rivers of the Ozarks which have escaped the Army Corps of Engineers." The 1965 float down the Missouri River was covered by *The Saturday Evening Post*, which then published, in October, an article by Robert Wernick that included candid color photographs of Benton sketching on the banks of the river. The piece was part publicity stunt—Wernick opens with a description of the "crusty" artist "rustling out of his sleeping bag with a *pro forma* resolution to definitely henceforth cut out drinking after the evening meal"—and part environmental politics: Benton was "ever ready with his Missouri muleskinner vocabulary to curl the

hairy ears of the Corps of Engineers men running the boats." Wernick
explains that the purpose of the trip was to cover the route of the 1805
Lewis and Clark expedition from Omaha to the river's headwaters at
Three Forks, Montana. "But," he writes, "the Engineers have built so
many giant dams that most of the river is blue lake water now, and the
landmarks of the old exploring and pioneering days have mostly been
drowned." Apparently, the corpsmen who accompanied Benton on the
float had designs to build a new $360 million dam on one last unspoiled
stretch of the river. "No, no, no," Benton reportedly shouted, before spitting a gob of tobacco juice in the muddy river. "Let the sons of bitches
go up the canyon the hard way."

The travelers, it seems, also got an earful about abstract art, and
Wernick, who peppers his article with some choice Benton declara-
tions, astutely draws a connection between the painter's river philosophy and his aesthetic theory. "The careers of abstract artists so often
end in a kind of bitter emptiness," he quotes Benton. "It's the emptiness
of a person looking into himself all the time. But the objective world is
always rich: There is always something round the next bend of the
river." Robert F. Jones, in a *Sports Illustrated* article he wrote reporting
on Benton's 1970 float down the Buffalo River in Arkansas, struck
many of the same chords. "Time is working against both Tom Benton
and the Buffalo River," he remarks. Benton was eighty-one at the time,
had suffered a heart attack in 1966, and could pour only four weak
bourbons a day; the Army Corps of Engineers, meanwhile, was at it
again, threatening to add the Buffalo to its "beaver complex" of dams
in the Ozarks. "Sooner or later the river lovers will give up and then the
river-straighteners will go to work," Jones surmises.

In both of these peculiar profiles, which combine hagiography, travelogue, and ecology, an elegiac tone laces together three unmistakable
facts: Benton was closing in on mortality, the Ozark rivers were under
siege, and abstraction had doomed regionalist painting. But before
these ends were finalized, Benton enjoyed the rivers and the experiences and companionship they provided. His usual gang of float partners accompanied him on the 1970 Buffalo River trip, for instance:
John Callison, a thirty-five-year-old Kansas City stockbroker; Fred Mc-
Craw, a computer executive; and Harold and Margaret Hedges, expert
canoeists who guided Benton on several trips. "After a day's run," Benton writes in a piece for *Travel and Leisure*, "when the shadows begin to

lengthen and cool comes over the water, you arrive at some of the best moments of a float. Rounding a bend of the river you discover your camp, set up on a high bar by your cook . . . A wood fire, cut from flood-time drift, sends its blue smoke curling up into the trees . . . Then you sit around the table telling your fisherman's lies while the cook takes care of the fish you don't have to lie about."

Rivers meant many things to Benton: they evoked nostalgia for a frolicsome boyhood; they symbolized the sublime power of nature; they suggested an unspoiled but endangered past; and they offered a romantic respite from the bustle of city life. They were also another milieu in which to observe modern Americans at work. He devotes much of his river chapter in *An Artist in America* to the labor of river commerce, portraying his frequent journeys on board new propeller-driven towboats. He had mixed feelings about the modernization of river craft; he both admired the efficiency of the new vessels and lamented the passing of the old steamers he remembered from his youth. He describes, for instance, "an old Mississippi second mate who lost his place on one of the modern towboats because he insisted on maintaining the character of a rip-roaring old-style riverman, 'tough as a hickory nut' and 'mean as a rattlesnake.'" This man, he explains, "gave up his job, commenting scornfully on the decadence of company rules which were trying to inject an impractical and unworkable softness into river ways," an observation that evokes Benton's criticisms about museums. The new reality of river traffic, "with its modern boats and sanitary quarters, with its systems of mechanized loading where skill rather than brute force is the order of the day," ran counter to Benton's childhood memories. He describes his surprise when he boarded one of the new boats, in 1935 or 1936, and noticed that its men were pampered, eating good food and sleeping on clean sheets belowdecks rather than among the freight up top. Around the same time, after climbing aboard a "spick-and-span" towboat of the Mississippi Valley Barge Line Company heading for New Orleans, he was shocked to be shown to a guest cabin with "brightly colored bedcovers," "polished furniture," and a "private shower and toilet"; "I never thought," he remarks, "of any towboat as offering convenience or ease of travel." Benton points out, though, that these new boats came with their own romance. The captain of this boat impressed him, for instance, with some "neat work," maneuvering out of a rogue current by reversing his engines and speeding downstream. "The pilots of the towboat were good fellows," he says.

Many of Benton's easel paintings from 1935 onward depict waterways. Both *Persephone* and *Susanna and the Elders* are set along gentle streams, and *Shallow Creek* and *Moonlight on the Osage* (also from 1938 and featured in the Associated American Artists exhibition of 1939) feature flowing water. *Shallow Creek*, for instance, depicts T.P. wading in a shallow stream in the Ozarks and recalls Benton's own boyhood, and *Moonlight on the Osage* is an intensely romantic work that recalls the dark, mystical paintings of Albert Pinkham Ryder, the artist whom both Benton and Pollock admired.

Several of Benton's later murals also include river themes. The earliest of these, contracted in 1946 for Harzfeld's, a Kansas City department store specializing in ready-to-wear women's fashions, was his first mural commission in ten years, likely owing to the difficulties he faced over the Missouri capitol project. A few years after he finished the Harzfeld's mural, Benton admitted that it was a little peculiar to see one of his works "in an atmosphere of silk nighties, pink slips and perfume," but once Lester Siegel, the president of Harzfeld's, promised not to interfere with the project, so long as Benton promised not to make a scandalous picture, it made sense to both of them. Made in 1947, the mural, titled *Achelous and Hercules*, shows the river god Achelous, who turned into a raging bull at flood season, in combat with Hercules for the affections of Deianira, a symbol of delta fertility. Benton depicts Hercules as a muscular frontiersman getting the best of the bull just before he tears off one of his horns, "which is magically transformed into a cornucopia, spilling harvest abundance." The action takes place on a verdant slope full of colorful fruits and vegetables, and in the background can be seen a calm river with an old-fashioned steamboat. At the time, Benton apparently had yet to turn against the Army Corps of Engineers, for in a pamphlet that was available in the store, he explains, "The story is thus applicable to our own land. It fits our Missouri River, which yet needs the attention of a Hercules."

Benton's fondness for rivers made him a logical choice for a commission by the River Club—an exclusive enclave for the Kansas City elite situated on a two-hundred-foot bluff above the Missouri River in the city's Quality Hill district. In 1956, the River Club hired Benton to make a mural for an empty space above a mantel in its lounge, and to satisfy the taste of its clientele, he produced a traditional image of Manifest Destiny reminiscent of his great-uncle and nineteenth-century landscapes by William S. Jewett (*The Promised Land—the Grayson Family*, 1850) and Emanuel Leutze (*Westward the Course of Empire Takes Its Way*, 1862). The mural, *Old Kansas City, Trading at Westport Landing*, depicts a view near the River Club as it might have looked in the nineteenth century, when American Indian and European traders would meet there. Similar to its likely art historical models, the mural presents an untroubled history—"a pageant of mythic Turnerism," in the words of Karal Ann Marling—suggesting that American progress depended on the mutual goodwill of natives and Europeans: a white settler offers a bejeweled necklace to an Indian warrior in exchange for an Indian bride. This cooperation, Benton implies, results in the peaceful habitation of the Missouri's Westport Landing, situated below the River Club and shown here in the background as the idyllic commercial seat of early Kansas City: steamboats docked at the landing link the regions along the quiet river to the settlers, depicted driving cattle and coaxing a wagon up the steep hill from the river to the future city.

After Benton completed *Old Kansas City*, Robert Moses, New York's principal architectural planner and chairman of the New York Power Authority, contacted him about doing a mural for the powerhouse building of the St. Lawrence–Franklin D. Roosevelt Power Project in Massena, New York—the state's first hydropower facility. Always interested in the grand gesture, Moses believed a Benton mural would properly distinguish the massive project and asked Benton to create two mural panels illustrating Jacques Cartier's discovery of the St. Lawrence River in 1534. Because, as Benton confessed, "what I knew of . . . Cartier's Canadian expedition could be put in a thimble," both parties agreed that he should travel to Quebec to research the history of the event. In Montreal, Benton discovered an English translation of the *Relation Originale du Voyage de Jacques Cartier au Canada en 1534*. Based on his reading of this text, he decided that one panel would illustrate "Cartier and his people, with their arms, ships, and European dress," as they came upon the Indian inhabitants of the land; the second panel would show the Indians, "with their own arms and equipment," as they came into contact with Cartier's expedition. Having heard that Moses could be a "tough cookie," Benton carried out a lot of additional research, even observing Seneca Indians, the tribe Cartier first encountered, in western New York and Oklahoma, where some had been obliged to settle by the U.S. government. In this latter endeavor Charles Banks Wilson, an American portraitist and book illustrator who lived in Oklahoma and was particularly interested in Native American subjects, aided Benton, and the two became good friends. Wilson knew many Senecas and "also knew what kind of persuasions to put in play to get them to pose for me," Benton explains.

Benton completed the murals quickly, in 1957, and by his own account need not have worried about getting along with Moses, who proved easy to work for. In Benton's words, the seven-by-six-foot panel *The Seneca Discover the French* "represents the excitement of an Indian community . . . when its people descried the French." Based on descriptions in Cartier's *Relation*, the mural illustrates a "great fire on the shore, the dancing and gesturing thereabouts by the Indians, the canoe visits to the French ships, the structure of the fortified village"—Hochelaga, near Montreal—and "the corn and tobacco fields" adjacent to the village. Benton explains that "surprise, excitement, [and] wonder on the part of the Indian discoverers" are the subject of the panel, though a Seneca figure in the foreground, "painted for war," suggests "some of the savage retributions of later times."

The second panel, *Jacques Cartier Discovers the Indians*, represents the event from the French point of view, a narrative strategy that he employed in *The American Historical Epic*, almost forty years earlier, to represent history as it was experienced from diverse perspectives. The panel depicts Cartier and his armed followers as they greet an Indian chief and a group of skeptical Senecas. According to Benton, the *Relation* includes frequent mention of "a certain tenseness" on the part of the two groups, an apprehension certainly exacerbated by the actions of Cartier's associates, whom Benton depicts in the background planting a cross and the banner of Francis I on native soil. This is romantic history, to be sure, but Benton understood that the ownership and taming of these waterways were fraught with mistrust and violence.

In 1959, Benton received a letter from Moses requesting that he do another mural, this time for the New York Power Authority's Niagara Power Project in Lewiston. Moses had constructed a dam—at the time, the largest in the Western world—across the Niagara River, four and a half miles downstream from Niagara Falls, and wanted Benton to do the mural for its administrative building, which he hoped would become a tourist destination. Moses stated his desires for the mural in a letter to a manager of the project. "I don't want any phoney, primitive, abstract or other freak stuff," he explained. Benton, though, had just signed on to paint a mural for the Harry S. Truman Library in Independence, Missouri, so Moses was compelled to secure Truman's permission to contract Benton for the project. In order to convince Truman, Moses invited him to tour the hydropower project in Massena and view the murals in place there. Truman, who as president had supported the 1950 Niagara River Water Diversion Treaty, the arrangement that dictated the amount of water that must flow over Niagara Falls and made Moses's project possible, was impressed and acquiesced to his request. Moses again dictated the subject of the mural, which was the discovery of the falls, in December 1678, by Father Louis Hennepin, the Belgian Franciscan priest who also is believed to be the first European to set foot in Hannibal, Missouri, the hometown of Mark Twain. Benton's seven-by-twenty-foot mural, *Father Hennepin at Niagara Falls*, was completed in 1961 and represents Hennepin, surrounded by members of the exploration party and Seneca Indians, holding a cross and blessing the falls. This mural includes none of the tensions of the earlier panels, as both the European explorers and the Native Americans appear to genuflect behind Hennepin's imperial gesture.

Benton recalls that when, in the mid-1930s, he was a guest on the Mississippi Valley Barge Line Company towboat traveling to New Orleans, he "got restless" and jumped ship in Arkansas, "where I left the river and made for the hills." In between his various river journeys and summer vacations on Martha's Vineyard, Benton took to the Ozarks, the rural South, and the mountains of the American West. There was hardly a region of the country, in fact, that he didn't visit during the last forty years of his life: he journeyed to southern Georgia, northeastern Oklahoma, Los Angeles and New Orleans again, the Grand Tetons, the Canadian Rockies, the Old Santa Fe Trail from Missouri to New Mexico, and even returned to Europe—Italy, France, and Spain.

Rita explained that she didn't mind that he usually traveled alone. "A man has his work to do and his own life to live," she told a reporter

in 1942. "When he's deep in the Ozarks or taking his time on Mississippi boats, it would be silly of me to expect him to find a post office." It
would be easy to get the impression from *An Artist in America* that
these trips were vagabond wanderings like the ones he took during the
1920s, when he discovered his interest in the American scene. In reality, he undertook these later jaunts mostly as guided vacations or for
professional reasons—on assignment for magazines or advertising work
arranged by Reeves Lewenthal, the head of Associated American Artists. Benton acknowledges that these travels were distinct from his
"earlier adventuring about the country," when he formulated the motifs
of his regionalism. "With the new urbanist developments," he explains,
his purposes for traveling changed: he set out either to document the
increasing industrialization of the countryside or to record life as it was
lived before urbanization. "I became more and more a painter of history," he writes.

Benton took one such trip in the summer of 1938 with James Fitzgerald, "a burly, hard-drinking Irishman" who taught watercolor at the Art
Institute. The two men started their trip in New Orleans, traveled west
to Oklahoma, and then to Tennessee and North Carolina. Benton
made about forty drawings on the trip, some of which he then published in an article he wrote for *Scribner's Magazine* on Disney, Oklahoma, located in the northeast corner of the state and precisely the sort
of boomtown he had in mind when he wrote about the urbanization
creeping into the countryside. "Fast-growing, industrial and recreation
center of the future—enterprising people—beautiful streets, beautiful
homes" is how Mr. Cohen, the president of the Disney Chamber of
Commerce, described the town to Benton in a barroom conversation.
"We call this the Venice of America," Cohen added.

The town's boom was made possible by Wesley E. Disney, the U.S.
congressman who successfully lobbied the Public Works Administration for twenty million dollars to build the Pensacola Dam on the
Grand River. Once the federal government approved the dam project, a
real estate speculator bought up land and began advertising the town of
Disney, "prosperous city in the making." Though construction on the
dam had yet to begin when Benton arrived, he explains that a "large
and loud population of itching palms" had settled there to wait for the
money to pour in. Benton was skeptical, noting the bitterness of the
"propertyless hopefuls" who occupied the low-lying land to be flooded—

the so-called bottoms. During his stay, he came across a grumpy man digging ditches for water lines. "Thirty-five cents a' hour," the man complained, "through these here roots with a god-damn dust plummer hollerin' like a wampus cat when yuh cain't do three hundred feet a minute." Benton concludes the article with a poignant image of the past's resistance to the future: "Away from the voice of Disney the tree frogs sang their interminable chorus. I heard them on my way to bed. They were singing that same chorus back in 1907, when Oklahoma became a state. They were singing it in the early 1800's when the Indian tribes of the locality were moved westward to a tune of desolation and death . . . They were singing it earlier than that."

The changes in rural America that Benton observes in the *Scribner's* article—that is, the creeping of a corporate mind-set into the hinterland—contributed to the end of regionalism's popularity in the 1940s. In the 1930s, the regionalist style and American scene subjects remained enormously appealing, thanks to media coverage of the aesthetic and political debates of the era, the appeal of New Deal arts projects and cultural nationalism during the Depression, the success of Associated American Artists, and press coverage of the always quotable Benton—and of Wood and Curry as well. But during the early 1940s, sensing that the market for his art was changing, Benton relied more heavily on Lewenthal and Associated American Artists for income. Despite the successes this relationship made possible, Benton grew uneasy, due in part to his growing sense that Lewenthal's organization was becoming more and more business-oriented, and "business and art, in its living form," he explains, "have too many differences for a long-time wedding."

Some of these differences became apparent to Benton in 1941 and 1942, when he worked on an advertising campaign for the American Tobacco Company. In 1940, George Washington Hill, the president of the company, grew worried that sales of his leading product, Lucky Strike, lagged behind those of Camel, R. J. Reynolds's brand. Hill believed that an advertising campaign featuring the artwork of popular American artists would propel sales and so arranged with Associated American Artists for Benton, Curry, and others to paint pictures of tobacco production that would be used in magazine ads. Both clever businessmen, Lewenthal and Hill believed that regionalist art, with its homespun style and subjects, was the ideal genre with which to promote cigarettes.

The project began well enough. At a meeting in New York, Benton, Lewenthal, and Hill decided that the pictures ought to portray the realities of tobacco production; they all agreed, Benton writes, that these pictures would "replace the usual photographs of pretty models holding tobacco leaves." In other words, initially it seemed that Hill understood Benton's brand of regionalism to be a kind of realism rather than a kind of sentimentality. So in 1942, Benton traveled to southern Georgia with two other artists commissioned to work on the campaign; he was enthusiastic, later describing the trip as "interesting" and the scene as "full of rich color," and filled a sketchbook with drawings of the black sharecroppers who farmed tobacco in that region of Georgia. However, upon returning to New York and showing the drawings to the advertising executives handling the account, he ran into "a most horrified protestation." The executives rejected the drawings on the grounds, according to Benton's recollection, that they depicted the black sharecroppers "doing what looks like old-time slave work" and "we don't want realism that will foul up our sales." Benton fought back, pointing out that you can't fiddle with reality, but the executives countered that race was too thorny an issue for them to touch and asked him to avoid depicting blacks altogether.

He would later regret it, but Benton complied, traveling to North Carolina, where white "hillbillies" handled the tobacco. Upon showing the men a painting of an old farmer and his granddaughter sorting tobacco leaves, they professed to like it but asked for an alteration: the girl was too skinny, apparently, and they instructed him that "everything about tobacco must look healthy." Fed up, Benton arranged a meeting with Hill to air his grievances. He lobbied hard on behalf of the painting, arguing that it was a fine picture. "Why I'd buy it myself," he said. But Hill wasn't sold and called the bluff: "Well then, Mr. Benton, I'll just sell it to you. It's yours." Benton was stuck and so bought the painting back for three thousand dollars.

The American Tobacco Company eventually used two quaint paintings, including *Outside the Curing Barn* (1942), in advertisements that appeared in *Time* and *The Saturday Evening Post* in 1942, but he'd been burned, having surrendered his cherished autonomy to a corporate mandate. Erika Doss views this as a pivotal episode in Benton's career, the moment when "he recognized that he had allowed his art, originated to challenge the status quo and transform America, to become complicitous propaganda for big business." She points out that the two paintings "portray tobacco country as an agricultural paradise full of bountiful fields and enthusiastic farmers."

Doss believes that Benton accepted advertising commissions both because they offered a "healthy income" and "because he believed his art could transform the institutions of labor and mass media," but very soon after completing the commission for Hill, he expressed his displeasure with the project and with advertising work in general. In February 1943, for example, in response to an interviewer's question, Benton stated, "Cheap people have cheap ideas. The advertising business is full of them . . . One of the horrible casualties of individual initiative is the advertising business." Later he put it more bluntly: "I thought the series of paintings the American Tobacco Company used in its advertising was a failure . . . The challenge we're making to business is, 'Are you willing to proceed on the basis of complete freedom for the artist?'" For an artist who had excoriated the "Business First" mentality of corporate America in the 1920s, playing into the hands of a giant like the American Tobacco Company must have been a disappointment. But desperate, perhaps, for his art to be accepted at the moment that regionalism was waning as the most visible mode of populism, Benton kept at it, continuing to do magazine illustrations, to work for corporations (Abbott Laboratories, for instance), and to make murals that boosted commercial businesses (the colorful vegetables spilling from the bull's horn in the Harzfeld's mural, for example, are a transparent symbol of the department store's merchandise).

Nevertheless, after another project brokered by Lewenthal fell apart, Benton abandoned Associated American Artists. In 1946, Lewenthal arranged for him to travel to Hollywood yet again, this time to work with Walt Disney. Since Benton's 1937 visit to Los Angeles for *Life*, he'd made promotional images, in deals also brokered by Lewenthal, for three big Hollywood films. He'd visited Hollywood in 1940, for instance, to make lithographs for the advertising campaigns for John Ford's *Grapes of Wrath* and *Long Voyage Home*, and the following year Twentieth Century–Fox hired him to produce lithographs for the promotion of *Swamp Water*, Jean Renoir's first American film. But the 1946 trip to

Hollywood was less successful. Disney and Lewenthal concocted a plan for Benton to illustrate the characters for an "American folk operetta on the theme of Davy Crockett." Salvador Dalí, who was already at the Disney studios working on illustrations for the short film *Destino* (telling of a tragic love between Chronos and a mortal woman, the film was canceled due to lack of funding but eventually released in 2003), encouraged Benton to collaborate with the cartoon impresario. As Benton recalls, "I had a few conversations with Dalí on the subject and he seemed very confident about such possibilities in so far as his own art was concerned." After just two weeks, however, Benton grew frustrated with Disney's objections, which mostly had to do with the international marketability of Benton's ideas: "I saw what a tough . . . balancing act Disney was entangled with and realized that I was just too 'sot' in my ways to learn to cope with it. So I gave up."

Upon his return home the fifty-seven-year-old Benton was exhausted from drinking too much at Hollywood parties. "Working all day and partying all night," he says, "wasn't my game anymore, but I'd forgotten it." Then, in August 1946, just when his doctors in Kansas City reprimanded him for drinking and smoking and chewing tobacco, his brother, Nat, died from a heart attack. Nat's "death so depressed me in my run-down condition," he remembers, "I thought I was about ready to go too." The trauma of these events prompted Benton to reconsider the wisdom of moonlighting for Associated American Artists—what he called his "public hoopla"—and later that year he informed Lewenthal that he was breaking from the organization.

Benton had made enough money on the Harzfeld's mural (and for a film that documented its execution, produced by *Encyclopaedia Britannica*) to fund a family trip to Europe in 1949—his first visit there in thirty-eight years. The principal reason for the trip was to help settle twenty-two-year-old T.P. in France, where he'd earned a yearlong scholarship at the Conservatoire de Paris to study the flute. The family flew to Italy, where Rita had not visited since leaving when a child, and she and Jessie stayed while Tom escorted his son to Paris. Benton recalled the vacation fondly and describes being tickled by his fame in Italy, the result, apparently, of the *Britannica* film, which was shown in cinemas around the country. "*Il pittore Benton*," as the Italians called him, even received honorary memberships in the ancient academies of Florence and Siena (he was inducted into the Accademia degli Intronati, or the Academy of the Bewildered, in Siena, as "Tomaso di Missouri"). On another Italian sojourn, twenty-five years later, Tom and Rita settled for an autumn in the medieval town of Pietrasanta (famous for its marble, which Michelangelo used in his sculptures) between Pisa and La Spezia. Harry Jackson, a colorful western painter and sculptor, had a large studio in the town and had invited Benton to borrow the space and the workmen that came with it to execute a bronze sculpture he had in mind.

In the spring of 1952, Benton's mother, Lizzie, who'd been suffering from a degenerative brain disease that caused hallucinations and had been moved to a state hospital in Massachusetts, died at age eighty-seven after a series of strokes. Shaken by death yet again, Benton began seeking refuge more frequently in the landscape of the American West. He'd traveled out west in 1944 to make illustrations for an edition of Francis Parkman's epic travelogue *The Oregon Trail* (1849)—the pastel-hued watercolors depict pioneers and Indians straining to subsist on the frontier—but when he returned in the 1950s and 1960s, he focused more on the land itself than the people who lived on it, a consequence, he says wistfully, of urbanization's influence on "traditional behavior." "The easy-going friendliness of the American people," he writes, "especially rural people, seemed to become more cautious, more reserved . . . It was getting so you needed an introduction to start even a barroom conversation." With the new "urbanist developments," he adds, "easy contacts became more and more difficult to initiate. I found that attempts to butt myself into talking groups began to be met with curious stares . . . that asked quite plainly, 'What's that old goat after?'" "I was simply getting too old," he concludes, "for the newly developing human situations of our country—too old to penetrate into their meanings."

Benton visited the Grand Tetons in 1958, Wyoming in 1963 (and again two years later), and the Canadian Rockies in 1965, and as he explained it earlier, he responded viscerally to these places, which swept away his egotism. Writing about the Great Plains that extend eastward from the Rockies, he muses, "I like the way they make thought seem futile and ideas but the silly vapors of the physically disordered . . . The indifference of the physical world to all human effort stands revealed as hard inescapable fact . . . Contrasting what is within me with the immensity outside, I get a proper sense of the consequence and significance of my concerns." His increasing concentration on the western landscape, whatever it indicated about the effects of urbanization, resulted in some remarkably sensitive easel paintings. One of these, *The Sheepherder*, completed in 1958 after his trip to Wyoming's Grand Tetons, includes memento mori in the form of a cow's skull in the foreground and folded-over hillsides in the background that resemble the corporeal bulges of the elderly, but these romantic associations are offset by the down-to-earth labors of the sheepherder who tends to his flock in the central valley. The metaphor appears straightforward enough: the shepherd cannot ignore the threat of death, of either himself or his sheep, but imminent responsibilities and conditions demand his immediate focus. Intellectual associations are dangerous, Benton suggests, and the present environment is all that matters. A second landscape, *Trail Riders*, finished in 1965 after the trip to the Banff region, contains a similar symbolism. Though landscape was a new genre for Benton, he used it to communicate familiar messages.

Benton's most deliberate statement about the West, however, was the mural he made for the Truman Library, *Independence and the Opening of the West*, which was contracted in 1958, after protracted negotiations with Truman, and completed three years later. In the spring of 1957, as he was finishing the Cartier mural, Benton received a visit at his Kansas City studio from David Lloyd, secretary of the Truman Library, and Wayne Grover, the archivist of the United States. The men studied the Cartier mural and informed Benton that they wanted something similar for the library. "Why not?" Benton responded, and the group retreated to the house to discuss the idea over a few highballs. Secretly, though, Benton had misgivings. He'd met Truman twice before, and both encounters were inauspicious. On February 24, 1949, Benton and a Kansas City lawyer friend, Jerome Walsh, visited the White House to pay their respects to the Missouri president. As Truman finished a press conference, Benton was introduced to him and was startled by the president's question. "Are you still making those controversial pictures?" Truman asked. "He put this question in a bantering sort of way," Benton recalls, "but there was not much humor in the look of his eyes, nor did he laugh when I replied, 'When I get the chance.'" Benton left Truman that day with a suspicion that "he did not quite approve of me." The two met again six years later, in the spring of 1955, at a cocktail party for Truman hosted by Randall Jessee, a Kansas City newscaster. Though many well-to-do Kansas Citians, mostly Republicans, disapproved of the Democratic president, Jessee's party was a success and everyone treated Truman respectfully. Benton introduced Rita to Truman and his wife, Bessie, both of whom addressed them "affably," but later, sitting together at a table with a large group, Truman was asked how he felt about Benton's Missouri mural. "How do you like our Missouri artist?" Jessee asked the former president. "I don't know whether I like that fellow or not," Truman responded. "You know, Randall, I have a long memory."

Shortly after the cocktail party, Truman wrote his daughter a letter that mentioned meeting Benton. "It seems that Tom Benton thinks your pa is a top-notch president," he explained. "It made me ashamed of my opinion of him as a mural painter." Two years later, after Lloyd and Grover suggested the library project to him, Benton discovered that Truman had been upset about the inclusion of Tom Pendergast in the Missouri mural. Apparently, Truman believed that Benton had included Pendergast, who'd given Truman his start in politics, against Pendergast's will. In addition, Truman had criticized Benton's *Kentuckian* (1954), a painting of Burt Lancaster playing the namesake of a 1955 film, on the grounds that he looked too handsome with his chiseled chin and blond locks. In a letter to the producer of the film, Truman wrote, "I don't like Mr. Benton's Kentuckian. It looks like no resident of or emigrant from that great State that I've ever seen."

Benton was nervous when Lloyd and Grover brought Truman to his studio in May 1957 to look at his progress on the Cartier mural. Still unsure as to why the president disapproved of him and his art, Benton was apprehensive and anticipated another embarrassing encounter. But Truman was friendly, greeting Benton cordially in the front yard of his Kansas City home. Once in the studio, however, the first panel of the Cartier mural, which depicted a life-size representation of a Seneca Indian clad only in moccasins and a loincloth, unsettled Truman. "The figure stood out," Benton recalls, "its muscular nakedness almost as real as life itself. Too real for the President." Upon seeing the panel, Truman reeled and turned away. At that point, Lloyd and Grover guided him to the second panel, the one depicting Cartier claiming St. Lawrence County for the French. Benton explained that he was stuck on one detail, the emblem on the French banner, which he wanted to depict with historical accuracy. The men discussed the problem for a few minutes, and Truman seemed to relax, stating, "I never knew that artists could be so careful about historical facts." Sensing that his stance was softening, Lloyd mentioned the possibility of Benton painting a mural for the library. Truman failed to commit but did invite Benton to call on him at the library in Independence, Missouri.

Though Benton started researching the mural immediately, he had to endure a long period of indecision by Truman, who apparently still had misgivings about the artist. After several more meetings and a few glasses of bourbon at Truman's office in Independence, the two finally came to terms on June 6, 1958, and signed a contract, for the healthy sum of sixty thousand dollars, for a mural to be installed in the library's lobby. In the year since his visit to the studio, Truman had warmed to Benton. "I was now his man," Benton remembers, "and as such he was going to protect me whether I liked it or not." Like Benton, Truman enjoyed bourbon, and the two men bonded over many highballs and a shared midwestern pragmatism. Benton's impressions of Truman conform to most sketches of his personality. "I discovered that beneath the rather formidable Presidential aura," Benton writes, "there was a simple, straightforward, essentially friendly man, without an iota of pretentiousness in his makeup." Nevertheless, Benton recognized in Truman some of his own traits: Truman was obstinate, feisty, and fractious. "I sensed that he was very much used to making up his own mind," Benton recalls, "and I quickly discerned a quality of stubbornness there which I didn't want to activate." Truman, who had a humble background, surely recognized the irony that his artist had been born to political greatness, and so the two also bonded over shared memories of Benton's brother and father. Truman knew Nat during the 1930s, seeing him often in Springfield, Missouri, at Democratic Party rallies. "Too bad," Benton remembers Truman telling him, "he . . . died so young, so good a Democrat and so dependable." And though he never met the Colonel, Truman knew of him and described him as "another loyal and dependable Democrat. A man of the people." Benton claims, in fact, that Truman reminded him of his father: both men were "stocky" and had "outthrust" stomachs, "slightly spread legs," and an "overall emphatic presence." He also explains that both men possessed an inherent skepticism of hype, a strain, perhaps, of "Protestant iconoclasm."

Benton comments that Truman was more than just an ordinary achiever, however: "He was also a thinker, even an intellectual, though he took care that his language disguised that most of the time." In one interview, Benton went so far as to call Truman "a first class historian." On the one hand, Truman's intellectualism permitted the men to have lively conversations about the historical theme of the mural; on the other, Truman's ideas, because more verbal than "imagistic," caused Benton some grief during the planning stages of the project. Two of Truman's ideas in particular gave Benton pause: he demanded that his face not be shown in the mural and wanted Thomas Jefferson to be its subject. From the moment he first learned of the mural project, Benton had supposed it would depict a history of Independence, specifically the onetime frontier town's role in the opening of the West, and Lloyd, Grover, and Benton all imagined that it would include a portrait of Truman as well. But during their third meeting at the library, Truman proposed to Benton that the subject should be Jefferson and Jeffersonian democracy, which would "provide an important historical lesson, of interest to all Americans." Though a great admirer of Jefferson, Benton was "appalled" by the idea—"there was no way I could make an interesting picture with such a theme," he argues. His main concern was that the subject was too abstract to paint; he was more comfortable depicting actions than grand concepts, and a theme as theoretical as Jeffersonian democracy, he felt, was unmanageable. Benton prevailed, eventually persuading Truman of the suitability of his frontier theme, and thereafter the president left him alone. "In all the time I worked on the mural he never kibitzed once," Benton recollects. "Maybe he wanted to now and then, but he never did. I call that a good patron."

Independence, "Queen City of the Trails," was the departure point for the Santa Fe, California, and Oregon Trails. Each spring the city had bustled with pioneers stocking up on supplies, preparing wagons, and forming traveling parties to better defend against Indian attacks. To prepare for the mural, Benton made two trips to points west, the first to research costumes and weapons in libraries and museums, the second, in May 1959, to travel along the Santa Fe Trail. Charles Banks Wilson accompanied Benton on this latter trip to help him, once again, meet Native Americans. In Tulsa, Oklahoma, for instance, Wilson arranged a meeting between Benton and Brummett Echohawk, a Pawnee artist. Benton had learned that pioneers starting out from Independence likely would meet Pawnee Indians before members from any other tribe, and he wanted to sketch one for the mural. Echohawk took the men to a Pawnee church where they found an appropriate model, a thirty-year-old lay preacher. Leaving Tulsa, Benton and Wilson headed into Cheyenne territory in western Oklahoma, where they met a white farmer in a restaurant who arranged to introduce them to some of his Cheyenne farmhands. Putting up in a "rickety motel," the men were visited by a group of Indians, including some "young squaws" eager to pose for the artist for free. "Indian men and women waited for their turn to be drawn by the little white man," Wilson recalls. "Our motel court was a busy place." Too busy, apparently, for the motel's owner, who, convinced that the men were arranging trysts with the Cheyenne women, hollered at them to leave. "I've read about artists," the man yelled, "and you ain't foolin' me a bit."

The men continued west, traveling through Boise City, Oklahoma, on the way to Bent's Old Fort, near La Junta, Colorado, where Benton sketched the ruins and spotted the Spanish Peaks in the distance. "Since he is never one to be satisfied with a written or pictured account if personal contact is possible," Wilson observes, "I was not surprised by our destination." After a two-hour hike, Benton located his desired vantage point and "polished off [a drawing of] the 13,623 foot peaks in about 10 minutes." At this point, Wilson returned home, leaving Benton to travel with an ex-student, Aaron Pyle, to western Nebraska, where he sketched Chimney and Courthouse Rocks, landmarks on the Oregon Trail.

Benton began working in the library lobby on November 16, 1959. With the help of Sidney Larson and Duard Marshall, another former student, he lined the wall with heavy linen and drew a grid to square up the composition. He was a daily presence at the library, taking a lunch break each day with the staff to eat Rita's homemade soup, which he brought in a thermos. On the day that he started painting, Benton invited Truman to climb the scaffolding and put down the first few strokes on the wall, a task he gladly performed for the clicking cameras and the applause of the crowd. Benton's labors were witnessed and photographed by large crowds on Sunday afternoons; so many visitors blinded him with their flashes that the guards had to intervene. Benton also had to contend with terrible bursitis in his back and shoulder, which required cortisone injections; the guards had to pick him up off the floor each day, and because he could no longer drive, the Kansas City police escorted him to and from the library. But Benton finished the mural on April 15, 1961, and at the opening ceremony Truman praised it, and

Chief Justice Earl Warren addressed the crowd. "As our people come to visit the Truman Library," Warren said, "their eyes will fall upon this great mural, and if they see it with eyes brightened by a knowledge of our own history every figure in it will have meaning for them and will help to build within their hearts a deep and abiding patriotism. The knowledge of our heroic past will open vistas for them into our future."

Warren had little choice but to speak such platitudes, for *Independence and the Opening of the West* illustrates a hackneyed history. One wishes, in fact, that Benton had painted either a more specific episode or a paean to Jeffersonian democracy. As it is, the mural, despite its typical dynamism, narrates a general and banal history. Like the River Club mural, the Truman Library mural is an anachronistic romanticization of Manifest Destiny. The right side of the mural depicts stock pioneer figures setting out from Independence, armed with guns and axes, and encountering Native Americans on the western plains, illustrated to the left. At the center, the whites and the Indians make a tentative peace: a Cheyenne offers a peace pipe to a gun-toting settler standing on a hill at the apex of the composition. In the predella below, Benton depicts Independence during a quieter time, in the 1840s, when the town was not aware yet of the coming bustle.

A month before the mural's dedication, *The New York Times* noted its epic grandiosity, reporting that it depicted "America's 'continental destiny'" and "symbolic—not actual—figures and happenings." Matthew Baigell also comments on the mural's generalized version of history, remarking that "in the 1920s and 1930s the American past, and its relation to the American present, was a viable subject of concern. People, whether they praised or condemned the earlier era, were searching out those elements of continuity that linked periods together." When Baigell adds that after World War II "the American past lost importance as a conscious influence on or modifier of current thought and behavior," and that "those who, like Benton, were intimately involved with the past became, in effect, antiquarians," he means not that history had become irrelevant, of course, but that by the 1960s a widespread understanding emerged that historical myths could not remain so uncomplicated.

Truman, however, was pleased with the mural. At the opening ceremony he told the crowd that Benton was "the best muralist in the country" and that he got along with the pugnacious artist—"that's hard for anyone to do," he quipped. Benton, meanwhile, had concluded that he and Truman "had found for all of our differences of temperament and outlook a kind of psychological kinship . . . that makes it possible for two men to sit together with a drink and say nothing." So it was that on December 27, 1972, Benton found himself standing next to Truman's casket, on view in the library lobby, with tears running down his face.

11

AT WAR

In the summer of 1969, a *Life* magazine writer visited Martha's Vineyard to prepare a profile of Benton. Appearing that fall, the hokily titled article—"Tom Benton at 80, Still at War with Bores and Boobs"—observed that while America had made peace with Benton, he had yet to do so with America. Though by 1969 he'd become a "quaint grandpappy" of American culture, Benton "is still waging his constant war," the author claims. Among the people whom Benton continued to rail against were the "crude, insensitive, rich" collectors who bought his paintings and the "cultural leaders" and "museum directors" who exhibited them. In addition, Benton was displeased with the state of the nation (though not with the counterculture of the 1960s, with which he had a passing familiarity—in the mid-1960s his daughter, Jessie, a musician, became involved with Mel Lyman, a folkie agitator and founder of a Boston commune). The *Life* reporter explains that "the other part of Benton's war is his own estrangement from . . . the contours of both the land and its people he once reported so handsomely." Benton agreed, telling him, "I was once able to walk all over the backwoods of the South and the West. But there's the difficulty of making contacts now," due, he explained, to the increased indifference of people—"because they can get around so rapidly, people don't give a damn about a stranger coming in to talk to them." Some of his indignation, then, we can attribute to his feeling ignored, but his more habitual and smoldering resentment had emerged almost thirty years earlier and reflected the cultural and political changes that spelled the end of regionalism, that ill-defined art movement with which he'd been associated since the early 1930s.

In 1933, while working at the Ferargil Galleries in New York, the art dealer Maynard Walker organized an exhibition titled *American Painting Since Whistler* that was shown at the Kansas City Art Institute. The exhibition was the first to show Benton, John Steuart Curry, and Grant Wood all together, and Walker worked hard to promote them as indigenous but modern artists who were uniquely suited to illustrating the life of the nation. As the art historian James Dennis notes, by 1935 regionalism had received a lot of press with "commercial significance to its 'triumvirate.'" In December 1934, for instance, less than two years after Walker's exhibition, *Time* magazine ran its cover story on the three painters, declaring them the most relevant and virile artists in the United States.

But from the moment of its inception regionalism was a deeply conflicted movement; it both emphasized the values particular to specific geographical areas and sought to identify a national ethos. According to Susan Hegeman, Benton worked at cross-purposes: he attacked what he saw as an increasingly standardized America yet promoted the region as a national culture; his art and rhetoric were stuck between provincialism and nationalism. But this fact reveals not so much the weakness of Benton's theories as the contradictions inherent to regionalism itself. "While this attention to folk roots thus helped . . . [to imagine] America as complete and undivided," Hegeman asserts, "it also suggested the existence of distinctive local cultures, each with their own folk traditions and lores." Some might conclude, therefore, that regionalism was dead on arrival—a half-baked movement founded on contradictions. Whatever regionalism may have been, Benton recognized long before the *Life* profile that it had vanished from the national consciousness and was no longer a viable foundation on which to build an art movement, which compelled him, not surprisingly, to lash out.

As early as 1940 the art critic Peyton Boswell observed that the "American scene" had vanished along with "the thirties"; now, he claimed, "the cry is for beauty," for a "return to aesthetics." Writing in 1951, E. P. Richardson, director of the Detroit Institute of Arts, observed that the movement had "disintegrated" and had been "a relatively superficial phenomenon in the field of American painting, compared with its strong, objective existence in other fields," such as literature. Erika Doss remarks that "it is no surprise that Benton wrote that 'gnawing suspicions of failure' gripped him at this time," for regionalism "was seen as a failed style by the late thirties," and David W. Noble claims that once Benton understood that "the promise of the Virgin Land had not been fulfilled," he expressed "dismay." For his part, Benton, remember, acknowledges that he grew "almost completely frustrated" by 1941, after realizing that he, Curry, and Wood had been "well off the beam" to assume that their movement had succeeded at holding back the colonization of America by European aesthetics and intellectualism, a fact evidenced by the ascendancy of abstract expressionism in the 1940s. In the end, then, Benton was comfortably situated as an "in" artist for only about the ten years that coincided with the Depression. "We found the bottom knocked out from under us," he writes, adding that "our interior images lost public significance" and "the critical world of art had, by and large, as little use for our group front as it had for me as an individual."

In his essays and autobiographies, Benton expresses embittered anger about these cultural shifts. He blasts "the coteries of high-brows, of critics, college art professors and museum boys" who failed to "accommodate our populist leanings." Ultimately, Benton claims, these groups "succeeded in destroying our Regionalism and returning American art to that desired position of obscurity." His critics, he concludes, were variously "neurotic," "cultist," and "anarchic." "The transfer of American attention from the national to the international scene," he argues, only bred "conflict" and "contradictory assumptions": "All meanings were confused." Later he added, "Without a belief in the reality of things there can certainly be no background for a realistic art."

The demise of regionalism was hastened by the deaths of Grant Wood (in 1942, on the eve of his fifty-first birthday) and John Steuart Curry (in 1946, at the age of forty-eight), which shook Benton to the core. As long as these men were alive, he could believe that he belonged to a robust movement; their deaths, besides devastating him personally, alienated him even further from the national mood. But their deaths also gave Benton the opportunity to sound off on the cultural changes that so infuriated him. Just after Wood died of liver cancer, Benton wrote, "When this new America looks back for landmarks to help gauge its forward footsteps, it will find a monument standing up in the midst of much wreckage . . . This monument will be made out of Grant Wood's works." This "wreckage," he maintains, is the "refuse of America's prewar decadence"; it is the "petty critical artifices and pretenses, the cultural frauds, the cultural imitations," and "cultural tourism." Writing a few years later, Benton went so far as to imply that regionalism's passing contributed to Wood's; he explains that when Wood was sitting in his hospital bed, his "worry over . . . his artistic self doubts" caused him to develop the "curious idea of changing his identity . . . It was as if he wanted to destroy what was in him and become an empty soul before he went out into the emptiness of death."

Benton amplified these points in his obituary for Curry, who died from a heart attack. Curry, he reminisces, "never learned to cover himself, and . . . as his reputation grew, he suffered much from the stings of critical assault. His humility was public and it laid him wide open to the shafts of little and jealous men." Benton later recounted his last conversation with Curry, which occurred on Martha's Vineyard just months before his death. Benton tried to boost his friend's spirits by calling attention to his successes. "You must feel pretty good now," he remarked, "after all your struggles, to know that you have come to a permanent place in American art. It's a long way from a Kansas farm to fame like yours." But Curry, clearly bitter about regionalism's misfortunes, was unmoved. "I don't know about that," he replied; "maybe I'd have done better to stay on the farm. No one seems interested in my pictures. Nobody thinks I can paint. If I *am* any good, I lived at the wrong time." As late as 1951, Benton was still lamenting the deaths of Wood and Curry and harping on the supposed connivances of cultural elites. They "put inventive method rather than a search for the human meaning of one's life at the center of artistic endeavor," he writes, "and made it appear that aesthetic creation was a matter for intellectual rather than intuitive insight." Such attitudes, the historian Richard Hofstadter demonstrates in *Anti-intellectualism in American Life* (1963), may have been prevalent in the political and cultural discourses of the 1940s and 1950s, but Benton emerged as one of their most vocal proponents, thus firming up his reputation as a crank.

In 1954, the collapse of regionalism was confirmed yet again, as was Benton's acrimony about the nation's cultural condition. That year officials at the Whitney Museum informed him that they were moving, from their original location at West Eighth Street in Greenwich Village to West Fifty-fourth Street, and had no room for *The Arts of Life in America* panels in the new building; they suggested that he take them back. "This was somewhat of a shock," Benton later recalled, adding, understatedly, "I had not expected the paintings to be so completely repudiated." Though the panels eventually found a home in Connecticut, at the New Britain Institute (today the New Britain Museum of American Art), the message was clear: regionalism had come and gone.

•

In their obituaries of Wood, both Benton and Curry imply that the war played a role in the defeat of regionalism, and Benton discussed the consequences of the war on American culture and politics in several other writings as well. In 1951, for example, he recalled that in the early 1940s, "I could feel the winds from Europe blowing with accelerating force toward conflict." He was angry, he explains, because "old-fashioned isolationist sentiment . . . was rising and particularly in the middle west. So also was a peculiar brand of acquiescence in the rise of Nazi power." Benton, who held strong isolationist views until Pearl Harbor, admits that he struggled with his decision to abandon some of his "anti-European" sentiments in favor of U.S. intervention: "The American scene which had furnished the content and motivations of my work for some twenty years was outweighed by the world one." As he put it in a 1942 letter to his writer friend John D. Weaver, "I have myself succumbed to the general pressure of the war. After Pearl Harbor I was traveling around lecturing and got so disgusted with Pullman car optimism and overconfidence that I started a series of war pictures intended to wake people up."

To distract himself from his anxiety regarding the impending war, and to earn some extra money after his firing from the Kansas City Art Institute, Benton started lecturing more frequently. He was in Cincinnati to deliver one such lecture when he heard the news of the Japanese attack on Pearl Harbor. Though he might have been delighted on the morning of December 7, 1941, to note that *The New York Times* included that day a big reproduction of his painting *Hollywood* in an article on the movie industry, he was too distressed by the attack to take any pleasure from the painting's public exposure. His mind was elsewhere, he says, for he "had an idea," which was to "wake up the middle west to the grimness of our national situation." To achieve this, Benton left Cincinnati immediately, returned to Kansas City, and began sketching designs for a series of paintings he called *The Year of Peril*. These tense, violent, and overwrought paintings were aimed at two targets—fascist sympathizers and American isolationists—and he spared nothing to make his case. "These, departing from any of my precedents," he writes, "were deliberate propaganda pictures, cartoons in paint, dedicated solely to arousing the public mind." Benton's original intent was to exhibit the series in Kansas City's Union Station, but when Reeves Lewenthal of Associated American Artists learned that he was working on a group of war pictures, he showed up at Benton's Kansas City studio to see them for himself. "Tom," Lewenthal exclaimed, "this is no local affair you have there. It's a national one." Lewenthal promptly arranged for one of his clients, Abbott Laboratories, an international pharmaceutical firm based in Chicago, to purchase *The Year of Peril*. The firm began collecting art in 1930 and during the war commissioned work by many artists, including Curry and Reginald Marsh, that it believed could build support for the war effort. Together, Lewenthal and Abbott Laboratories enlisted the help of the U.S. Office of Facts and Figures (which became the Office of War Information in June 1942) to disperse reproductions of the Benton paintings all over the world. In the end, Benton was paid handsomely (twenty thousand dollars) and received enormous publicity in the United States and Europe.

The eight paintings in the series (*Starry Night, Again, Indifference, Casualty, The Sowers, The Harvest, Invasion,* and *Exterminate!*) were completed in 1942 and then quickly disseminated. Abbott's advertising department worked hard to get high-quality reproductions, going so far as to bring Benton to Chicago to monitor the printing process. "All in all," Benton claims, "the circulation of actual single reproductions . . . came to well over fifty-five million." *Starry Night*, based on press photographs of the USS *Shaw* and the USS *West Virginia*, ships bombed at Pearl Harbor, depicts a terrified sailor slipping beneath water ablaze with burning oil. One of the more sensational paintings, *Again*, shows an emaciated Christ on the cross, just as he's speared by gross caricatures of the three fascist powers and strafed by a Nazi warplane. Benton, who had very little use for religion, must have been desperately agitated to use such an image, even if, according to Cécile Whiting, author of *Antifascism in American Art*, this was a common symbolism at the time. "For many Americans," she explains, "the war formed a clear-cut battle between democracy and fascism, barbarism and civilization, pagan ignominy and Christianity." *Indifference* and *Casualty* represent wounded and dismembered soldiers in the wreckage of, respectively, two downed planes and a sinking battleship, a rendering of the apocalyptic consequences of acquiescence. Recalling Millet's realist painting *The Sower* (1850), *The Sowers* depicts a massive, antiheroic monster sprinkling human skulls across a wasted landscape, and in the words of Doss,

Exterminate!, the most extravagant of the paintings, "shows enthusiastic G.I. Joes disemboweling a jaundiced ogre clutching the tattered remnants of the Rising Sun."

The critics were appalled by the feral paintings. An *Art Digest* writer observes that Benton must have painted them in a "white heat" and describes them as "grim," "strident," and "bitter." Writing in *The New Republic*, the critic Manny Farber, though impressed that the pictures depict "war as war, and not as pattycake pattycake," excoriates "Benton's bad painting." Of *The Harvest*, Farber says, "There is so little emotional truth in the painting that you expect a curtain to go down and the figures to get up and walk off the stage"; of the series in general he claims that Benton "starts with a story and never stops talking," a criticism we've heard many times before. More recently, Henry Adams described *The Year of Peril* as a "psychotic outburst" and remarked that Benton may have gone "off the deep end" as he worked on the paintings. For what it's worth, Benton never pretended that these paintings were anything other than bitter expressions. "There are no bathing beauties dressed up in soldier outfits in these pictures," he writes. "There are no silk-stockinged legs. There are no pretty boys out of collar advertisements to suggest that this war is a gigolo party. There is no glossing over of the kind of hard ferocity that men must have to beat down the evil that is now upon us." Doss describes *The Year of Peril* as a "hysterical reaction to American unpreparedness" and wonders whether it was as successful at stimulating support for intervention as its distribution numbers suggest. She identifies in the series something more than a violent revenge fantasy. The paintings, she claims, exhibit "magic realism or pseudo-surrealism," a fascination with the "creepy underbelly of human consciousness" that was ill suited to "engineering prowar sentiment."

Two paintings in the series, *The Harvest* and *Invasion*, conflate wartime and regional themes. Each depicts good rural folk visited by the horrors of war. In *The Harvest,* a woman clutches her head in grief: her husband and daughter have been killed by bombers, shown circling overhead, which also have set the family's farm on fire. *Invasion* represents bloodthirsty fascists maiming and torturing another rural family in front of their barn. Benton's message here is plain: unless isolationist farmers come to their senses and join the war against evil and the battle for reform, they will be overrun by brutality. Doss's implication, it's worth emphasizing, is that Benton expresses so much anger in the paintings that they are rendered ineffective. In the end, his fears about war and the state of the regionalist ethos trump any capacity the series has to move us. Benton, it seems, was so overcome by an all-around frustration that he couldn't produce anything other than what the *Art News* editor Alfred Frankfurter called "vague Baroque mannerism" and "ridiculous" propaganda. Benton had tripped over his temper many times in the 1930s, but now his resentment became so conspicuous, and pointed in so many directions, as to render his art a little bit silly.

The board of Abbott Laboratories felt otherwise, however, and in 1943 commissioned Benton (and some lesser-known illustrators) to travel the country to sketch troops, military bases, and industrial contributions to the war effort; the company then lent these images to the U.S. government for use in propaganda campaigns. Benton documented the first embarkation of troops for Africa, the fluid catalytic crackers at an oil refinery in Baton Rouge, and submarine maneuvers in New London, Connecticut. These excursions offered him a way both to perpetuate his regionalist working methods and to express his support for the war effort. In New London, for instance, he immersed himself in all aspects of the "silent service," the often-secret drills on board military submarines. He was a guest on the *Dorado*, which later was lost at sea with all hands, and sketched its crewmen conducting war games and relaxing in a mess hall; these illustrations were included in a 1944 *Collier's* article describing life aboard the submarines.

But while in Natchez, Mississippi, Benton was reminded yet again of his growing irrelevance. He recalls how he went out one night with some soldiers from a nearby training camp to a nightclub. He spent most of his time sketching but after a few highballs got the notion to dance with one of the women at the bar. After an embarrassing performance on the dance floor, the girl turned to him and said, "Looky here Pop, you take care of the drawin' angle at this table and let the soldiers take care of the dancin' angle from now on." Eventually, Benton says, he came to the conclusion that the war effort "was almost too wholly a young man's affair for me to follow it," and so "I began losing interest in it." He had hoped to make a definitive war painting, but feeling too old and frail to travel overseas for research, he looked for local subjects before concluding that he wasn't able to make pictures "conclusive to the maintenance of a sense of crisis" and abandoning wartime subjects altogether. The decision reveals an interesting aspect of Benton's method for choosing subjects; even at this stage of his career he still insisted that his pictures must be utilitarian—that is, they must be instrumental for some specific purpose or they weren't worth making.

Shortly after completing *The Year of Peril*, Benton received a surprising letter from his old friend Lewis Mumford. Since the late 1930s Mumford had been, in his words, a one-man "national propaganda department," producing antifascist writings with what one of his biographers describes as "white hot rancor and desperate urgency." "I want you to know how deeply impressed I am with your war pictures," Mumford wrote to Benton; "they are the best paintings on the theme that have been done since Goya." Mumford added a cautionary reminder, however: "Those who are unable to face the brutality of the world and who have no will to resist it, will turn on you the hate they ought to direct against our enemies."

Mumford, who would be virulently opposed to Lyndon Johnson's escalation policy in Vietnam, later became president of the American Academy of Arts and Letters and would use his cultural authority to issue political protests. On February 28, 1965, for instance, he addressed an open letter to the president, vilifying him and his policies. "Your professed aims are emptied of meaning by your totalitarian tactics and your nihilistic strategy," he stated. "We are ashamed by your actions, and revolted by your dishonest excuses and pretexts."

Johnson never responded to the letter, but Mumford continued to speak out against the war, especially at the various cultural ceremonies he attended. In May 1965, for example, he received the prestigious Emerson-Thoreau Medal from the American Academy of Arts and Sciences in Cambridge, Massachusetts, and blasted the administration's war policy in his acceptance speech. A couple of weeks later, on May 19, Mumford was in New York to chair the spring ceremony of the American Academy of Arts and Letters. Benton, who became a member of the academy in 1962, was there too. As president of the academy, Mumford knew that politics was off-limits during these events, but in his introductory remarks he criticized Johnson again. He stated that he could not maintain his "self-respect" if he was silent on the issue; because U.S. policy was "an assault upon . . . basic moralities" and an "abject failure," he was, he explained, compelled to speak out. Upon hearing these remarks, Benton, who was wary of the war but supported the government's stated intentions, leaped up and shouted, "I'm not going to listen to this shit!" Benton was briefly restrained, but broke free and stormed off the stage.

"I left because I was afraid of what I'd say if I stayed, I was so damned mad," Benton stated the next day. Nevertheless, before the day of the ceremony was over, Benton shot Mumford a personal telegram. "I protest your talk," he wrote, adding, "unless the academy . . . repudiates concurrence with your expressed views . . . I feel that I must resign from the academy." After sending the telegram, Benton returned to the Midwest for a trip on the Buffalo River in Arkansas. On that trip he told a *Saturday Evening Post* writer who was along for the ride that "the sad thing about the fracas with Lewis is, we used to be friends . . . Then he got up and gave that damfool speech . . . [H]e was calling the U.S. Government a bunch of blackguards . . . Oh, I'd had a few, but I knew what I was doing. I was mad." Just over a week after Mumford's speech, Benton returned from the river to learn that the academy hadn't repudiated Mumford, so he resigned from the institution.

In an undated notebook entry, titled "Lewis Mumford Affair," Benton tried to come to terms with the episode. He expresses regret about the feud, noting that he and Mumford had, "if not a friendship, at least an old toleration of one another." He also explained that he knew as well as Mumford that "armed violence is evil." "Nor do I believe," he continued, "that the questions of Vietnam . . . are not debatable." But Mumford sounded like a "fanatic" that day, he argued; he showed "blind acceptance" of an idea and "complete indifference . . . to violence in the communist world." Apparently, though, Benton never contacted Mumford to apologize or discuss the matter, and so after Benton was reinstated to the academy the next year, Mumford grew bitterly angry. As late as 1988, Mumford's wife, Sophia, was still sensitive about the episode: that year she wrote a letter to Henry Adams that quoted from entries in her diary for October 1967. "It was pretty dreadful," she wrote, upon learning that the academy had reinstated Benton without consulting Lewis. "Their taking Benton back was tantamount to rejecting Lewis," she explained, "and I thoroughly agreed he should himself resign." After waiting a couple of weeks, Mumford sent a brief letter of resignation to the academy. In closing her letter, Sophia added that she still gets "a bit carried away by the memory of that occasion."

·

Benton's quarrel with his old friend Mumford demonstrates, yet again, that he would do battle with anyone. There had been rancorous feuds with Alfred Stieglitz and Stuart Davis, of course, but he'd also alienated other allies over the years, including Max Eastman, Juliana Force, and the administration of the Kansas City Art Institute, to name just a few. One rivalry, however—that with Jackson Pollock—has loomed larger in the critical and public imagination than it did in reality. The men's relationship has its share of myths, but two of the most stubborn are that Pollock totally dismissed his mentor and that Benton despised his student's paintings. Pollock certainly rejected regionalism in favor of a shamanistic symbolism, but despite his cutting remarks about reacting against Benton (first expressed in 1944, and again in 1951, in a Hans Namuth film about Pollock), he continued to seek his advice, frequently calling him in Kansas City, even after the Christmastime debacle in 1937. As Adams suggests, Pollock likely understood that he was indebted to Benton for teaching him how to "harness the power of myth and national identity."

To be sure, there were rejections on both sides from the beginning. For instance, when Benton received commissions in 1932 to paint murals for the Whitney Museum and the state of Indiana, he refused to enlist Pollock as an assistant, later stating, "Jack would not have been qualified for such work." Pollock, who showed Benton maquettes he had made, apparently in an attempt to get work on the Whitney mural, was hurt by the rejection, as well as by Benton's refusal to take any students with him to Indiana. And later, in 1940, after Pollock learned of the death of his friend and benefactor, Helen Marot, he flew into a drunken rage and took a knife to dozens of his own paintings—focusing especially on those that showed Benton's influence—throwing the bits of canvas out of his studio window. But these outbursts, as legendary as they are, hardly tell the whole story of their relationship. For instance, despite what he believed were real "deficiencies" in Pollock's painting, Benton claims that he felt a "considerable satisfaction in Jack's final success." While he admits to being frustrated by his student's disavowal of objective experience, he also acknowledges that the "very original" aspect of Pollock's art was in how it "represents, not the objects we experience in the act of seeing, but the *way* we see them, in continuing, unending shifts of focus." Teacher and student definitely had their differences, and each certainly uttered a few choice remarks regarding the other, but Benton's nemesis was modernism in general, not Pollock. As entertaining as it may be to conjure images of Benton and Pollock drunk on whiskey and brawling over the relative merits of realism and abstraction, the truth is that they loved each other too much to let their divergent aesthetic philosophies ruin their mutual admiration.

After Pollock left New York Hospital in White Plains, in late September 1938, he had to wait five years for his first major success. In the summer of 1943, he signed a contract with the wealthy art collector Peggy Guggenheim—who'd been collecting modern art since 1938 under the guidance of Marcel Duchamp and Alfred H. Barr Jr., then director of the Museum of Modern Art—that obliged him to make a large mural for her house and exhibit exclusively at her New York gallery, called Art of This Century, for one year. In November, Guggenheim's gallery opened Pollock's first one-man show, which included his strongest work to date, large canvases such as *Male and Female* (1942–1943), *Guardians of the Secret* (1943), and *The She-Wolf* (1943). Aside from their familiar "bumps and hollows" and overall dynamism, the paintings show that Pollock had moved on from Benton's influence and abandoned regionalism and literal narrative in favor of a raw and primal mysticism. He borrowed from surrealism, indigenous art of the American Southwest, and Jungian notions of the collective unconscious to fashion a mythic world of archaic totems and animistic energies. Clement Greenberg, the art critic who championed Pollock and abstract expressionism, lauded the exhibition in *The Nation*, calling some of the works "the strongest abstract paintings I have yet seen by an American," and Guggenheim responded to the strength of the show by increasing the length of his contract and giving him a three-hundred-dollar monthly stipend just as the Federal Art Project, which had sustained him for eight years, was closing.

Pollock married the painter Lee Krasner on October 25, 1945, just as he was poised to fulfill his threat to become more famous than Benton. The couple moved to East Hampton, Long Island, where Pollock converted a large barn on their property into a studio, and he spent most of 1947 painting at home. He was preparing large canvases for a one-man show at the Betty Parsons Gallery to open in January 1948. This exhibition proved to be another key event in Pollock's career, as it included his first drip paintings, iconic works such as *Cathedral* (1947) and *Full Fathom Five* (1947). No one knows for sure when he first moved from experimenting with dripping paint to treating it as a formal technique for making finished works, but it was sometime during the year that he was preparing for the exhibition. And though many artists could lay claim to being the first drip painter—Hans Hofmann, William Baziotes, and Joan Miró among them—Pollock is the one who got credit for it. In his review of the exhibition, for instance, Greenberg acknowledges that Pollock did not originate the method, only to claim that he alone was capable of taking it so far: "It is Pollock's culture as a painter that has made him so sensitive and receptive to a tendency that has brought with it . . . a greater concentration on surface texture and tactile qualities." Greenberg also anticipated what would become the principal critique of the drip paintings. "His new work," he writes, "is a puzzle to all those not sincerely in touch with contemporary painting. I already hear: 'wallpaper patterns,' 'the picture does not finish inside the canvas,' 'raw, uncultivated emotion,' and so on, and so on." Greenberg immediately assumed the role of enthusiast for Pollock and gestural abstract expressionism and introduced a discourse that continues to exert a powerful influence on the American imagination. Just several months after the exhibition, he wrote an essay titled "The Decline of Cubism" that addressed the waning of European cultural dominance and the rise of a vital American avant-garde in New York. "The conclusion forces itself, much to our own surprise," he writes, "that the main premises of Western art have at last migrated to the United States, along with the center of gravity of industrial production and political power." As he saw it, abstract expressionism was the supreme example of a postwar tendency to affirm principles of individual liberty as victorious over fascism and dogma. Harold Rosenberg's famous essay "The American Action Painters" made similar arguments. "The big moment came when it was decided to paint . . . just TO PAINT," Rosenberg maintains. "The gesture on the canvas was a gesture of liberation, from Value—political, aesthetic, moral." The editors of *Life* magazine deemed the American public ready for such arguments and ran a story on August 8, 1949, under the headline "Jackson Pollock: Is He the Greatest Living Painter in the United States?"

Some critics couldn't be persuaded, of course. Of the exhibition at the Betty Parsons Gallery, Robert Coates, art critic for *The New Yorker*, observed that at times "communication breaks down entirely," and a review of the same exhibition in *Art Digest* quipped that Pollock must have been "staring steadily up into the sky" as he made the paintings. Just as Greenberg had anticipated, the predominant theme in the negative appraisals of Pollock was that his paintings were disassociated from reality and had no practical instrumentality; they were mere patterns and webs of paint without any stable reference point. Despite his general support for Pollock as a friend and ex-student, Benton disapproved of the direction his art was taking and gave himself the task of attacking abstraction. In 1943, he told an interviewer that "the only excuse for the artist's existence lies in his responsibility to his culture . . . The artist must respond to life and represent it." And eight years later he lamented the end of regionalism, explaining that when artists initiated a "denial of all formal values, and . . . began pouring paint out of cans and buckets just to see what would happen," there arose an audience that "saw immediately the wonderful opportunities for their own ego advancement that this 'free expression' afforded."

But these were arguments that Benton had been making for some time, since the 1920s, and in fact he waited a long time, until 1968, to publish explicit critiques of Pollock's mature paintings—and even then he made sure to praise Pollock. In "And Still After," his final addendum to *An Artist in America*, Benton prefaced his remarks on his former student by reminding his readers that Pollock "was the most discussed artist on the international scene" and "an extraordinary natural colorist." He did express regret that Pollock abandoned regionalism—"judging from his early efforts," Benton writes, "he would have injected a mystic strain into the more generally prosaic characteristics of Regionalism"— but he quickly explains that once he saw Pollock's abstractions, he "recognized their sensuous attractiveness." In this same passage he genuinely tries hard to state his goodwill toward his troubled young friend, despite his more general conviction that 1940s and 1950s modernism suffered from severe deficiencies. And that goodwill was evident as well in Benton's actions: no matter how inconvenient it must have been, he answered Pollock's desperate late-night phone calls, refused to discourage his awkward infatuation with Rita, and supported his career. In one instance, in 1947, Benton sent a letter to the Guggenheim Foundation in support of Pollock's application for a fellowship. "Very much an artist," he wrote. "In my opinion one of the few original painters to come up in the last 10 years."

So it was Benton's battle against modernism, not Pollock specifically, that became the defining struggle of his career, and he fought against it on many fronts and with all the acridity he could muster. According to the art critic Donald Kuspit, "The regionalist ideal of the '30s was to raise the level of the Many, not to single out and exalt the One," and from the 1940s onward abstract expressionism "made the crucial transition from a regionalism of physical locale to one of psychic and spiritual locale." In other words, whereas regionalism had emphasized common experiences, abstract expressionism stressed the authentic individual and the significance of intuition. For Benton, who had spent the 1920s disentangling himself from modernist impulses in American art, the rise of abstract expressionism made a logical target and so brought out his habitual contrarianism. He certainly had the choice to accept the postwar ascendancy of abstraction as a vital alternative to his brand of realism, to view the two modes as related dialectically—the former as a representation of psychological experience and the latter as a representation of social experience. Instead, Benton dug in his heels and reacted as he had twenty years earlier, opting to describe regionalism and modernist abstraction as incompatible. One may conclude that Benton's opposition to abstract expressionism was the product of a healthy skepticism, of a necessary debate about national aesthetics at the dawn of an American moment, but his obstinate vehemence strikes me as sad more than anything else, first because it proved so distracting—it prevented him from even considering an alteration of his style or attitude—and second because it demonstrates what is a serious failing for any artist: a lack of imagination. To put it simply, Benton didn't "get" abstract expressionism.

In "And Still After," Benton states that "the most destructive tendency in artistic circles of our century [is] the dehumanization of art in favor of purely aesthetic formalism" and "cultural conformity." What he was unable or unwilling to discern was abstract expressionism's humanism, its laudatory confirmation of existence, no matter how fraught, and its insistence on finding forms that testify to the fact that most experiences are not only legitimate but also interesting. The truth is, as any student of art history can tell you, abstract expressionism did stand for the diversity of what we call collective experiences, not for unfamiliar ones. As Mark Rothko states so eloquently, "The picture must be for [the artist], as for anyone experiencing it later, a revelation, an unexpected and unprecedented resolution of an eternally familiar need." Here is that emphasis on experience and familiarity that Benton argued for, but he looked past these qualities and, mistakenly, focused instead only on what was "unexpected and unprecedented" in the new art.

Reading between the lines of his diatribes against abstraction, it's fairly easy to determine that the primary cause of Benton's rejection of postwar modernism was the "sideshow business" it engendered, "which the dealers and the art critics of the press serve as barkers." But what he chose to critique was not so much the conformist tendencies of the art market as the fundamental human urge to express oneself as a way of interrogating one's place in the world. What Benton couldn't comprehend, then, was that abstract expressionists were interested in examining what it meant to belong. Such belonging may have been for postwar abstract artists a matter more of personal responsibility—thus their interest in existential philosophy—than of adherence to democratic contracts, but it was as well, in accordance with Benton's beliefs, a manner of belonging that required a sustained corporeal commitment and a preference for action rather than reflection. That abstract expressionism was indeed pragmatic, to the degree that it sought to revitalize the spirit of American creativity and Yankee ingenuity, for instance, or represent the most functional alternative to fascism (namely, personal expression), should have appealed to Benton. One might ask, in fact, not what Pollock could have achieved as a regionalist but what Benton could have achieved as an abstractionist: imagine, for example, an abstract Benton painting; see the push and pull of his dynamic bumps and hollows, and see his vibrant, swirling colors and the anxious, tentative gestures he makes in the process of abandoning representational forms. It's alive and it's natural. But it's the step he never took, the work he never did.

EPILOGUE: AT EASE

In spite of his tenacious irritability, Benton made some peace and attained some contentment during his last decades. He was able, for instance, despite the egoism and occasional hostility that endangered them, to maintain two significant friendships: with Stanton Macdonald-Wright and Thomas Craven. When Macdonald-Wright departed for "the nut state"—he left New York in 1918 for California—Benton had felt "sincere regret," and they might have left it at that, choosing merely to reminisce occasionally about their zany years together in Paris and New York, but each made an effort to sustain a mature amity based on mutual respect. After settling in Santa Monica, Macdonald-Wright abandoned pure synchromism for a hybrid style, a mixture of bright colors, oriental themes, and 1930s representationalism. In 1935, he completed a large mural project for the Santa Monica Public Library under the auspices of the Public Works of Art Project, a short-lived New Deal program. "The subject matter," Macdonald-Wright states, "may be described as depicting the two streams of human development: one technical, the other imaginative. They coalesce and fuse in what perhaps holds the greatest potentialities for art expression invented by man—the medium of the moving picture." Though he had mixed feelings about American scene painting of the Depression era, Macdonald-Wright included in the *Prologue* panel of the mural a portrait of Benton, who appears in the guise of a prehistoric man trying to lasso a Makara, a mythological monster symbolizing the chaotic forces of nature. According to one critic, Macdonald-Wright was "complimenting Benton's personal heroism (acknowledgment of Benton's fight for a kind of art he believed in), but also equated Benton's pursuit with the pursuit of science—noble and useful, but inherently limited." Whatever the precise intent of the portrait reference, it pays tribute to Benton's tireless competition for control of powerful ideas and casts him in a central role within a larger drama about the relationship between art and nature.

Many years later Benton returned the favor by painting a portrait of Macdonald-Wright during a 1961 visit to Los Angeles. Completed the following year, the portrait depicts a wizened Macdonald-Wright posing before a large synchromist canvas. It's a quiet and tender portrait; the artist is at ease and thoughtful, yet his important role in the history of American modernism is confirmed by his confidence and the prominence given to the abstract painting in the background. Macdonald-Wright, who holds a paintbrush just above a sketch pad on his lap, sits between two worlds: even as the significance of his past work is emphasized, he carries on with new experiments. Taken together these portraits illustrate that Benton and Macdonald-Wright were kindred spirits: though they made different kinds of art, each man depicts the other as still committed to important work even as he must reckon with his past reputation. Macdonald-Wright, in fact, was one of just a few people to claim that Benton was capable of such sensitivity. In an interview conducted a few years after Benton painted his portrait, Macdonald-Wright stated, "I'm very fond of Tom and always have been; he's a very sweet fellow." In a twist to their friendship, after Benton's success at the 1939 Associated American Artists show, he finally paid Macdonald-Wright the three hundred dollars he'd borrowed in Paris twenty-eight years earlier. In the end, though, it's fair to say that each was indebted to the other, because of a mutual loyalty rooted in their shared experiences and memories of Paris.

Thomas Craven took his loyalty to Benton to the extreme. He published *Modern Art* on the eve of his friend's return to Missouri, and the book heaps lavish praise on Benton and defends him against all criticisms. Regarding those who see his paintings as debasing or "ignoble," Craven claims, "they will never know anything about America, for they are incapable of entering into any form of American life outside their own little circles." And whenever Benton got in trouble—during the controversies over the Missouri mural, for example, and his firing from the Kansas City Art Institute—there was Craven, prepared with a few bons mots for his friend's enemies. When some Missourians spoke out against the Jefferson City mural, Craven scolded them in a *Scribner's* profile of Benton. Their onslaught, he writes, was "mean, vindictive, and unintelligent," and he adds, "Standing out against this mediocrity of average mental performance, the murals . . . may well become one of the shrines of American cultural achievement." Craven was surely less enthusiastic about entering into the fray regarding his friend's employment at the Art Institute, but he came to his aid nonetheless, telling a Kansas City newspaper reporter that the city was "losing the best art teacher in the country."

Craven wrote many letters, articles, and essays in defense of Benton, going so far as to claim that in his illustrations for a 1940 edition of *The Grapes of Wrath* he was "more realistic than Steinbeck in his treatment of the Okies." And in 1958, when given another chance to consider his friend's place in American art, Craven yet again went as far as he could: "Thomas Hart Benton, secure in his eminence, has weathered the storms and caprices of popular and aesthetic tastes, and stands virtually in a class by himself today, foursquare and indefatigable, still extraordinarily productive, capable of defending himself when challenged, but above personalities—a character withal, picturesque and good-humored, and a sort of American phenomenon compared to the makers of amorphous patterns." Benton depended on Craven for help with more personal matters as well. In 1948, both Craven and Lizzie Benton moved to Martha's Vineyard year-round, and as Lizzie was suffering from hardening of the arteries and required supervision, Benton was grateful when Craven, who had always been fond of her, agreed to check in on her periodically.

For all their similarities it's remarkable that Benton and Craven were able to sustain such a close friendship. With Benton's constant battling and Craven's often stupid chauvinism and sloganeering, each certainly gave the other plenty of opportunities to jump ship and disavow their camaraderie. Professionally speaking, each would have benefited greatly from distancing himself from the other, for critics took constant shots at their long association. Through it all, though, they remained loyal, and it's fair to presume that for Benton maintaining the friendship became a matter of pride, a way of sticking it to the critics who believed their rapport was based more on convenience than genuine affection. In the end, Benton's ability to nurture his friendships with Macdonald-Wright and Craven serves as a counterargument to the popular image of him as a man incapable of tenderness or long-term loyalty. On Martha's Vineyard in particular, Benton nourished many alliances that belie his reputation as a dangerous friend.

•

Benton suffered a stroke and a heart attack in 1966. He'd been bothered by bad health for some time: he'd collapsed, broken down with exhaustion, and lost his stamina on numerous occasions. His mortality, and that of his friends and family, had been a frequent theme in his art and writing. As a young man, he was strong and athletic, but as early as 1932 or 1933, when he was in his early forties, he'd discerned a degree of physical decline while swimming off a Martha's Vineyard beach. He recalls that he'd swum out past the breakers with a friend, and when it was time to head back in, he couldn't make way against the riptide. "Suddenly I felt tired," he writes, "tired in my shoulders and down my back and, what was worse, in my stomach muscles." Approaching the shore, Benton was tumbled head over heels by a crashing wave: "I don't know how I got to shore, but I finally did and lay on the sand for a long time utterly exhausted and also utterly ashamed of myself."

Benton vacationed on Martha's Vineyard almost every summer until his death, and nothing demonstrates the inadequacy of the term "regionalism" more than his attachment to the New England island: he was just as fond of Martha's Vineyard as he was of Missouri or the West and made dozens of his most famous paintings there. He was "genuinely sensitive to the poetry of the Island," Polly Burroughs writes, where "that Midwestern chauvinism, anti-Eastern arrogance, and surge of vanity brought on by his success fell on deaf ears and he knew it." During his summers on the island, Benton reread his favorite books—Balzac, Twain, *The Arabian Nights*—swam and fished, spent quiet afternoons with his mother, and canoed on Squibnocket Pond. He grew to love the island's varied weather: its hot, sunny days, foggy nights, and occasional summer storms. In the evenings, Tom and Rita enjoyed cocktails with such friends as Alfred Eisenstaedt, Max Eastman, and Denys Wortman (a newspaper cartoonist), and on some nights Benton performed for guests with a makeshift band, which inspired James Cagney on several occasions to break into a "soft shoe routine to everyone's delight." Only the strained relationship between Lizzie and Rita threatened his summer idylls.

Benton did a lot of painting on Martha's Vineyard over the years; he made portraits of its salty residents, illustrated its beautiful coastlines, and painted its flora and fauna—"horses, mules, cows, goats, even cats and butterflies, as well as ferns, flowers, sumac, corn, mushrooms, grapes, the trumpet vine, and . . . contorted tree trunks." In 1937, however, he told a reporter from *The Vineyard Gazette*, "I know the Vineyard too well and too intimately to be able to paint it anymore." He was wrong, of course, and continued to paint on the island. In 1938, for instance, Benton made *Flight of the Thielens*, which, like his illustrations of midwestern floods, depicts the horror of a natural disaster. On September 21, Benton and T.P. were clearing brush on their property when the Great Hurricane of 1938 thundered onshore. To get a closer look at the massive surf, Benton went down to Hariph's Creek Bridge and watched as three tidal waves destroyed the house of Benedict "Bob" Thielen, a *New Yorker* writer. Of that terrible day, Thielen recalls, "We watched the hesitant, then rapid, then pausing, then flying-forward, yellow flecks of foam. It looked like the vomit foam of a sick animal." In the struggle to escape the rushing water, Thielen lost track of the family's Jamaican maid, Josephine Clarke, who drowned in the torrent. Upon reaching land, Bob and his wife were met by Benton, who'd witnessed the event. He invited them to his house, where he sat them in front of a fire and served them rum to help ease their shock. Benton made a sketch of the Thielens' calamity almost immediately; later he produced several paintings of the subject that show Bob straining to grab Josephine just before she disappears beneath the roiling water.

He also painted several portraits of Vineyarders during the 1940s that render the Yankee character of the island's local residents. In 1941, for instance, a summer country fair, the All-Island Cavalcade, was held in West Tisbury to benefit the Red Cross and a local hospital; the fair featured attractions such as Coast Guard drills, archery, and sheep-shearing and fly-casting contests. In addition, island artists set up demonstrations: Denys Wortman made cartoon sketches, Virginia Thielen painted abstractions, and Benton set up in a barn where, for ten cents, one could watch him paint portraits. In 1940, he produced a portrait this way of Zebulon "Zeb" Tilton, the legendarily tough ("course I ain't lived on butterfly wings and wind puddin'") captain of a freight schooner that sailed throughout the Northeast; at the fair the following year he painted a neighbor, Henry Look, as a typically weather-beaten and skeptical New England farmer.

During World War II, Benton worried about, among other things, the impact the war would have on the rural communities he'd come to love but, according to Burroughs, "was pleasantly reassured that not even a world war was going to disturb these [Vineyard] Yankees very much." As if to confirm that the island had retained its character during the war years, Benton made several pictures that illustrate typically bucolic Vineyard life: the painting *July Hay* (1943), for instance, represents island farmers hard at work, and the lithograph *White Calf* (1945) depicts Henry Look milking one of his cows in front of a ramshackle barn. But it was his portrait of George Hough, titled *New England Editor* (1946), that best testifies to the survival of the Yankee spirit.

Hough—the idiosyncratic but exacting former editor of the New Bedford *Standard-Times* who was reputed to despise error and injustice—posed for Benton in the summer home he'd retired to on the North Shore. Benton's portrait represents Hough sitting at a desk in a sparse room; he looks seriously upon a piece of paper on which he scribbles the word "Unless," a reference to the editor's refusal to print a story *unless* it was accurate and *unless* a reporter had exhausted all possible sources. On the wall behind Hough is a painting of the New Bedford whaling ship *Catalpa*, recalling the city's famed industry. Benton's admiration for the man, whom he called "one of the finest down to earth Yankees ever to come out of the soil, sharp, witty, and smart," is obvious: Hough is rugged, with sinewy muscles and crooked fingers; attentive to his craft; and perfectly at home in his milieu—the bare room holds only books, the painting, and Hough, sitting in a wicker chair at his desk, holding firmly on to his pencil. The painting may as well be a self-portrait, so similar is Hough to Benton, who designs the composition classically, to emphasize the sitter's equanimity, the perfect harmony between his head and hands, the right balance between craftsmanship and reflection. These were the qualities that Benton held dearest, and in Hough he found them embodied, which is ironic considering the harsh words Benton had for critics and editors throughout his career.

When Jessie was at college in the late 1950s, Tom and Rita started spending more time on the Vineyard, usually from early May to mid-October. They particularly enjoyed autumn on the island, when the summer tourists and humidity had gone and Rita gathered ripened cranberries from the bogs. The author of a 1969 *Life* magazine profile describes their daily routine: "The Bentons rise . . . with the sun which, in the early summer, is 4 a.m., swim and work until noon. Rita fastens herself to the ocean bed as if she had grown out of it, and clams . . . Tom paints or, when he can discover something before Rita has attended to it herself, putters." Benton also solidified old friendships and made some new ones. He frequently saw Craven, for instance, who moved to the island year-round in 1949, and hung around with Roger Nash Baldwin, who also accompanied him on some river trips. In the late 1940s, Benton met Charles B. Harding, a partner at Smith Barney and president of the New York Botanical Garden. They became fast friends, and Benton often joined him on his powerboat for fishing adventures; they'd leave the dock at 9:00 a.m., and by noon Benton would holler, "Where the hell's the gin, Charlie?" After a few drinks and lunch he'd disappear belowdecks for a nap.

In the spring of 1973, Mike Wallace interviewed Benton for an episode of *60 Minutes*. Wallace, who began visiting Vineyard Haven when he was a kid growing up in Brookline, Massachusetts, knew Benton only casually before the taping. Afterward, he observed that it was the "therapeutic absolutes of Martha's Vineyard that drew us both there." Apparently, the island's soothing therapy had mellowed Benton's attitude about death, for when Wallace asked him, just before his eighty-fourth birthday, if he hated "getting old," a wry, disheveled Benton snorted, "I don't care . . . I make no moves in contemplation of death." The next summer, Wallace reminisces, he was set to appear with Benton at an Edgartown church to raise money for the Martha's Vineyard Art Association when Benton approached him outside the church "with a case of the jitters." "Fully aware of his lifelong fondness for the sauce," Wallace continues, "I had come equipped with a flask that contained his favorite libation—cold and very dry gin martinis— and for the next half hour or so, we stood outside the church and gulped them down with the fervor of parched Bedouins quaffing at an oasis." Benton's comments touched on the familiar subjects: the dehumanizing tendencies of abstract art and out-of-touch curators. A letter appeared in *The Vineyard Gazette* the next day, written by a witness of the talk, that stated, "We accept your art, but it's not easy to accept your evaluations of our art institutions, contemporary art, and its critics . . . What have you got against museums? Is it fair to say they are dead? Aren't you thinking of them as they were in the 1920s and 30s? Have you been to a museum lately?" Benton didn't respond to the letter; he must have known how fortunate he'd been over the years to be left alone on the island. For the most part he was able to work and relax on the Vineyard without facing the sorts of controversies that dogged him elsewhere. But Martha's Vineyard was more than a refuge for Benton; it was yet another place, like the rivers and western plains and mountains, where he could achieve a level of coveted authenticity, where he could physically inhabit the kinds of experiences he'd championed in his paintings and prose. Every day he was on the island, he exhausted himself painting, hauling brush, building, fishing, swimming, and telling tales. Except for the occasional lecture or painting demonstration, he could do things on the Vineyard rather than merely philosophize about doing things. Simply put, Benton was himself on Martha's Vineyard.

The Benton biographer Polly Burroughs visited him during his last day on the island, in mid-October 1974. On that sparkling afternoon, talking with him in his studio, she said, "Thinking of you out here alone, working for hours on end, chewing tobacco and humming that old Hillbilly tune 'Prisoner For Life,' and looking at all your work, I've come to the conclusion you're a hopeless romantic at heart."

"That's your opinion—maybe so," he responded.

Benton died on January 19, 1975, just as he was to paint his signature on his mural *The Sources of Country Music*. After dinner that night he went to his studio to inspect the painting and sign it, but he dropped dead on the floor, from a massive heart attack, before he could do so. A few months later, a grief-stricken Rita passed away as well. The Country Music Foundation commissioned the painting in 1973 for the Country Music Hall of Fame and Museum in Nashville; the foundation's board members announced that Benton, "the distinguished American painter . . . [and] America's greatest muralist," should be hired to produce a major work for the building. To that end, several board members traveled to Benton's home in Kansas City, Missouri, and, over a bottle of Jack Daniel's, persuaded him to accept the commission. Though old and frail, Benton was enthusiastic about the project; long before, his art had been cast aside by critics—who called his popular realism quaint and irrelevant—and so he was happy for the opportunity to execute another public work that would address the folk culture he believed so superior to the "intellectual curiosities" and "infinitely shaded egotism" of modernist aesthetics.

William Ivey, the executive director of the Country Music Foundation, recalls that Benton decided right away that the painting "should
show the roots of the music—the sources—before there were records
and stars" and that "this idea of Benton's, that the painting should emphasize the folk cultures which produced country music, became the
guiding theme of the project." In the end, Benton received sixty thousand dollars for the project, with a third of the money coming from a
National Endowment for the Arts grant.

As was his custom, Benton developed the painting from drawings—in
this case, some old sketches that he'd made on walkabouts through the
Ozark Mountains in the 1920s and some new ones made on a trip south,
to Branson, Missouri, where he observed country musicians firsthand.
Earlier he had claimed to admire the "old boys, with their rheumatic
arms," who improvised and played in keys unlike those heard in the
canned music of the day. "I like their plaintive, slightly nasal voices," he
wrote, "and their way of short bowing the violin." The painting depicts
over a dozen figures divided into different vignettes: in the center, a
group dances to the sounds of two fiddlers; in the foreground, a man plays
guitar and a woman plays a dulcimer; and, alone in the background, an
African American man picks at a banjo. On an elevated stage to the
left, we see a choir, and behind it the Wabash Cannonball barreling
down the tracks. The composition is distinguished by Benton's trademark dynamism, achieved through the rhythmic postures of the figures; the complementary diagonals of fiddle bows, guitar necks, and
tilting telephone poles; and the visceral music itself, which seems to
swirl through the canvas shaping each material form. As the art historian Vivien Green Fryd puts it, "These compositional devices establish
a sense of stability amidst explosive energy and movement, suggesting
both the permanence and the powerful rhythms of the music."

The power of Benton's best murals—*America Today* (1930), *The Arts
of Life in America* (1932), and *A Social History of the State of Missouri*
(1936)—comes from his ability to transform seemingly mundane subjects from everyday America into something grand: dancing, harvesting,
theatergoing, and even drinking are invested with monumental significance simply because he treats them as constituents of a larger epic. At
his best, Benton integrates varied people and activities, and illustrates
the connections between individual practices and communal health,
thus revealing the Jeffersonianism that he cherished and that we find

ourselves returning to again and again for enlightenment. *The Sources of Country Music* is Benton's last stab at illustrating this romantic viewpoint. The anonymity of the players and the dancers is meant to tell us that our regional customs and spontaneous rituals, not our theories, account for the nation's dynamism. That this ideology comes from a man who could be so charming and so crude, who was an anti-intellectual intellectual, and who scorned a career in politics but was profoundly political is what makes Benton such a magnetic subject for the writer. We want to pin him down precisely because we cannot.

NOTES

Note: Full bibliographic information is omitted in the notes for works listed in the bibliography.

PROLOGUE: SKETCHES FROM LIFE

3 *"occasioned one of"*: Benton quoted in Burroughs, *Thomas Hart Benton*, 178.

3 *"the only place"*: Ibid., 194.

4 *Phenomenology*: See Hubert L. Dreyfus, *Being-in-the-World: A Commentary on Heidegger's "Being and Time," Division I* (Cambridge, Mass.: MIT Press, 1990).

5 *"strong and masculine"*: Schapiro, "Populist Realism," 57.

7 *"producerism"*: Doss, *Benton, Pollock, and the Politics of Modernism*, 15.

7 *"I believe I have wanted"*: Thomas Hart Benton, in *New Art in America*, ed. John I. H. Baur (Greenwich, Conn.: New York Graphic Society, 1951), 131.

8 *"They talked so often"*: Georgia O'Keeffe, *Georgia O'Keeffe* (New York: Viking Press, 1976), quoted in Corn, *Great American Thing*, 287–88.

8 *"destroyed dozens"*: Naifeh and Smith, *Jackson Pollock*, 359.

8 *"He didn't want"*: Kadish quoted ibid.

8 *"a truly glorious wake"*: Henderson quoted ibid.

11 *"make a fascinating pair"*: Jed Perl, "A Cool Heat: The Intrepid Genius of Edmund Wilson," *Harper's*, September 2005, 86.

12 *"You yourself seem"*: Wilson quoted in Virginia Spencer Carr, *Dos Passos: A Life* (Garden City, N.Y.: Doubleday, 1984), 396. On Dos Passos's politics, see Rosen, *John Dos Passos*.

12 *"regionalism"*: Benton, "American Regionalism," 148.

12 *"uplift psychologies"*: Benton, *Artist in America*, 77.

13 *"This was very much"*: Ibid., 362. Also see Austin C. Wehrwein, "Thomas Hart Benton Welcomed at Ozark Birthplace," *New York Times*, May 13, 1962.

13 *"debatable"*: Thomas Hart Benton Day described in "Tom Benton Welcomed Home by the Thousands," *Neosho Daily News*, May 13, 1962.

13 *"I've written it all"*: Benton quoted in "Benton Sharp and Witty at a Press Conference," *Neosho Daily News*, May 13, 1962.

14 *"would appear"*: Benton, "Boyhood," 1, microfilm reel 2325, Benton Papers. "Boyhood" is an undated typescript intended as part of Benton's unpublished memoir "The Intimate Story." From here on, I'll refer to the specific chapter titles (all undated)—"Boyhood," "Chicago," "The Life of Art in Paris," and "The Thirties"—that make up "The Intimate Story."

1. NEOSHO

17 *"a kind of compulsion"*: Benton, "Artist in America," interview by Robert S. Gallagher, 43–44. This is a condensed version of an interview Robert S. Gallagher conducted on Martha's Vineyard, September 20–23, 1972. For the typescript of the unedited interview, see "Reminiscences of Thomas Hart Benton," interview by Robert S. Gallagher, September 20–23, 1972, Oral History Collection of Columbia University.

17 *"I am bound to"*: Benton to his mother, January 24, 1907, microfilm reel 2325, Benton Papers.

17 *"family fated"*: Benton, "Boyhood," 2–3, reel 2325, Benton Papers.

17 *"a man of high"*: Roosevelt, *Thomas H. Benton*, 12, 31.

17 *"not necessarily one"*: Doss, *Benton, Pollock, and the Politics of Modernism*, 20.

18 *"the various coarse"*: Roosevelt, *Thomas H. Benton*, 24.

18 *"any puppy who"*: Senator Benton quoted in Charles van Ravenswaay, *St. Louis: An Informal History of the City and Its People, 1764–1865* (St. Louis: Missouri Historical Society Press, 1991), 196.

19 *"It is the character"*: Jackson to Benton, quoted in Smith, "'Now Defend Yourself,'" 45.

19 *"in capacity"*: Ibid., 44.

19 *"Now defend"*: Ibid.

19 *"The details were"*: Roosevelt, *Thomas H. Benton*, 26.

19 *"jabbing, repetitive"*: William Nisbet Chambers, *Old Bullion Benton: Senator from the New West* (Boston: Little, Brown, 1956), 184, 194.

19 *"bravely [accepted] defeat"*: Roosevelt, *Thomas H. Benton*, 13.

19 *"the heroic part"*: Ibid., 283.

19 *"the world's last hope"*: Senator Benton in a speech against his son-in-law, John Charles Frémont, *Jefferson (Mo.) Enquirer*, November 8, 1856.

20 *"I shall not fall"*: Senator Benton quoted in Smith, "'Now Defend Yourself,'" 798.

20 *"would sooner sit"*: Senator Benton, public letter, March 8, 1850, in *Jefferson Enquirer*, April 6, 1850.

20 *"helped, with pompous phrase"*: Benton, *Artist in America*, 5.

20 *relied on "power"*: Benton, "Boyhood," 46.

21 *"knocking the snakes"*: Benton, *Artist in America*, 4.

21 *"an individualistic and cocksure"*: Ibid., 5.

21 *"splendid American"*: Walter B. Stevens, *Missouri, the Center State* (St. Louis: S. J. Clarke, 1915), 710.

21 *"full measure of"*: Benton, *Artist in America*, 4.

21 *"addicted"*: Ibid., 3.

22 *"In the middle eighteen-nineties"*: Ibid., 3–4.

23 *"civic scientific"*: Doss, *Benton, Pollock, and the Politics of Modernism*, 31.

23 *"tall willowy black-haired"*: Benton, "Boyhood," 8.

23 *"the top town sport"*: Ibid., 7.

23 *"an epoch in Neosho"*: From a newspaper account included in Virginia Brady Hoare, ed., *Newton County Saga* 3, no. 1 (Neosho, Mo.: Newton County Historical Society, 1981), n.p., cabinet 1, drawer 1, Benton Curatorial Files.

23 *"Col. Benton like one"*: Ibid.

24 *"the Fifteen Bachelors"*: Ibid.

24 *"got her papers"*: Benton, "Boyhood," 8.

24 *"were able to choose"*: Ibid., 45.

24 *"made his own deals"*: Ibid., 17.

24 *"The farm house"*: Ibid., 39.

25 *"proud, intensely self-concerned"*: Ibid., 22.

25 *"I've never met anyone"*: Mildred Benton Small, interview by Henry Adams and Ken Burns, December 26, 1986, American Original Exhibition Records.

25 *"Oh, they hated me"*: Elizabeth Benton quoted in Benton, "Boyhood," 10.

25 *"The women . . . found"*: Benton, "Boyhood," 16.

26 *"My father"*: Ibid., 21.

26 *"I never had any feeling"*: Small, interview, December 26, 1986.

26 *"physical intimacies"*: Benton, "Boyhood," 20.

26 *"in spite of that"*: Ibid., ii–iii.

26 *"The boy"*: Maecenas Benton quoted in Yeo and Cook, *Maverick with a Paintbrush*, 4.

26 *"From the moment"*: Benton, *Artist in America*, 10.

27 *"immaculate white apron"*: "Missouri History Not Found in Textbooks," *Missouri Historical Review* 53, no. 1 (October 1958): 97.

27 *"she had a baby"*: "Midwife to Greatness," *Ozarks Mountaineer*, December 1975, 20, cabinet 1, drawer 1, Benton Curatorial Files.

27 *"up and down"*: Benton, "Boyhood," 11.

27 *"the seat barely"*: Ibid., 12.

27 *"We had no business"*: Stroop quoted in James and Jobe, *Neosho*, 124. Also see Benton, *Artist in America*, 9.

27 *he steps on a black snake*: Benton, "Boyhood," 12.

28 *"where you ran"*: Benton, *Artist in America*, 9.

28 *"game-shy"*: Adams, *American Original*, 6.

28 *"jump and howl"*: Benton, *Artist in America*, 10.

28 *"strawberry gaumer"*: Yeo and Cook, *Maverick with a Paintbrush*, 6.

28 *"Missouri values"*: Benton, *Artist in America*, 9.

29 *"men in wide black hats"*: Craven, "Thomas Hart Benton," 33.

29 *"Our dinner table"*: Benton, *Artist in America*, 5.

30 *"My father was a Populist"*: Mildred Benton Small, interview by Henry Adams and Ken Burns, December 27, 1986, American Original Exhibition Records.

30 *"The problem"*: Nye, *Midwestern Progressive Politics*, 27.

30 *"could be incredibly"*: Ibid., 161–62.

30 *"millions of Americans"*: Ibid., 162.

30 *"uphill struggle"*: Michael J. Steiner, "The Failure of Alliance/Populism in Northern Missouri," in *The Other Missouri History: Populists, Prostitutes, and Regular Folk*, ed. Thomas M. Spencer (Columbia: University of Missouri Press, 2004), 131–32.

31 *"make law into the major"*: David Thelen, *Paths of Resistance: Tradition and Dignity in Industrializing Missouri* (New York: Oxford University Press, 1986), 218.

31 *"blaring horns"*: Benton, *Artist in America*, 7.

31 *"Hold on Dad"*: Benton, "Boyhood," 33.

31 *"I guess you all"*: Yeo and Cook, *Maverick with a Paintbrush*, 5.

31 *"promise of adventure"*: Benton, *Artist in America*, 16.

32 *"The activity"*: Ibid., 6.

32 *"There was much about"*: Ibid., 10.

33 *"Looking back"*: Benton, "The Thirties," appendix 1 in Priddy, *Only the Rivers Are Peaceful*, 245. See also Benton, "American Regionalism," 145–92.

33 *"a variant of"*: Benton, *Artist in America*, 25.

33 *One Neosho native*: *Neosho Daily News*, April 29, 1962, 125.

33 *"Look what I've produced"*: Ibid.

33 *"Well, Cousin Maecenas"*: Yeo and Cook, *Maverick with a Paintbrush*, 3.

33 *"a very beautiful"*: Mildred Benton Small, interview by Henry Adams and Ken Burns, May 12, 1986, American Original Exhibition Records.

33 *"My father said"*: Benton, *Artist in America*, 25.

34 *"over-romantic reports"*: Oral History Interview with Benton, 3.

34 *"the dime novels"*: Benton, *Artist in America*, 11.

34 *"psychological failing"*: Burroughs, *Thomas Hart Benton*, 35.

34 *"What is it"*: Ibid., 31.

34 *"Engines"*: Benton, *Artist in America*, 13.

35 *"was the first intimation"*: Ibid.

35 *"Dad was profoundly"*: Ibid., 12.

36 *"pretty boy[s]"*: Benton, interview by Floyd Taylor, *New York World-Telegram*, reprinted in "Blast by Benton," 6.

2. WASHINGTON, D.C.

37 *"Navy Yart"*: Benton to Robison, January 23, 1898, quoted in *Thomas Hart Benton: Artist of America*, 23.

37 *"leisurely place"*: Benton, *Artist in America*, 29.

37 *"ugliest man in Congress"*: Benton, "Boyhood," 49, microfilm reel 2325, Benton Papers.

37 *"outtalk, outlaugh"*: Craven, "Thomas Hart Benton," 33.

37 *"the money power"*: Maecenas Benton, *Congressional Record*, 56th Cong., 1st sess., 309–10.

38 *"un-American, un-businesslike"*: Ibid.

38 *"gold bugs of Wall Street"*: Excerpts from Maecenas Benton's speech of October 11, 1886, and a biased summary of the scandal it engendered, were printed in "District Attorney Benton," *New York Times*, December 1, 1886, 4.

38 *"The public image"*: Benton, "Boyhood," 30–31.

38 *"chronicler of America's folk"*: Weintraub, *Thomas Hart Benton*.

39 *"dress herself"*: Benton, "Boyhood," 87.

39 *"mighty uppity"*: Ibid., 86.

40 *"prostrate on the floor"*: Adams, *American Original*, 10. Also see Benton, "Boyhood," 55.

40 *"red and grim-faced"*: Adams, *American Original*, 10.

40 *"In Washington"*: Henry Adams, *The Education of Henry Adams* (Boston: Houghton Mifflin, 1918), 320.

40 *"Play a tune"*: Maecenas Benton quoted in Adams, *American Original*, 11.

40 *"Miss Juliet"*: "Fashions at the White House," *Washington Post*, January 3, 1909.

41 *"I like best"*: Small, "'Sane People, Sane Life,'" 536.

41 *"The old man"*: Benton, "Boyhood," 79–80. This speech is not recorded in the *Congressional Record*, but there's no reason to doubt Benton's account.

42 *"I had come to"*: Benton, *Artist in America*, 16.

42 *"very tender with"*: Mildred Benton Small, interview by Henry Adams and Ken Burns, May 12, 1986, American Original Exhibition Records.

42 *"Well, I don't"*: Benton, "Boyhood," 77, 71.

42 *"was very sure"*: Small, interview, May 12, 1986.

42 *"At Oak Hill"*: Adams, *American Original*, 6.

43 *"encouraged the boy's"*: Ibid.

43 *"Now, my Dad"*: Benton, *Artist in America*, 10–11.

43 *"I was raised"*: Benton, "My American Epic in Paint," reprinted in Baigell, *Thomas Hart Benton Miscellany*, 19.

44 *"I ran into"*: Oral History Interview with Benton, 3.

44 *"I liked steam"*: Ibid.

45 *"spell of mythology"*: Ibid.

45 *"show an almost"*: Craven, *Descriptive Catalogue*, 10. Also see Adams, *Drawing from Life*, 40–46.

45 *"the very appearance"*: Benton, *American in Art*, 11.

45 *"What I didn't know"*: Benton, *Artist in America*, 13.

45 *"I had seen plenty"*: Ibid., 13–14.

46 *"two bits"*: Ibid., 14.

46 *"I may speak generally"*: Benton, statement in *Forum Exhibition of Modern American Painters*, reprinted in Baigell, *Thomas Hart Benton Miscellany*, 3.

47 *"The first paintings"*: Oral History Interview with Benton, 3.

47 *"Well," Tom responded*: Benton, "Boyhood," 70–71.

48 *"Here was an immense"*: William A. Coffin, "The Decorations in the New Congressional Library," *Century Magazine*, March 1897, 694.

49 *"Presidents, Senators"*: Truman to Berryman, reel D111, Berryman Family Papers, 1829–1984, Archives of American Art, Smithsonian Institution.

49 *"When my father"*: Benton, "Artist in America," interview by Robert S. Gallagher, 42.

49 *"It is plain to me"*: Benton quoted in Gruber, "Thomas Hart Benton: Teaching and Art Theory," 1–2.

49 *"As far back"*: Benton to Baigell, reel 2086, Baigell Papers.

50 *"sketches preserved"*: Marling, *Tom Benton and His Drawings*, 5.

50 *"taste"*: Benton, "Boyhood," 65–66.

50 *"You do not bite"*: Ibid., 101.

50 *"Why do you"*: Ibid., 100.

51 *"hysterics and faints"*: Ibid., 112.

3. JOPLIN

52 *"leaned against"*: Ellen Maury Slayden, *Washington Wife: Journal of Ellen Maury Slayden from 1897–1919* (New York: Harper and Row, 1963), 69.

52 *"This is your"*: Benton, "Boyhood," 112, microfilm reel 2325, Benton Papers.

53 *"was at times"*: Benton, *Artist in America*, 5.

53 *"The walls of"*: Ibid.

53 *"[we] drifted apart"*: Ibid., 16.

53 *"all the cockiness"*: Ibid.

53 *"The damned scoundrels"*: The Colonel quoted in Adams, *American Original*, 16.

54 *"slashing attack[s]"*: *Thomas Hart Benton: Artist of America*, 24.

54 *"I found my way"*: Benton, "Boyhood," 124–26.

54 *"hooked a southbound"*: Benton, *Artist in America*, 17.

54 *"faux-naive"*: Ellen G. Landau, "Classic in Its Own Little Way: The Art of Woody Guthrie," in *Hard Travelin': The Life and Legacy of Woody Guthrie*, ed. Robert Santelli and Emily Davidson (Middletown, Conn.: Wesleyan University Press, 1999), 90.

54 *"I'm gonna hug"*: Woody Guthrie, *Bound for Glory* (New York: Plume, 1983), 36.

54 *"The itch to be"*: Benton, *Artist in America*, 17.

55 *"I was raised"*: Benton, foreword to *Adventures of Huckleberry Finn*, by Mark Twain (New York: Limited Editions Club, 1942), lxxiii.

55 *"For Huck"*: Robert Penn Warren, "Mark Twain," in *New and Selected Essays* (New York: Random House, 1989), 118.

55 *"All one has"*: Benton, *Artist in America*, 144. Also see Karal Ann Marling, "Thomas Hart Benton's Epic of a Usable Past," in Hurt and Dains, *Thomas Hart Benton*, 117–37.

56 *"unwhitewashed"*: Mark Twain, *The Adventures of Tom Sawyer* (New York: Harper and Brothers, 1903), 26, 71. Also see Adams, *Drawing from Life*, 160.

56 *"Huckleberry came and went"*: Twain, *Tom Sawyer*, 71.

56 *"The foundation of"*: Robert Ingersoll, "Superstition," in *The Works of Robert G. Ingersoll* (New York: C. P. Farrell, 1900), 4:295.

57 *"Religion teaches"*: Robert Ingersoll, "What Is Religion?" ibid., 4:493.

57 *"It is not book-learning"*: Elbert Hubbard, *A Message to Garcia: Being a Preachment* (East Aurora, N.Y.: Roycrofters, 1908), 7.

57 *"wanted in every"*: Ibid., 15.

57 *"I would never become"*: Benton, "Boyhood," 118.

57 *"uneasiness"*: Benton, *Artist in America*, 25.

59 *"in the burning sun"*: Ibid., 18.

59 *"The saloon doors"*: Ibid.

59 *"in an independent frame"*: Ibid.

59 *"mysteries of sex"*: Ibid., 22.

59 *"The kid has been"*: Benton, "Boyhood," 135.

59 *"dim"*: Ibid., 133.

59 *"Although my head"*: Ibid.

60 *"I must have got"*: Benton, *Artist in America*, 19.

60 *"tied together"*: Ibid.

60 *"I went, strangely enough"*: Ibid., 20.

60 *"printer's ink"*: Ibid.

60 *"By the grace"*: Ibid., 21.

60 *"I would start"*: Ibid.

60 *"under the red-hot"*: Ibid.

61 *"easily the fastest"*: *St. Louis Post-Dispatch*, September 2, 1906.

61 *"Everyone was disappointed"*: Benton to his father, September 4, 1906, reel 2325, Benton Papers.

61 *"offered too many"*: Benton, *Artist in America*, 22.

61 *"strutting around"*: Ibid.

62 *"When we drove"*: Warten quoted in Wally Kennedy, "Man Who Helped Arrange for Mural Recalls Its History," *Joplin Globe*, March 8, 2005.

62 *"Every old codger"*: Benton, "The Mural," in Warten, *Thomas Hart Benton*, 31.

62 *"ladder climbing"*: Ibid., 32.

62 *"the young booming"*: Ibid.

63 *"worried that with"*: Sidney Larson, "Personal Reminiscences," in Hurt and Dains, *Thomas Hart Benton*, 103.

63 *"at least"*: Benton, "Mural," 36.

63 *"plainer and more"*: Benton quoted in Albert Christ-Janer, *George Caleb Bingham of Missouri: The Story of an Artist* (New York: Dodd, Mead, 1940), viii. Also see Benton, preface to *George Caleb Bingham, Frontier Painter of Missouri*, by Albert Christ-Janer (New York: Abrams, 1975). For a deeper analysis of the Bingham-Benton link, see Wallach, "Regionalism Redux," 88–104.

63 *"made [Joplin] boom"*: Benton quoted in John Canaday, "3 Shows Trace the Path of American Art," *New York Times*, April 19, 1969, 29.

64 *"Mr. Benton's weak"*: Ibid.

64 *"few snorts"*: Larson, "Personal Reminiscences," 103.

64 *"[T]he sweetest sight"*: Canaday, "Tom Benton of Mazura Comes Back to Joplin— Grown Up," 181.

65 *"Remember, we sign"*: Warten, preface to *Thomas Hart Benton*, 11.

65 *"soliciting preachers"*: Benton, *Artist in America*, 18–19.

65 *"I am still open"*: Warten, preface to *Thomas Hart Benton*, 11.

66 *"academic harness"*: Benton, *Artist in America*, 22.

66 *"The restriction"*: Benton to his mother, September 21, 1906, reel 2325, Benton Papers.

66 *"There are a lot"*: Benton to his mother, October 7, 1906, reel 2325, Benton Papers.

66 *"Of course they don't"*: Benton to his parents, October 14, 1906, reel 2325, Benton Papers.

67 *"a world of serious"*: Benton to Morris Leopold Ernst, March 18, 1963, reel 2325, Benton Papers.

67 *"So my little"*: Benton to his father, December 17, 1906, reel 2325, Benton Papers.

67 *"I rec'd Mama's letter"*: Benton to his parents, January 24, 1907, reel 2325, Benton Papers.

4. CHICAGO

69 *"first in violence"*: Lincoln Steffens, "Chicago: Half-Free and Fighting On," *McClure's Magazine*, October 1903, 563–77. See also Lisa Krisshoff Boehm, *Popular Culture and the Enduring Myth of Chicago, 1871–1968* (New York: Routledge, 2004).

69 *"I am looking out"*: Benton to his parents, February 4, 1907, microfilm reel 2325, Benton Papers.

70 *"Here is a town"*: Henry Blake Fuller, *The Cliff-Dwellers* (New York: Harper and Brothers, 1893), 42.

70 *"sausage & hominy"*: Benton to his parents, [mid-February] 1907, reel 2325, Benton Papers.

71 *"something was always"*: Oral History Interview with Benton, 6.

71 *"dirty, slovenly"*: Benton to his father, March 24, 1907, reel 2325, Benton Papers.

71 *"It is impossible"*: Benton to his mother, March 25, 1907, reel 2325, Benton Papers.

72 *"amusement[s]"*: Observations from *The Dial* quoted in Boehm, *Popular Culture and the Enduring Myth of Chicago*, 58. For more on the Midway, see ibid., 54–62.

72 *"In the center"*: Benton, "Chicago—1907–08," 32, manuscript, reel 2326, Benton Papers.

73 *"demon rum"*: "Water Scarce; Beer Plenty," *Chicago Daily Tribune*, August 7, 1907.

73 *"compassionate"*: Benton, "Chicago," 25.

73 *"plain and cold"*: Ibid., 10.

73 *"perverse"*: Ibid.

74 *"in all directions"*: Ibid., 11.

74 *"older men can have"*: Ibid.

74 *"arrogant and superior"*: Ibid., 33.

74 *"They're the German"*: Ibid.

74 *"old time's sake"*: Ibid., 52.

74 *"I looked at him"*: Ibid.

74 *"Still the only"*: Ibid., 53.

75 *"I can't sleep"*: Ibid.

75 *"Shut the door"*: Ibid.

75 *"Eventually, not only"*: Naifeh and Smith, *Jackson Pollock*, 185.

75 *"a macho bastard"*: Philip Pavia quoted in Potter, *To a Violent Grave*, 36.

75 *"shrill"*: Naifeh and Smith, *Jackson Pollock*, 185.

75 *"I was put to"*: Benton, *Artist in America*, 30.

76 *"The beautiful"*: Ibid.

76 *"I revolted"*: Ibid., 31.

76 *"practical ability"*: Roger Gilmore, ed., *Over a Century: A History of the School of the Art Institute of Chicago, 1866–1981* (Chicago: School of the Art Institute of Chicago, 1982), 76.

76 *"life, history"*: Benton to his parents, February 25, 1907, reel 2325, Benton Papers.

76 *"I am very confident"*: Benton to his parents, March 1907, reel 2325, Benton Papers.

77 *"As to working"*: L. B. Sidway to Maecenas Benton, May 14, 1907, reel 2325, Benton Papers.

77 *"If necessary"*: Benton to his father, [Spring 1907], reel 2325, Benton Papers.

77 *"artistic"*: Benton, "Chicago," 5–6.

77 *"It was thus"*: Ibid., 7.

77 *"was one of"*: Oral History Interview with Benton, 5.

77 *"dressed up"*: Benton, "Chicago," 12.

78 *"your stroke"*: Benton to his father, April 23, 1907, reel 2325, Benton Papers.

78 *"by dropping little"*: Benton, "Chicago," 12.

78 *"Why are you looking"*: Ibid.

78 *"Oh, look at"*: Ibid., 15.

78 *"For some reason"*: Benton to his parents, March 1, 1907, reel 2325, Benton Papers.

78 *"it made me"*: Benton, "Chicago," 21.

78 *"I obtained also"*: Benton, *American in Art*, 12.

78 *"Japanese prints were"*: Ibid.

79 *"arrangement of objects"*: Benton, "Chicago," 22.

79 *"rich in a big-time"*: Benton, *Artist in America*, 23.

79 *"I want to be"*: Vytlacil quoted in Burroughs, *Thomas Hart Benton*, 40.

79 *"It is well"*: *Bulletin of the Art Institute of Chicago* 2 (July 1908): 6.

80 *"design and execute"*: Gilmore, *Over a Century*, 77.

80 *"slippery, buttery"*: Benton, *American in Art*, 13.

80 *"From the moment"*: Benton, *Artist in America*, 31.

80 *"was a standard"*: Oral History Interview with Benton, 6.

81 *"Some of the fellows"*: Benton, "Chicago," 31.

81 *"You all who"*: Benton to his parents, July 1907, reel 2325, Benton Papers.

81 *"class and kind"*: Benton, *Artist in America*, 24.

81 *"Every artist"*: Ibid., 26.

81 *"parvenu spirit"*: Ibid., 27.

82 *"secret"*: Benton to his father, May 25, 1907, reel 2325, Benton Papers.

82 *"a big feed"*: Benton to his father, February 1908, reel 2325, Benton Papers.

82 *"nursing probably"*: Benton, "Chicago," 41.

82 *"indifferent"*: Ibid.

82 *"they are all"*: Benton to his mother, July 1, 1907, reel 2325, Benton Papers.

82 *"forum for mighty"*: Benton, "Chicago," 44.

82 *"one of our crowd"*: Ibid.

83 *"could be alone"*: Benton, *Artist in America*, 32.

83 *"Are you a religious"*: Benton, "Chicago," 60.

83 *"Look at that crazy"*: Benton, *Artist in America*, 32.

83 *"Though I was among"*: Ibid., 31.

83 *"a gangling six footer"*: Benton, "Chicago," 36.

84 *"needler"*: Ibid., 49.

84 *"but the boil"*: Ibid.

84 *"crying with humiliation"*: Ibid., 50.

84 *"By the time"*: Benton, *Artist in America*, 25–26.

85 *"The majority of"*: Ibid., 31–32.

85 *"He had a high"*: Craven, "Thomas Hart Benton," 35.

85 *"unoccupied pedestal"*: Benton to his parents, March 18, 1907, reel 2325, Benton Papers.

85 *"As each day"*: Benton to his parents, February 1907, reel 2325, Benton Papers.

86 *"Just the other"*: Benton to his parents, February 24, 1908, reel 2325, Benton Papers.

86 *"watching the donkey"*: Benton, *Artist in America*, 29.

86 *"I am aware"*: Ibid.

87 *"I am excited"*: Benton to his mother, October 1, 1907, reel 2325, Benton Papers.

87 *"I feel in my very"*: Benton to his parents, March 9, 1908, reel 2325, Benton Papers.

87 *"I've always felt"*: Oral History Interview with Benton, 7.

88 *"I feel the pull"*: Benton to his mother, January 20, 1908, reel 2325, Benton Papers.

88 *"There [Paris] the almighty"*: Benton to his parents, January 27, 1908, reel 2325, Benton Papers.

88 *"a lizard that"*: Benton, "Chicago," 65.

88 *"the best"*: Benton to his mother, June 8, 1908, reel 2325, Benton Papers.

88 *"The pink dress"*: Benton to Clark, [1908], Crowder College Archives, Neosho, Mo., quoted in Adams, *American Original*, 35.

5. PARIS

90 *"It sounds like"*: Henry James, "John S. Sargent," *Harper's New Monthly Magazine*, October 1887, 683.

91 *"with incredible patience"*: James R. Mellow, *Charmed Circle: Gertrude Stein and Company* (New York: Henry Holt and Company, 1974), 183.

91 *"One was quite certain"*: Gertrude Stein, *Two: Gertrude Stein and Her Brother and Other Early Portraits* (New Haven, Conn.: Yale University Press, 1951), 337.

91 *"ill-assorted pair"*: Mellow, *Charmed Circle*, 183.

91 *"standing in front"*: Macdonald-Wright quoted in Mellow, *Charmed Circle*, 184.

92 *"These people were"*: Benton, *Artist in America*, 34–35; Benton quoted in Craven, "Thomas Hart Benton," 35.

92 *"Whom did I meet"*: Hopper quoted in Brian O'Doherty, "Portrait: Edward Hopper," *Art in America*, December 1964, 73.

92 *"I was very uneasy"*: Benton, "Ali," 75.

93 *"a kindly voice"*: For the following dialogue and quotations, see ibid., 75–89.

95 *"He introduced himself"*: Ibid.

96 *"heroic seascapes"*: Abel G. Warshawsky, *The Memories of an American Impressionist* (Kent, Ohio: Kent State University Press, 1980), 36.

96 *"lived on good"*: Ben L. Bassham, introduction to ibid., xviii, xii.

96 *"There was the usual"*: Warshawsky, *Memories of an American Impressionist*, 107–108.

96 *"disconcerting"*: Ibid., 49.

97 *"short, swarthy, compact"*: Ibid., 47.

97 *"who in his quiet"*: Bassham, introduction, xiv.

97 *"Tommy Benton"*: Warshawsky, "My Brush with Life," 121, reel 3893, Abel G. Warshawsky Papers, Archives of American Art, Smithsonian Institution.

97 *"walk[ed] him about"*: Warshawsky, *Memories of an American Impressionist*, 47.

97 *"yell obscenities"*: Benton, "The Life of Art in Paris," unpaginated manuscript, microfilm reel 2326, Benton Papers.

98 *"frontier tradition"*: Craven, "Thomas Hart Benton," 35.

98 *"astonishing"*: Benton, "Life of Art in Paris."

98 *"I got a quick reputation"*: Ibid.

98 *"convolutions"*: Ibid."

98 *"a big chest"*: Benton, *Artist in America*, 35. For more on Thompson, see Charles F. Ramus, "John E. Thompson, Dean of Colorado Painters," in *John Edward Thompson, 1882–1945*, exhibition catalog (Denver: Denver Art Museum, 1945). Also see Michael Paglia, "Fresh Start," *Westword*, April 21, 2005; and the John Edward Thompson Papers, Collection of the Denver Public Library.

99 *"a stiff entry examination"*: Catherine Fehrer, "History of the Julian Academy," in *The Julian Academy, Paris, 1868–1939* (New York: Shepherd Gallery, 1989), 2. Also see Gabriel P. Weisberg and Jane R. Becker, eds., *Overcoming All Obstacles: The Women of the Académie Julian* (New York: Dahesh Museum and Rutgers University Press, 1999).

99 *"The art language"*: Warshawsky, *Memories of an American Impressionist*, 52.

99 *"These students"*: Robert Henri, *The Art Spirit* (1923; Boulder, Colo.: Westview Press, 1984), 78–79.

100 *"meaningful subject"*: Benton, "Life of Art in Paris."

100 *"exercise"*: Benton, *American in Art*, 13.

100 *"deeply rooted"*: Warshawsky, "My Brush with Life," 124.

100 *"was certain that"*: Benton, *American in Art*, 14.

100 *"My pride was assaulted"*: Benton, "Life of Art in Paris."

100 *"flashy lady companions"*: Ibid.

101 *"a sunlit scene"*: Benton, *American in Art*, 15.

101 *"recognize that some"*: Benton, "Life of Art in Paris."

101 *"somber French histories"*: Benton, *American in Art*, 15, 16.

102 *"broad brushing manner"*: Ibid., 17.

102 *"opposed and contradictory"*: Ibid., 16.

102 *"Tommy"*: Benton, "Life of Art in Paris."

102 *"I wallowed in every"*: Benton quoted in Craven, "Thomas Hart Benton," 35.

102 *"The art of James McNeil* [sic] *Whistler"*: Benton to his mother, February 24, 1908, reel 2325, Benton Papers.

103 *"Because of my revolt"*: Benton, *Artist in America*, 34.

104 *"One of the curious sights"*: Warshawsky, *Memories of an American Impressionist*, 57.

104 *"mature and even famous"*: Benton, *American in Art*, 16.

104 *"You're Benton"*: Benton, "Life of Art in Paris."

104 *"George"*: Warshawsky, *Memories of an American Impressionist*, 111.

104 *"He carried his head"*: Benton, "Life of Art in Paris."

105 *"an erratic, somewhat inarticulate"*: Benton, *American in Art*, 16.

105 *"had become a student"*: Ibid.

105 *"I was not only seeing"*: Benton, "Life of Art in Paris."

106 *"Show me how"*: Ibid.

106 *"I feel I owe"*: Benton, *Artist in America*, 35. Also see Adams, *American Original*, 42.

107 *"book worm"*: Benton, "Life of Art in Paris."

107 *"Well, Benton, I hear"*: Ibid.

107 *"The story of my life"*: Benton, *Artist in America*, 33.

107 *"uncomfortably"*: Benton, "Life of Art in Paris."

107 *"I was too young"*: Benton, "Artist in America," interview by Robert S. Gallagher, 43–44.

108 *"because it took the color"*: Benton, *American in Art*, 17.

108 *"a deeper appreciation"*: Ibid.

108 *"great trees"*: Benton to his mother, postmarked May 2[?], 1909, and June 29, 1909, reel 2325, Benton Papers.

108 *"everything was O.K."*: Benton, note preceding his letters from Paris, reel 2325, Benton Papers.

108 *"To begin with"*: Benton to his father, July 20, 1909, reel 2325, Benton Papers.

109 *"That I have succeeded"*: Benton to his mother, July 20, 1909, reel 2325, Benton Papers.

110 *"brown gravy"*: Mildred Benton Small, interview by Henry Adams and Ken Burns, December 27, 1986, American Original Exhibition Records.

110 *"These pictures are bad"*: Benton to his parents, December 26, 1909, reel 2325, Benton Papers.

110 *"paralyzed"*: Benton, "Life of Art in Paris."

111 *"Funniest God damned thing"*: Ibid.

111 *"repellent"*: Ibid.

111 *"There have been four"*: Macdonald-Wright quoted in South, "Early Life," in *Color, Myth, and Music*, 15.

112 *"was very much"*: Henry Clausen, "Recollections of SMW," *American Art Review*, January/February 1974, 56. For a quick summary of Macdonald-Wright's childhood and arrival in Paris, see South, "Early Life," 15–23.

112 *"There's a woman here"*: Benton, "Life of Art in Paris."

112 *"This one was to be"*: Benton, *Artist in America*, 36.

113 *"ham out the French poets"*: Benton, "Life of Art in Paris."

113 *"Steinitis"*: Stanton Macdonald-Wright, Paris journal, Manuscripts Department, Alderman Library, University of Virginia.

113 *"fat-assed kike"*: Macdonald-Wright quoted in Adams, *American Original*, 55.

113 *"made a lot of anti-Semitic"*: Clinton Adams, interview by Paul J. Karlstrom, August 2–3, 1995, Archives of American Art, Smithsonian Institution.

113 *"[I was] a Missouri Democrat"*: Benton, "Life of Art in Paris."

113 *"we could not talk"*: Benton, *Artist in America*, 36.

114 *"two races"*: John Ruskin, *The Crown of Wild Olive: Four Lectures on Industry and War* (London: George Allen, 1907), 126–27.

115 *"it made a deep"*: Benton, *American in Art*, 25.

115 *"In the artistic milieus"*: Ibid., 25–26.

115 *"the old and the new"*: Benton to his parents, [late] 1909, reel 2325, Benton Papers.

115 *"years later the trends"*: Benton, *American in Art*, 26.

116 *"the literature circulating"*: Ibid.

116 *"under the great spreading"*: Benton, *Artist in America*, 36.

116 *"loved the rich"*: William C. Agee, "New Perspectives: Stanton Macdonald-Wright in the Twentieth Century," in South, *Color, Myth, and Music*, 2.

116 *"in abstract problems"*: Benton, *American in Art*, 20.

116 *"'ultramodern' experimenters"*: Ibid., 21.

116 *"The pattern of my"*: Ibid., 27.

117 *"that pasty-faced prick"*: Thompson quoted in Adams, *American Original*, 50.

117 *"The poets say"*: Benton quoted in Lyman Field, *". . . When Thy Summons Comes . . .": Eulogy to Tom Benton* (Kansas City, Mo.: Bob McDonald, 1975), 1.

117 *"landscape 'motifs' "*: Benton, *American in Art*, 24.

117 *"all conscious theorizing"*: Benton, "Life of Art in Paris."

117 *"direct imitation"*: Adams, *American Original*, 52.

118 *"This effort at self-promotion"*: Benton, "Life of Art in Paris."

118 *"the fat heads"*: Ibid.

119 *"Either I would paint"*: Benton, *American in Art*, 26.

119 *"It may be"*: Robert Motherwell, "How Inner Torment Feeds the Creative Spirit," *New York Times*, November 17, 1985, sec. 2, 1.

120 *"What was the son"*: Benton, "Life of Art in Paris."

120 *"a man of great intelligence"*: Stanton Macdonald-Wright, interview by Betty Lochrie Hoag, April 13, 1964, Archives of American Art, Smithsonian Institution.

121 *"was soon living"*: Adams, *American Original*, 54.

121 *"It tore me apart"*: Benton, "Life of Art in Paris."

121 *"We will go together"*: Ibid.

121 *"spiderish"*: Mildred Benton Small, "Paris Memoir," American Original Exhibition Records.

122 *"Oh, Tom, it's true"*: Benton, "Life of Art in Paris."

122 *"She flatly refused"*: Small, "Paris Memoir."

122 *"Why give the bitch"*: Benton, "Life of Art in Paris."

122 *"It was plain"*: Small, "Paris Memoir."

123 *"I had gotten myself"*: "Reminiscences of Thomas Hart Benton," 45.

123 *"Her affectionate acts"*: Benton, "Life of Art in Paris."

123 *"it was Dejeuner"*: Small, "Paris Memoir."

123 *"cocky"*: Ibid.

124 *"That year Mother built"*: Ibid.
124 *"romantic"*: Craven, "Thomas Hart Benton," 35.
124 *"he had enormous energy"*: Craven, *Modern Art*, 333.
125 *"it has always been"*: Small, "Paris Memoir."

6. EXPERIMENTS
129 *"streaks and spots"*: Benton, *American in Art*, 28.
129 *"was glad, in a way"*: Ibid.
129 *"the Missouri environment"*: Ibid.
130 *"an agile, nervous"*: "In the Studio of a Kansas City Stage Artist," *Kansas City Star*, February 4, 1912.
130 *"But Mr. Benton paints"*: Ibid.
131 *"psychologically equivalent terms"*: South, "Synchromism: Theoretical Beginnings," in *Color, Myth, and Music*, 31.
131 *"luminosity octaves"*: Tudor-Hart quoted ibid., 32.
131 *"When the colors"*: Macdonald-Wright to Benton, August 29, 1911, Benton Curatorial Files.
131 *"women's underwear"*: Benton, "Artist in America," interview by Robert S. Gallagher, 88.
132 *"Latin Quarter in itself"*: Van Wyck Brooks, *John Sloan: A Painter's Life* (London: J. M. Dent, 1955), 42.
132 *"The doors of its long"*: Benton, *Artist in America*, 37.
133 *"that nest of youthful genius"*: Craven, *Modern Art*, 332.
133 *"been in love"*: Barton quoted in Charles G. Shaw, "Through the Magnifying Glass," *New Yorker*, November 5, 1927, 21.
133 *"Underneath the pretensions"*: Benton, *Artist in America*, 40.
133 *"He had a fancy"*: Ibid.
134 *"denned up"*: Hunt quoted in Page Smith, *America Enters the World: A People's History of the Progressive Era and World War I* (New York: McGraw-Hill, 1985), 281–82.
134 *"decorative adaptations"*: Benton, *American in Art*, 30.
134 *"The general 'pull'"*: Ibid.
134 *"a sort of snobbery"*: Benton, "The Thirties," appendix 1 in Priddy, *Only the Rivers Are Peaceful*, 241.
134 *"go to Paris"*: Ibid., 242.
135 *"I would be more willing"*: Benton to his parents, July 10, 1912, microfilm reel 2325, Benton Papers.
135 *"these new idioms"*: "Reminiscences of Thomas Hart Benton," 48.
136 *"layman"*: Theodore Roosevelt, "A Layman's Views of an Art Exhibition," *Outlook*, March 29, 1913, 719; and Julian Street, *Everybody's Magazine*, quoted in Richard Guy Wilson, Dianne H. Pilgrim, and Dickran Tashjian, *The Machine Age in America, 1918–1941* (New York: Brooklyn Museum and Harry N. Abrams, 1986), 211.
136 *"the most hideous"*: Harriet Monroe quoted in Milton Brown, *The Story of the Armory Show* (New York: Joseph H. Hirshhorn Foundation, 1988), 172.
137 *"It must have been the top"*: Mildred Benton Small, interview by Henry Adams and Ken Burns, September, 28, 1987, American Original Exhibition Records.

137 *"two very sympathetic"*: Benton to his parents, July 2, 1912, ibid.

137 *"grave, high-tempered"*: Craven, *Modern Art*, 241.

138 *"the pioneer spirit"*: Ibid., 245. Also see Wayne Lloyd Roosa, "American Art Theory and Criticism During the 1930s: Thomas Craven, George L. K. Morris, Stuart Davis" (Ph.D. diss., Rutgers, 1989).

138 *"They used to think"*: Oral History Interview with Benton, 21.

138 *"begged, borrowed, sponged"*: Craven, "Thomas Hart Benton," 35.

138 *"We were very young"*: Craven, *Modern Art*, 250.

138 *"neat as an old-maid"*: Burroughs, *Thomas Hart Benton*, 7.

139 *"keen and indefatigable"*: Lewis Mumford, "Paint," *New Republic*, April 4, 1923, 169.

139 *"infested with grubbers"*: Thomas Craven, *Paint* (New York: Harcourt, Brace, 1923), 7.

139 *"rogue's tale"*: Mumford, "Paint," 170.

139 *"The nostalgia of Verlaine"*: Craven, *Modern Art*, 332.

140 *"For ten years"*: Ibid.

140 *"tried everything"*: Craven, "Thomas Hart Benton," 35.

140 *"straight realistic portraits"*: Benton, *American in Art*, 32.

140 *"half-witted, talentless imbeciles"*: Benton to his parents, July 2, 1912, American Original Exhibition Records.

141 *"It was obvious"*: Benton, *American in Art*, 32–33.

141 *"artistic ideals"*: Benton to his parents, July 15, 1912, American Original Exhibition Records.

141 *"He hung around gymnasiums"*: Craven, "Thomas Hart Benton," 35.

141 *"Every time I returned"*: Ibid.

142 *"when the city failed"*: Benton, *Artist in America*, 38.

142 *Synchromism*: South, "Synchromism," 3. Also see Abraham A. Davidson, *Early American Modernist Painting, 1910–1935* (New York: Harper and Row, 1981), 121–32; and Amy Dempsey, *Art in the Modern Era: A Guide to Styles, Schools, and Movements, 1860 to the Present* (New York: Harry N. Abrams, 2002), 98.

142 *"subject is deep blue"*: Russell quoted in Loughery, *Alias S. S. Van Dine*, 74–75.

143 *"playing poor"*: Benton, "Mysterious Years," American Original Exhibition Records.

143 *"hold their art"*: Willard Huntington Wright, "Impressionism to Synchromism," *Forum* 50 (July–December 1913): 770.

143 *"craze for the static"*: Ibid., 766–67. Also see Howard Risatti, "Music and the Development of Abstraction in America: The Decade Surrounding the Armory Show," *Art Journal* 39 (Autumn 1979): 12; and Loughery, *Alias S. S. Van Dine*, 82.

143 *"intelligible"*: "In the Art Galleries," *New York Times*, March 14, 1914, 10.

143 *"marked a revolution"*: Wright, *Modern Painting*, 291.

143 *"desired to express"*: Ibid., 294.

144 *"agony of effort"*: Craven, *Modern Art*, 218.

144 *"used . . . abstract properties"*: Benton, *American in Art*, 76.

144 *"For all his talk"*: Benton, "American Regionalism," 184. Also see Doss, *Benton, Pollock, and the Politics of Modernism*, 38–41.

144 *"What most captured"*: Benton, *American in Art*, 33.

144 *"the spectral coloration"*: Ibid.

145 *"usual enthusiasm"*: Ibid., 36.

145 *"If one admitted"*: Ibid., 39. For more on synchromism, see Gail Levin, "Thomas Hart Benton, Synchromism, and Abstract Art," 144–48.

145 *"Its purpose"*: H. L. Mencken, "A Review of Reviewers," in *H. L. Mencken's "Smart Set" Criticism*, ed. William H. Nolte (Washington, D.C.: Gateway, 1987), 299.

146 *"full of theatrical romance"*: Benton, *Artist in America*, 38. For more on Rex Ingram, see André Soares, *Beyond Paradise: The Life of Roman Navarro* (New York: St. Martin's Press, 2002), 27–28; and Liam O'Leary, *Rex Ingram: Master of the Silent Cinema* (New York: Barnes and Noble Imports, 1980).

146 *"great knockdown and drag-out fight"*: Benton, *Artist in America*, 38

147 *"black and white thing"*: Benton, "Artist in America," interview by Robert S. Gallagher, 43.

147 *"parlance of popular culture"*: Doss, *Benton, Pollock, and the Politics of Modernism*, 42–44.

147 *"more important in my life"*: Oral History Interview with Benton, 25.

148 *"the revolutionary path"*: Balken, *After Many Springs*, 47.

148 *"There is a feeling"*: John Weichsel, "Artists and Others," *Camera Work* 46 (April 1914): 13–17, quoted in Stavitsky, "John Weichsel and the People's Art Guild," 14. For more on Weichsel, see Antliff, *Anarchist Modernism*, 53–58; and John Weichsel Jr., "The People's Art Guild" (master's thesis, Hunter College, 1965).

148 *"the prevailing detachment"*: Weichsel, open letter, February 12, 1916, Weichsel Papers, quoted in Antliff, *Anarchist Modernism*, 55.

148 *"'socialization' of art"*: "Art Notes: The People's Art Guild," *New York Times*, November 14, 1915, 18.

148 *"quite as important"*: Benton, "Note for Baigell," reel 2086, Baigell Papers.

149 *"learned man"*: Benton, *Artist in America*, 41–42.

149 *"didn't want to be"*: "Reminiscences of Thomas Hart Benton," 49.

149 *"voted socialist"*: Ibid.

150 *"when the artist concentrates"*: Ibid., 55.

150 *"narrowly 'aesthetic'"*: Benton, *American in Art*, 41.

150 *"There is no real"*: "Reminiscences of Thomas Hart Benton," 57.

151 *"to turn public attention"*: *The Forum Exhibition of Modern American Painters, March 13th to March 25th, 1916* (New York: Anderson Galleries, 1916), n.p.

151 *"will run a month"*: Macdonald-Wright to Russell quoted in Agee, "Willard Huntington Wright and the Synchromists," 11.

151 *"It will be seen"*: Marsden Hartley, explanatory note in *Forum Exhibition of Modern American Painters*, n.p.

152 *"to give in form and color"*: Arthur G. Dove, ibid.

152 *"the inherent aesthetic qualities"*: Willard Huntington Wright, foreword to ibid.

152 *"just enough plausibility"*: Benton, *American in Art*, 39.

152 *"In speaking of the works"*: Ibid., 37.

153 *"it was bruited about"*: Ibid., 38.

153 *"I was interested"*: Oral History Interview with Benton, 17. Also see Brennan, *Painting Gender, Constructing Theory*, 207; and Gail Levin, "The Tradition of the Heroic Figure in Synchromist Abstraction," *Arts Magazine*, June 1977, 138–42.

153 *"is more than a search"*: John Weichsel, "Another New Art Venture: The Forum Exhibition," *International Studio* 58 (June 1916): 116–17.

153 *"the irascible dynamism"*: Ibid.

153 *"nonbodily bodies"*: Brennan, *Painting Gender, Constructing Theory*, 209. Also see Doss, *Benton, Pollock, and the Politics of Modernism*, 41–42.

153 *"I believe the representation"*: Benton, statement, *Forum Exhibition of Modern American Painters*, reprinted in Baigell, *Thomas Hart Benton Miscellany*, 3–4.

154 *"it would appear"*: Benton to Matthew Baigell, quoted in Agee, "Willard Huntington Wright and the Synchromists," 90.

154 *"One thing that will"*: "Current News of Art and the Exhibitions," *New York Sun*, March 12, 1916, quoted in Raverty, *Struggle over the Modern*, 33.

154 *"abstract purity"*: Willard Huntington Wright, "The Truth About Painting," *Forum* 54 (October 1915): 450, quoted in Raverty, *Struggle over the Modern*, 36.

154 *"blind to the big spirit"*: Robert J. Coady, "Current News," *New York Sun*, March 19, 1916, and "American Art," *Soil: A Magazine of Art*, December 1916, 4, both quoted in Raverty, *Struggle over the Modern*, 38–39, 40.

155 *"quite in vogue"*: Benton to Weichsel, [ca. 1917], reel N60-2, frame 43, Newark Museum Papers, Archives of American Art, Smithsonian Institution.

155 *"sort of regret"*: Benton, *Artist in America*, 46.

155 *"I thought he was a pain"*: Oral History Interview with Benton, 22.

155 *"social as well as the artistic"*: Benton, *American in Art*, 35.

155 *"a hot house of artistic"*: Ibid., 40. For more on Daniel, see Davidson, *Early American Modernist Painting*, 177–78.

156 *"considered himself"*: Benton, *American in Art*, 41.

156 *"pretensions"*: Ibid.

157 *"treated with the injustice"*: Willard Huntington Wright, "Modern Art: An American Painter of Promise," *International Studio* 61 (May 1917): xcv–xcvi.

157 *"eclectic combination"*: Benton, *Artist in America*, 42.

157 *"trying interval"*: Craven, "Thomas Hart Benton," 35.

158 *"There is really not much"*: Benton to Baigell, March 15, 1972, Baigell Papers.

158 *"I'm tired of chasing"*: Macdonald-Wright, quoted by Benton in Oral History Interview with Benton, 20.

158 *"flat broke"*: Benton to Weichsel, [ca. 1917], Newark Museum Papers.

7. EXPERIENCES

159 *"between big capitalists"*: "Reminiscences of Thomas Hart Benton," 71.

159 *"a cubist's holiday"*: "Whistler and Others on Exhibition: Art at Home and Abroad," *New York Times*, December 22, 1918, 46.

159 *"relished the idea"*: Benton, *Artist in America*, 42–43.

159 *"I have landed"*: Benton to his mother, [1918], American Original Exhibition Records.

160 *"Well Craven"*: Benton to Craven, July 28, 1918, ibid.

160 *"poor ring psychology"*: Benton, *Artist in America*, 44.

160 *"must be more accurate"*: Benton to his mother, [1918], American Original Exhibition Records.

160 *"own purposes"*: Ibid.

160 *"I have not time"*: Benton to his mother, September 7, 1918, microfilm reel 2325, Benton Papers.

160 *"the last vestiges of French influence"*: Craven, *Modern Art*, 334.

161 *"career since the War"*: Ibid., 334–35.

161 *"among boys"*: Benton, *Artist in America*, 44, 45.

161 *"The strenuous life"*: "T. H. Benton's Naval Pictures Unique in Expressing Force," *New York Herald*, December 22, 1918.

161 *"did not care"*: Benton, *American in Art*, 43.

161 *"In their sinister"*: "Whistler and Others on Exhibition," 46.

162 *"Why," he asks*: Benton, *American in Art*, 44. For an analysis of the frontispiece see Ann Uhry Abrams, "Visions of Columbus: The 'Discovery' Legend in Antebellum American Paintings and Prints," *American Art Journal* 25, nos. 1–2 (1993): 87.

162 *"things existed in the world"*: Benton, *Artist in America*, 45.

162 *"a religious fact"*: Waldo Frank, *Our America* (New York: Boni and Liveright, 1919), 184.

163 *"rigid taboos"*: Benton, *Artist in America*, 45, 48.

163 *"spontaneity"*: Benton to Stieglitz, September 21, 1919, Alfred Stieglitz/Georgia O'Keeffe Archive.

163 *"Never, even when I became"*: Benton, "Artist in America," interview by Robert S. Gallagher, 48. Also see Benton, *American in Art*, 55–56.

164 *"concrete references"*: Benton, *American in Art*, 46–47.

164 *"the actual forms"*: Ibid., 47.

164 *"pallid abstractionists"*: Craven, "Thomas Hart Benton," 36.

164 *"would arouse sharp animosities"*: Benton, *American in Art*, 49.

164 *"These are no damn good"*: Rita Benton quoted in Burroughs, *Thomas Hart Benton*, 4.

164 *"too Michelangelese"*: Ibid.

165 *"She was slim"*: Benton, *Artist in America*, 48–49.

165 *"We thought that he"*: Santo Piacenza quoted in Adams, *American Original*, 104.

165 *"delicious beach plums"*: Burroughs, *Thomas Hart Benton*, 3.

165 *"drenching in the nakedness"*: Mumford, *Sketches from Life*, 453.

165 *"Situated on the western"*: Burroughs, *Thomas Hart Benton*, 6, 21.

166 *"getting out of the damn city"*: "Reminiscences of Thomas Hart Benton," 87.

166 *"The relaxing sea air"*: Benton, *Artist in America*, 63.

166 *"resplendent physical condition"*: Craven, "Thomas Hart Benton," 36.

166 *"all goes well here"*: Craven to Lizzie Benton quoted in Burroughs, *Thomas Hart Benton*, 10.

166 *"hard workers"*: Burroughs, *Thomas Hart Benton*, 92.

167 *"for all their crotchety ways"*: Benton, *Artist in America*, 62–63.

167 *"the uncanny palpability"*: Craven, *Modern Art*, 336.

168 *"defended Modernism"*: Ibid.

168 *"classical composition"*: Thomas Craven, "The Awakening of the Academy," *Dial*, June 1921, 677, 673. On the shift in Craven's criticism, see Raverty, *Struggle over the Modern*, 45–67.

168 *"opulent design"*: "World of Art: Later Tendencies at the Philadelphia Exhibition," *New York Times Book Review*, April 24, 1921, 8.

168 *"I think he did"*: "Reminiscences of Thomas Hart Benton," 84–85.

169 *"inexhaustible"*: A. H. Shaw, "Profiles: De Medici in Merion," *New Yorker*, September 22, 1928, 29.

169 *"my cockiness"*: Benton, "Artist in America," interview by Robert S. Gallagher, 48. Also see Mary Ann Meyers, *Art, Education, and African-American Culture: Albert Barnes and the Science of Philanthropy* (New Brunswick, N.J.: Transaction, 2004), 88–89.

169 *"significant form"*: Wright, *Modern Painting*, 93.

169 *"the parts . . . must be held"*: Benton, "Mechanics of Form Organization" *Arts* 10 (November 1926): 285–89.

169 *"There are here"*: Benton, "Mechanics of Form Organization," *Arts* 11 (February 1927): 95.

170 *"design"*: Thomas Craven, "Thomas H. Benton," *Shadowland*, September 1921, 11, 66.

170 *"enormous picture"*: Craven to Lizzie Benton, September 6, 1921, quoted in Burroughs, *Thomas Hart Benton*, 24.

170 *"form and the subject"*: Benton, "Form and the Subject," reprinted in Baigell, *Thomas Hart Benton Miscellany*, 9–11.

171 *"environmental experience"*: Benton, "The Dead and the Living," 172. Benton uses the term "environmentalism" in "American Regionalism," 150. Also see Benton, *Artist in America*, 63.

171 *"a locality exists"*: John Dewey, "Americanism and Localism," in *Characters and Events: Popular Essays in Social and Political Philosophy*, 2:540–41.

171 *"The 'eternal' quality"*: John Dewey, "Experience, Nature, and Art," *Journal of the Barnes Foundation* 1 (October 1925): 7.

171 *"that interaction of organism"*: Dewey, *Art as Experience*, 22.

172 *"issued in the conviction"*: William Carlos Williams, *Contact* 1 (1920): 1; and William Carlos Williams, "Yours, O Youth," *Contact* 3 (1921): 14. Also see Matthew Baigell, "Recovering America for American Art: Benton in the Early Twenties," in Weintraub, *Thomas Hart Benton*, 14–15. For more on Dewey's influence on Williams, see John Beck, *Writing the Radical Center: William Carlos Williams, John Dewey, and American Cultural Politics* (Albany: State University of New York Press, 2001); and Ann Mikkelsen, "'The Truth About Us': Pastoral, Pragmatism, and *Paterson*," *American Literature* 75 (September 2003): 601–27.

172 *"If Americans are to be blessed"*: William Carlos Williams, "Sample Critical Statement," *Contact* 4 (1921): 18.

172 *"We are here"*: Williams, *Contact* 1 (1920): 1.

172 *"interdependent individualism"*: Beck, *Writing the Radical Center*, 19. For more on *Contact*, see Eric White, "Advertising Localist Modernism: William Carlos Williams, 'Aladdin Einstein,' and the Transatlantic Avant-Garde in *Contact*," *European Journal of American Culture* 28, no. 2 (2009): 141–65.

172 *"attempt[ed] to humanize knowledge"*: Ron Loewinsohn, introduction to *The Embodiment of Knowledge*, by William Carlos Williams (New York: New Directions, 1974), xv.

172 *"a somatic awareness"*: Charles Tomlinson, introduction to *William Carlos Williams: Selected Poems*, ed. Charles Tomlinson (New York: New Directions, 1985), viii.

172 *"the region provides"*: Lewis Mumford, "Regional Planning" (1931), in *Lewis Mumford Reader*, 211.

172 *"sweeping national crusades"*: Donald L. Miller, *Lewis Mumford*, 166.

173 *"definite, verifiable"*: Mumford, *Story of Utopias*, 281.

173 *"Art in its social setting"*: Ibid., 293. For more on Mumford's influence on Benton, see Dreishpoon, introduction to *Benton's America*, 11.

173 *"They never spoke"*: Burroughs, *Thomas Hart Benton*, 12.

173 *"You learned things"*: Benton, *Vineyard Gazette*, August 1940, quoted ibid., 26.

173 *recent dissertation*: Bailly, "Painting the *American Historical Epic*," 73.

174 *"we lived from hand to mouth"*: Benton, *Artist in America*, 49.

174 *"abject squalor and chaos"*: Dick Craven, interview by Henry Adams and Ken Burns, n.d., American Original Exhibition Records.

175 *"She never faltered"*: Jessie Benton, ibid.

175 *"If it wasn't for her"*: Santo Piacenza quoted in Adams, *American Original*, 104.

175 *"an infamous character"*: Suzanne Muchnic, "Culture Monster: Who's That Guy Behind the Wheel at the Huntington?" http://latimesblogs.latimes.com/culture-monster/2009/05/whos-that-guy-behind-the-wheel-at-the-huntington.html, May 10, 2009, accessed March 28, 2010.

176 *"draws people out"*: Lewis Mumford, "An American Epic in Paint," *New Republic*, April 6, 1927, 197.

176 *"We got down there"*: Benton quoted in Burroughs, *Thomas Hart Benton*, 89.

176 *"hell-raisin' parties"*: Kingsbury quoted ibid.

176 *"She wasn't one to mind"*: Mumford quoted ibid., 90.

176 *"political liberalism"*: Doss, *Benton, Pollock, and the Politics of Modernism*, 32.

176 *"something less than nothing"*: Benton, *Artist in America*, 51–52.

177 *"Although politically"*: Benton, "American Regionalism," 165.

177 *"an open and pluralistic theory"*: Hofstadter, *Progressive Historians*, 186.

177 *"It seemed to those"*: Benton, "American Regionalism," 166–67.

178 *"economic elements"*: Beard, *Economic Interpretation of the Constitution*, 6.

178 *"I had agreed"*: Benton, "American Regionalism," 168. For more references to Beard and Benton's association with him, see Emily Braun, "Thomas Hart Benton and Progressive Liberalism: An Interpretation of the New School Murals," in Braun and Branchick, *Thomas Hart Benton*, 31nn10–12.

178 *"Wild strawberries"*: Craven to Lizzie Benton, June 16, 1921, quoted in Burroughs, *Thomas Hart Benton*, 16–17.

178 *"that hangout for radicals"*: Burroughs, *Thomas Hart Benton*, 22.

178 *"They always had a punch"*: Benton quoted ibid.

179 *"emerged as the orphic bard"*: John P. Diggins, "Getting Hegel out of History: Max Eastman's Quarrel with Marxism," *American Historical Review* 79 (February 1974): 39.

179 *"the immediate qualities"*: Ibid., 41.

179 *"It was not God"*: Max Eastman, "John Dewey: My Teacher and Friend," *Great Companions: Critical Memoirs of Some Famous Friends* (New York: Farrar, Straus and Cudahy, 1942), 261.

179 *"dispassionate respect"*: Diggins, "Getting Hegel out of History," 41.

179 *"a friend and helper"*: Benton, *American in Art*, 51.

179 *"This was an important meeting"*: Ibid.

180 *"staring out to sea"*: Burroughs, *Thomas Hart Benton*, 85.

180 *"He did the first experimentation"*: Robinson quoted in Albert Christ-Janer, *Boardman Robinson* (Chicago: University of Chicago Press, 1946), 43.

180 *"a psychological condition"*: Benton, *Artist in America*, 63.

180 *"part of the world"*: Benton, "Form and the Subject," 16.

180 *"a concern with"*: Doss, *Benton, Pollock, and the Politics of Modernism*, 93.

181 *"I am certainly interested"*: Pfeiffer to Benton, March 26, 1922, American Original Exhibition records. The letter is signed "Pfeiffer" and was sent from Redlands, California. Edward Heyman Pfeiffer was secretary of the Chelsea Neighborhood Association and moved to Redlands in the early 1920s, where he worked as a

translator, poet, novelist, and nonfiction writer. For more on the sequencing of the series, see Benton, "My American Epic in Paint," xxxi–xxxvi; Bailly, "Painting the *American Historical Epic*," 292–304; and Erika Doss, "American Moderns and the American Scene," paper presented at the symposium Remapping the New: Modernism and the Midwest, 1893–1945, organized by the Terra Museum of American Art and the Union League Club of Chicago, September 18, 2004.

181 *"the organic ever-onward-pressing"*: Pfeiffer to Benton, March 26, 1922.

181 *"artificial, transitory concoctions"*: Ibid.

181 *"My original purpose"*: Benton, "American Regionalism," 149.

182 *"proclaimed in downright"*: Thomas Craven, "American Month in the Galleries," *Arts* 11 (March 1927): 151.

182 *"While these [paintings]"*: "The Art World," *New York American*, February 20, 1927, 119.

182 *"shocking"*: Boardman Robinson, "A Shocking Exhibit," letter to the editor, *Nation*, February 20, 1927, 211.

183 *"Although Benton believed"*: Baigell, *Thomas Hart Benton*, 70.

183 *"Mumford's revisionism"*: Corn, *Great American Thing*, 318–19.

183 *"Mr. Benton"*: Lewis Mumford, *Thomas H. Benton*, exhibition catalog (New York: New Gallery, 1927), n.p.

183 *"The idiom in which"*: Mumford, "American Epic in Paint," 197.

183 *"Mr. Benton holds"*: Ibid.

184 *"was often referred to"*: Craven, "Thomas Hart Benton," 36.

184 *"Mr. Benton's major paintings"*: Mumford, *Thomas H. Benton*, n.p.

184 *"If this art does not belong"*: Mumford, "American Epic in Paint," 197.

184 *"vain and snobbish"*: Anonymous neighbor of the Bentons' quoted in Burroughs, *Thomas Hart Benton*, 79.

184 *"wouldn't let Rita"*: Jessie Benton, interview with the author, October 24, 2003, Martha's Vineyard, Mass.

185 *"pitiful"*: Benton to his mother, April 1924, reel 2325, Benton Papers.

185 *"I listened to old-timers"*: Benton, *Artist in America*, 75.

186 *"In the conflict"*: Baigell, "Thomas Hart Benton and the Left," in Hurt and Dains, *Thomas Hart Benton*, 27. Also see Burroughs, *Thomas Hart Benton*, 93.

186 *"The flavor of a premachine-age"*: Benton, *Artist in America*, 75–76.

186 *"He has struck"*: Lloyd Goodrich, "In Missoura," *Arts* 6, no. 6 (1924): 338.

186 *"outsiders may laugh"*: Benton, *Artist in America*, 75.

186 *"All of this poking"*: Ibid., 60, 77.

187 *"foot itch"*: Ibid., 66–67.

187 *"Experience in the degree"*: Dewey, *Art as Experience*, 18.

187 *"beginnings and cessations"*: Ibid., 41.

188 *"shaggy, unprepossessing toughs"*: Benton, *Artist in America*, 89.

188 *"The industrial South"*: Ibid., 95.

188 *"paps a-stickin' up"*: Ibid., 97.

188 *"in the middle of my back"*: Ibid., 117.

189 *"fat like a pillow"*: Ibid., 118.

189 *"peculiar brand"*: Ibid., 97.

189 *"Dionysiac madness"*: Ibid., 100–101.

189 *"cultural organicism"*: Raverty, *Struggle over the Modern*, 63–67.

189 *"The modern painter"*: Thomas Craven, "Have Painters Minds?" *American Mercury*,

March 1927, 262. Also see Thomas Craven, "Daumier and the New Spirit," *Dial*, March 1925, 241.

189 *"In the parade"*: Craven, "American Month in the Galleries," 151–52.

190 *"by tough experience"*: Mumford, foreword to *The South*, exhibition catalog (New York: Delphic Studios, 1929), n.p.

190 *"Regional Survey"*: Mumford, *Story of Utopias*, 279.

190 *"non-political grouping"*: Ibid., 222–23.

190 *"region by region"*: Mumford quoted in Donald L. Miller, *Lewis Mumford*, 201.

190 *"were caught in a linguistic bind"*: Michael Kazin, *The Populist Persuasion: An American History* (New York: Basic Books, 1995), 66.

191 *"democratic critique"*: Michael Hardt, "Jefferson and Democracy," *American Quarterly* 59 (March 2007): 41.

191 *"productive and [the] burden-bearing"*: Senator Thomas Hart Benton quoted in Kazin, *Populist Persuasion*, 13.

191 *"ingenious"*: Benton, "New York Exhibitions," *Arts* 10 (1926): 343–44.

191 *"Culture is not bought"*: John C. Van Dyke, "The Art Students' League of New York," *Harper's New Monthly Magazine* 83 (June–November 1891): 697–98.

192 *"a sort of Left Bank"*: Robert Beverly Hale quoted in Judd Tully, "The Art Students League of New York," *American Artist*, August 1984, 74.

192 *"livelier, freer, noisier"*: Raphael Soyer, *Diary of an Artist* (Washington, D.C.: New Republic Books, 1977), 212.

192 *"permitted complete freedom"*: Landgren, *Years of Art*, 97.

192 *"pugnacious"*: Stewart Klonis, interview by Paul Cummings, in Cummings, "Art Students League, Part I," 6.

192 *"What I taught"*: Oral History Interview with Benton, 28.

192 *"Benton's style"*: Fairfield Porter, interview by Cummings, in Cummings, "Fairfield Porter," *Archives of American Art Journal* 12, no. 2 (1972): 15. See also Justin Spring, *Fairfield Porter: A Life in Art* (New Haven, Conn.: Yale University Press, 2000), 52–53.

192 *"I didn't treat them"*: Oral History Interview with Benton, 30.

193 *"whatever talent I had"*: Charles Pollock quoted in Naifeh and Smith, *Jackson Pollock*, 152.

193 *"genial"*: Charles Pollock quoted in Potter, *To a Violent Grave*, 31.

193 *"was almost a member"*: Ibid., 33. For more on Charles Pollock, see Terence Maloon, *The Art of Charles Pollock: Sweet Reason* (Muncie, Ind.: Ball State University Museum of Art, 2002).

193 *"Rita"*: Frank Pollock quoted in Potter, *To a Violent Grave*, 31.

194 *"humanistic"*: Benton, *American in Art*, 61–62.

8. EXPRESSIONS

195 *"operations"*: Benton, "American Regionalism," 149.

195 *"As an artist"*: Lloyd Goodrich, "New Benton Drawings," *New York Times*, October 27, 1929, sec. 9, 13.

196 *"[The drawings] are comparatively free"*: Lloyd Goodrich, "The Delphic Studios," *Arts* 16, no. 3 (1929): 185.

196 *"Slot machines banged"*: Benton, *Artist in America*, 202.

196 *"demonstrates the waste"*: Baigell, *Thomas Hart Benton*, 76. There's some debate

as to whether Benton visited Borger in 1926 or 1928—or both. See also Adams, *Drawing from Life*, 194n21; and Adams, *American Original*, 138–39 and 151–53.

197 *"calculated mixture"*: Marling, "Thomas Hart Benton's *Boomtown*," 74.

197 *"the hermetic integrity"*: Ibid., 78.

197 *"In lieu of familiar aspects"*: James M. Dennis, *Grant Wood: A Study in American Art and Culture* (New York: Viking Press, 1975), 194.

197 *"caricatured . . . cartoony images"*: Dennis, *Renegade Regionalists*, 14.

198 *"Tarted Up"*: Robert Hughes, "Tarted Up till the Eye Cries Uncle: Reviving the Vulgarity of Thomas Hart Benton," *Time*, May 1, 1989, 80.

198 *"new experiences"*: Frederick Jackson Turner, *The Frontier in American History* (New York: Henry Holt, 1920), 38.

198 *"flight westward"*: Marling, "Thomas Hart Benton's *Boomtown*," 79.

198 *"Turner's 'Frontierism'"*: Benton, "Letter to Matthew Baigell," November 22, 1967, reprinted in Baigell, *Thomas Hart Benton Miscellany*, 33.

199 *"who have no standing"*: Beard to N. M. Butler, October 8, 1917, *Minutes of the Trustees of Columbia University* 38 (1917–1918): 88–90, reprinted in Richard Hofstadter and Wilson Smith, eds., *American Higher Education: A Documentary History* (Chicago: University of Chicago Press, 1961), 2:882.

199 *"I have no reforms"*: James Harvey Robinson, *The Mind in the Making: The Relation of Intelligence to Social Reform* (New York: Harper and Brothers, 1921), 28. For more background on the Columbia controversy, see Peter M. Rutkoff and William B. Scott, *New School: A History of the New School for Social Research* (New York: Free Press, 1986), 1–11.

199 *"either political or religious"*: Butler quoted in Rutkoff and Scott, *New School*, 17.

200 *"intelligent men and women"*: Advertisement for the New School in *The New Republic*, December 28, 1918, iii.

200 *"clubiness"*: Rutkoff and Scott, *New School*, 23.

200 *"house an idea"*: Agnes de Lima quoted ibid., 49.

200 *"straightforward, rational"*: Johnson quoted in Emily Braun, "Thomas Hart Benton and Progressive Liberalism: An Interpretation of the New School Murals," in Braun and Branchick, *Thomas Hart Benton*, 16.

201 *"modern technology"*: Bender, *New York Intellect*, 313.

201 *"stumped by the Marxist picture"*: Benton, "American Regionalism," 167.

201 *"Paint me a picture"*: Alvin Johnson, *Pioneer's Progress* (New York: Viking Press, 1952), 328.

202 *"the Mexican concern"*: Benton, *American in Art*, 61.

202 *"no history book"*: Johnson quoted in Braun, "Thomas Hart Benton and Progressive Liberalism," 15.

202 *"very frigidly"*: Benton, *American in Art*, 63.

202 *"bankrupted"*: Johnson, *Pioneer's Progress*, 329.

202 *"little garden"*: Ibid.

203 *"draftsman's medium"*: Thomas Branchick and Emily Braun, "The Restoration of America Today," in Braun and Branchick, *Thomas Hart Benton*, 68.

203 *"When I first got acquainted"*: Reginald Marsh, "Thomas Benton," *Demcourier*, February 1943, 9–11.

204 *"a Marxist"*: Denning, *Cultural Front*, 172.

204 *"The only excuse"*: Dos Passos quoted ibid., 170.

204 *"contained no specifically"*: Benton, *American in Art*, 67.

204 *"destined for difficulties"*: Johnson, *Pioneer's Progress*, 329.

205 *"I too have seen"*: Ibid.

205 *"reveals the power"*: Rita Susswein, "The New School for Social Research," *Parnassus* 3 (January 1931): 11.

205 *"What is chaotic"*: Craven, *Modern Art*, 339.

205 *"These pictures"*: Edmund Wilson, "Aladdin's Lecture Palace," *New Republic*, June 10, 1931, 91. In 1931, Lewis Mumford praised the murals as well: see Mumford, *The Brown Decades: A Study of the Arts in America* (New York: Dover, 1971), 109.

205 *"progressive liberalism"*: See Braun, "Thomas Hart Benton and Progressive Liberalism," 24–25.

205 *"escapist"*: Broun, "Thomas Hart Benton," 59.

206 *"in modern America"*: Doss, *Benton, Pollock, and the Politics of Modernism*, 69, 71, 81.

206 *"Populist/Capitalist Realism"*: Robert Hughes, *American Visions: The Epic History of Art in America* (New York: Knopf, 2006), 445.

206 *"synthesis of the national"*: Noble, *Death of a Nation*, 160.

206 *"In this high-spirited"*: Broun, "Thomas Hart Benton," 64.

206 *"having an occupation"*: Michael Kazin, *The Populist Persuasion: An American History* (New York: Basic Books, 1995), 13.

207 *"American populism"*: Ibid., 2.

207 *"grand form"*: Ibid.

207 *"The freedom with which"*: Benton, *Artist in America*, 249.

208 *"intellectual harmony"*: Benton, "American Regionalism," 167.

208 *"There was no way out"*: Leo Huberman, *We, the People*, rev. ed. (New York: Harper and Brothers, 1947), 224.

208 *"Huberman," he writes*: Louis M. Hacker, "History Made Straight," *New Republic*, March 22, 1933, 165.

208 *"how ill-used he was"*: Marling, *Tom Benton and His Drawings*, 77.

209 *"Benton will be with me"*: Delaney quoted in Sam Yates, *Joseph Delaney: Retrospective Exhibition* (Knoxville, Tenn.: Ewing Gallery of Art and Architecture, 1986), n.p. Also see Justin Spring, *Fairfield Porter: A Life in Art* (New Haven, Conn.: Yale University Press, 2000), 66.

209 *"the role of the 'man's man'"*: Naifeh and Smith, *Jackson Pollock*, 171.

210 *"an artist or a teacher"*: Darrow quoted in Burroughs, *Thomas Hart Benton*, 114.

210 *"Even if it's wrong"*: Alexander Calder, *Calder: An Autobiography with Pictures* (New York: Pantheon, 1966), 67.

210 *"was rigorous about drawing"*: Wilson quoted in Potter, *To a Violent Grave*, 37.

210 *"hard-boiled, rough-fellow"*: Simonds quoted ibid., 37.

210 *"menopause crowd"*: Jules quoted in Naifeh and Smith, *Jackson Pollock*, 228.

210 *"he never said"*: Simonds quoted in Potter, *To a Violent Grave*, 37.

210 *"tell everyone that Tom"*: Anonymous Benton neighbor quoted in Burroughs, *Thomas Hart Benton*, 79.

211 *"They were always hollerin'"*: Margo Henderson quoted in Naifeh and Smith, *Jackson Pollock*, 194.

211 *"Whatever abuse she got"*: Maria Piacenza quoted ibid.

211 *"to articulate and express"*: Axel Horn, "Jackson Pollock," 80–81.

211 *"to identify the direction"*: Ibid., 81.

211 *"You know," Frank recalls*: Frank Pollock quoted in Potter, *To a Violent Grave*, 27.

211 *"four-square drinker"*: Charles Pollock quoted ibid., 33.

212 *"a revelation from heaven"*: Benton, *Artist in America*, 256.

212 *"As the music spread"*: Charles Seeger, *Reminiscences of an American Musicologist*, 205–206, interview by Adelaide G. Tusler and Ann M. Briegleb, November 3, 1966, Oral History Program, University of California, Los Angeles, 1972. For more on Benton and Seeger, see Archie Green, "Charles Louis Seeger (1889–1979)," *Journal of American Folklore* 92 (October–December 1979): 393–94; Fryd, "'The Sad Twang of Mountain Voices'"; and Ann M. Pescatello, *Charles Seeger: A Life in American Music* (Pittsburgh: University of Pittsburgh Press, 1992), xi, 133–35.

213 *"sounds have the power"*: Dewey, *Art as Experience*, 247.

213 *"believed was vanishing"*: Leo G. Mazow, "Banjo Cultures," in *Picturing the Banjo* (University Park: Palmer Museum of Art and the Pennsylvania State University Press, 2005), 33.

213 *"The old music cannot last"*: Benton, *Artist in America*, 114. Also see Archie Green, "Tom Benton's Folk Depictions," in *Torching the Fink Books and Other Essays on Vernacular Culture* (Chapel Hill: University of North Carolina Press, 2001), 108–33.

213 *"had an almost comic"*: Naifeh and Smith, *Jackson Pollock*, 247.

214 *"muttered"*: Ibid.

214 *"Pollock was a born artist"*: Benton quoted in Burroughs, *Thomas Hart Benton*, 118. See also Carter Ratcliff, *The Fate of a Gesture: Jackson Pollock and Postwar American Art* (Boulder, Colo.: Westview Press, 1998), 16.

214 *"produced a family"*: Naifeh and Smith, *Jackson Pollock*, 68.

214 *"weak and absent father"*: Ratcliff, *Fate of a Gesture*, 15–16.

214 *"a fragile creature"*: Ibid., 15.

214 *"struggling to draw"*: Ibid., 16.

215 *"Jackson was very macho"*: McNeil quoted in Potter, *To a Violent Grave*, 34.

215 *"There was a rhythm"*: Ibid., 36.

215 *"With such news"*: Benton, *Artist in America*, 331.

215 *"as something against which"*: Pollock, interview, *Arts and Architecture*, February 1944, 14.

215 *"personality was such"*: Benton, *Artist in America*, 332.

216 *"shadowy white wolves"*: Ibid., 338.

216 *"intense interest"*: Ibid., 332.

216 *"Benton was a strange shot"*: Delaney quoted in Naifeh and Smith, *Jackson Pollock*, 183.

216 *"tailed after Benton"*: Holtzman quoted in Solomon, *Jackson Pollock*, 56.

216 *"an intuitive sense"*: Benton, *Artist in America*, 333–34. Also see Jackson Pollock to Charles Pollock, July 1931, in Frances V. O'Connor, *Jackson Pollock* (New York: Museum of Modern Art, 1967), 16.

217 *"Benton is beginning"*: Jackson Pollock to his father, February 3, 1933, quoted in Ratcliff, *Fate of a Gesture*, 22.

217 *"Perhaps Pollock's upbringing"*: Doss, *Benton, Pollock, and the Politics of Modernism*, 325.

217 *"Trying to wring"*: Sanford "Sande" McCoy (born Pollock) to Kadish quoted in Naifeh and Smith, *Jackson Pollock*, 265.

218 *"took to [Pollock] immediately"*: Benton, *Artist in America*, 332.

218 *"I was unused to that sort of thing"*: Frank Pollock quoted in Naifeh and Smith, *Jackson Pollock*, 209.

218 *"violent and baffling"*: Ratcliff, *Fate of a Gesture*, 15.

218 *"loved a good party"*: Anonymous friend quoted in Burroughs, *Thomas Hart Benton*, 95.

218 *"You know how dogs are"*: Benton quoted ibid.

218 *"used to fuck"*: Pollock quoted in Naifeh and Smith, *Jackson Pollock*, 211.

219 *"cult of nudity"*: Benton, *Artist in America*, 307.

219 *"as if they were making"*: Ibid.

219 *"John Deweyites, Marxist radicals"*: Ibid., 334.

220 *"the arts and their role"*: Ronald J. Onorato, introduction to *Thomas Hart Benton, Frank Lloyd Wright*, iv.

220 *"colonial heritage"*: Ibid., v.

221 *"cantankerous"*: Ibid., vi.

221 *"Therefore, in my case"*: Benton, in *Thomas Hart Benton, Frank Lloyd Wright*, 1.

221 *"process"*: Ibid.

221 *"has demanded that"*: Ibid.

222 *"aesthetic emotion"*: Ibid., 2.

222 *"with subjects which"*: Ibid.

222 *"return to 'Mother'"*: Ibid., 3.

222 *"You want to tie"*: Ibid.

222 *"Mr. Benton"*: Ibid.

222 *"structures to unify"*: Ibid.

222 *"unregenerate bad boy"*: Paul Rosenfeld, "Ex–Reading Room," *New Republic*, April 12, 1933, 246.

223 *"they do protest too much"*: Paul Rosenfeld, "American Painting," *Dial*, December 1921, 661.

223 *"I have done a lot"*: Benton to Stieglitz, December 9, 1921, Alfred Stieglitz/Georgia O'Keeffe Archive.

223 *"specially made"*: Benton, *Artist in America*, 250. Also see Avis Berman, *Rebels on Eighth Street: Juliana Force and the Whitney Museum of American Art* (New York: Atheneum, 1990), 319–25.

224 *"Appalachian Oread"*: Benton, *Artist in America*, 98.

224 *"The arts which today"*: Dewey, *Art as Experience*, 4–5.

225 *"popular outpourings"*: Benton, *Arts of Life in America*, reprinted in Baigell, *Thomas Hart Benton Miscellany*, 22.

225 *"the arts of life"*: Ibid.

225 *"In the process of correlating"*: Ibid., 27.

225 *"are evidently giving"*: Rosenfeld, "Ex–Reading Room," 246.

225 *"fetish of purity"*: Benton, *Arts of Life in America*, 31. For more on the viewers' experiences of the mural, see Brennan, *Painting Gender, Constructing Theory*, 216–19.

226 *"through the rejuvenation"*: Doss, *Benton, Pollock, and the Politics of American Modernism*, 91.

226 *"In the Whitney panels"*: Ibid., 92.

226 *"The welfare and the soundness"*: Franklin D. Roosevelt, nomination speech, in *The Public Papers and Addresses of Franklin D. Roosevelt* (New York: Random House, 1938), 1:657.

226 *"are the spiritual values"*: Ibid.

226 *"I am very certain"*: Roosevelt, radio address, ibid., 788.

226 *"The cold truth"*: Charles Beard, "The Myth of Rugged American Individualism," *Harper's Monthly Magazine*, December 1931, 22.

226 *"vulgarity"*: Henry McBride, "Thomas Hart Benton's Murals at the Whitney Museum," *New York Sun*, December 10, 1932, quoted in Dennis, *Renegade Regionalists*, 22.

227 *"environment, not in isolation"*: Davis, "Davis's Rejoinder to Thomas Benton," 12.

227 *"an escape from the demands"*: Schapiro, "Populist Realism," 55.

227 *"should have no trouble"*: Davis, "Davis's Rejoinder to Thomas Benton," 13.

228 *"vicious caricature"*: Ibid.

228 *"In life, the claim to purity"*: Benton, *Arts of Life in America*, 29.

228 *"This mural"*: Ibid., 30.

228 *"the viewer is not"*: Brennan, *Painting Gender, Constructing Theory*, 219.

228 *"tight as a jay bird"*: Benton, *Artist in America*, 250–51.

229 *"lead-ass"*: Lieber quoted in Kathleen A. Foster, "Thomas Hart Benton and the Indiana Murals," in Foster, Brewer, and Contompasis, *Thomas Hart Benton and the Indiana Murals*, 7.

229 *"a social history"*: Benton quoted ibid., 10. See also Benton, *Artist in America*, 252.

229 *"How does an artist"*: Marilyn, "The Girl About Town: A Muralistic Conception of Indiana," *Indianapolis Star*, April 23, 1933.

230 *"I hardly know how"*: Benton, *Artist in America*, 254–55.

230 *"unroll progressively"*: Benton, "A Dream Fulfilled," reprinted in Foster, Brewer, and Contompasis, *Thomas Hart Benton and the Indiana Murals*, following p. 32.

230 *"a critical whaling"*: Benton, *Artist in America*, 254.

231 *"was merely realism"*: Benton quoted in Foster, "Thomas Hart Benton and the Indiana Murals," 21.

231 *"just civic sphere"*: Erika Doss, "Action, Agency, Affect: Thomas Hart Benton's Hoosier History," *Indiana Magazine of History*, June 2009, 135.

231 *"socialist tendencies"*: Anonymous quoted in Foster, "Thomas Hart Benton and the Indiana Murals," 21.

231 *"we have been extremely"*: Richards quoted in Doss, *Benton, Pollock, and the Politics of Modernism*, 111.

231 *"not all that is shown"*: Richards quoted in Virginia Gardner, "Indiana's Story Is Narrated to Its Daughters at Fair," *Chicago Tribune*, September 13, 1933. For a history of the Klan, see Patsy Sims, *The Klan* (Lexington: University Press of Kentucky, 1996), esp. 287; and for more on Benton's treatment of race, see Austen Barron Bailly, "Art for America: Race in Thomas Hart Benton's Murals, 1919–1936," *Indiana Magazine of History*, June 2009, 150–66, esp. 164.

231 *"I had milked"*: Benton, *Artist in America*, 256.

232 *"I loved to squeak"*: Ibid.

232 *"I knew the regionalists"*: Lewenthal quoted in Doss, *Benton, Pollock, and the Politics of Modernism*, 162. For more on Associated American Artists, see Doss, "Catering to Consumerism."

233 *"the crazy parade"*: "U.S. Scene," *Time*, December 24, 1934, 24.

233 *"opposition to such"*: Ibid., 25.

233 *"To them"*: Ibid., 26.

233 *"is the most virile"*: Ibid., 27.

233 *"regionalism became"*: Hegeman, *Patterns for America*, 138.

233 *"most vital modern art"*: Maynard Walker, statement in *Art Digest*, September 1, 1933, 10. Also see Adams, *American Original*, 216–21.

234 *"experience-based"*: Raverty, *Struggle over the Modern*, 63.

234 *"inevitably linked"*: Thomas Craven, "The Progress of Painting: The Modern Background," *Dial*, April 1923, 358.

234 *"the context of art"*: Ibid., 593.

234 *"fetish"*: Thomas Craven, "The Curse of French Culture," *Forum* 82 (July 1929): 60.

234 *"is the artificial prolongation"*: Thomas Craven, "The Bohemians of Paris," *Harper's Monthly Magazine*, February 1933, 335.

234 *"insistence on the superior"*: Thomas Craven, "Our Art Becomes American: We Draw Up Our Declaration of Independence," *Harper's Monthly Magazine*, September 1935, 435.

234 *"highly controversial"*: Benton, *American in Art*, 29.

234 *"never went quite as far"*: "Reminiscences of Thomas Hart Benton," 67.

234 *"vivid exponent"*: Craven, "Thomas Hart Benton," 33, 40.

234 *"to build an art"*: Craven, *Modern Art*, 335.

234 *"vicious and windy"*: Davis, "New York American Scene in Art," reprinted in Patricia Hills, *Modern Art in the U.S.A.: Issues and Controversies of the 20th Century* (Upper Saddle River, N.J.: Prentice Hall, 2001), 133.

235 *"slight burp"*: Ibid.

235 *"Is the well-fed farm hand"*: Ibid.

235 *"No verbiage can"*: Benton, letter to the editor, *Art Front* 1 (April 1935): 4. On the gendered discourse of such debates, see Brennan, *Painting Gender, Constructing Theory.*

235 *"'aesthetic' values"*: Benton, "Answers to Ten Questions," reprinted in Shapiro, *Social Realism*, 98.

235 *"It is now clear"*: Davis, "Davis's Rejoinder to Thomas Benton," 13.

235 *"frenetic and sometimes heavy-footed"*: Edward Alden Jewell, "When the Cobblers Turn from the Last," *New York Times*, April 7, 1935.

236 *"the fictions of political nationalism"*: Benton, "Art and Nationalism," reprinted in Baigell, *Thomas Hart Benton Miscellany*, 50.

236 *"Craven never minced"*: Benton, "The Thirties," appendix 1 in Priddy, *Only the Rivers Are Peaceful*, 223.

236 *"A work of art"*: Stuart Davis, "The Artist Today: The Standpoint of the Artists' Union," *American Magazine of Art*, August 1935, 478. For more on Davis's interest in Dewey, see Christ, "Stuart Davis and the Politics of Experience."

236 *"life's dynamic nature"*: Christ, "Stuart Davis and the Politics of Experience," 53.

236 *"I thought it possible"*: Benton, "Thirties," 242. Also see Benton, "American Regionalism," 168.

237 *"writer, artist, and worker"*: The constitution of the New York John Reed Club quoted in Hemingway, *Artists on the Left*, 20.

237 *"to struggle against"*: Ibid. Also see Denning, *Cultural Front*, 205–208.

237 *"You make good priests"*: Benton, "Art and Nationalism," 56.

238 *"To conclude"*: Ibid., 57.

238 *"I always knew you"*: Benton, "Thirties," 238.

238 *"enraged Commie"*: Benton, "American Regionalism," 171.

238 *"the dark and bloody"*: Lionel Trilling, *The Liberal Imagination: Essays on Literature and Society* (New York: New York Review of Books, 2008), 11.

238 *"Life for the vital"*: Benton, "Confessions of an American I: Why I Don't Like Marxism," *Common Sense* 6 (July 1937): 7.

239 *"I am an amateur thinker"*: Ibid.

239 *"Truth, manhandled"*: Ibid.

239 *"the entrance of the"*: Ibid., 8.

239 *"intellectual methods"*: Ibid.

239 *"I believe in the collective"*: Benton, "Interview in *Art Front*," April 1935, reprinted in Baigell, *Thomas Hart Benton Miscellany*, 62. Also see "Reminiscences of Thomas Hart Benton," 49–60; and "Benton Goes Home," *Art Digest*, April 15, 1935, 13.

239 *"relatively illogical"*: Benton, "Philosophy," undated typed manuscript, microfilm reel 2326, Benton Papers.

239 *"would scorn the conclusions"*: Ibid.

239 *"an alteration in"*: John Dewey, "What Pragmatism Means by Practical," in *John Dewey: The Middle Works, 1899–1924*, ed. Jo Ann Boydston (Carbondale: Southern Illinois University Press, 1977), 4:100. Also see John Dewey, "The Development of American Pragmatism," in *John Dewey: The Later Works, 1925–1953*, ed. Jo Ann Boydston (Carbondale: Southern Illinois University Press, 1984), 2:12.

240 *haunted by a Stalinist "spectre"*: Burck, "Benton Sees Red."

240 *"Particularly unacceptable"*: John Dewey, "Why I Am Not a Communist," *Modern Monthly* 8 (April 1934), reprinted in *American Anxieties: A Collective Portrait of the 1930s*, ed. Louis Filler (New Brunswick, N.J.: Transaction, 1993), 81.

240 *"uniform theory of revolutionary"*: Ibid., 82.

240 *"rightful heir of John Reed"*: Denning, *Cultural Front*, 165.

241 *"It was not easy"*: Louis Filler, *A Question of Quality: Popularity and Value in Modern Creative Writing* (Bowling Green, Ohio: Bowling Green University Popular Press, 1976), 116.

241 *"habitual disorder"*: Leon Edel, *Writing Lives: Principia Biographica* (New York: W. W. Norton, 1984), 15.

9. AT WORK

246 *"And a man shall be"*: Isaiah 32:2 (King James Bible).

246 *"carried the fullest load"*: William Carlos Williams, "The American Background," in Frank, *America and Alfred Stieglitz*, 26.

246 *"If anything is done"*: Gertrude Stein, "Stieglitz," ibid., 136.

246 *"And so Stieglitz to me"*: Sherwood Anderson, "City Plowman," ibid., 148.

246 *"unusual experiment"*: Eric Estorick, "The Career of Alfred Stieglitz," *Nation*, January 23, 1935, 110–11.

246 *"has fostered a sort"*: Edward Alden Jewell, "Alfred Stieglitz and Art in America," *New York Times Book Review*, December 23, 1934, 4.

247 *"idiosyncrasy rather than"*: Frank Jewett Mather Jr., "Photographer and Champion of Art," *Saturday Review of Literature*, December 8, 1934, 337.

247 *"I think that Stieglitz"*: Thomas Craven, "Art and the Camera," *Nation*, April 16, 1924, 456–57.

247 *"Art is not a philosophical system"*: Craven, *Modern Art*, xx.

247 *"every Jean, Jacques"*: Ibid., 318, 311.

247 *"half-baked philosophies"*: Ibid., 312.

247 *"Stieglitz," Craven concludes*: Ibid.

247 *"I was born in Hoboken"*: Stieglitz quoted in Brennan, *Painting Gender, Constructing Theory*, 212.

248 *"I suppose you have"*: Stieglitz to Cheney, May 10 and 25, 1934, Sheldon Cheney Papers, Archives of American Art, Smithsonian Institution.

248 *"Craven's attack"*: Lewis Mumford, "Books: General," *New Yorker*, May 12, 1934, 94. For an analysis of these exchanges, see Brennan, *Painting Gender, Constructing Theory*, 207–14.

248 *"I was deeply antagonized"*: Benton, "My American Epic in Paint," reprinted in Baigell, *Thomas Hart Benton Miscellany*, 17.

248 *"ever-dwindling elite"*: Alan Lawson, review of *The New American Radicalism: Alfred M. Bingham and the Non-Marxian Insurgency in the New Deal Era*, by Donald L. Miller, in *American Historical Review* 85 (October 1980): 1011. See also Alfred M. Bingham, *Insurgent America: Revolt of the Middle-Classes* (New York: Harper, 1935).

249 *"For the benefit"*: Benton, "America and/or Alfred Stieglitz," 22.

249 *"lovable"*: Ibid.

249 *"has a mania for self"*: Ibid.

249 *"I am certain"*: Ibid.

249 *"Knowledge of life"*: Ibid., 23.

249 *"like boys addicted"*: Ibid., 24.

249 *"Can you imagine"*: Ibid., 23.

249 *"And ye Gods"*: Stieglitz to Benton, December 29, 1934, Alfred Stieglitz/Georgia O'Keeffe Archive. Also see Edward Abrahams, "Alfred Stieglitz and/or Thomas Hart Benton," *Arts Magazine*, June 1981, 108–13.

249 *"And, believe me"*: Benton to Stieglitz, January 1, 1935, Alfred Stieglitz/Georgia O'Keeffe Archive.

250 *"foolish"*: Stieglitz to Benton, January 2, 1935, Alfred Stieglitz/Georgia O'Keeffe Archive.

250 *"break upon him"*: Mather Jr., "Photographer and Champion of Art," 337.

250 *"a man with a great appetite"*: Lewis Mumford, "The Art Galleries: The Three Bentons," *New Yorker*, April 20, 1935, 68.

250 *"more human"*: Ibid., 70.

251 *"Afraid of being highbrow"*: Ibid.

251 *"place has lost its masculinity"*: Benton quoted in "Mr. Benton Will Leave Us Flat," *New York Sun*, April 12, 1935, reprinted as "Interview in New York *Sun*," in Baigell, *Thomas Hart Benton Miscellany*, 78.

251 *"Don't get the idea"*: Benton quoted in "Benton Goes Home," *Art Digest*, April 15, 1935, 13.

251 *"ethic of responsibility"*: Max Weber, "Politics as a Vocation," in *From Max Weber: Essays in Sociology*, ed. Hans Gerth and C. Wright Mills (New York: Routledge, 2007), 120.

251 *"exemplary value"*: Ibid.

251 *"acids of modernity"*: Walter Lippmann, *A Preface to Morals* (New York: Macmillan, 1929), 19.

252 *"To be caught unwittingly"*: Andrew Nelson Lytle, "The Hind Tit," in *I'll Take My*

Stand: The South and the Agrarian Tradition, by Twelve Southerners (Baton Rouge: Louisiana State University Press, 2006), 201.

252 *"what we did after"*: Ibid., 244.

252 *"siege mentality"*: Robert L. Dorman, *Revolt of the Provinces: The Regionalist Movement in America, 1920–1945* (Chapel Hill: University of North Carolina Press, 1993), 107.

252 *"The conviction that our"*: Lyle H. Lanier, "A Critique of the Philosophy of Progress," in *I'll Take My Stand*, 123.

252 *"to make a democratic"*: Dorman, *Revolt of the Provinces*, 118. Also see Donald B. Kuspit, "Regionalism Reconsidered," *Art in America*, July–August 1974, 64–69.

252 *"home-grown, grass-roots artistry"*: Benton, "American Regionalism," 151.

253 *"provincial"*: This essay is reprinted in Benton, *Artist in America*, 262–63.

253 *"people I learned to like"*: Ibid., 269.

253 *"I wouldn't have missed"*: Ibid.

253 *"My known attitudes"*: Benton, "The Thirties," appendix 1 in Priddy, *Only the Rivers Are Peaceful*, 235.

253 *"below the surface"*: Stephen Alexander, "Art," *New Masses*, April 23, 1935, 29.

254 *"spinning"*: Benton, *Artist in America*, 258.

254 *"pretensions"*: Benton, "Thirties," 250.

254 *"this part of the country"*: Benton quoted in Joseph Hanlon, "Thomas Hart Benton to Live in Missouri," *St. Louis Post-Dispatch*, March 31, 1935.

255 *"Now get me right"*: Benton quoted in Priddy, *Only the Rivers Are Peaceful*, 39.

255 *"Gee," Larson recalls*: Larson quoted ibid., 41.

256 *"Interesting faces"*: Reporter quoted ibid., 56.

256 *"The average businessman"*: Ibid.

256 *"Your garage man"*: Ibid., 57.

256 *"gaped earnestly"*: "Legislators' Lounge," *Time*, January 11, 1937.

256 *"I do not want"*: Benton quoted in Priddy, *Only the Rivers Are Peaceful*, 60.

256 *"The 'realness' of this"*: Ibid., 68.

256 *"God damn it"*: Ibid., 69.

257 *"Mr. Sharkey," Benton said*: Benton, "Thirties," 256.

258 *"characteristic aspects"*: Benton, "The Missouri Mural and Its Critics," reprinted in appendix 1 in Priddy, *Only the Rivers Are Peaceful*, 268.

258 *"inadequacies of democracy"*: Doss, *Benton, Pollock, and the Politics of Modernism*, 131.

258 *"tempered by the values"*: Ibid., 127.

258 *"sometimes inspiring"*: *Kansas City Star*, December 21, 1936.

258 *"Missouri is not proud"*: Holland quoted in Priddy, *Only the Rivers Are Peaceful*, 84.

258 *"The work of true"*: Field quoted ibid., 85.

258 *"Benton's shown Missouri"*: Legislator quoted in Edelman, *Thomas Hart Benton Murals in the Missouri State Capitol*, 1.

258 *"Not a brush mark"*: Ibid.

259 *"Shame on you"*: *Tulsa Tribune*, January 27, 1937, quoted in Bob Priddy, "Public Art and Political Controversy," in Hurt and Dains, *Thomas Hart Benton*, 151.

259 *"I wouldn't hang"*: Murray quoted in Jerre Gerlando Mangione, *The Dream and the Deal: The Federal Writers' Project, 1935–1943* (Syracuse, N.Y.: Syracuse University Press, 1996), 195.

259 *"just a bunch"*: Benton, "Artist in America," interview by Robert S. Gallagher, 88.

259 *"I see mural painting"*: Benton, "Missouri Mural and Its Critics," 265.

259 *"virile"*: Eleanor Jewett, "Benton Exhibit Is Worthy of Public Notice," *Chicago Tribune*, October 31, 1937.

260 *"the combination of a machine"*: Benton quoted in Adams, *American Original*, 284. Also see Diane Kirkpatrick, "See You at the Movies: The Cinema in Art," in *The Movies: Texts, Receptions, Exposures*, ed. Laurence Goldstein and Ira Konigsberg (Ann Arbor: University of Michigan Press, 1996), 228–29.

261 *"blond sex bomb"*: Adams, *American Original*, 284. See Doss, *Benton, Pollock, and the Politics of Modernism*, 217–19.

261 *"Here is a rare thing"*: Sinclair Lewis, "Slim, Jim, and Lem," *Newsweek*, November 1, 1937, 25.

262 *"all Missouri"*: Clifton Fadiman, "Books," *New Yorker*, October 23, 1937, 89.

262 *"vigorous and provocative"*: Grant Wood, "Hard-Hitting Artist," *Saturday Review of Literature*, November 6, 1937, 6.

262 It's been suggested: Elizabeth Schultz, *"An Artist in America*: Thomas Hart Benton's 'Song of Himself,'" in Hurt and Dains, *Thomas Hart Benton*, 165.

262 *"despite his frankness"*: Schapiro, "Populist Realism."

262 *"romantic view"*: Benton, "Artist in America," interview by Robert S. Gallagher, 48.

263 *"puckish zest"*: Clarence R. Decker, "Tom Benton—the Kansas City Years," foreword to *An Artist in America*, by Benton (New York: University of Kansas City Press/Twayne Publishers, 1951), viii.

263 *"being the average"*: Walt Whitman, *Democratic Vistas, and Other Papers* (London: Walter Scott, 1888), 83. For more on Whitman's influence on Benton, see Schultz, *"An Artist in America,"* 183–87; and for more on Whitman's influence on Guthrie, see Richard Pascal, "Walt Whitman and Woody Guthrie: American Prophet-Singers and Their People," *Journal of American Studies* 24, no. 1 (1990): 41–59, and Craig Werner, "Democratic Visions, Democratic Voices: Woody as Writer," in *Hard Travelin': The Life and Legacy of Woody Guthrie*, ed. Robert Santelli and Emily Davidson (Middletown, Conn.: Wesleyan University Press, 1999), 69–82.

263 *"vernacular"*: Ellen G. Landau, "Classic in Its Own Little Way: The Art of Woody Guthrie," in Santelli and Davidson, *Hard Travelin'*, 90.

263 *"The world got twice"*: Woody Guthrie, *Bound for Glory* (New York: Plume, 1983), 140.

264 *"much too nude"*: Rogers quoted in "Thomas Benton's Nudes People the Ozarks," *Life*, February 20, 1939, 40.

264 *"The nude is stark"*: Ellis quoted in Adams, *American Original*, 290.

264 *"That's funny"*: Benton quoted ibid., 292.

265 *"even Benton has achieved"*: Archie Musick, "West of the Mississippi," *Magazine of Art*, September 1938, 538.

265 *"You flea-bitten red rock"*: Benton's letter quoted in Archie Musick, *Musick Medley: Intimate Memories of a Rocky Mountain Art Colony* (Colorado Springs: Creative Press, 1971), 87–88.

265 *"the Moscow subway"*: Robert Hughes, *American Visions: The Epic History of Art in America* (New York: Knopf, 2006), 445.

265 *"cheap and trivial"*: Emily Genauer quoted in Adams, *American Original*, 290.

265 *"one of the great works"*: Marling in *Thomas Hart Benton*, dir. Ken Burns.

266 *"protesting screams"*: Benton, "Boyhood," 20, microfilm reel 2325, Benton Papers. Also see Adams, *American Original*, 289–90.

266 *"was a beautiful girl"*: Benton quoted in "Very Nude Girl Irks Art Critics," *Indianapolis Sunday Star*, February 19, 1939.

266 *"a profound lack"*: Doss, *Benton, Pollock, and the Politics of Modernism*, 253.

266 *"there came over me"*: Benton, "After," in *Artist in America*, 296–97.

266 *"an art of fantasy"*: Doss, *Benton, Pollock, and the Politics of Modernism*, 258.

267 *"more enthusiasm today"*: Fillmore quoted in Milton S. Katz, *A History of the Kansas City Art Institute: A Century of Excellence and Beyond* (Kansas City, Mo.: Kansas City Art Institute, 2005), 26.

268 *"Grand Design"*: Earl Fred Bennett in *Thomas Hart Benton*, dir. Ken Burns.

268 *"it runs too frequently"*: Benton, "The Dead and the Living," 173.

268 *"If you have a good"*: Voegele quoted in Henry Adams, "Thomas Hart Benton as a Teacher," in Berardi, *Under the Influence*, 8.

268 *"as a terrier"*: Marshall quoted ibid., 9.

268 *"Tom had a wonderful"*: Barber quoted ibid., 10.

268 *"good-natured growl"*: Medearis, "Student of Thomas Hart Benton," 48.

268 *"When all has been said"*: Ibid., 50.

269 *"was like the sun"*: Bennett quoted in Berardi, *Under the Influence*, 37.

269 *"corrupt Pied Piper"*: Medearis, "Student of Thomas Hart Benton," 50. Also see Berton Rouche, "Rare Adventure for Art Students on Journey to Ozarks with Benton," *Kansas City Times*, May 13, 1940.

269 *"Experience"*: Benton, interview in the *New York Sun*, April 12, 1935, reprinted in Baigell, *Thomas Hart Benton Miscellany*, 78.

269 *"He was just interested"*: Peet quoted in Adams, "Thomas Hart Benton as a Teacher," 10.

270 *"Tom set this"*: Bransby quoted in Berardi, *Under the Influence*, 53.

270 *"What the hell"*: Graham quoted in Joseph Popper, "Artist Broke Free at Last of His Towering Mentor," *Kansas City Star*, September 2, 1995, A1.

270 *"great master of design"*: Howard quoted in Katz, *History of the Kansas City Art Institute*, 27.

270 *"odd man"*: William T. Kemper quoted in Adams, *American Original*, 279.

270 *"low type of painting"*: Huselton quoted ibid., 269.

270 *"I have read quite"*: Huselton to the Board of Governors of the Art Institute, June 1938, American Original Exhibition Records.

271 *"Never before or since"*: Adams, "Thomas Hart Benton as a Teacher," 18–19.

271 *"American Regionalism"*: Thomas Hart Benton, introduction to *Kansas City Regional Art*, exhibition catalog (New York: Associated American Artists Galleries, 1940), reprinted as appendix in Berardi, *Under the Influence*, n.p.

271 *"Do you want to know"*: "Blast by Benton," reprinted in Baigell, *Thomas Hart Benton Miscellany*, 79. The original interview appeared in Floyd Taylor, "Thomas Hart Benton Says Art Belongs in Clubs and Saloons, Not Museums," *New York World-Telegram*, April 5, 1941, 4.

272 *"He strikes out"*: Peyton Boswell, "Benton Sounds Off," *Art Digest*, April 15, 1941, 3.

272 *"All this a little"*: Benton statement in *Kansas City Journal-Post*, April 29, 1941.

272 *"And now after"*: Mike Amrine, *Kansas City Week-End Feature Journal*, May 3, 1941, quoted in Adams, *American Original*, 308–9.

272 *"fat men"*: Benton, unpublished statement quoted in Kenneth W. Rendell Gallery, *Autograph Letters, Manuscripts, Documents*, catalog no. 182 (1987), 3.

272 *"stuffed shirts and sissies"*: "Benton Ousted," *Art Digest*, May 15, 1941, 14.

273 *"Our present museums"*: Dewey, *Art as Experience*, 6, 8.

273 *"a couple of highballs"*: Benton, "Art vs. the Mellon Gallery," reprinted in Baigell, *Thomas Hart Benton Miscellany*, 79.

273 *"Museum people"*: Ibid., 82–83.

273 *"If I teach it will"*: Benton to Weaver, July 8, 1941, cabinet 1, drawer 3, Benton Curatorial Files.

273 *"I was too obviously"*: Benton, "After," 284.

274 *"these homosexuals are quite"*: Benton, "Artist in America," interview by Robert S. Gallagher, 88–89.

274 *"swift decline in terms"*: Doss, *Benton, Pollock, and the Politics of Modernism*, 281.

274 *"were bitter revelations"*: Ibid.

275 *"By linking the nightclub"*: Lewis Erenberg, "Impresarios of Broadway Nightlife," in *Inventing Times Square: Culture and Commerce at the Crossroads of the World*, ed. William R. Taylor (New York: Russell Sage Foundation, 1991), 174. For more on the Diamond Horseshoe, see Stephen Nelson, *"Only a Paper Moon": The Theatre of Billy Rose* (Ann Arbor, Mich.: UMI Research Press, 1987), 88–91.

275 *"I've got a saloon"*: "Benton Rejoices as Art Is Hung in 'Saloon': 'Persephone' Adorns the Diamond Horseshoe," *New York Times*, April 9, 1941, 27.

275 *"had also sneaked out"*: Benton, "After," 282.

275 *"exhilarating years"*: Ibid., 290.

276 *"I still can't figure out"*: Bennett quoted in Berardi, *Under the Influence*, 38.

10. AFIELD

277 *"Missourians are notoriously"*: Charles van Ravenswaay, preface to *Missouri: A Guide to the "Show Me" State* (New York: Duell, Sloan, and Pearce, 1941), n.p.

277 *"half-hobo"*: Craven, "Thomas Hart Benton," 38.

277 *"They lisp the same"*: Benton, *Artist in America*, 274.

277 *"taken as a whole"*: Ibid., 275.

277 *"I like Kansas City"*: Benton, *Kansas City Journal-Post*, April 29, 1941, quoted in Adams, *American Original*, 306.

278 *"Here was the city"*: Henry C. Haskell Jr. and Richard B. Fowler, *City of the Future: A Narrative History of Kansas City, 1850–1950* (Kansas City, Mo.: Frank Glen, 1950), 132.

278 *"They were shouting"*: Rosenberg quoted in Naifeh and Smith, *Jackson Pollock*, 268.

278 *"laboratory for experimentation"*: Harold Lehman quoted in Hurlburt, *Mexican Muralists in the United States*, 222.

279 *"a way out of his lack"*: Horn quoted in Naifeh and Smith, *Jackson Pollock*, 288.

279 *"forbidden longings"*: Naifeh and Smith, *Jackson Pollock*, 313.

279 *"God-damn you"*: Pollock quoted ibid.

280 *"didn't leak"*: Benton quoted in Hilary Iris Lowe, review of the Thomas Hart Benton Home and Studio State Historic Site, *Public Historian* 27 (Autumn 2005): 100–101.

280 *"fascinating"*: Sidney Larson, "Personal Reminiscences," in Hurt and Dains, *Thomas Hart Benton*, 101.

281 *"short tractor"*: Robert Bly, "Visiting Thomas Hart Benton and His Wife in Kansas City," in *The Morning Glory: Prose Poems by Robert Bly* (New York: Harper and Row, 1975), 61. The poem was first published in *New Letters* 38, no. 4 (1972): 29.

281 *"Tom! Come to bed"*: Blanche Carstensen quoted in Naifeh and Smith, *Jackson Pollock*, 312.

281 *"We were different"*: Benton, "After," in *Artist in America*, 314, 319–20. Also see Benton, "Death of Grant Wood," and Benton, "John Curry," 87.

282 *"From where I live"*: Benton, *Artist in America*, 275.

282 *"There is a high rugged"*: Ibid., 275–76.

282 *"River tradition runs"*: Ibid., 127.

283 *"The river and atmospheric"*: Mazow, *Shallow Creek*, 14.

283 *"pure romance and"*: Benton, *Artist in America*, 128.

283 *"some proud but bedraggled"*: Ibid., 29.

283 *"Description can give"*: Ibid., 146. Benton's official report appeared in "The Great Flood in Missouri as Seen and Recorded by Thomas Hart Benton," *Kansas City Star*, February 14, 1937.

283 *"ironically pitted the flood"*: Mazow, *Shallow Creek*, 26.

284 *"went into the waste baskets"*: Benton, "Disaster on the Kaw," *New Republic*, November 19, 1951, 9.

284 *"Hadn't Congress"*: Ibid., 10–11. For a full account of the flood, see Daniel Serda, *A Blow to the Spirit: The Kaw River Flood of 1951 in Perspective* (Kansas City, Mo.: Midwest Research Institute, 1993).

284 *"As I've said lots"*: Benton to Lyle Woodcock, August 24, 1969, quoted in Mazow, *Shallow Creek*, 29.

284 *"rustling out of his"*: Robert Wernick, "Down the Wide Missouri with an 'Old S.O.B.,'" *Saturday Evening Post*, October 23, 1965, 93–94.

285 *"But," he writes*: Ibid., 94.

285 *"No, no, no"*: Ibid.

285 *"The careers of abstract"*: Ibid., 95.

285 *"Time is working against"*: Robert F. Jones, "The Old Man and the River," *Sports Illustrated*, August 10, 1970, 28.

285 *"Sooner or later"*: Ibid.

285 *"After a day's run"*: Benton, "The Ozarks," *Travel and Leisure*, June–July 1973, 32–33.

286 *"an old Mississippi second mate"*: Benton, *Artist in America*, 127.

286 *"gave up his job"*: Ibid.

286 *"with its modern boats"*: Ibid.

286 *"spick-and-span"*: Ibid., 131.

287 *"The pilots of the towboat"*: Ibid., 133.

287 *"in an atmosphere of silk"*: Ibid., 321.

287 *"which is magically transformed"*: Broun, "Thomas Hart Benton," 73.

287 *"The story is thus"*: Benton pamphlet quoted ibid.

288 *"a pageant of mythic"*: Marling, *Tom Benton and His Drawings*, 67. Benton agreed that it's a "possibility" that the white man is trading for the Indian woman: see "The Missouri Murals," *Missouri Life*, March–April 1973, 30. For more on the River Club, see Roger Swanson, *The River Club: Its History and Development* (Kansas City, Mo.: River Club, 1956).

288 *"what I knew of"*: Benton, "And Still After," in *Artist in America*, 344.

288 *"Cartier and his people"*: Ibid., 345.

289 *"tough cookie"*: Ibid.

289 *"also knew what kind"*: Ibid., 347.

289 *"represents the excitement"*: Benton, "Murals for the Administration Building of the Power Authority of the State of New York, Located at Massena, New York," typescript, reel 2086, Baigell Papers.

289 *"great fire on the shore"*: Ibid.

289 *"surprise, excitement"*: Ibid.

289 *"a certain tenseness"*: Ibid.

290 *"I don't want any"*: Moses to William Chapin quoted in Ginger Strand, *Inventing Niagara: Beauty, Power, and Lies* (New York: Simon and Schuster, 2009), 189.

290 *"got restless"*: Benton, *Artist in America*, 134.

290 *"A man has his work"*: Rita Benton quoted in Sally McDougall, "Benton the Artist a Wild Man to the Critics but a Lamb to His Wife, Who Doesn't Nag," *New York World-Telegram*, April 15, 1942.

291 *"earlier adventuring"*: Benton, "And Still After," 329–30.

291 *"a burly, hard-drinking"*: Adams, *Drawing from Life*, 177.

291 *"Fast-growing"*: Mr. Cohen quoted in Benton, "Thirty-six Hours in a Boom Town," *Scribner's Magazine*, October 1938, 16.

291 *"large and loud population"*: Benton, "Thirty-Six Hours in a Boom Town," 17.

292 *"Away from the voice"*: Ibid., 53.

292 *"business and art"*: Benton, "After," 314.

293 *"replace the usual photographs"*: Ibid., 294.

293 *"interesting"*: Ibid.

293 *"hillbillies"*: Ibid., 295.

293 *"everything about tobacco"*: Ibid.

293 *"Why I'd buy it"*: Ibid., 296.

294 *"he recognized that"*: Doss, *Benton, Pollock, and the Politics of Modernism*, 232. Also see Doss, "Catering to Consumerism."

294 *"portray tobacco country"*: Doss, *Benton, Pollock, and the Politics of Modernism*, 233.

294 *"healthy income"*: Ibid., 239.

294 *"Cheap people have"*: "Thomas Benton Answers Questions," *Demcourier*, February 1943, reprinted in Baigell, *Thomas Hart Benton Miscellany*, 98–99.

294 *"I thought the series"*: "Business and Art as Tom Benton Sees It," *PM*, December 24, 1945, quoted in Doss, *Benton, Pollock, and the Politics of Modernism*, 239. For more on the "Business First" mentality, see Benton, "American Regionalism," 158–60.

295 *"American folk operetta"*: Benton, "After," 312.

295 *"I had a few conversations"*: Ibid.

295 *"I saw what a tough"*: Ibid. For more on Benton's Hollywood projects, see Doss, *Benton, Pollock, and the Politics of Modernism*, 240–52.

295 *"Working all day"*: Benton, "After," 312.

295 *"death so depressed me"*: Ibid., 313.

295 *"public hoopla"*: Ibid.

295 *Benton recalled the vacation fondly*: Ibid., 323–24.

296 *"traditional behavior"*: Benton, "And Still After," 328.

296 *"The easy-going friendliness"*: Ibid., 328–29.

296 *"urbanist developments"*: Ibid., 329.

296 *"I like the way they"*: Benton, *Artist in America*, 200.

297 *"Why not"*: Benton, "And Still After," 347.

297 *"Are you still making"*: Benton, "The President and Me: The Intimate Story," in "Highballs and High Stakes: The President, the Painter, and the Truman Library Mural," ed. Tim Fox, *Gateway Heritage* 16 (Winter 1995–1996): 5.

298 *"affably"*: Ibid., 6.

298 *"I don't know whether"*: Ibid.

298 *"It seems that Tom Benton"*: Truman letter quoted in Raymond H. Geselbracht, *"Independence and the Opening of the West*: Harry S. Truman, Thomas Hart Benton, and the Making of the Mural," *Prologue: Quarterly of the National Archives and Records Administration* 41 (Spring 2009): 14.

298 *"I don't like Mr. Benton's"*: Truman letter quoted ibid., 16.

298 *"The figure stood out"*: Benton, "President and Me," 6.

298 *"I never knew that artists"*: Ibid., 7.

299 *"I was now his man"*: Ibid., 11.

299 *"I discovered that beneath"*: Benton, "And Still After," 349.

299 *"I sensed that he"*: Ibid., 350.

299 *"Too bad"*: Benton, "President and Me," 9.

299 *"another loyal and dependable"*: Ibid.

299 *"stocky"*: Ibid., 7.

299 *"Protestant iconoclasm"*: Ibid.

299 *"He was also a thinker"*: Ibid., 14.

300 *"a first class historian"*: Benton in Milton F. Perry, "Oral History Interview with Thomas Hart Benton," April 21, 1964, Truman Presidential Museum and Library, http://www.trumanlibrary.org/oralhist/benton.htm, accessed July 14, 2009.

300 *"imagistic"*: Benton, "President and Me," 14.

300 *"provide an important"*: Ibid., 12.

300 *"appalled"*: Ibid.

300 *"In all the time I worked"*: Benton in Perry, "Oral History Interview with Thomas Hart Benton."

301 *"rickety motel"*: Benton, "And Still After," 358.

301 *"Indian men and women"*: Charles Banks Wilson, "On the Trail with Tom Benton," *Oklahoma's Orbit*, May 13, 1962, 27.

301 *"I've read about artists"*: Ibid.

301 *"Since he is never"*: Ibid., 28.

301 *"polished off"*: Ibid.

302 *"As our people come"*: Warren quoted in Geselbracht, *"Independence and the Opening of the West,"* 21.

302 *"America's 'continental destiny'"*: "Mural for Truman," *New York Times*, March 12, 1961, SM52.

302 *"in the 1920s and 1930s"*: Baigell, *Thomas Hart Benton*, 180–83.

302 *"the best muralist"*: Truman quoted in Geselbracht, *"Independence and the Opening of the West,"* 21.

303 *"had found for all of our"*: Benton, "President and Me," 13.

11. AT WAR

304 *"quaint grandpappy"*: William A. McWhirter, "Tom Benton at 80, Still at War with Bores and Boobs," *Life*, October 3, 1969, 66.

304 *"crude, insensitive, rich"*: Ibid.

304 *"the other part of Benton's war"*: Ibid., 68.

304 *"I was once able"*: Ibid.

305 *"commercial significance"*: Dennis, *Renegade Regionalists*, 60.

305 *"While this attention"*: Hegeman, *Patterns for America*, 129. For more on this topic, see Louis Wirth, "The Limitations of Regionalism," in *Regionalism in America*, ed. Merrill Jensen (Madison: University of Wisconsin Press, 1965), 382–84.

305 *"American scene"*: Boswell quoted in Harris, *Federal Art and National Culture*, 154.

305 *"disintegrated"*: E. P. Richardson, "Regionalism in American Painting," in Jensen, *Regionalism in America*, 270, 272.

305 *"it is no surprise"*: Doss, *Benton, Pollock, and the Politics of Modernism*, 281. Doss quotes Benton, "And Still After," in *Artist in America*, 368.

305 *"was seen as a failed style"*: Ibid., 301.

305 *"the promise of the Virgin Land"*: Noble, *Death of a Nation*, 161.

306 *"almost completely frustrated"*: Benton, "After," in *Artist in America*, 297.

306 *"well off the beam"*: Ibid., 315.

306 *"We found the bottom"*: Ibid., 316.

306 *"the coteries of high-brows"*: Ibid.

306 *"succeeded in destroying"*: Ibid.

306 *"neurotic"*: Ibid., 317.

306 *"The transfer of American"*: Benton, "And Still After," 326–27.

306 *"Without a belief"*: Benton, "American Regionalism," 191.

306 *"When this new America"*: Benton, "Death of Grant Wood," 148.

306 *"refuse of America's"*: Ibid.

306 *"worry over"*: Benton, "After," 320–21.

307 *"never learned to cover"*: Benton, "John Curry," 88.

307 *"You must feel"*: Benton, "After," 321.

307 *"I don't know"*: Curry quoted ibid.

307 *"put inventive method"*: Ibid., 318.

307 *"This was somewhat"*: Benton, "And Still After," 330.

308 *"I could feel the winds"*: Benton, "After," 296.

308 *"old-fashioned isolationist"*: Ibid., 297.

308 *"The American scene"*: Ibid.

308 *"I have myself succumbed"*: Benton to Weaver, March 18, 1942, Benton Correspondence, cabinet 1, drawer 3, Benton Curatorial Files.

308 *"had an idea"*: Benton, "After," 298.

308 *"These, departing from any"*: Ibid.

309 *"this is no local"*: Lewenthal quoted ibid.

309 *"All in all"*: Ibid., 299.

309 *"For many Americans"*: Whiting, *Antifascism in American Art*, 117.

310 *"shows enthusiastic G.I. Joes"*: Doss, *Benton, Pollock, and the Politics of Modernism*, 283.

310 *"white heat"*: "The War and Thomas Benton," *Art Digest*, April 15, 1942, 13.

310 *"war as war"*: Manny Farber, "Thomas Benton's War," *New Republic*, April 20, 1942, 542.

310 *"There is so little emotional"*: Ibid., 543.

310 *"psychotic outburst"*: Henry Adams in *Thomas Hart Benton*, dir. Ken Burns.

310 *"There are no bathing beauties"*: Benton, "The Year of Peril," reprinted in Baigell, *Thomas Hart Benton Miscellany*, 94. Benton published two versions of this essay: the one cited here and another for the Abbott Laboratories pamphlet. See Benton, *The Year of Peril: A Series of War Paintings by Thomas Hart Benton* (Chicago: Abbott Laboratories, 1942).

310 *"hysterical reaction"*: Doss, *Benton, Pollock, and the Politics of Modernism*, 289.

310 *"magic realism"*: Ibid.

311 *"vague Baroque mannerism"*: Frankfurter quoted ibid., 297.

311 *"Looky here Pop"*: Anonymous woman quoted in Benton, "After," 302. Also see Quentin Reynolds, "Take 'Er Down," *Collier's*, November 4, 1944, 16–19, 42, 44. Abbott Laboratories eventually donated the illustrations to the Naval Historical Center, Washington, D.C., and they are available to view in an online exhibition at http://www.history.navy.mil/ac/benton/benton1.htm.

311 *"was almost too wholly"*: Benton, "After," 309.

311 *"conclusive to the maintenance"*: Ibid., 310.

312 *"national propaganda"*: Mumford quoted in Donald L. Miller, *Lewis Mumford*, 389.

312 *"white hot rancor"*: Ibid.

312 *"I want you to know"*: Mumford to Benton, April 25, 1942, Benton Correspondence, cabinet 1, drawer 3, Benton Curatorial Files.

312 *"Your professed aims"*: Mumford to Johnson, February 28, 1965, quoted in Donald L. Miller, *Lewis Mumford*, 513.

312 *"an assault upon"*: Mumford quoted in Sanka Knox, "Mumford Speech Rankles Benton," *New York Times*, May 20, 1965, 40.

312 *"I'm not going to"*: Benton quoted in Norman Mailer, "Rounding Camelot," in Louis Auchincloss and John Updike, *A Century of Arts and Letters: The History of the National Institute of Arts and Letters and the American Academy of Arts and Letters* (New York: Columbia University Press, 1998), 187.

313 *"I left because"*: Benton quoted in Knox, "Mumford Speech Rankles Benton," 40.

313 *"I protest your talk"*: Benton to Mumford, telegram, May 19, 1965, Lewis Mumford Papers, Rare Book and Manuscript Library, University of Pennsylvania.

313 *"the sad thing"*: Benton quoted in Robert Wernick, "Down the Wide Missouri with an 'Old S.O.B.,'" *Saturday Evening Post*, October 23, 1965, 96.

313 *"if not a friendship"*: Benton, "Lewis Mumford Affair," notebook entry, microfilm reel 2327, Benton Papers.

313 *"It was pretty dreadful"*: Sophia Mumford to Adams, April 4, 1988, American Original Exhibition Records.

314 *"harness the power"*: Adams, *Tom and Jack*, 14.

314 *"Jack would not"*: Benton quoted in Naifeh and Smith, *Jackson Pollock*, 229.

314 *"deficiencies"*: Benton, "And Still After," 341.

314 *"very original"*: Ibid., 340.

315 *"the strongest abstract paintings"*: Clement Greenberg, "Art," *Nation*, November 27, 1943, 621.

316 *"It is Pollock's culture"*: Clement Greenberg, "Art," *Nation*, January 24, 1948, 107.

316 *"His new work"*: Ibid., 108.

316 *"The conclusion forces"*: Clement Greenberg, "The Decline of Cubism," *Partisan Review* 10, no. 3 (March 1948): 369.

316 *"The big moment"*: Rosenberg, "American Action Painters," 22.

316 *"The gesture on the canvas"*: Ibid., 23.

316 *"communication breaks"*: Robert Coates, "The Art Galleries," *New Yorker*, January 17, 1948, 57.

317 *"staring steadily"*: Alonzo Lansford, "Fifty-seventh Street in Review: Automatic Pollock," *Art Digest*, January 15, 1948, 19.

317 *"the only excuse"*: Benton, interview in *Demcourier*, February 1943, reprinted in Baigell, *Thomas Hart Benton Miscellany*, 97.

317 *"denial of all formal"*: Benton, "What's Holding Back American Art?" *Saturday Review of Literature*, December 15, 1951, reprinted in Baigell, *Thomas Hart Benton Miscellany*, 107.

317 *"was the most discussed"*: Benton, "And Still After," 332–33.

317 *"judging from his early"*: Ibid., 338.

317 *"recognized their sensuous"*: Ibid., 339.

317 *"Very much an artist"*: Benton to the Guggenheim Foundation quoted in Solomon, *Jackson Pollock*, 171.

318 *"The regionalist ideal"*: Donald Kuspit, "Regionalism Reconsidered," *Art in America*, July–August 1976, 66.

318 *"the most destructive tendency"*: Benton, "And Still After," 341–42.

318 *"The picture must be"*: Mark Rothko, "The Romantics Were Prompted," in Herschel B. Chipp, *Theories of Modern Art: A Source Book by Artists and Critics* (Berkeley: University of California Press, 1968), 549.

319 *"sideshow business"*: Benton, "And Still After," 343.

EPILOGUE: AT EASE

321 *"sincere regret"*: Benton, *Artist in America*, 48.

321 *"The subject matter"*: Stanton Macdonald-Wright, *Santa Monica Library Murals* (Los Angeles: Angelus Press, 1935), 2.

321 *"complimenting Benton's"*: South, "Invention and Imagination," 17.

322 *"I'm very fond of Tom"*: Oral History Interview with Stanton Macdonald-Wright.

322 *"they will never know anything"*: Craven, *Modern Art*, 344.

322 *"mean, vindictive"*: Craven, "Thomas Hart Benton," 38–39.

323 *"losing the best art teacher"*: Craven quoted in Adams, *American Original*, 308.

323 *"more realistic than"*: Thomas Craven, "Thomas Hart Benton and *The Grapes of Wrath*," preface to *The Grapes of Wrath*, by John Steinbeck (New York: Limited Editions Club, 1940), xxii.

323 *"Thomas Hart Benton"*: Thomas Craven, "A Letter to the University About Thomas Hart Benton," in *Thomas Hart Benton*, exhibition catalog (Lawrence: University of Kansas Museum of Art, 1958), n.p.

324 *"Suddenly I felt tired"*: Benton, "After," in *Artist in America*, 303–304.

324 *"genuinely sensitive to the poetry"*: Burroughs, *Thomas Hart Benton*, 113.

324 *"soft shoe routine"*: Ibid., 124.

324 *"horses, mules, cows"*: Ibid., 129.

325 *"I know the Vineyard"*: Ibid.

325 *"We watched the hesitant"*: Thielen quoted in "The Hurricane of '38: People and Events: Benedict Thielen Tries to Save His Maid, Josephine Clarke," PBS, http://www.pbs.org/wgbh/amex/hurricane38/peopleevents/p_thielen.html, accessed July 21, 2009.

325 *"course I ain't lived on"*: Tilton quoted in Burroughs, *Thomas Hart Benton*, 142.

326 *"was pleasantly reassured"*: Ibid., 156.

326 *"one of the finest"*: Elliot Bostwick Davis et al., *MFA Highlights: American Painting* (Boston: MFA Publications, Museum of Fine Arts, 2003), 200.

326 *"The Bentons rise"*: William A. McWhirter, "Tom Benton at 80, Still at War with Bores and Boobs," *Life*, October 3, 1969, 66.

327 *"Where the hell's"*: Harding quoted in Burroughs, *Thomas Hart Benton*, 188.

327 *"therapeutic absolutes"*: Wallace quoted in "'60 Minute' Reflection on Benton the Artist," *Kansas City Star*, October 8, 1978, 13C.

327 *"getting old"*: Mike Wallace with Gary Paul Gates, *Between You and Me: A Memoir* (New York: Hyperion, 2005), 145.

327 *"with a case"*: Ibid., 147.

327 *"Fully aware of"*: Ibid., 147–48.

327 *"We accept your art"*: Letter to *The Vineyard Gazette* quoted in Burroughs, *Thomas Hart Benton*, 189–90.

328 *"Thinking of you"*: Burroughs, *Thomas Hart Benton*, 197.

328 *"That's your opinion"*: Ibid.

328 *"the distinguished American painter"*: Tex Ritter and Joe Allison quoted in Fryd, "'The Sad Twang of Mountain Voices,'" 303–304.

328 *"intellectual curiosities"*: Benton, *Artist in America*, 46.

329 *"should show the roots"*: Ivey quoted in Fryd, "'Sad Twang of Mountain Voices,'" 306.

329 *"old boys"*: Benton, *Artist in America*, 112.

329 *"I like their plaintive"*: Ibid., 113.

329 *"These compositional devices"*: Fryd, "'Sad Twang of Mountain Voices,'" 308.

SELECTED BIBLIOGRAPHY

ARCHIVES

Alfred Stieglitz/Georgia O'Keeffe Archive. Yale Collection of American Literature. Beinecke Rare Book and Manuscript Library.

Associated American Artists Records, ca. 1934–1981. Archives of American Art. Smithsonian Institution.

Charles Pollock Papers, 1902–1990. Archives of American Art. Smithsonian Institution.

Eleanor Piacenza Papers regarding Thomas Hart Benton, 1915–1988. Archives of American Art. Smithsonian Institution.

John Weichsel Papers, 1905–1922. Archives of American Art. Smithsonian Institution.

Lewis Mumford Papers, ca. 1905–1987. Annenberg Rare Book and Manuscript Library. University of Pennsylvania, Philadelphia.

Matthew Baigell Papers. Archives of American Art. Smithsonian Institution.

Maynard Walker Gallery Records, 1847–1973. Archives of American Art. Smithsonian Institution.

Oral History Interview with Stanton Macdonald-Wright, April 13–September 16, 1964. Archives of American Art. Smithsonian Institution.

Oral History Interview [conducted by Paul Cummings] with Thomas Hart Benton, July 23–24, 1973. Archives of American Art. Smithsonian Institution.

Reminiscences of Thomas Hart Benton, September 20–23, 1972. Columbia University Oral History Research Office Collection.

Stanton Macdonald-Wright Papers, 1907–1973. Archives of American Art. Smithsonian Institution.

Thomas Hart Benton: An American Original Exhibition Records, 1985–1990. Nelson-Atkins Museum of Art Archives, Kansas City, Mo.

[Thomas Hart] Benton Curatorial Files. Nelson-Atkins Museum of Art, Kansas City, Mo.

Thomas Hart Benton Miscellaneous Printed Material, 1935–1978. Archives of American Art. Smithsonian Institution.

Thomas Hart Benton Papers, 1906–1975. Archives of American Art. Smithsonian Institution.

BY BENTON

"Ali." *New Letters: A Continuation of the University Review* 38, no. 1 (Fall 1971): 75–91.

"America and/or Alfred Stieglitz." *Common Sense* 4 (January 1935): 22–25.

An American in Art: A Professional and Technical Autobiography. Lawrence: University Press of Kansas, 1969.

"American Regionalism: A Personal History of the Movement." *University of Kansas City Review* 18 (1951): 41–75. Reprinted as appendix in Benton, *An American in Art: A Professional and Technical Autobiography.* Lawrence: University Press of Kansas, 1969, 145–92.

"America's Yesterday: In the Ozark Mountains—Life and Customs on a Forgotten Frontier." *Travel,* July 1934, 6–11, 45–56.

"Answers to Ten Questions." *Art Digest,* March 15, 1935, 20–21.

"Art and Nationalism." *Modern Monthly* 8 (May 1934): 232–36.

"Art and Reality: Reflections on the Meaning of Art in the Social Order." *University of Kansas City Review* 16 (Spring 1950): 198–216.

"Art and Social Struggle: A Reply to Rivera." *University Review* 2 (Winter 1935): 71–78.

An Artist in America. 4th rev. ed. Columbia: University of Missouri Press, 1983.

"An Artist in America." Interview by Robert S. Gallagher. *American Heritage,* June 1973, 40–48, 90.

The Arts of Life in America: A Series of Murals by Thomas Hart Benton. New York: Whitney Museum of American Art, 1932.

"Art vs. the Mellon Gallery." *Common Sense* 10 (June 1941): 172–73.

"Blast by Benton." *Art Digest,* April 15, 1941, 6, 19.

"Confessions of an American." *Common Sense* 6 (July 1937): 7–9; *Common Sense* 6 (August 1937): 10–14; *Common Sense* 6 (September 1937): 19–22.

"The Dead and the Living." *University Review* 7 (March 1941): 171–76.

"Death of Grant Wood." *University Review* 8 (Spring 1942): 147–48.

"Disaster on the Kaw." *New Republic,* November 19, 1951, 9–11.

"A Dream Fulfilled." In *Indiana: A Hoosier History Based on the Mural Paintings of Thomas Hart Benton,* by David Laurance Chambers, 49. Indianapolis: Bobbs-Merrill, 1933.

"Form and the Subject." *Arts* 5 (June 1924): 303–8.

"The Intimate Story." Unpublished typescript. Thomas Hart and Rita Piacenza Testamentary Trusts, UMB Bank, Kansas City, Mo.

"John Curry." *University of Kansas City Review* 12 (Winter 1946): 87–90.

"The Mechanics of Form Organization in Painting." *Arts* 10 (November 1926): 285–89; 10 (December 1926): 340–42; 11 (January 1927): 43–44; 11 (February 1927): 95–96; 11 (March 1927): 145–48.

"My American Epic in Paint." *Creative Art,* December 1928, xxx–xxxvi.

"On the American Scene." *Art Front* 1, no. 4 (1935): 3, 8.

"Painting and Propaganda Don't Mix." *Saturday Review of Literature,* December 24, 1960, 16–17.

"What's Holding Back American Art?" *Saturday Review of Literature,* December 15, 1951, 9–11, 38.

"The Year of Peril." *University Review* 8 (Spring 1942): 178–88.

OTHER SOURCES

Abrahams, Edward. "Alfred Stieglitz and/or Thomas Hart Benton." *Arts Magazine* 55 (June 1981): 108–13.

Adams, Henry. *Boardman Robinson: American Muralist and Illustrator, 1876–1952*. Exhibition catalog. Colorado Springs: Colorado Springs Fine Arts Center, 1996.

———. *Thomas Hart Benton: An American Original*. New York: Knopf, 1989.

———. *Thomas Hart Benton: Drawing from Life*. New York: Abbeville Press, in association with the Henry Art Gallery, University of Washington, Seattle, 1990.

———. *Tom and Jack: The Intertwined Lives of Thomas Hart Benton and Jackson Pollock*. New York: Bloomsbury Press, 2009.

Agee, William C. "Willard Huntington Wright and the Synchromists: Notes on the Forum Exhibition." *Archives of American Art Journal* 30, nos. 1–4 (1990): 88–93. Reprint of vol. 24, no. 2 (1984): 10–15.

Alexander, Thomas M. *John Dewey's Theory of Art, Experience, and Nature: The Horizons of Feeling*. Albany: State University of New York Press, 1987.

American Life and Lore: Thomas Hart Benton and the Associated American Artists. Exhibition catalog. Tempe: Arizona State University Art Museum, 1989.

Antliff, Allan. *Anarchist Modernism: Art, Politics, and the First American Avant-Garde*. Chicago: University of Chicago Press, 2001.

———. "Cosmic Modernism: Elie Nadelman, Adolf Wolff, and the Materialist Aesthetics of John Weichsel." *Archives of American Art Journal* 38, no. 4 (1998): 20–29.

"Artist Thomas Hart Benton Hunts Communists and Fascists in Michigan." *Life*, July 26, 1937, 22–25.

Baigell, Matthew. *Artist and Identity in Twentieth-Century America*. New York: Cambridge University Press, 2000.

———. *Thomas Hart Benton*. New York: Abrams, 1974.

———. "Thomas Hart Benton in the 1920's." *Art Journal* 29, no. 4 (Summer 1970): 422–29.

———. ed. *A Thomas Hart Benton Miscellany: Selections from His Published Opinions, 1916–1960*. Lawrence: University Press of Kansas, 1971.

Baigell, Matthew, and Milly Heyd, eds. *Complex Identities: Jewish Consciousness and Modern Art*. New Brunswick, N.J.: Rutgers University Press, 2001.

Bailly, Austen Barron. "Painting the *American Historical Epic*: Thomas Hart Benton and Race, 1919–1936." Ph.D. diss., University of California, Santa Barbara, 2009.

Balken, Debra Bricker. *After Many Springs: Regionalism, Modernism, and the Midwest*. Des Moines: Des Moines Art Center, distributed by Yale University Press, 2009.

Beard, Charles. *An Economic Interpretation of the Constitution of the United States*. 1913. Reprint, Mineola, N.Y.: Dover, 2004.

Beard, Charles A., and William Beard. *The American Leviathan: The Republic in the Machine Age*. New York: Macmillan, 1930.

Bender, Thomas. *New York Intellect: A History of Intellectual Life in New York City, from 1750 to the Beginnings of Our Own Time*. Baltimore: Johns Hopkins University Press, 1988.

Benton in the Ozarks: Selections from the Thomas Hart and Rita P. Benton Testamentary Trusts. Exhibition catalog. Little Rock: Arkansas Arts Center, 1986.

Benton on the Vineyard. New York: Owen Gallery, 2008.

"Benton Quits Arts Academy over Remarks by Mumford." *New York Times*, May 28, 1965.

Benton's Bentons: Selections from the Thomas Hart Benton and Rita P. Benton Trusts. Exhibition catalog. Lawrence: Spencer Museum of Art, University of Kansas, 1980.

Berardi, Marianne. *Under the Influence: The Students of Thomas Hart Benton*. Exhibition catalog. St. Joseph, Mo.: Albrecht-Kemper Museum of Art, 1993.

Berube, Maurice R. "John Dewey and the Abstract Expressionists." *Educational Theory* 48, no. 2 (June 1998): 211–27.

Best, Gary Dean. *The Retreat from Liberalism: Collectivists Versus Progressives in the New Deal Years*. Westport, Conn.: Praeger, 2002.

Boswell, Peyton, Jr. *Modern American Painting*. New York: Dodd, Mead, 1940.

Braun, Emily, and Thomas Branchick. *Thomas Hart Benton: The America Today Murals*. New York: Equitable Life Assurance Society of the United States, 1985.

Brennan, Marcia. *Painting Gender, Constructing Theory: The Alfred Stieglitz Circle and American Formalist Aesthetics*. Cambridge, Mass.: MIT Press, 2001.

Brewer, Nanette Esseck. "A Hoosier History Lesson: Thomas Hart Benton's Indiana Murals, John Dewey, and Progressivism." Master's thesis, Indiana University, 1998.

Brooks, Van Wyck. "On Creating a Usable Past." *Dial*, April 1918, 337–41.

Broun, Elizabeth. "Thomas Hart Benton: A Politician in Art." *Smithsonian Studies in American Art* 1, no. 1 (Spring 1987): 59–77.

Brown, Elizabeth, and Homer Brown. "Thomas Hart Benton Comes Home." *Midwest Quarterly* 4, no. 4 (1963): 315–33.

Burck, Jacob. "Benton Sees Red." *Art Front* 1, no. 4 (1935): 4.

Burroughs, Polly. *Thomas Hart Benton: A Portrait*. Garden City, N.Y.: Doubleday, 1981.

Canaday, John. "Tom Benton of Mazura Comes Back to Joplin—Grown Up." *New York Times*, April 8, 1973.

Chafe, William Henry. *The Achievement of American Liberalism: The New Deal and Its Legacies*. New York: Columbia University Press, 2003.

Christ, John X. "Stuart Davis and the Politics of Experience." *American Art* 22, no. 2 (Summer 2008): 42–63.

Commemorating the 50th Anniversary of the Forum Exhibition of Modern American Painters, March 1916. New York: ACA Heritage Gallery, 1966.

Connor, Celeste. *Democratic Visions: Art and Theory of the Stieglitz Circle, 1924–1934*. Berkeley: University of California Press, 2001.

Corn, Wanda M. *The Great American Thing: Modern Art and National Identity, 1915–1935*. Berkeley: University of California Press, 1999.

Coss, Louis. "Missouri Murals Split Home Critics." *New York Times*, January 17, 1937.

Cozad, Mary. *Neosho, the Story of a Missouri Town: A Short History*. Neosho, Mo.: Safeway Stores, 1965.

Craven, Thomas. *Catalogue of a Loan Exhibition of Drawings and Paintings by Thomas Hart Benton, with an Evaluation of the Artist and His Work*. Chicago: Lakeside Press Galleries, 1937.

———. *A Descriptive Catalogue of the Works of Thomas Hart Benton, Spotlighting the Important Periods During the Artist's Thirty-Two Years of Painting*. New York: Associated American Artists, 1939.

———. *Men of Art*. New York: Simon and Schuster, 1931.

———. *Modern Art: The Men, the Movements, the Meaning*. New York: Simon and Schuster, 1934.

———. "Thomas Hart Benton," *Scribner's Magazine*, October 1937, 33–40.

Cummings, Paul. *Artists in Their Own Words: Interviews*. New York: St. Martin's Press, 1979.

————. "The Art Students League, Part 1." *Archives of American Art Journal* 13, no. 1 (1973): 1–25.

Czestochowski, Joseph. *John Steuart Curry and Grant Wood: A Portrait of Rural America.* Columbia: University of Missouri Press, 1981.

Davis, Stuart. "Davis's Rejoinder to Thomas Benton." *Art Digest,* April 1, 1935, 12, 13, 26.

————. "The New York American Scene in Art." *Art Front* 1 (February 1935): 6.

"A Debate: Benton vs. Rivera." *New York Times,* December 22, 1935.

Denning, Michael. *The Cultural Front: The Laboring of American Culture in the Twentieth Century.* New York: Verso, 1998.

Dennis, James M. *Renegade Regionalists: The Modern Independence of Grant Wood, Thomas Hart Benton, and John Steuart Curry.* Madison: University of Wisconsin Press, 1998.

Dewey, John. "Americanism and Localism." In *Characters and Events: Popular Essays in Social and Political Philosophy.* New York: Henry Holt, 1929, 537–41.

————. *Art as Experience.* 1934. Reprint, New York: Perigee, 1980.

Dickstein, Morris. *Dancing in the Dark: A Cultural History of the Great Depression.* New York: W. W. Norton, 2009.

Dos Passos, John. *U.S.A.: The 42nd Parallel/1919/The Big Money.* New York: Library of America, 1996.

Doss, Erika. "The Art of Cultural Politics: From Regionalism to Abstract Expressionism." In *Recasting America: Culture and Politics in the Age of Cold War,* edited by Larry May. Chicago: University of Chicago Press, 1989.

————. *Benton, Pollock, and the Politics of Modernism: From Regionalism to Abstract Expressionism.* Chicago: University of Chicago Press, 1991.

————. "Catering to Consumerism: Associated American Artists and the Marketing of Modern Art, 1934–1958." *Winterthur Portfolio* 26, no. 2 (1991): 143–67.

————. "New Deal Politics and Regionalist Art: Thomas Hart Benton's *A Social History of the State of Indiana.*" *Prospects* 17 (1992): 353–78.

Dreishpoon, Douglas. Introduction to *Benton's America: Works on Paper and Selected Paintings.* New York: Hirschl and Adler Galleries, 1991.

Edelman, Nancy. *The Thomas Hart Benton Murals in the Missouri State Capitol: A Social History of the State of Missouri.* [Jefferson City]: Missouri State Council on the Arts, 1975.

Eldredge, Charles C. *John Steuart Curry's Hoover and the Flood: Painting Modern History.* Chapel Hill: University of North Carolina Press, 2007.

Fath, Creekmore. *The Lithographs of Thomas Hart Benton.* Austin: University of Texas Press, 1979.

Fletcher, John Gould. "The Stieglitz Spoof." *American Review* 4 (March 1935): 588–602.

The Forum Exhibition of Modern American Painters. New York: Mitchell Kennerley, 1916.

Foster, Kathleen A., Nanette Esseck Brewer, and Margaret Contompasis. *Thomas Hart Benton and the Indiana Murals.* Bloomington: Indiana University Art Museum, in association with Indiana University Press, 2000.

Fox, Tim. "Highballs and High Stakes: The President, the Painter, and the Truman Library Mural." *Gateway Heritage* 16, no. 3 (1995–1996): 2–17.

Frank, Waldo, et al. *America and Alfred Stieglitz: A Collective Portrait.* Garden City, N.Y.: Doubleday, Doran, 1934.

Fryd, Vivien Green. "'The Sad Twang of Mountain Voices': Thomas Hart Benton's *Sources of Country Music*." In "Readin' Country Music: Steel Guitars, Opry Stars and Honky Tonk Bars," ed. Cecelia Tichi, special issue, *South Atlantic Quarterly* 94, no. 1 (1995): 301–35.

Glass, Newman Robert. "Theory and Practice in the Experience of Art: John Dewey and the Barnes Foundation." *Journal of Aesthetic Education* 31, no. 3 (1997): 91–105.

Goodwyn, Lawrence. *Democratic Promise: The Populist Movement in America*. New York: Oxford University Press, 1976.

Greenberg, Clement. *Clement Greenberg: The Collected Essays and Criticism*. Chicago: University of Chicago Press, 1986.

Greenough, Sarah. *Modern Art and America: Alfred Stieglitz and His New York Galleries*. Washington, D.C.: National Gallery of Art, 2000.

Grieve, Victoria. *The Federal Art Project and the Creation of Middlebrow Culture*. Urbana: University of Illinois Press, 2009.

Gruber, Richard J. *Thomas Hart Benton and the American South*. Exhibition catalog. Augusta, Ga.: Morris Museum of Art, 1998.

———. "Thomas Hart Benton: Teaching and Art Theory." Ph.D. diss., University of Kansas, 1987.

Guedon, Mary Scholz. *Regionalist Art: Thomas Hart Benton, John Steuart Curry, and Grant Wood: A Guide to the Literature*. Metuchen, N.J.: Scarecrow Press, 1982.

Hamby, Alonzo L. *Beyond the New Deal: Harry S. Truman and American Liberalism*. New York: Columbia University Press, 1973.

Harris, Jonathan. *Federal Art and National Culture: The Politics of Identity in New Deal America*. New York: Cambridge University Press, 1995.

Hegeman, Susan. *Patterns for America: Modernism and the Concept of Culture*. Princeton, N.J.: Princeton University Press, 1999.

Hemingway, Andrew. *Artists on the Left: American Artists and the Communist Movement, 1926–1956*. New Haven, Conn.: Yale University Press, 2002.

———. "Meyer Schapiro and Marxism in the 1930s." *Oxford Art Journal* 17, no. 1 (1994): 13–29.

Hills, Patricia. "1936: Meyer Schapiro, *Art Front*, and the Popular Front." *Oxford Art Journal* 17, no. 1 (1994): 30–41.

Hofstadter, Richard. *Anti-intellectualism in American Life*. New York: Knopf, 1963.

———. *The Progressive Historians: Turner, Beard, Parrington*. New York: Knopf, 1968.

Horn, Axel. "Jackson Pollock: The Hollow and the Bump." *Northfield (Minn.) Carleton Miscellany* 7, no. 3 (Summer 1966): 80–87.

Huntington, Gale. "Chilmark's Deaf: Valued Citizens." *Dukes County Intelligencer* 21 (1981): 98–102.

Hurlburt, Laurance P. *The Mexican Muralists in the United States*. Albuquerque: University of New Mexico Press, 1989.

Hurt, Douglas R., and Mary K. Dains, eds. *Thomas Hart Benton: Artist, Writer, and Intellectual*. Columbia: State Historical Society of Missouri, 1989.

Hyland, Douglas. "Benton's Images of American Labor." In *Benton's Bentons: Selections from the Thomas Hart Benton and Rita P. Benton Trusts*, 23–31. Lawrence: Spencer Museum of Art, University of Kansas, 1980.

Jackson, Phillip W. *John Dewey and the Lessons of Art*. New Haven, Conn.: Yale University Press, 1998.

James, Larry A., and Sybil Jobe, comps. *Neosho: Tom Benton's All-America City: A Tribute to "The Neosho Daily News."* Neosho, Mo.: Newton County Historical Society, 1997.

Jewell, Edward Alden. *Have We an American Art?* New York: Longmans, Green, 1939.

Joplin's First 100 Years. Joplin, Mo.: Published as a centennial souvenir by the Joplin Globe Publishing Co., 1973.

Junker, Patricia A. *John Steuart Curry: Inventing the Middle West.* New York: Hudson Hills Press, 1998.

Karmel, Pepe, and Kirk Varnedoe, eds. *Jackson Pollock: Interviews, Articles, and Reviews.* New York: Museum of Modern Art, distributed by Harry N. Abrams, 1999.

Kellner, Bruce. *The Last Dandy, Ralph Barton: American Artist, 1891–1931.* Columbia: University of Missouri Press, 1991.

Kendall, M. Sue. *Rethinking Regionalism: John Steuart Curry and the Kansas Mural Controversy.* Washington, D.C.: Smithsonian Institution Press, 1986.

Klinkenborg, Verlyn. "Thomas Hart Benton Came from Missouri—and He Showed 'Em." *Smithsonian* 20, no. 1 (1989): 82–101.

Kushner, Marilyn S. *Morgan Russell.* New York: Hudson Hills Press, 1990.

Ladner, Barbara E. "Thomas Hart Benton's 'Jealous Lover' and the Ballad of Middle-Brow Culture." *Prospects* 15 (1990): 283–324.

Landau, Ellen G. *Jackson Pollock.* New York: Abrams, 1989.

Landgren, Marchal E. *Years of Art: The Story of the Art Students League of New York.* New York: Robert M. McBride, 1940.

Langa, Helen. *Radical Art: Printmaking and the Left in 1930s New York.* Berkeley: University of California Press, 2004.

Lears, Jackson. *Fables of Abundance: A Cultural History of Advertising in America.* New York: Basic Books, 1994.

Leja, Michael. *Reframing Abstract Expressionism: Subjectivity and Painting in the 1940s.* New Haven, Conn.: Yale University Press, 1993.

Levin, Gail. *Synchromism and American Color Abstraction, 1910–1925.* New York: G. Braziller, 1978.

———. "Thomas Hart Benton, Synchromism, and Abstract Art." *Arts Magazine* 56 (December 1981): 144–48.

Lewison, Jeremy. *Interpreting Pollock.* London: Tate Gallery, 1999.

Lieban, Helen. "Thomas Benton: American Mural Painter." *Design* 36 (December 1934): 26, 31–34.

"*Life* Goes to a Party: With Tom Benton, Grant Wood, and John Curry at the Kansas City Beaux Arts Ball." *Life,* March 21, 1938, 62–64.

Lofton, Kathryn, and Matthew Pratt Guterl, eds. "Thomas Hart Benton's Indiana Murals at 75." Special issue, *Indiana Magazine of History,* June 2009.

Loughery, John. *Alias S. S. Van Dine: The Man Who Created Philo Vance.* New York: Charles Scribner's Sons, 1992.

Lowe, Sue Davidson. *Stieglitz: A Memoir/Biography.* New York: Farrar, Straus and Giroux, 1983.

Marcell, David W. *Progress and Pragmatism: James, Dewey, Beard, and the American Idea of Progress.* Westport, Conn.: Greenwood Press, 1974.

Marchand, Roland. *Advertising the American Dream: Making Way for Modernity, 1920–1940.* Berkeley: University of California Press, 1986.

Marling, Karal Ann. "Thomas Hart Benton's *Boomtown*: Regionalism Redefined." *Prospects* 6 (1981): 73–137.

————. *Tom Benton and His Drawings: A Biographical Essay and a Collection of His Sketches, Studies, and Mural Cartoons.* Columbia: University of Missouri Press, 1985.

Mazow, Leo G. "Regionalist Radio: Thomas Hart Benton on Art for Your Sake." *Art Bulletin* 90 (March 2008): 101–22.

————. *Shallow Creek: Thomas Hart Benton and American Waterways.* Exhibition catalog. University Park: Palmer Museum of Art, Pennsylvania State University, distributed by Pennsylvania State University Press, 2007.

————. *Thomas Hart Benton and the American Sound.* University Park: Pennsylvania State University Press, forthcoming.

McKinzie, Robert D. *The New Deal for Artists.* Princeton, N.J.: Princeton University Press, 1973.

Medearis, Roger. "Student of Thomas Hart Benton." *Smithsonian Studies in American Art* 4, no. 3 (1990): 46–61.

Menand, Louis. *The Metaphysical Club.* New York: Farrar, Straus and Giroux, 2001.

Mencken, H. L., George Jean Nathan, and Willard Huntington Wright. *Europe After 8:15.* New York: John Lane, 1914.

Meyer, Richard E. "The Outlaw: A Distinctive American Folktype." *Journal of the Folklore Institute* 17, nos. 2–3 (1980): 94–124.

Miller, Donald L. *Lewis Mumford: A Life.* New York: Grove Press, 1989.

Miller, John E. "Midwestern Regionalism During the 1930s: A Democratic Art with Continuing Appeal." *Mid America* 83, no. 2 (2001): 71–93.

————. "Rose Wilder Lane and Thomas Hart Benton: A Turn Toward History During the 1930s." *American Studies* 37, no. 2 (1996): 83–101.

Moore, David Ryan. "Exiled America: Sherwood Anderson, Thomas Hart Benton, Benjamin A. Botkin, Constance Rourke, Arthur Raper, and the Great Depression." Ph.D. diss., Brown University, 1992.

Mumford, Lewis. *The Lewis Mumford Reader*, edited by Donald L. Miller. New York: Pantheon Books, 1986.

————. *Mumford on Modern Art in the 1930s.* Edited by Robert Wojtowicz. Berkeley: University of California Press, 2007.

————. *Sketches from Life: The Autobiography of Lewis Mumford: The Early Years.* New York: Dial Press, 1982.

————. *The Story of Utopias.* New York: Boni and Liveright, 1922.

————. "The Three Bentons." *New Yorker,* April 20, 1935, 48.

Naifeh, Steven, and Gregory White Smith. *Jackson Pollock: An American Saga.* New York: Clarkson N. Potter, 1989.

Noble, David W. *Death of a Nation: American Culture and the End of Exceptionalism.* Minneapolis: University of Minnesota Press, 2002.

Norman, Dorothy. *Alfred Stieglitz: An American Seer.* New York: Random House, 1973.

Nye, Russel B. *Midwestern Progressive Politics: A Historical Study of Its Origins and Development, 1870–1958.* East Lansing: Michigan State College Press, 1951.

O'Connor, Francis V. *Federal Support for the Visual Arts: The New Deal and Now.* Greenwich, Conn.: New York Graphic Society, 1969.

————. "The Genesis of Jackson Pollock: 1912–43." *Artforum,* May 1967, 16–23.

Piacenza, Eleanor. "Rita Piacenza Benton: 'Without Her, I'd Have Been a Bum!'" *Dukes County Intelligencer* 31, no. 2 (1989): 87–111.

Platt, Susan. *Art and Politics in the 1930s: Modernism, Marxism, and Americanism.* New York: Midmarch Arts Press, 1999.

Polcari, Stephen. "Thomas Hart Benton and Jackson Pollock." *Arts Magazine*, March 1979, 120–24.

Potter, Jeffrey. *To a Violent Grave: An Oral Biography of Jackson Pollock.* Wainscott, N.Y.: Pushcart, 1987.

Powers, Sarah G. "Images of Tension: City and Country in the Work of Charles Sheeler, Thomas Hart Benton, and Edward Hopper." Ph.D. diss., University of Pennsylvania, 2010.

Priddy, Bob. *Only the Rivers Are Peaceful: Thomas Hart Benton's Missouri Mural.* Independence, Mo.: Independence Press/Herald Publishing House, 1989.

Railton, Arthur R. "Tom Benton: Chilmarker." *Dukes County Intelligencer* 31, no. 2 (1989): 51–86.

Raverty, Dennis. *Struggle over the Modern: Purity and Experience in American Art Criticism, 1900–1960.* Madison, N.J.: Fairleigh Dickinson University Press, 2005.

Reed, Alma. *Orozco.* New York: Oxford University Press, 1946.

Renner, G. K. *Joplin: From Mining Town to Urban Center.* Northridge, Calif.: Windsor Publications, in association with the Joplin Historical Society, 1985.

Richter, Annett Claudia. "Fiddles, Harmonicas, and Banjos: Thomas Hart Benton and His Role in Constructing Popular Notions of American Folk Music and Musicians." Ph.D. diss., University of Minnesota, 2008.

Roosevelt, Theodore. *Thomas H. Benton.* Boston: Houghton, Mifflin, 1899.

Rose, Barbara. *American Art Since 1900: A Critical History.* London: Thames and Hudson, 1967.

Rosen, Robert C. *John Dos Passos: Politics and the Writer.* Lincoln: University of Nebraska Press, 1981.

Rosenberg, Harold. "The American Action Painters." *Art News*, December 1952, 24–28.

Saab, A. Joan. *For the Millions: American Art and Culture Between the Wars.* Philadelphia: University of Pennsylvania Press, 2004.

Schack, William. *Art and Argyrol: The Life and Career of Dr. Albert C. Barnes.* New York: Thomas Yoseloff, 1960.

Schapiro, Meyer. "Populist Realism." *Partisan Review* 4, no. 2 (January 1938): 53–57.

Schiller, Joyce K. *Passion, Politics, Prohibition: Benton's Bootleggers.* Winston-Salem, N.C.: Reynolda House Museum of American Art, 2002.

Shapiro, David. *Social Realism: Art as a Weapon.* New York: Ungar, 1973.

Shusterman, Richard. *Pragmatist Aesthetics: Living Beauty, Rethinking Art.* Oxford: Blackwell, 1992.

Small, Mildred. "'Sane People, Sane Life': The Death of Elizabeth Wise Benton." *Massachusetts Review* 22, no. 3 (1981): 519–36.

Smith, Elbert B. "'Now Defend Yourself, You Damned Rascal.'" *American Heritage*, February 1958, 44–47, 106.

———. "Thomas Hart Benton: Southern Realist." *American Historical Review* 58, no. 4 (1953): 795–807.

Solomon, Deborah. *Jackson Pollock: A Biography.* New York: Simon and Schuster, 1987.

South, Will. *Color, Myth, and Music: Stanton Macdonald-Wright and Synchromism.* Exhibition catalog. Raleigh: North Carolina Museum of Art, 2001.

———. "Invention and Imagination: Stanton Macdonald-Wright's Santa Monica Library Mural." *Archives of American Art Journal* 39, nos. 3–4 (1999): 11–20.

Stavitsky, Gail. "John Weichsel and the People's Art Guild." *Archives of American Art Journal* 31, no. 4 (1991): 12–19.

Szalay, Michael. *New Deal Modernism: American Literature and the Invention of the Welfare State.* Durham, N.C.: Duke University Press, 2000.

Thomas Hart Benton. VHS. Directed by Ken Burns. New York: PBS Home Video, 1988.

Thomas Hart Benton and the Indiana Murals: The Making of a Masterpiece. Exhibition catalog. Bloomington: Indiana University Art Museum, 1989.

Thomas Hart Benton: A Retrospective of His Early Years, 1907–1929. Exhibition catalog. New Brunswick, N.J.: Rutgers University Art Gallery, 1972.

Thomas Hart Benton: Artist of America. Neosho, Mo.: Printed by Neosho Printing Co., 1962.

Thomas Hart Benton, Frank Lloyd Wright: A Transcript of the Addresses and Exchanges Between Frank Lloyd Wright and Thomas Hart Benton, Providence, Rhode Island, November 11, 1932. Introduction and notes by Ronald J. Onorato; edited and with an afterword by Thomas Weston Fels. Williamstown, Mass.: Williams College Museum of Art, 1985.

"Thomas Hart Benton Paints the History of Missouri—Starts a Civil War." *Art Digest,* February 1, 1937, 10–11.

Wallach, Alan. "Regionalism Redux." In *Exhibiting Contradiction: Essays on the Art Museum in the United States.* Amherst: University of Massachusetts Press, 1998.

Warten, Mary Curtis, ed. *Thomas Hart Benton: A Personal Commemorative.* Exhibition catalog. Kansas City, Mo.: Burd and Fletcher, 1973.

Watkins, Paul. "Thomas Hart Benton Remembered." *Missouri Life* 3 (March–June 1975): 46–57.

Weichsel, John. "Cosmism or Amorphism?" *Camera Work,* nos. 42–43 (April–July 1913): 69–82.

Weintraub, Linda, ed. *Thomas Hart Benton: Chronicler of America's Folk Heritage.* Exhibition catalog. Annandale-on-Hudson, N.Y.: Edith C. Blum Art Institute, 1984.

Whiting, Cécile. *Antifascism in American Art.* New Haven, Conn.: Yale University Press, 1989.

Wilkin, Karen. *Stuart Davis.* New York: Abbeville Press, 1987.

Wilson, Kristina. "The Intimate Gallery and the Equivalents: Spirituality in the 1920s Work of Alfred Stieglitz." *Art Bulletin* 85 (December 2003): 746–68.

Wojtowicz, Robert. *Lewis Mumford and American Modernism: Eutopian Theories for Architecture and Urban Planning.* Cambridge: Cambridge University Press, 1996.

World War II Through the Eyes of Thomas Hart Benton. Exhibition catalog. San Antonio: Marion Koogler McNay Art Museum, 1991.

Wright, Willard Huntington. *The Creative Will: Studies in the Philosophy and the Syntax of Aesthetics.* New York: John Lane, 1916.

———. *Modern Painting: Its Tendency and Meaning.* New York: John Lane, 1915.

Yeo, Wilma, and Helen K. Cook. *Maverick with a Paintbrush: Thomas Hart Benton.* Garden City, N.Y.: Doubleday, 1977.

INDEX

A NOTE ABOUT THE AUTHOR

Justin Wolff is an assistant professor of art history at the University of Maine. He is the author of *Richard Caton Woodville: American Painter, Artful Dodger.*